VOL. 15
Action Edition

Story and Art by
RUMIKO TAKAHASHI

English Adaptation by Gerard Jones

Translation/Mari Morimoto
Touch-Up Art & Lettering/Bill Schuch
Cover Design/Hidemi Sahara
Graphics & Design/Sean Lee
Editor/Julie Davis

Managing Editor/Annette Roman
Editor in Chief/William Flanagan
Dir. of Licensing and Acquisitions/Rika Inouye
VP of Sales and Marketing/Liza Coppola
Sr. VP of Editorial/Hyoe Narita
Publisher/Seiji Horibuchi

© 1997 Rumiko Takahashi/Shogakukan, Inc. First published
by Shogakukan, Inc. in Japan as "Inuyasha."

Printed in Canada.

Published by VIZ, LLC
P.O. Box 77010
San Francisco, CA 94107

Action Edition
10 9 8 7 6 5 4 3 2 1
First printing, September 2003

store.viz.com

www.viz.com

InuYasha

VOL. 15 — Action Edition

STORY AND ART BY
RUMIKO TAKAHASHI

CONTENTS

THE STORY THUS FAR

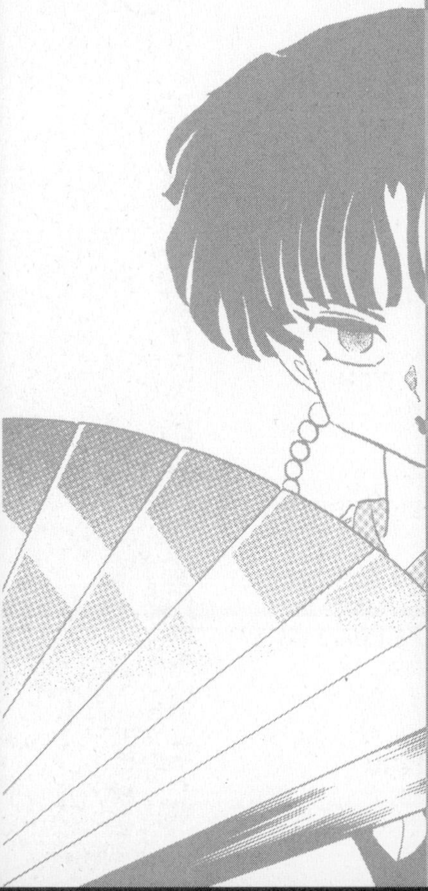

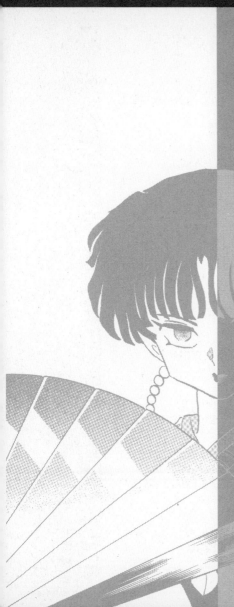

Long ago, in the "Warring States" era of Japan's Muromachi period (Sengoku-jidai, approximately 1467-1568 CE), a legendary doglike half-demon called "Inu-Yasha" attempted to steal the Shikon Jewel, or "Jewel of Four Souls," from a village, but was stopped by the enchanted arrow of the village priestess, Kikyo. Inu-Yasha fell into a deep sleep, pinned to a tree by Kikyo's arrow, while the mortally wounded Kikyo took the Shikon Jewel with her into the fires of her funeral pyre. Years passed.

Fast forward to the present day. Kagome, a Japanese high school girl, is pulled into a well one day by a mysterious centipede monster, and finds herself transported into the past, only to come face to face with the trapped Inu-Yasha. She frees him, and Inu-Yasha easily defeats the centipede monster.

The residents of the village, now fifty years older, readily accept Kagome as the reincarnation of their deceased priestess Kikyo, a claim supported by the fact that the Shikon Jewel emerges from a cut on Kagome's body. Unfortunately, the jewel's rediscovery means that the village is soon under attack by a variety of demons in search of this treasure. Then, the jewel is accidentally shattered into many shards, each of which may have the fearsome power of the entire jewel.

Although Inu-Yasha says he hates Kagome because of her resemblance to Kikyo, the woman who "killed" him, he is forced to team up with her when Kaede, the village leader, binds him to Kagome with a powerful spell. Now the two grudging companions must fight to reclaim and reassemble the shattered shards of the Shikon Jewel before they fall into the wrong hands.

THIS VOLUME Kagome returns home to the modern day until Inu-Yasha apologizes; meanwhile, back in the past, a new threat is rising.

CHARACTERS

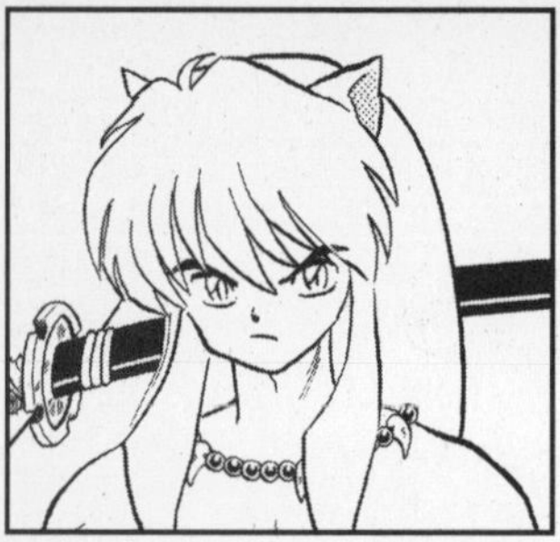

KAGOME
Working with Inu-Yasha to recover the shattered shards of the Shikon Jewel, Kagome routinely travels into Japan's past through an old, magical well on her family's property. All this time travel means she's stuck with living two separate lives in two centuries. Will she *ever* be able to catch up to her schoolwork?

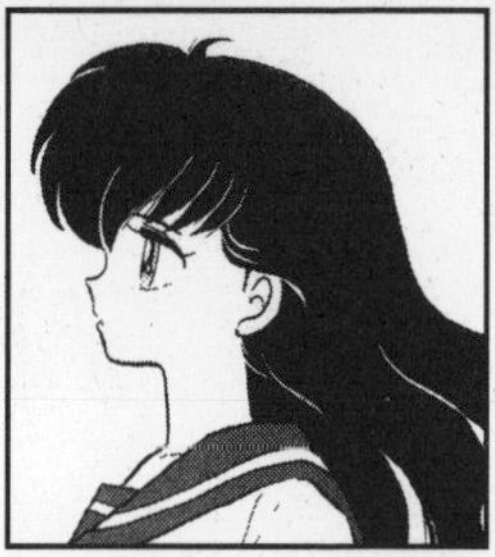

INU-YASHA
A half-human, half-demon hybrid son of a human mother and a demon father, Inu-Yasha has the claws of a demon, a thick mane of white hair, and ears rather like a dog's. The necklace he wears carries a powerful spell that allows Kagome to control him with a single word. Thanks to his human half, Inu-Yasha's powers are different from those of full-blooded monsters—a fact that the Shikon Jewel has the power to change.

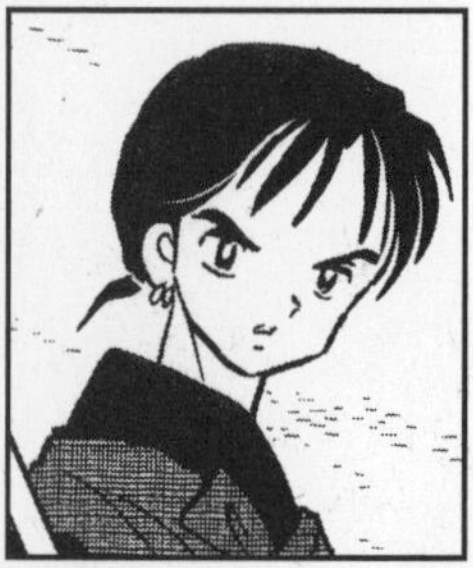

MIROKU
An easygoing Buddhist priest (also somewhat of a ladies' man), Miroku carries a "hellhole" in his hand, a curse that was originally inflicted on his grandfather by the demon Naraku.

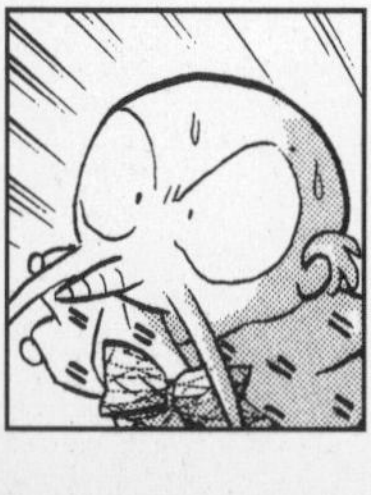

MYOGA
Flea-demon servant to Inu-Yasha, Myoga is both wise and cowardly. His bloodsucking seems to have the ability to weaken certain spells.

KOGA
The powerful, charismatic leader of a wolf-demon clan, Koga covets both the Shikon Jewel and Kagome's affections.

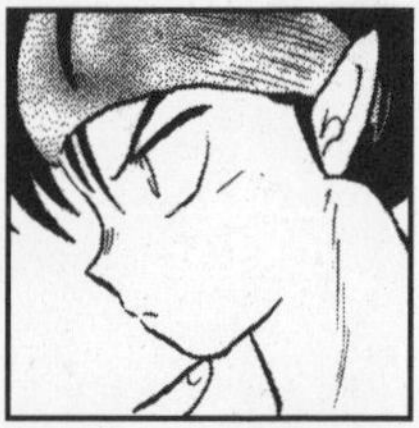

SANGO
A "Demon Exterminator" from the village where the Shikon Jewel was first born, Sango lost her father and little brother to a demon attack arranged by the mysterious Naraku.

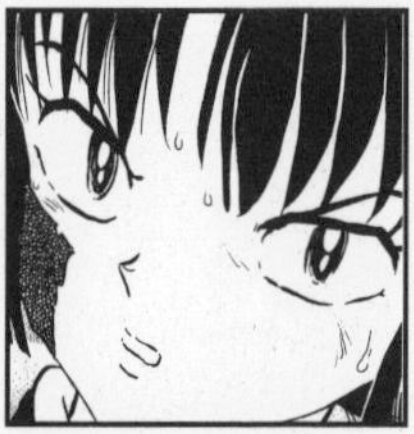

NARAKU
An enigmatic demon whose machinations have affected nearly everyone in the story at one time or another—what is his ultimate plan?

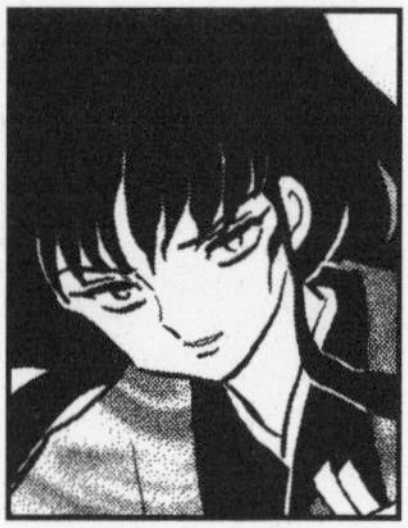

SHIPPO
An orphaned young fox-demon, the mischievous Shippo likes to goad Inu-Yasha and play tricks with his shape-changing.

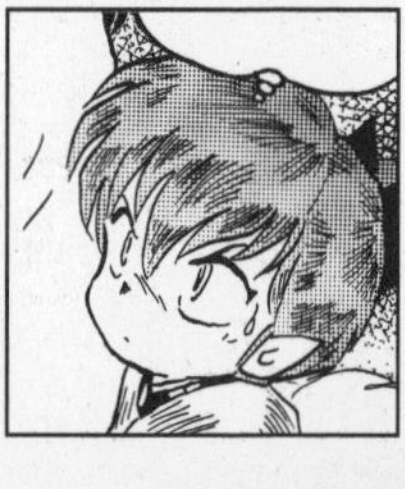

SCROLL ONE

DUELING EMOTIONS

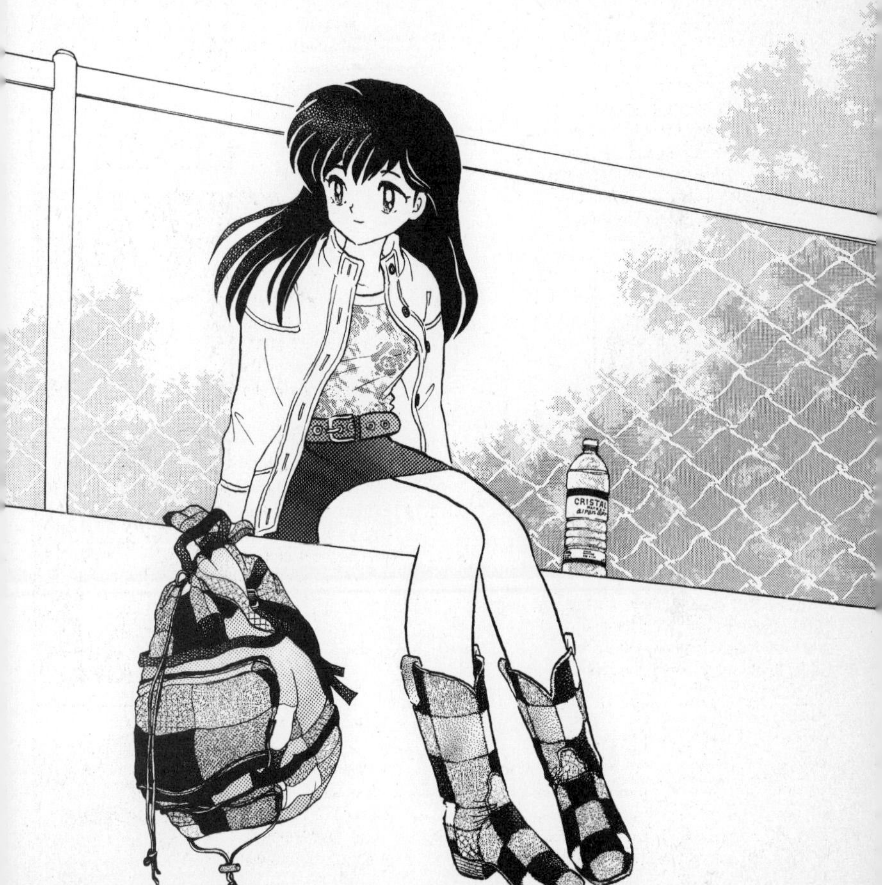
CRISTAL

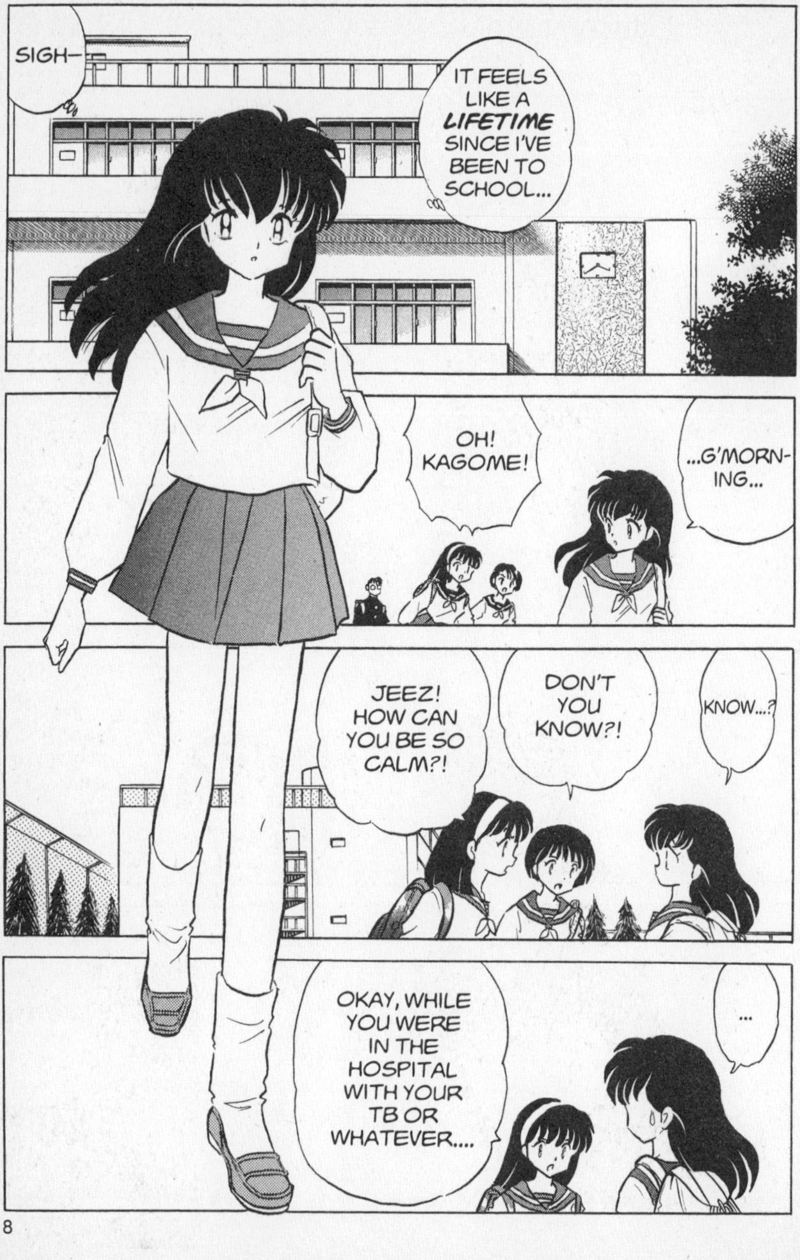
SIGH—
IT FEELS LIKE A *LIFETIME* SINCE I'VE BEEN TO SCHOOL...
OH! KAGOME!
...G'MORN-ING...
JEEZ! HOW CAN YOU BE SO CALM?!
DON'T YOU KNOW?!
KNOW...?
OKAY, WHILE YOU WERE IN THE HOSPITAL WITH YOUR TB OR WHATEVER....
...

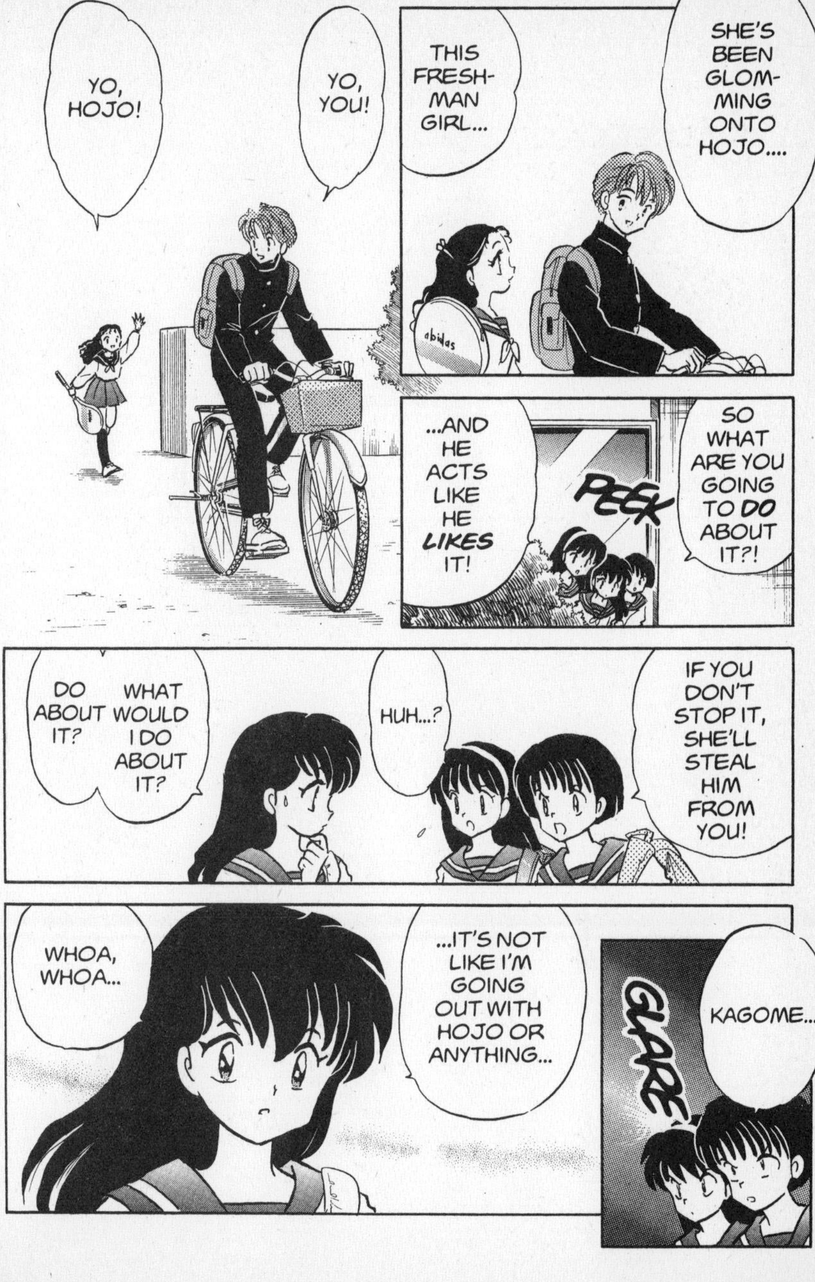
YO, HOJO!
YO, YOU!
THIS FRESH-MAN GIRL...
SHE'S BEEN GLOM-MING ONTO HOJO....
...AND HE ACTS LIKE HE **LIKES** IT!
PEEK
SO WHAT ARE YOU GOING TO **DO** ABOUT IT?!
DO ABOUT IT?
WHAT WOULD I DO ABOUT IT?
HUH...?
IF YOU DON'T STOP IT, SHE'LL STEAL HIM FROM YOU!
WHOA, WHOA...
...IT'S NOT LIKE I'M GOING OUT WITH HOJO OR ANYTHING...
GLARE
KAGOME...

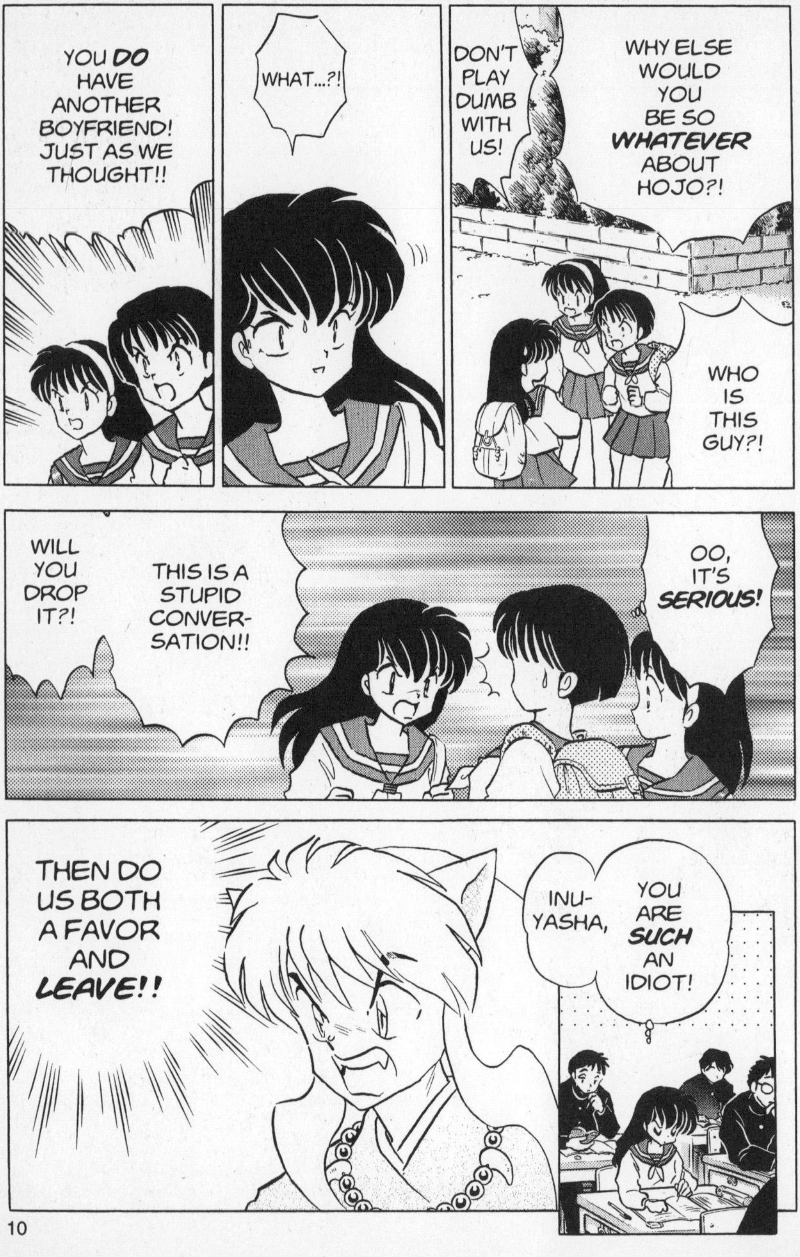
YOU DO HAVE ANOTHER BOYFRIEND! JUST AS WE THOUGHT!!
WHAT...?!
DON'T PLAY DUMB WITH US!
WHY ELSE WOULD YOU BE SO WHATEVER ABOUT HOJO?!
WHO IS THIS GUY?!
WILL YOU DROP IT?!
THIS IS A STUPID CONVER-SATION!!
OO, IT'S SERIOUS!
THEN DO US BOTH A FAVOR AND LEAVE!!
INU-YASHA,
YOU ARE SUCH AN IDIOT!

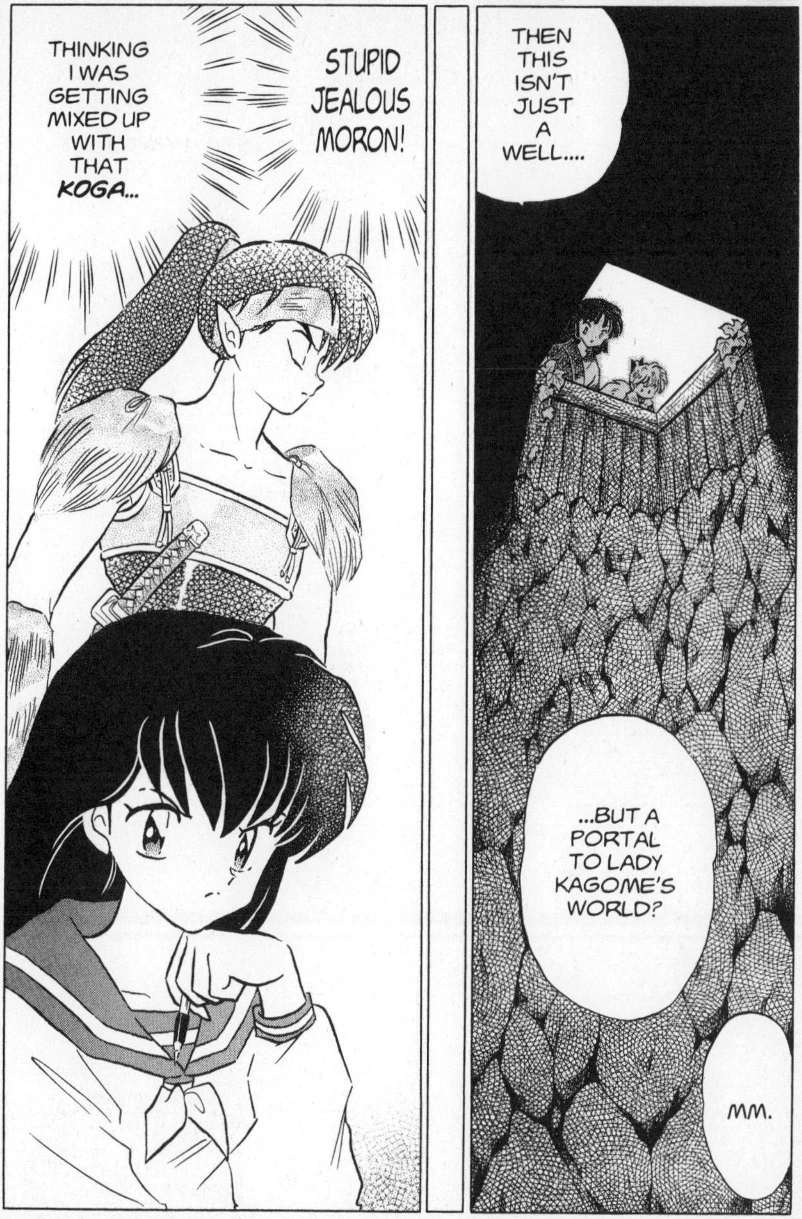
THINKING I WAS GETTING MIXED UP WITH THAT *KOGA*...
STUPID JEALOUS MORON!
THEN THIS ISN'T JUST A WELL....
...BUT A PORTAL TO LADY KAGOME'S WORLD?
MM.

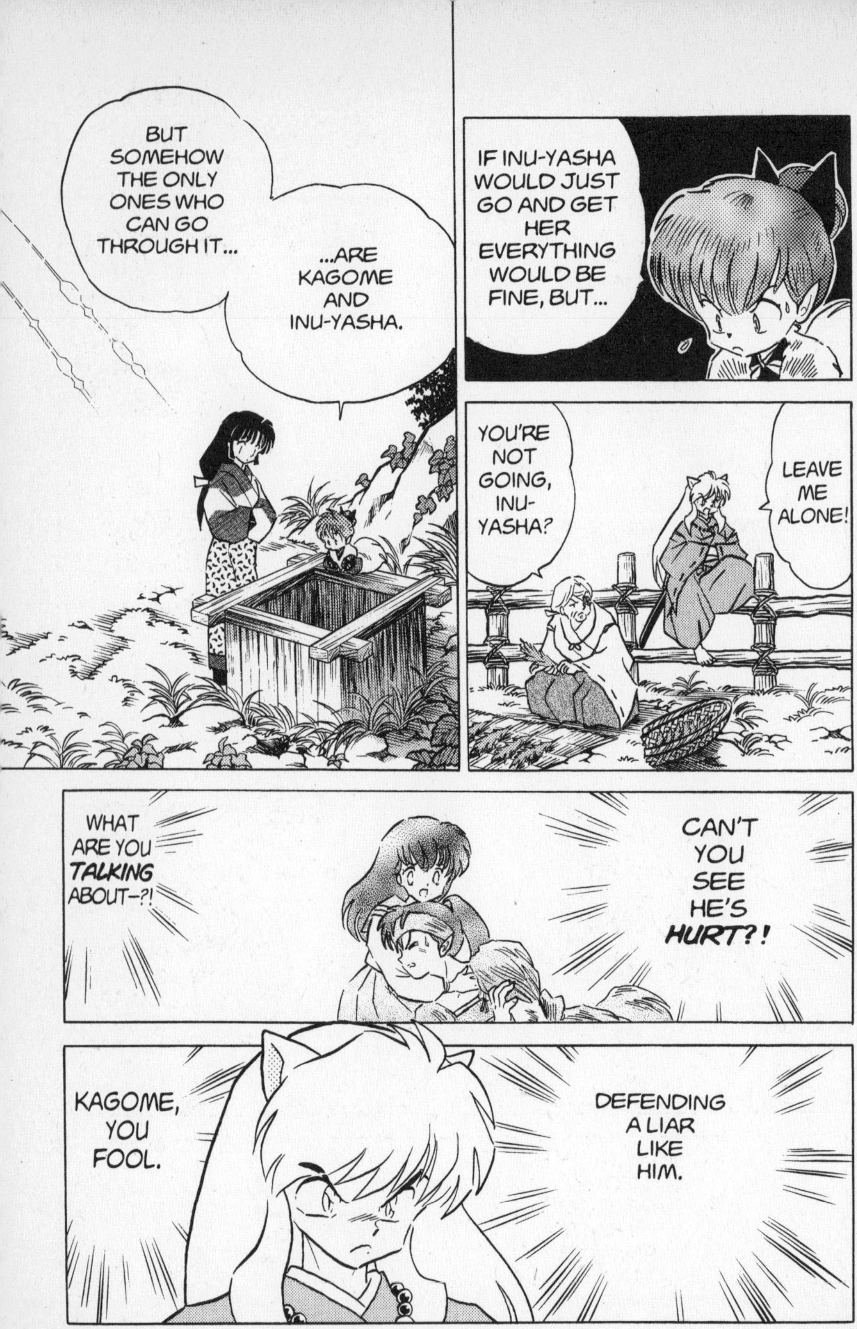
BUT SOMEHOW THE ONLY ONES WHO CAN GO THROUGH IT...
...ARE KAGOME AND INU-YASHA.
IF INU-YASHA WOULD JUST GO AND GET HER EVERYTHING WOULD BE FINE, BUT...
YOU'RE NOT GOING, INU-YASHA?
LEAVE ME ALONE!
WHAT ARE YOU TALKING ABOUT-?!
CAN'T YOU SEE HE'S HURT?!
KAGOME, YOU FOOL.
DEFENDING A LIAR LIKE HIM.

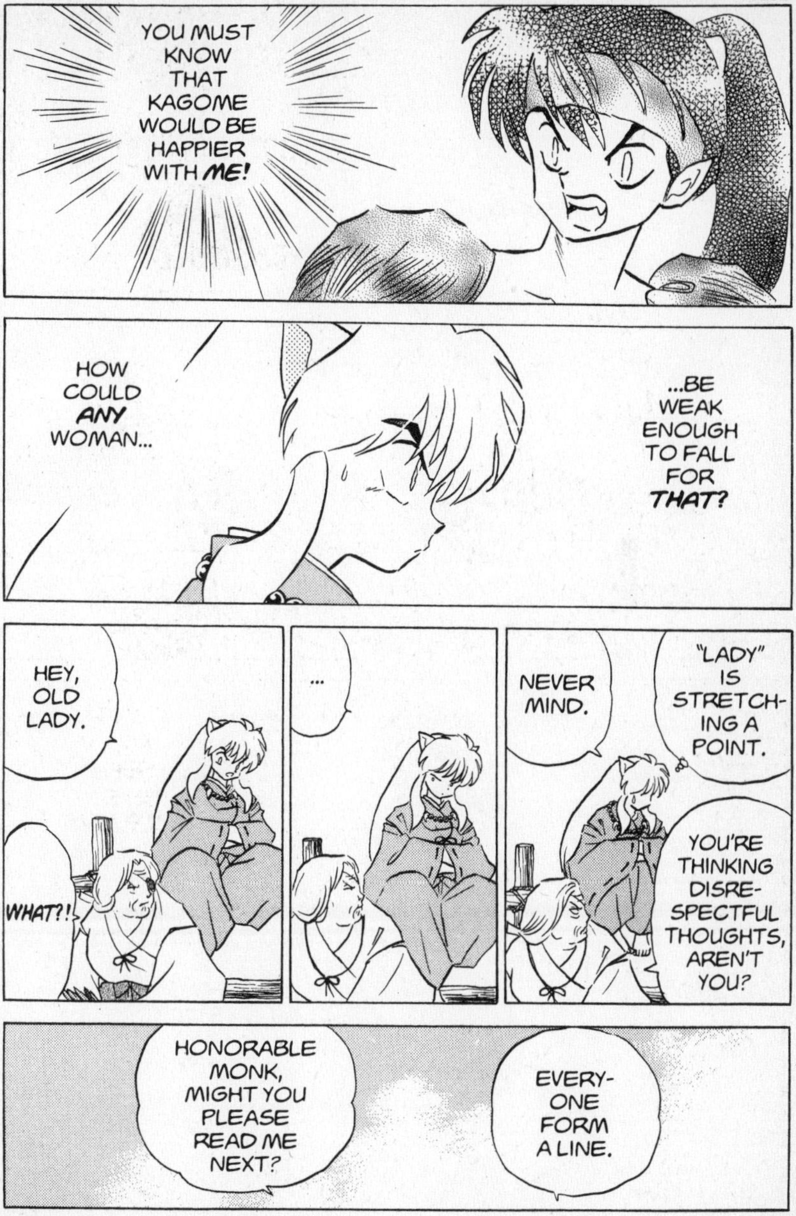
YOU MUST KNOW THAT KAGOME WOULD BE HAPPIER WITH ME!
HOW COULD ANY WOMAN...
...BE WEAK ENOUGH TO FALL FOR THAT?
HEY, OLD LADY.
WHAT?!
...
NEVER MIND.
"LADY" IS STRETCH-ING A POINT.
YOU'RE THINKING DISRE-SPECTFUL THOUGHTS, AREN'T YOU?
HONORABLE MONK, MIGHT YOU PLEASE READ ME NEXT?
EVERY-ONE FORM A LINE.

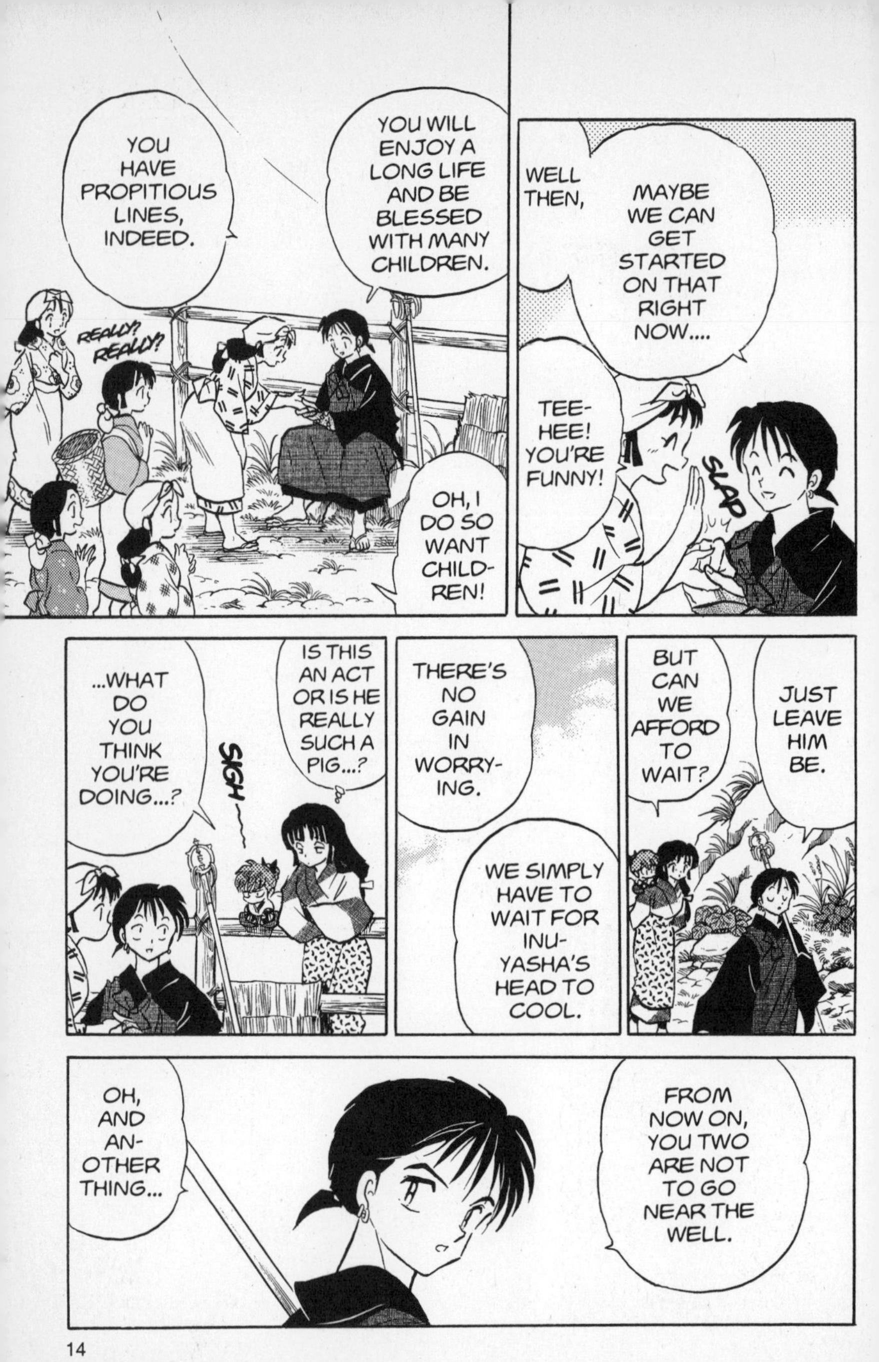
YOU HAVE PROPITIOUS LINES, INDEED.
YOU WILL ENJOY A LONG LIFE AND BE BLESSED WITH MANY CHILDREN.
REALLY? REALLY?
OH, I DO SO WANT CHILD-REN!
WELL THEN,
MAYBE WE CAN GET STARTED ON THAT RIGHT NOW....
TEE-HEE! YOU'RE FUNNY!
SLAP
...WHAT DO YOU THINK YOU'RE DOING...?
SIGH
IS THIS AN ACT OR IS HE REALLY SUCH A PIG...?
THERE'S NO GAIN IN WORRY-ING.
WE SIMPLY HAVE TO WAIT FOR INU-YASHA'S HEAD TO COOL.
BUT CAN WE AFFORD TO WAIT?
JUST LEAVE HIM BE.
OH, AND AN-OTHER THING...
FROM NOW ON, YOU TWO ARE NOT TO GO NEAR THE WELL.

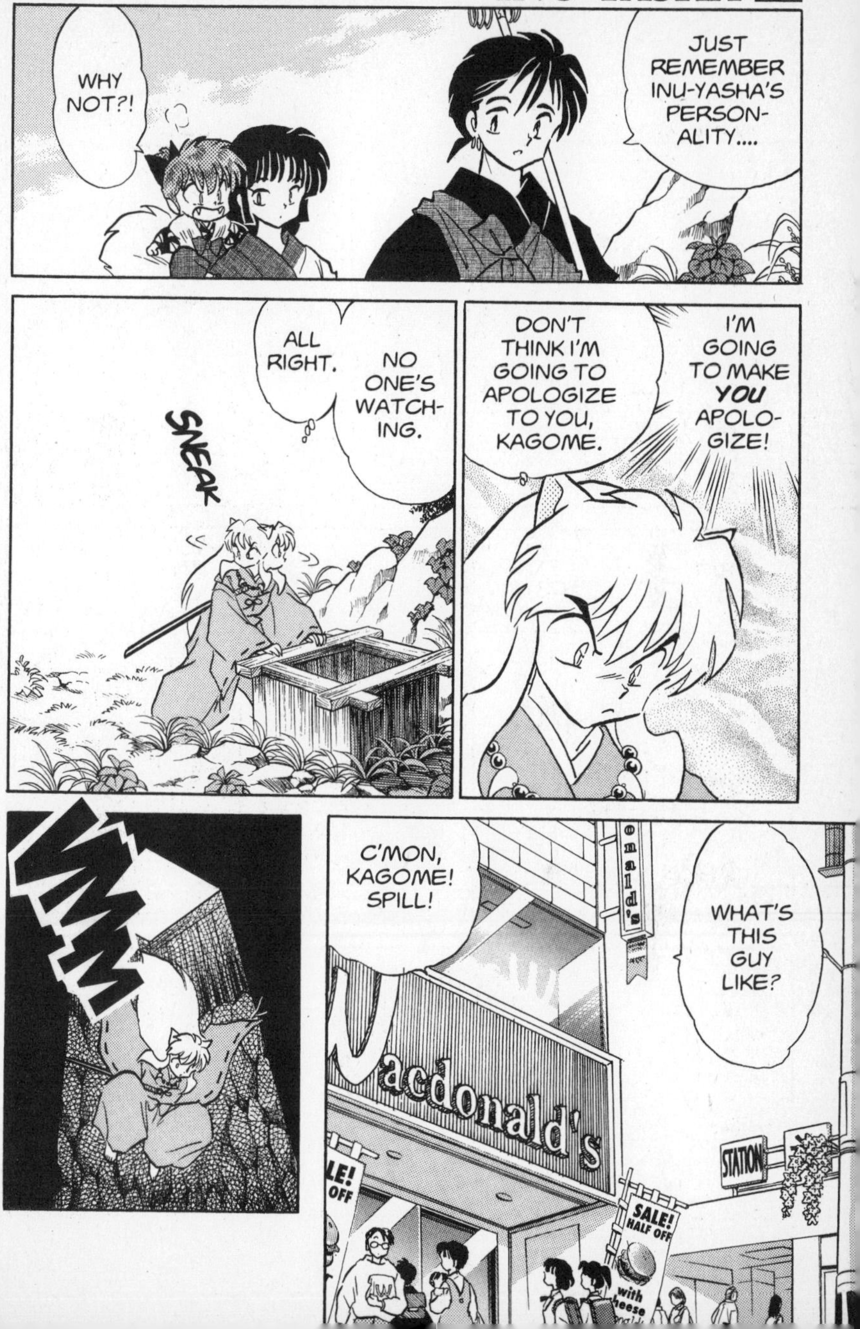
WHY NOT?!
JUST REMEMBER INU-YASHA'S PERSON-ALITY....
ALL RIGHT.
NO ONE'S WATCH-ING.
SNEAK
DON'T THINK I'M GOING TO APOLOGIZE TO YOU, KAGOME.
I'M GOING TO MAKE ***YOU*** APOLO-GIZE!
C'MON, KAGOME! SPILL!
WHAT'S THIS GUY LIKE?
acdonald's
STATION
SALE! HALF OFF

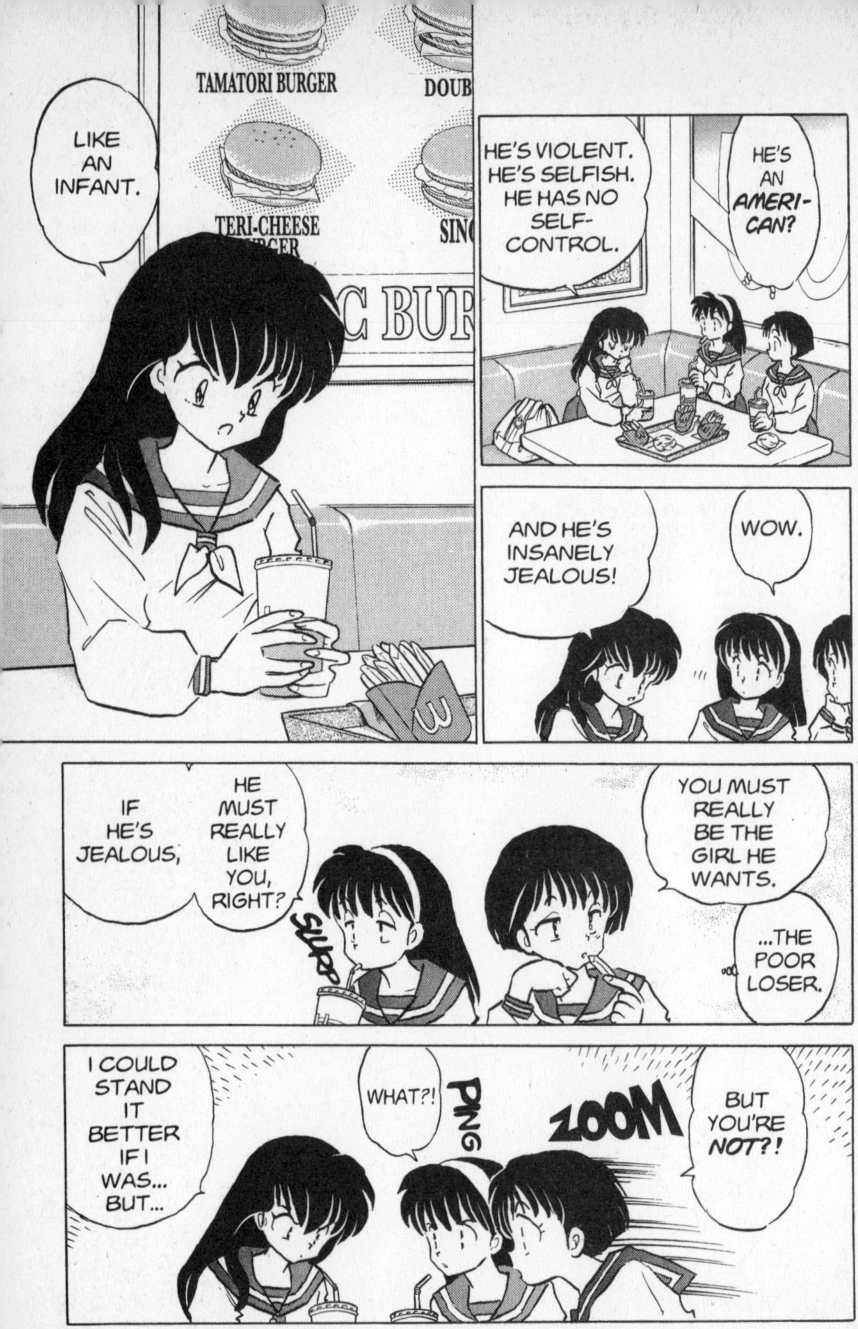
TAMATORI BURGER
DOUB
TERI-CHEESE BURGER
SING
C BUR
LIKE AN INFANT.
HE'S VIOLENT. HE'S SELFISH. HE HAS NO SELF-CONTROL.
HE'S AN *AMERI-CAN?*
AND HE'S INSANELY JEALOUS!
WOW.
IF HE'S JEALOUS,
HE MUST REALLY LIKE YOU, RIGHT?
SLURP
YOU MUST REALLY BE THE GIRL HE WANTS.
...THE POOR LOSER.
I COULD STAND IT BETTER IF I WAS... BUT...
WHAT?!
PING
ZOOM
BUT YOU'RE *NOT?!*

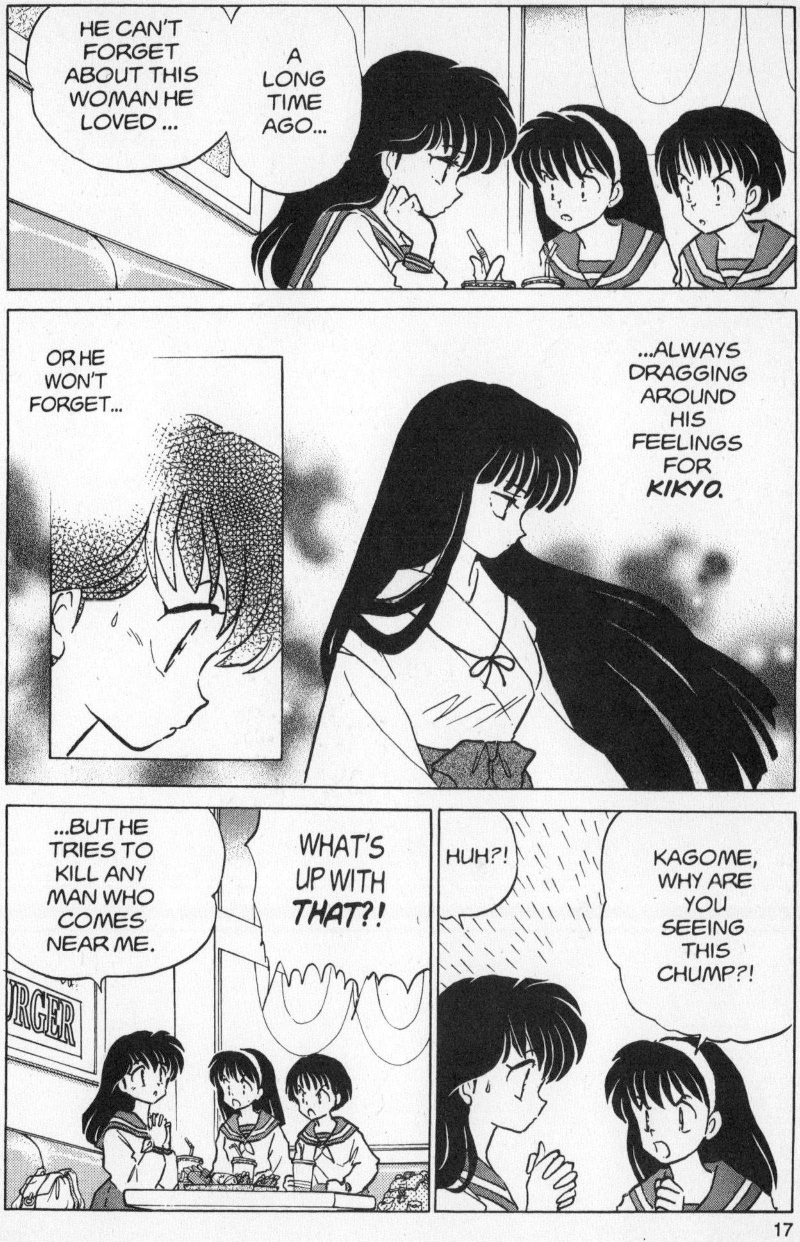
HE CAN'T FORGET ABOUT THIS WOMAN HE LOVED ...
A LONG TIME AGO...
OR HE WON'T FORGET...
...ALWAYS DRAGGING AROUND HIS FEELINGS FOR ***KIKYO.***
...BUT HE TRIES TO KILL ANY MAN WHO COMES NEAR ME.
WHAT'S UP WITH ***THAT?!***
HUH?!
KAGOME, WHY ARE YOU SEEING THIS CHUMP?!

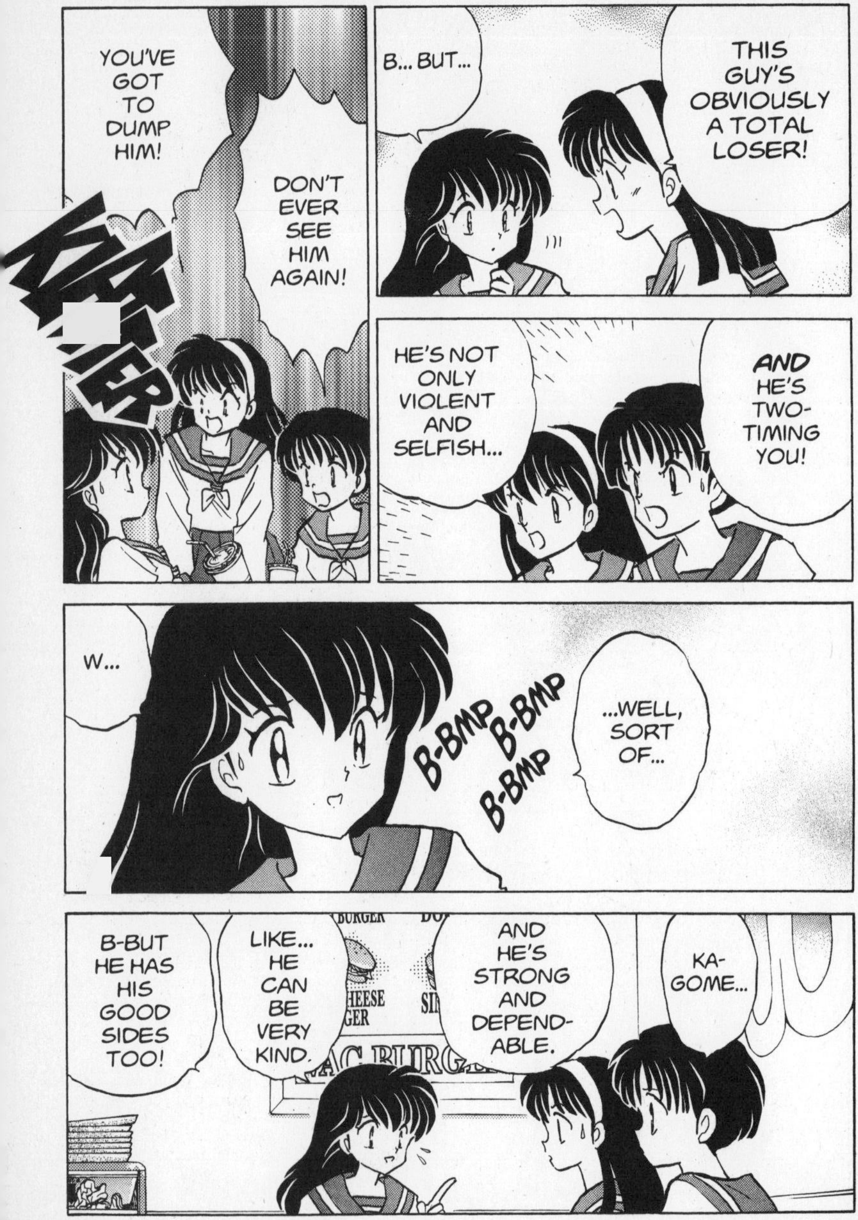
YOU'VE GOT TO DUMP HIM!
DON'T EVER SEE HIM AGAIN!
B... BUT...
THIS GUY'S OBVIOUSLY A TOTAL LOSER!
HE'S NOT ONLY VIOLENT AND SELFISH...
AND HE'S TWO-TIMING YOU!
W...
B-BMP B-BMP B-BMP
...WELL, SORT OF...
B-BUT HE HAS HIS GOOD SIDES TOO!
LIKE... HE CAN BE VERY KIND.
AND HE'S STRONG AND DEPEND-ABLE.
KA-GOME...

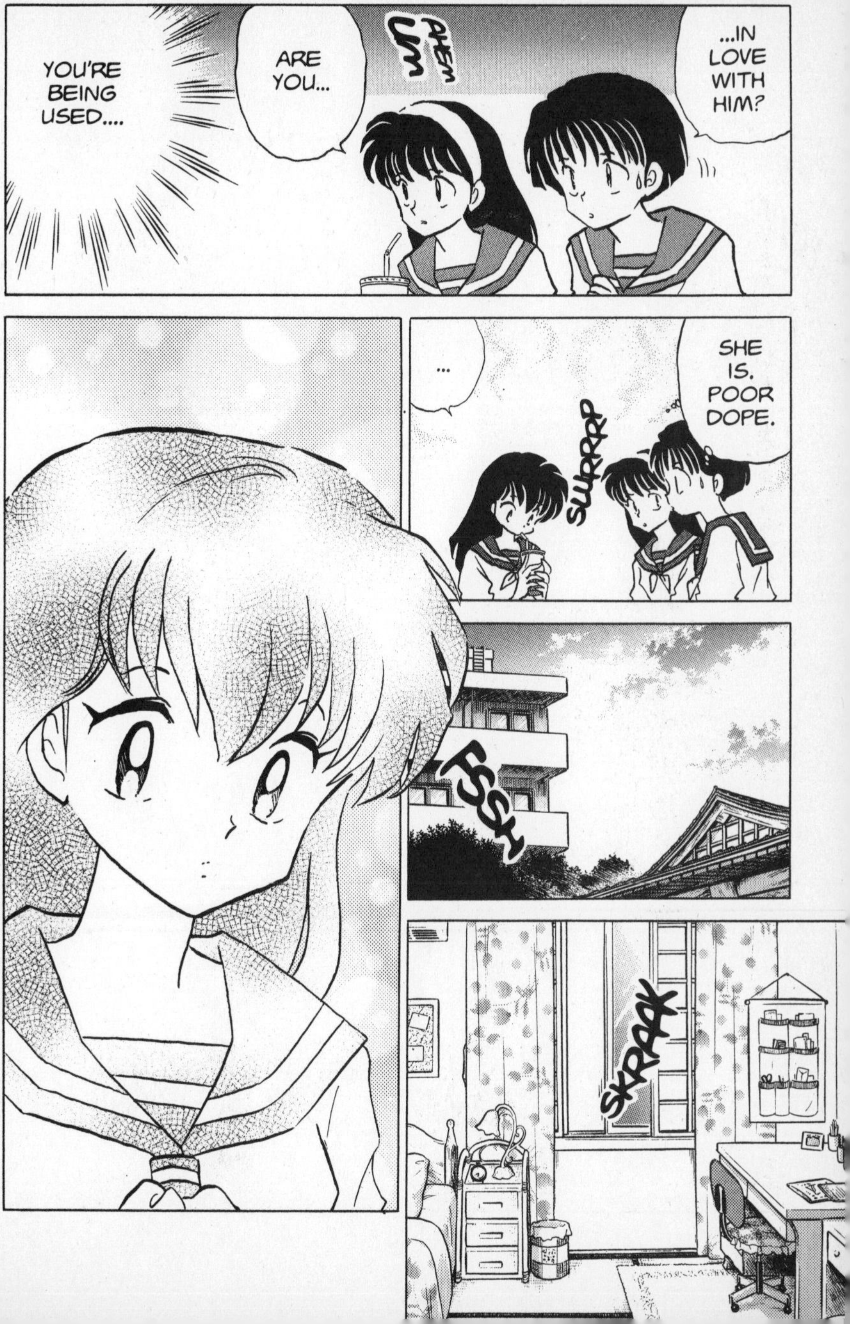
YOU'RE BEING USED....
ARE YOU...
AHEM UM
...IN LOVE WITH HIM?
...
SLURRRP
SHE IS. POOR DOPE.
FSSH
SKRAAK

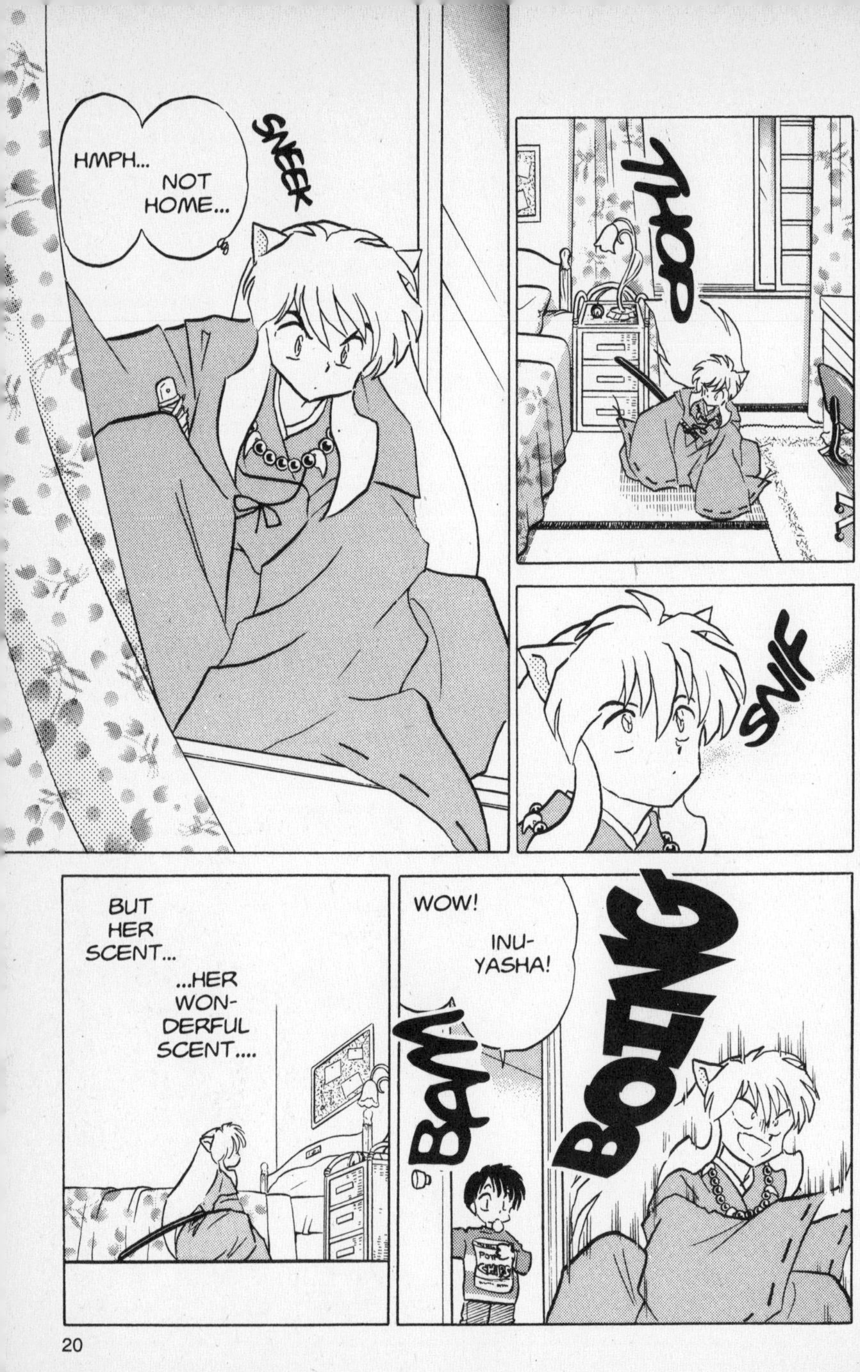
HMPH... NOT HOME...
SNEEK
THOP
SNIF
BUT HER SCENT...
...HER WON-DERFUL SCENT....
WOW! INU-YASHA!
BAM
BOING

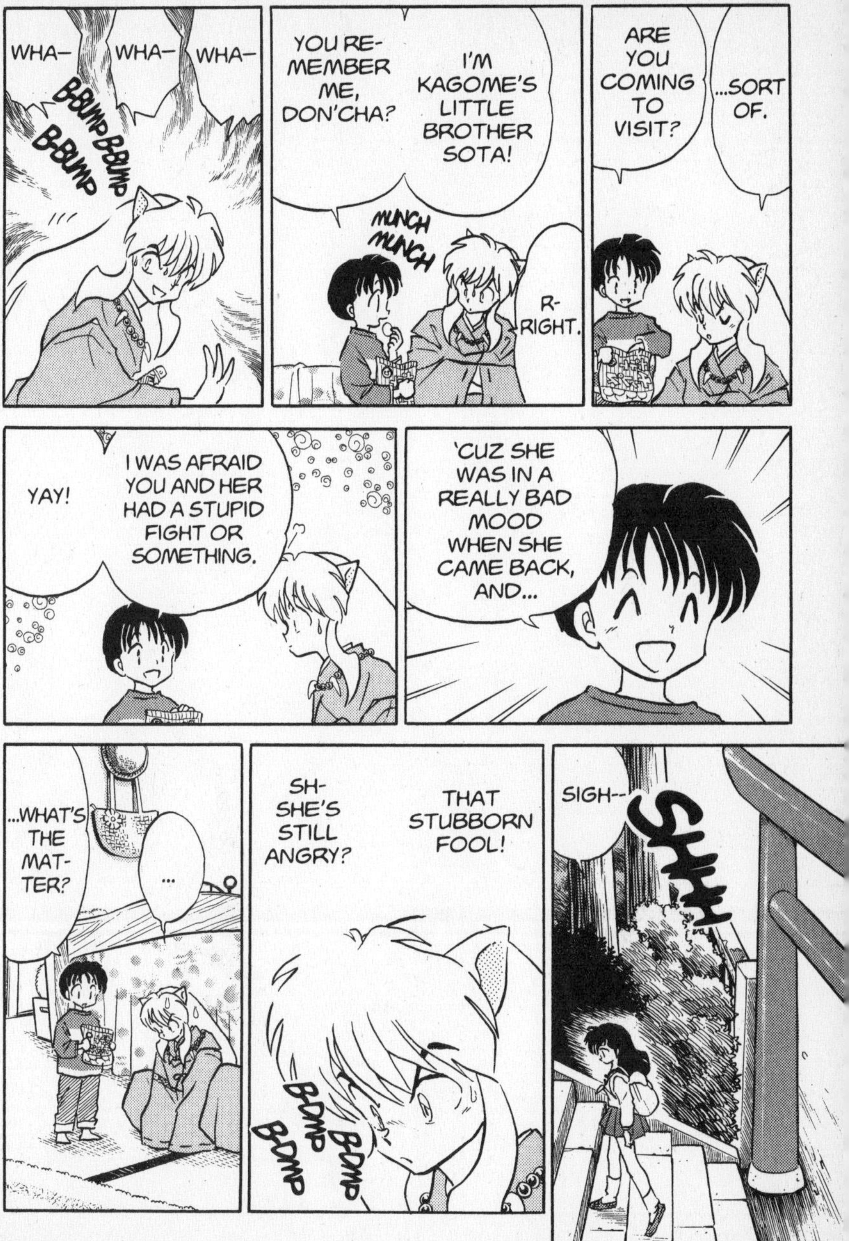
WHA–
WHA–
WHA–
B-BUMP B-BUMP B-BUMP
YOU RE-MEMBER ME, DON'CHA?
I'M KAGOME'S LITTLE BROTHER SOTA!
MUNCH MUNCH
R-RIGHT.
ARE YOU COMING TO VISIT?
...SORT OF.
YAY!
I WAS AFRAID YOU AND HER HAD A STUPID FIGHT OR SOMETHING.
'CUZ SHE WAS IN A REALLY BAD MOOD WHEN SHE CAME BACK, AND...
...WHAT'S THE MAT-TER?
...
SH-SHE'S STILL ANGRY?
THAT STUBBORN FOOL!
B-DMP B-DMP B-DMP B-DMP
SIGH--
SHHH

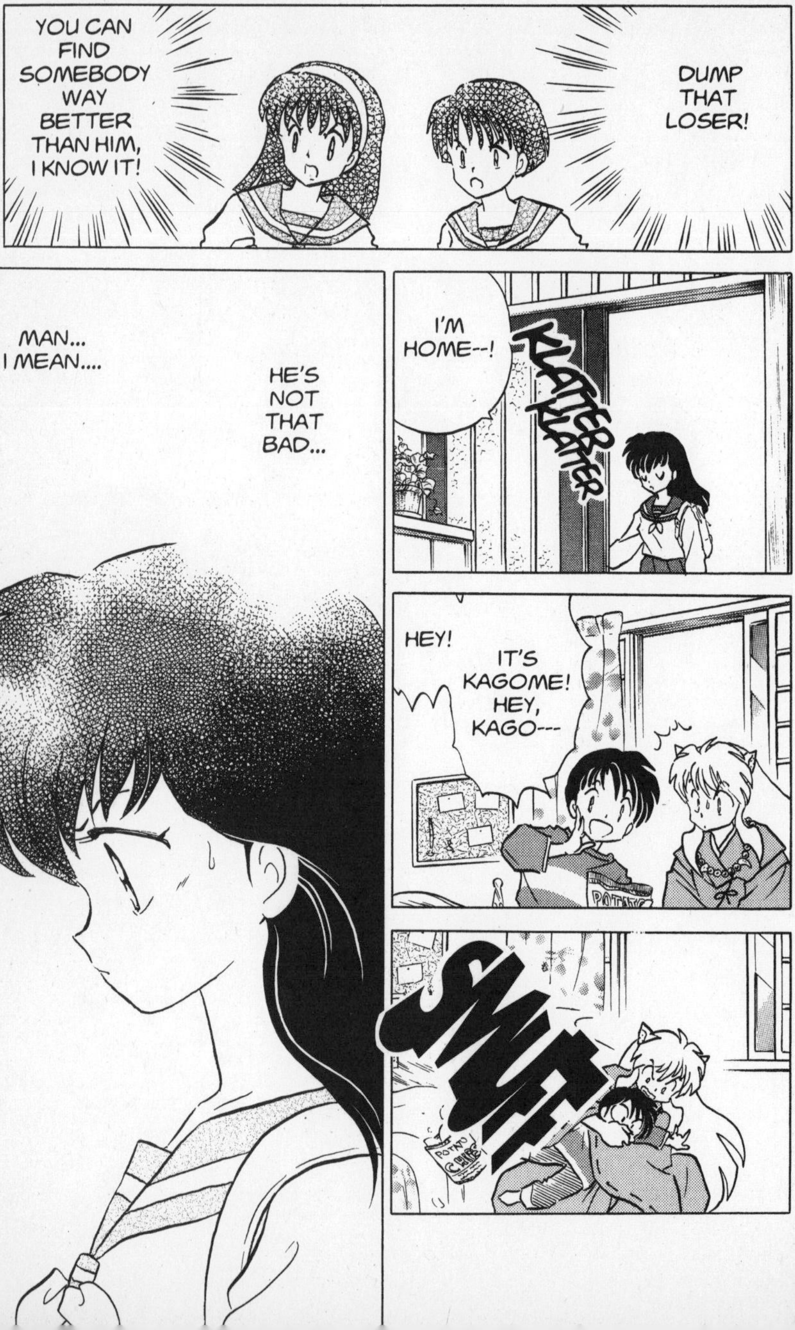
YOU CAN FIND SOMEBODY WAY BETTER THAN HIM, I KNOW IT!
DUMP THAT LOSER!
MAN... I MEAN....
HE'S NOT THAT BAD...
I'M HOME--!
KLATTER KLATTER
HEY!
IT'S KAGOME! HEY, KAGO---

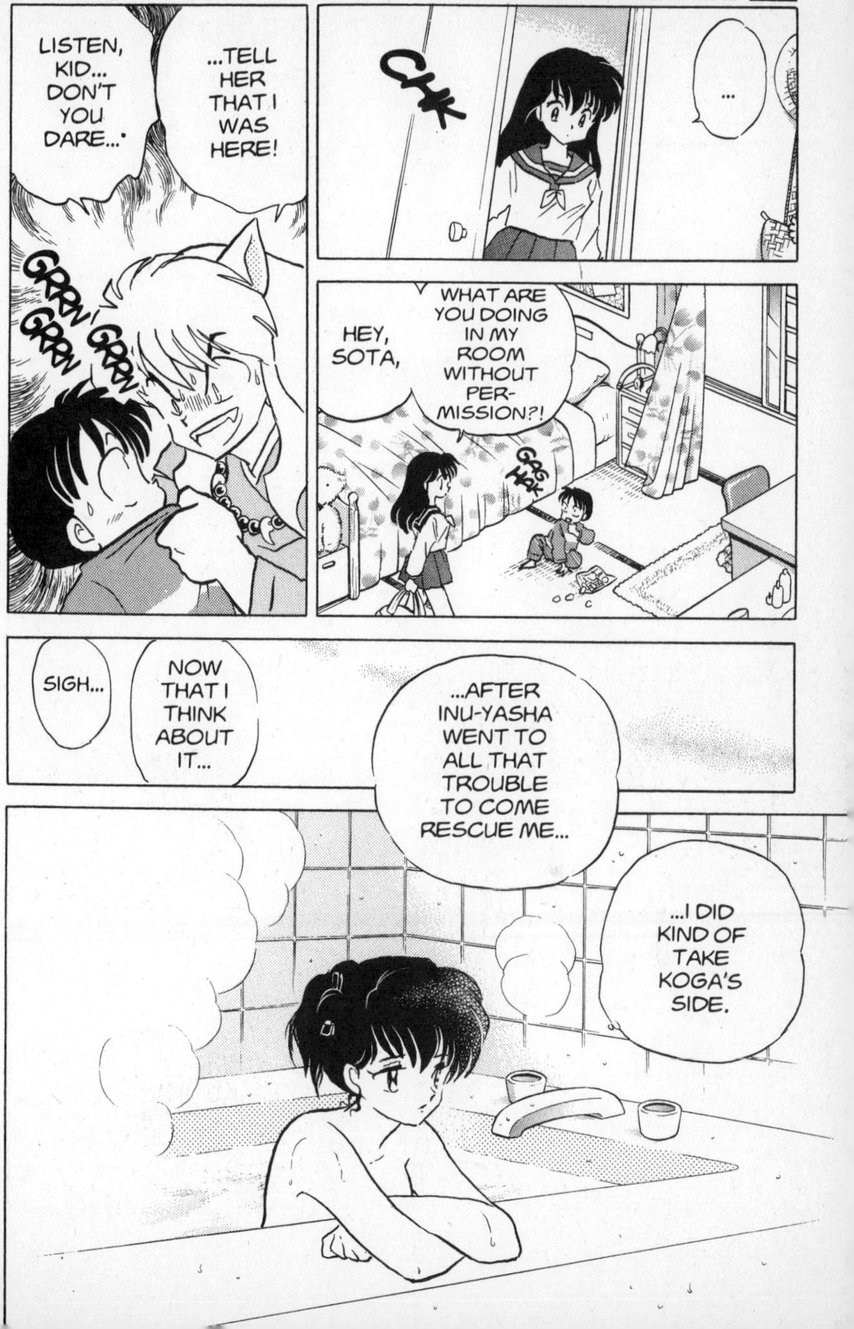
LISTEN, KID... DON'T YOU DARE...
...TELL HER THAT I WAS HERE!
GRRN GRRN GRRN
CLIK
...
HEY, SOTA,
WHAT ARE YOU DOING IN MY ROOM WITHOUT PER-MISSION?!
SIGH...
NOW THAT I THINK ABOUT IT...
...AFTER INU-YASHA WENT TO ALL THAT TROUBLE TO COME RESCUE ME...
...I DID KIND OF TAKE KOGA'S SIDE.

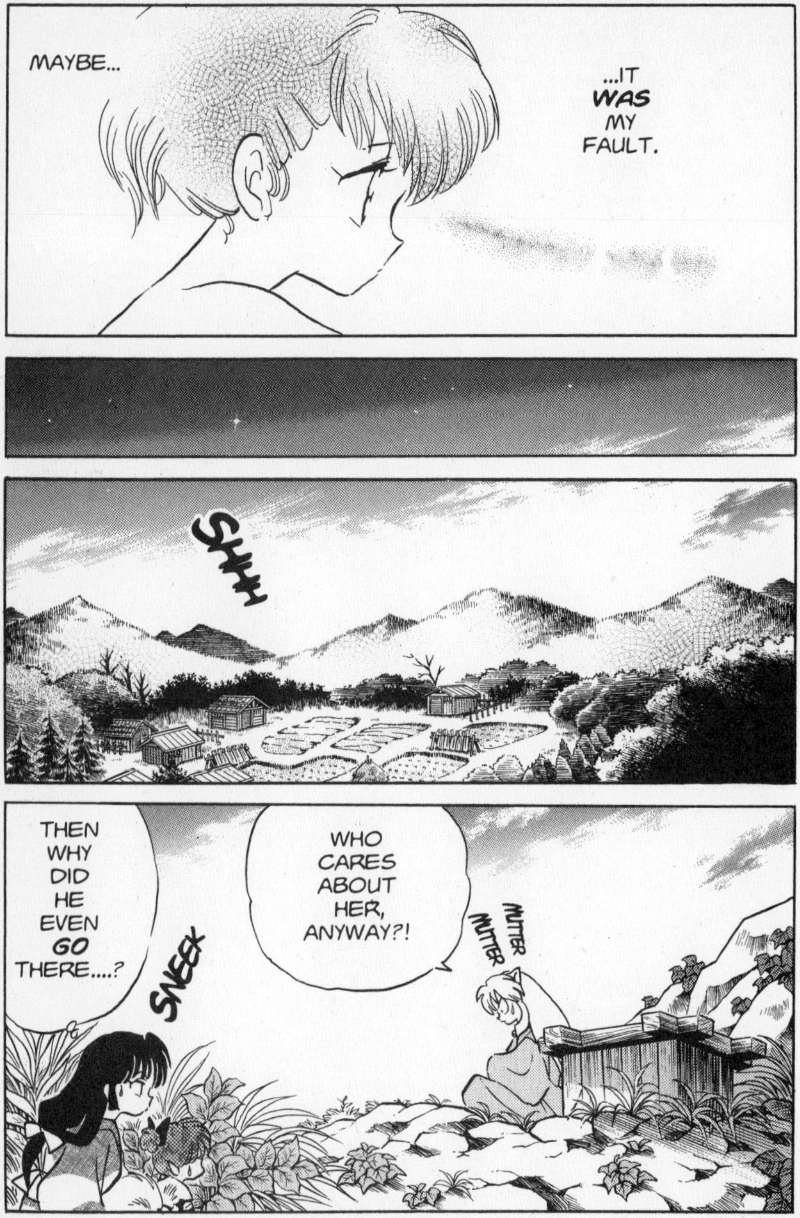
MAYBE...
...IT WAS MY FAULT.
SHHH
THEN WHY DID HE EVEN GO THERE....?
SNEEK
WHO CARES ABOUT HER, ANYWAY?!
MUTTER MUTTER

SCROLL TWO
THE OTHER SIDE OF THE WELL

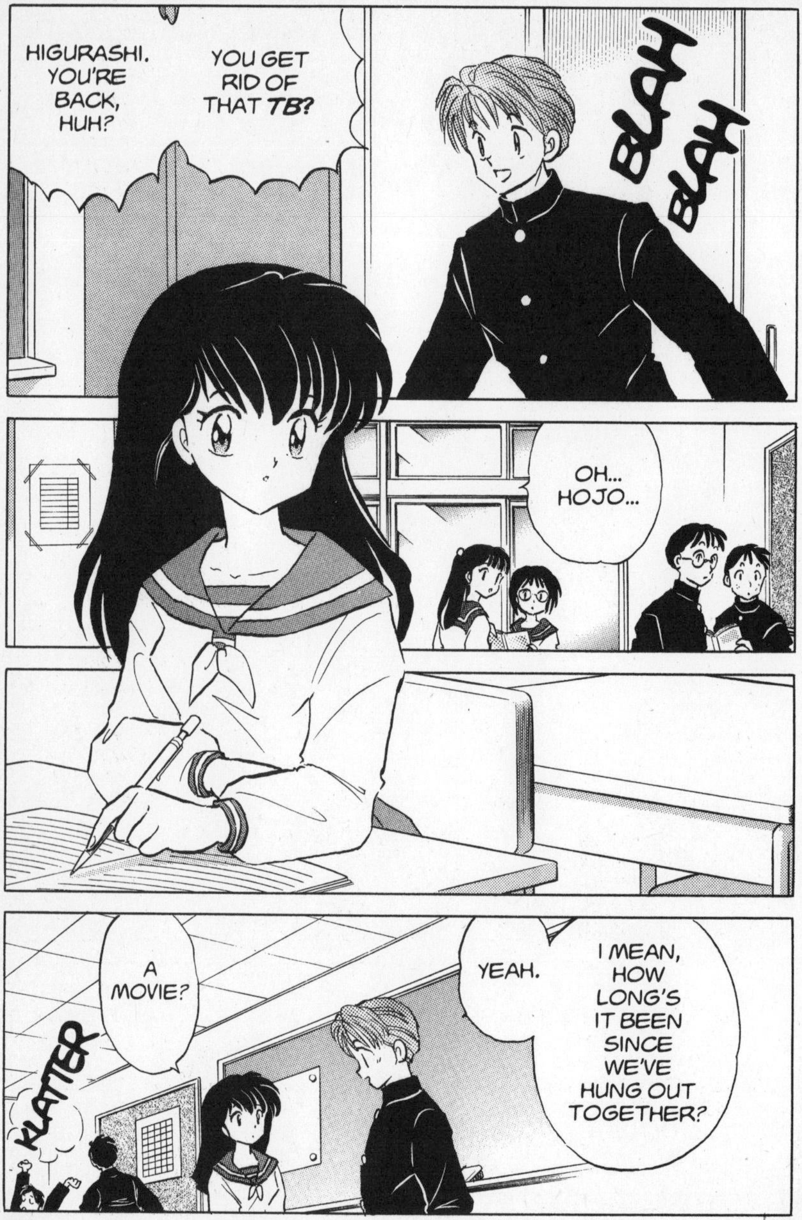
HIGURASHI. YOU'RE BACK, HUH?
YOU GET RID OF THAT TB?
BLAH BLAH
OH... HOJO...
A MOVIE?
KLATTER
YEAH.
I MEAN, HOW LONG'S IT BEEN SINCE WE'VE HUNG OUT TOGETHER?

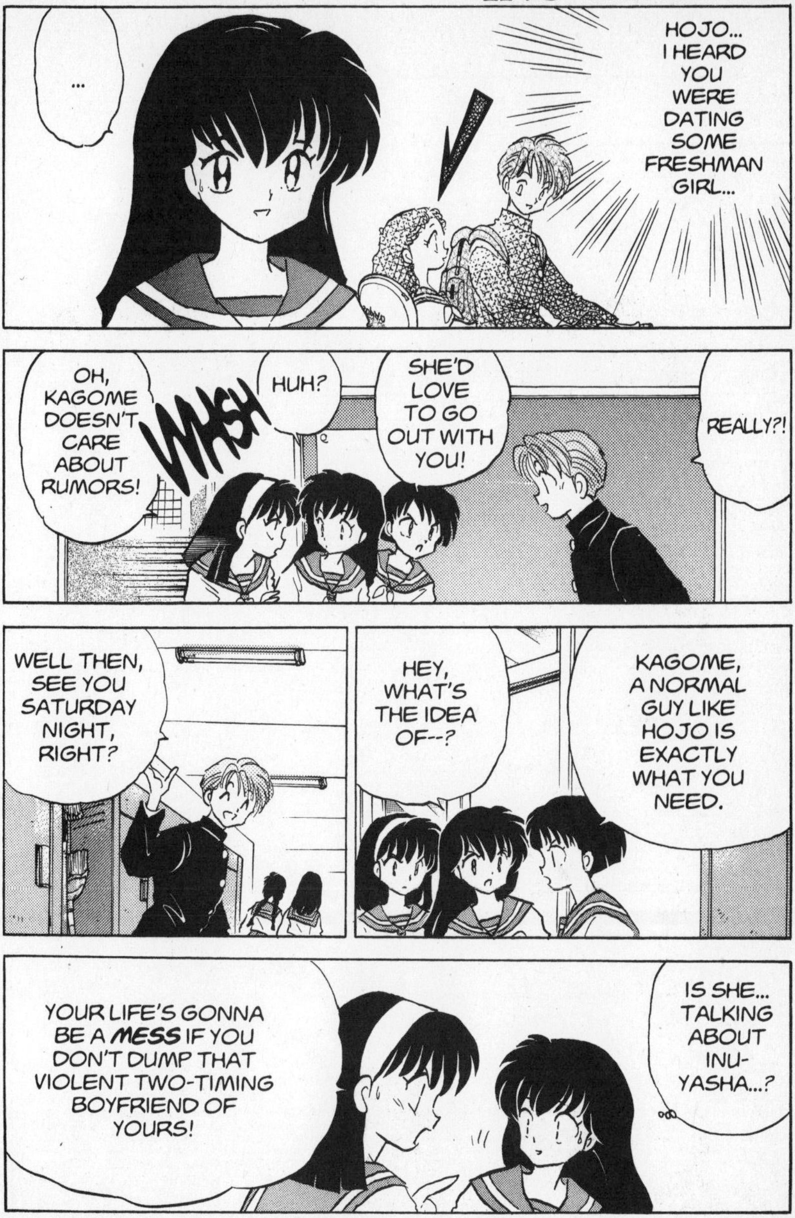
...
HOJO... I HEARD YOU WERE DATING SOME FRESHMAN GIRL...
OH, KAGOME DOESN'T CARE ABOUT RUMORS!
WHSH
HUH?
SHE'D LOVE TO GO OUT WITH YOU!
REALLY?!
WELL THEN, SEE YOU SATURDAY NIGHT, RIGHT?
HEY, WHAT'S THE IDEA OF--?
KAGOME, A NORMAL GUY LIKE HOJO IS EXACTLY WHAT YOU NEED.
YOUR LIFE'S GONNA BE A MESS IF YOU DON'T DUMP THAT VIOLENT TWO-TIMING BOYFRIEND OF YOURS!
IS SHE... TALKING ABOUT INU-YASHA...?

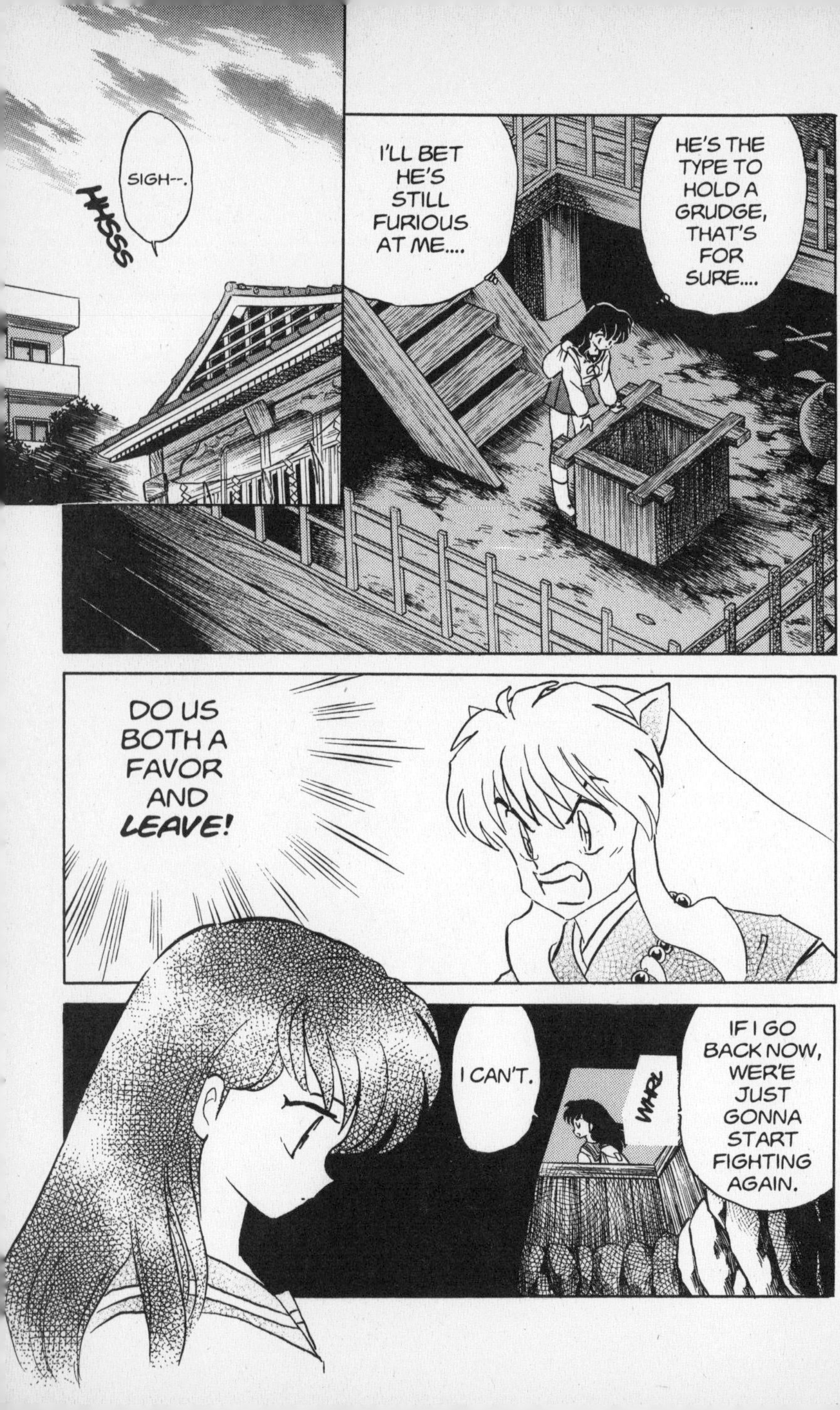
SIGH--.
HHSSS
I'LL BET HE'S STILL FURIOUS AT ME....
HE'S THE TYPE TO HOLD A GRUDGE, THAT'S FOR SURE....
DO US BOTH A FAVOR AND *LEAVE!*
I CAN'T.
WHRL
IF I GO BACK NOW, WER'E JUST GONNA START FIGHTING AGAIN.

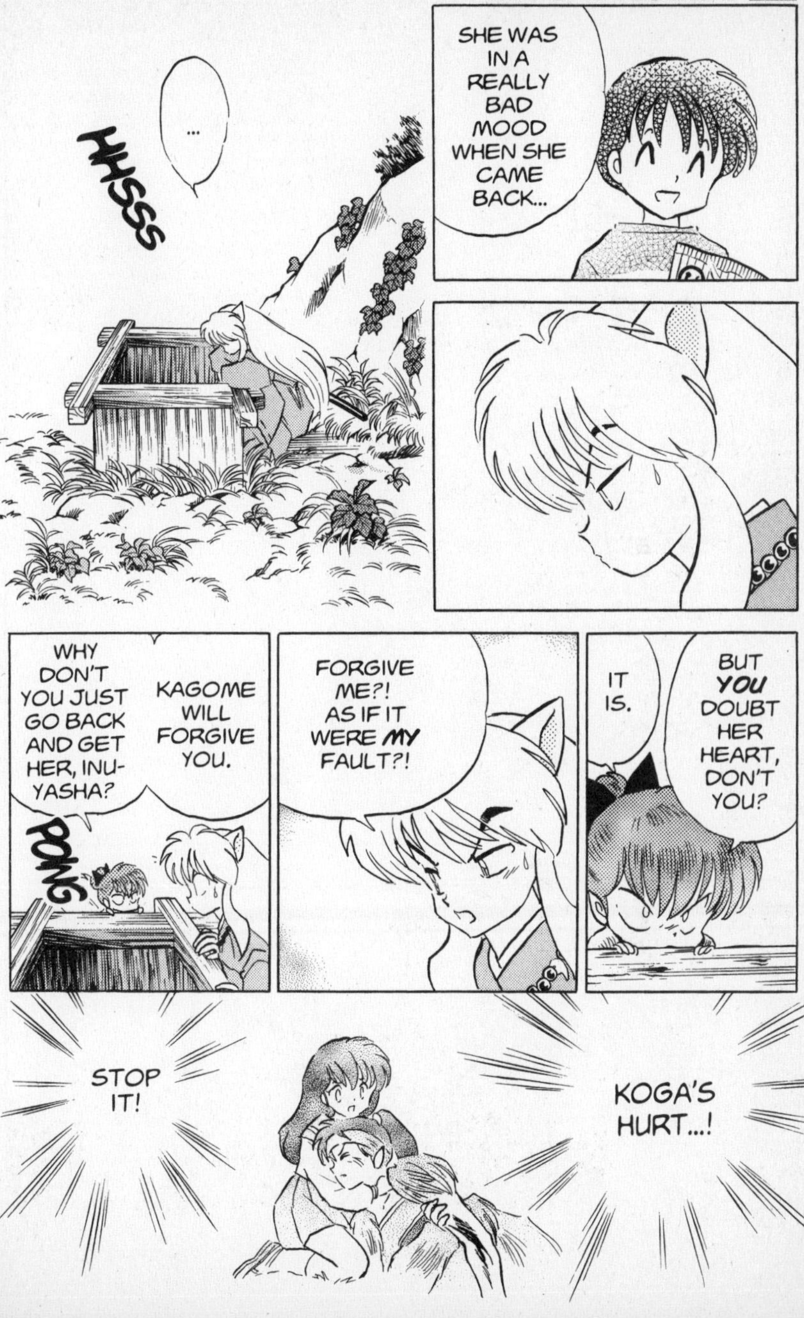
HHSSS
...
SHE WAS IN A REALLY BAD MOOD WHEN SHE CAME BACK...
WHY DON'T YOU JUST GO BACK AND GET HER, INU-YASHA?
KAGOME WILL FORGIVE YOU.
POING
FORGIVE ME?! AS IF IT WERE *MY* FAULT?!
IT IS.
BUT *YOU* DOUBT HER HEART, DON'T YOU?
STOP IT!
KOGA'S HURT...!

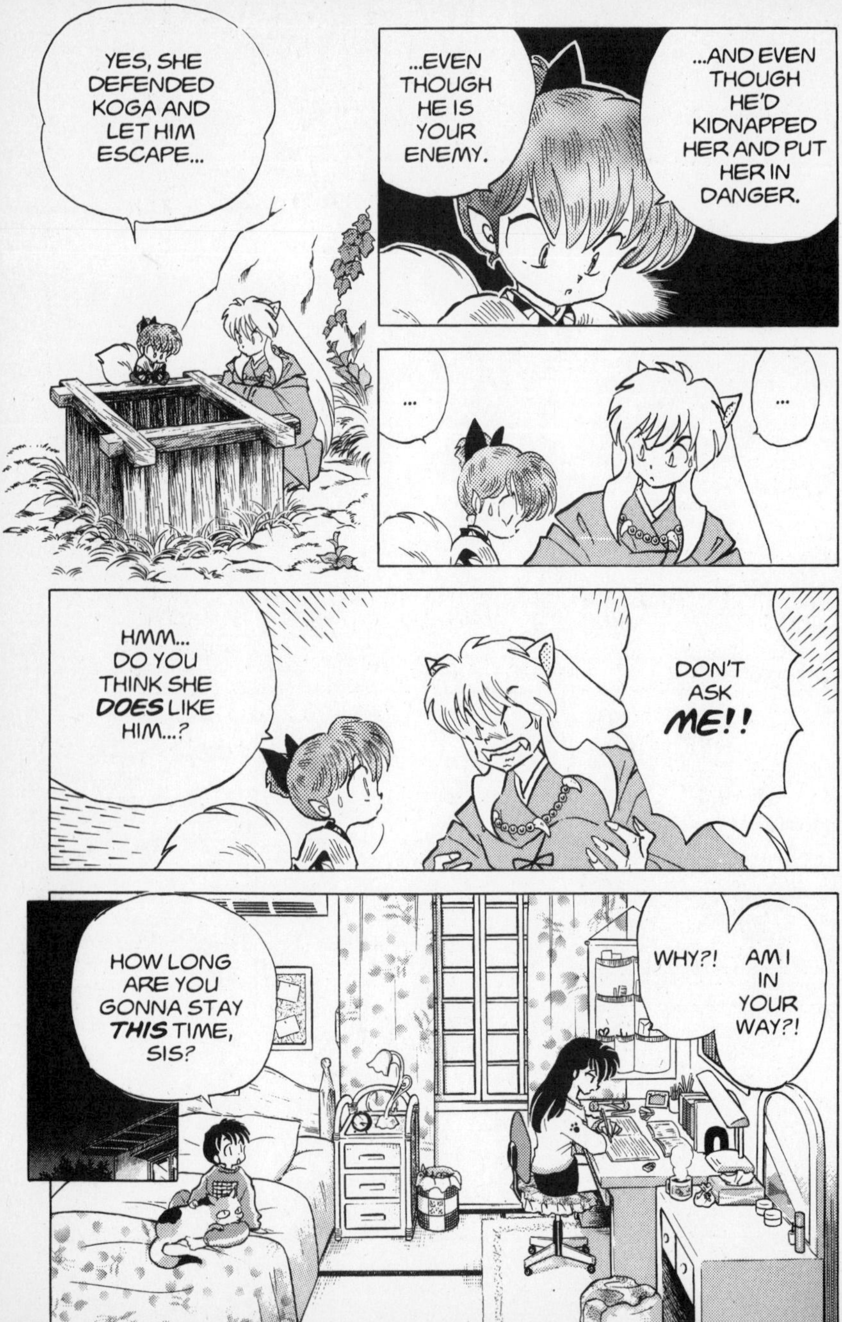
YES, SHE DEFENDED KOGA AND LET HIM ESCAPE...
...EVEN THOUGH HE IS YOUR ENEMY.
...AND EVEN THOUGH HE'D KIDNAPPED HER AND PUT HER IN DANGER.
...
...
HMM... DO YOU THINK SHE DOES LIKE HIM...?
DON'T ASK ME!!
HOW LONG ARE YOU GONNA STAY THIS TIME, SIS?
WHY?! AM I IN YOUR WAY?!

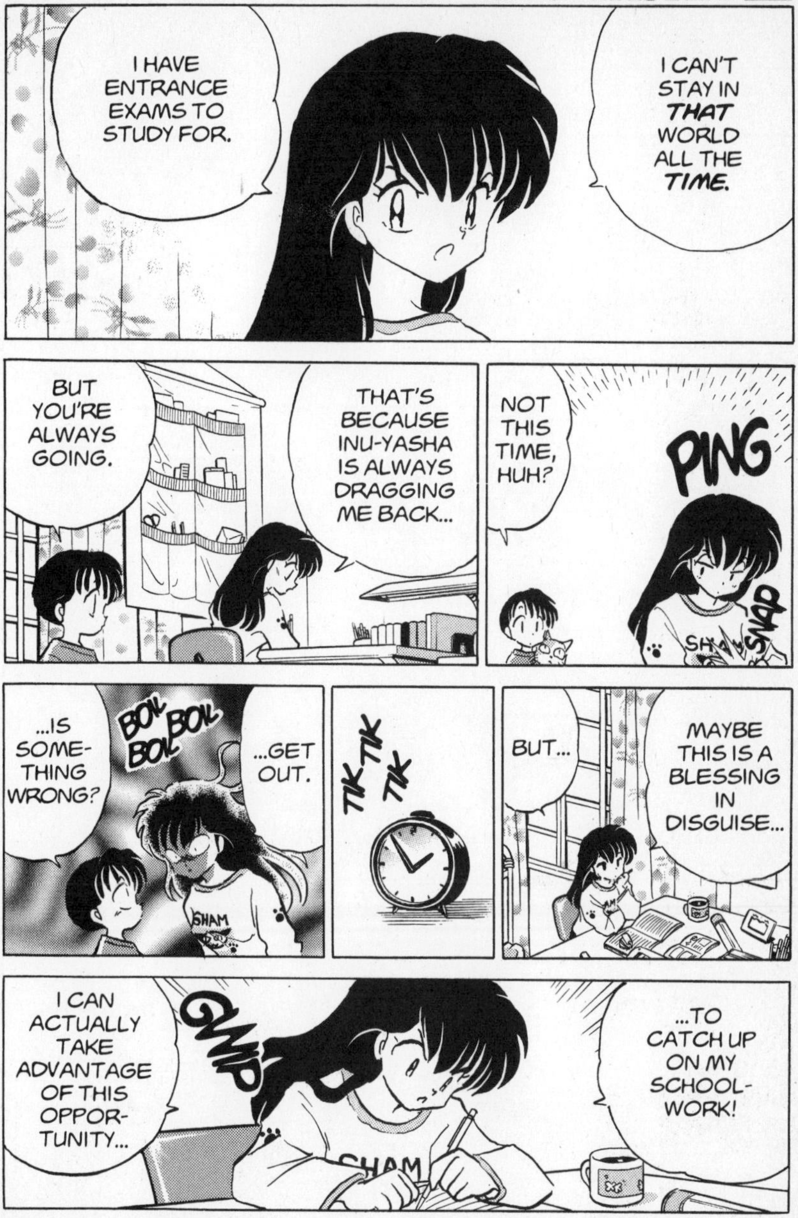
I HAVE ENTRANCE EXAMS TO STUDY FOR.
I CAN'T STAY IN *THAT* WORLD ALL THE *TIME.*
BUT YOU'RE ALWAYS GOING.
THAT'S BECAUSE INU-YASHA IS ALWAYS DRAGGING ME BACK...
NOT THIS TIME, HUH?
PING
SNAP
...IS SOME-THING WRONG?
BON BON BON
...GET OUT.
TIK TIK TIK
BUT...
MAYBE THIS IS A BLESSING IN DISGUISE...
I CAN ACTUALLY TAKE ADVANTAGE OF THIS OPPOR-TUNITY...
...TO CATCH UP ON MY SCHOOL-WORK!

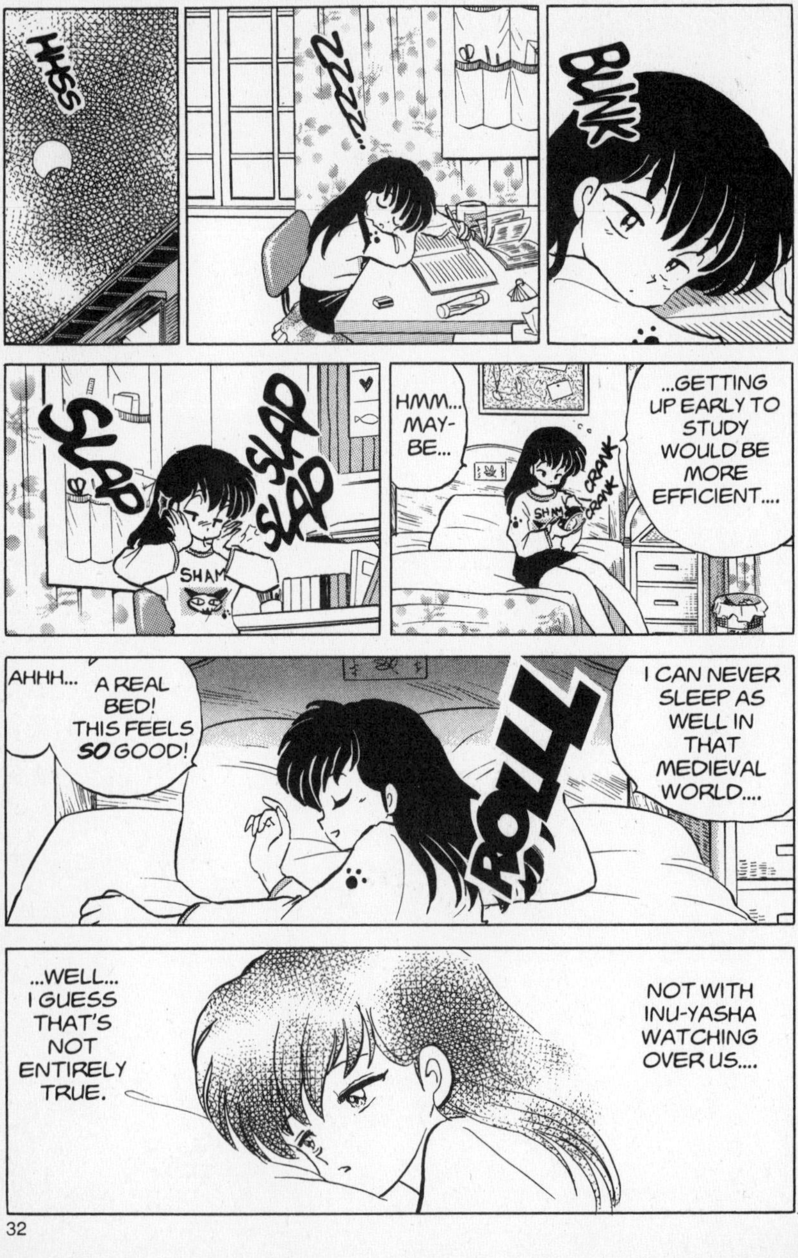
HISS
ZZZZ...
BLINK
SLAP
SLAP SLAP
SHAM
HMM... MAY-BE...
CRANK CRANK
...GETTING UP EARLY TO STUDY WOULD BE MORE EFFICIENT....
AHHH...
A REAL BED! THIS FEELS SO GOOD!
ROLL
I CAN NEVER SLEEP AS WELL IN THAT MEDIEVAL WORLD....
...WELL... I GUESS THAT'S NOT ENTIRELY TRUE.
NOT WITH INU-YASHA WATCHING OVER US....

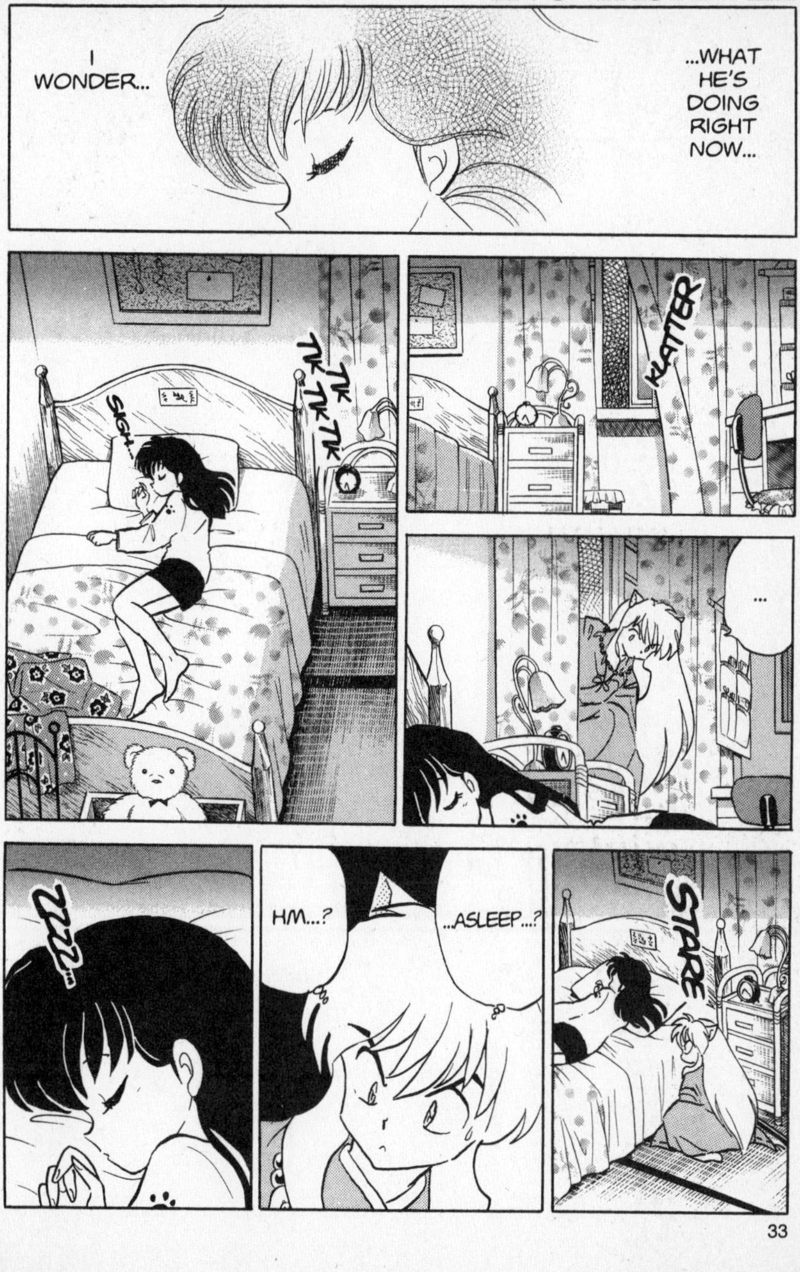
I WONDER...
...WHAT HE'S DOING RIGHT NOW...
SIGH...
TIK TIK TIK TIK
KLATTER
...
ZZZZ...
HM...?
...ASLEEP...?
STARE

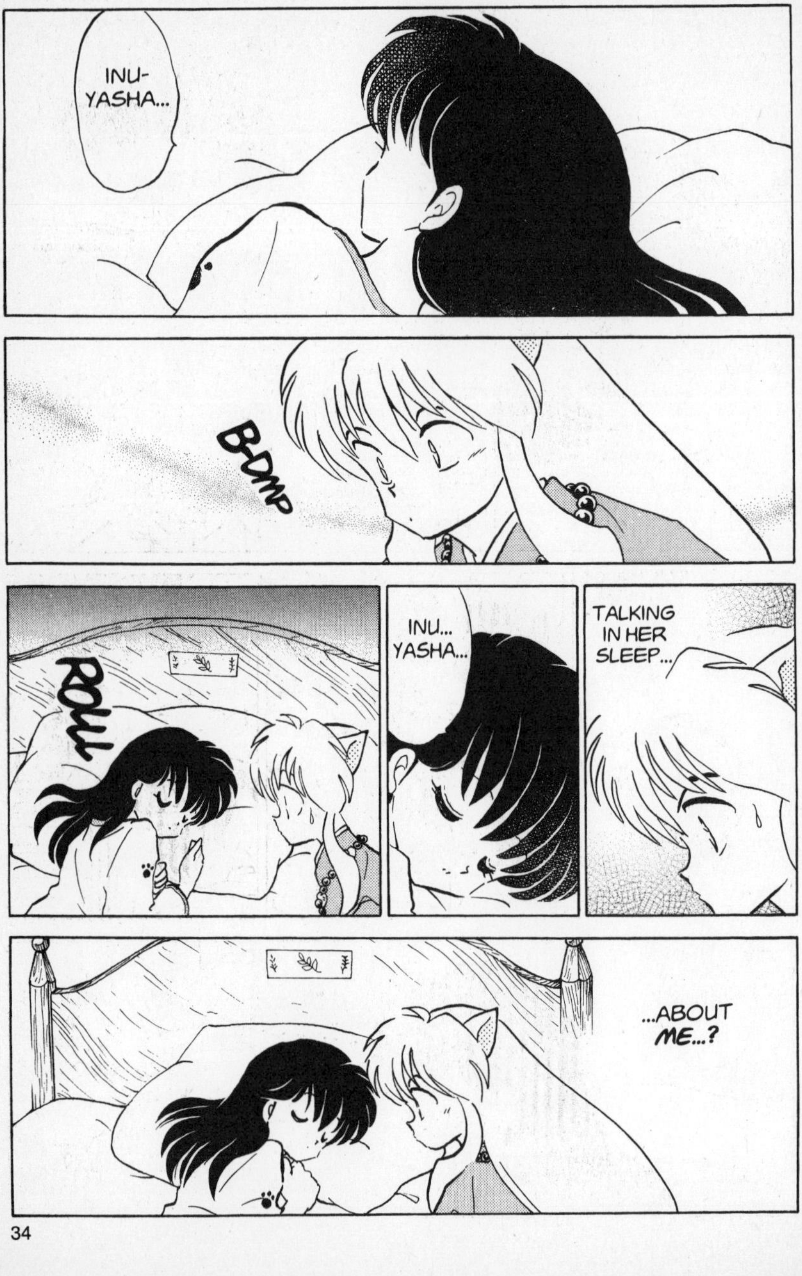
INU-
YASHA...
B-DMP
ROLL
INU...
YASHA...
TALKING
IN HER
SLEEP...
...ABOUT
ME...?

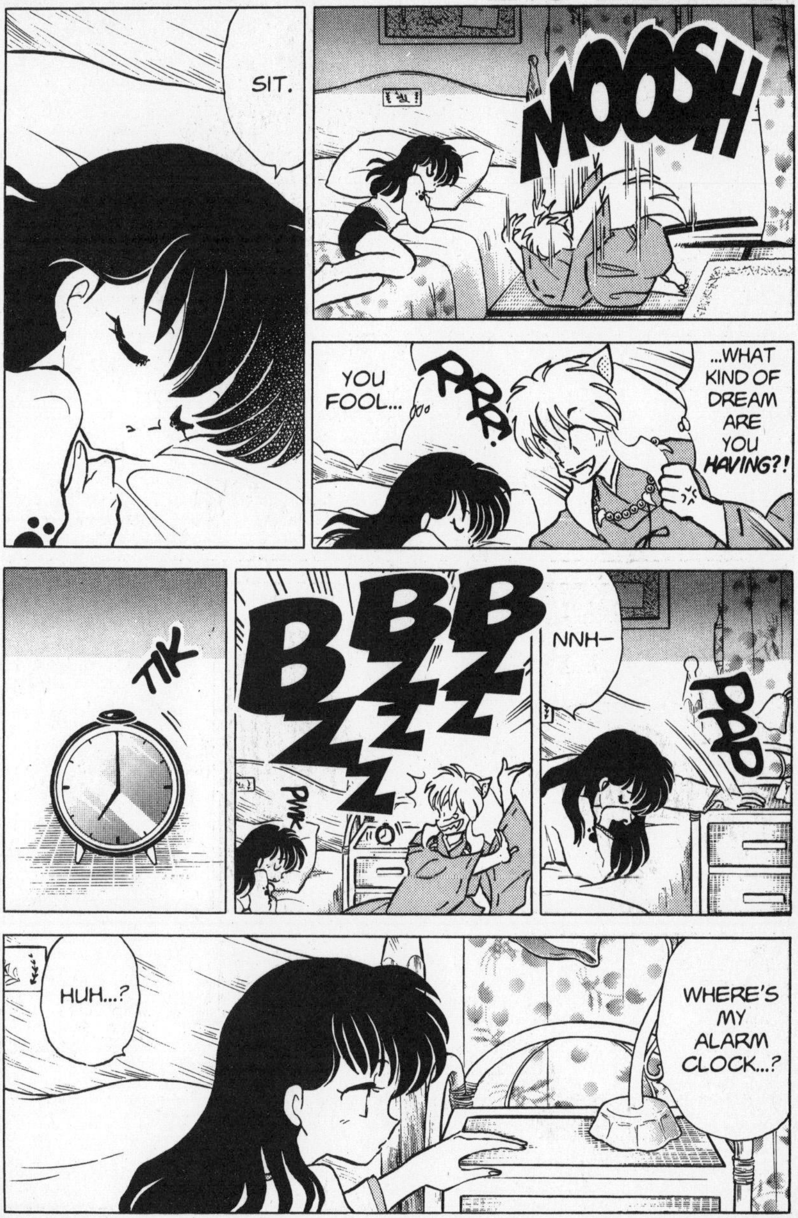
SIT.
MOOSH
YOU FOOL...
RRR!
...WHAT KIND OF DREAM ARE YOU *HAVING?!*
TIK
BBBZZZ
PWK
NNH–
PAP
HUH...?
WHERE'S MY ALARM CLOCK...?

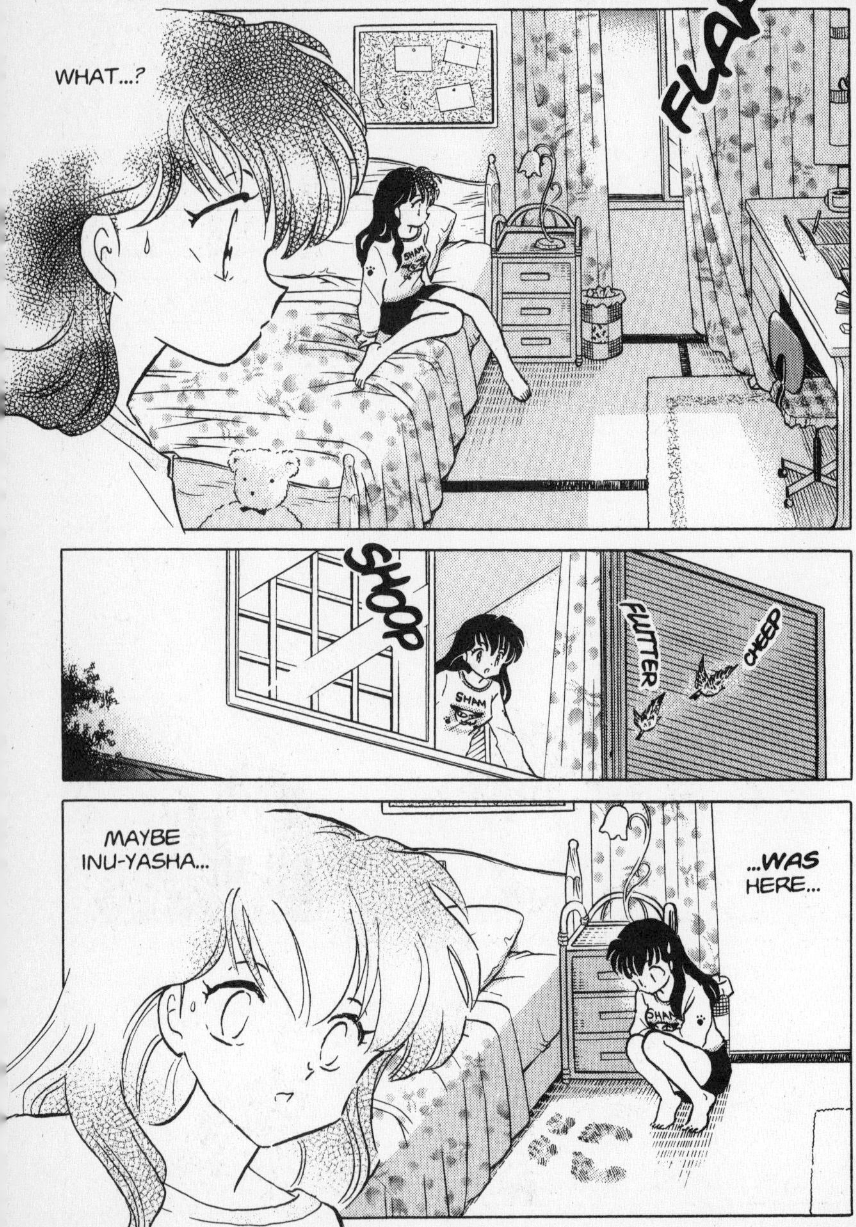
WHAT...?
FLAP
SHOOP
FLUTTER
CHEEP
MAYBE INU-YASHA...
...WAS HERE...

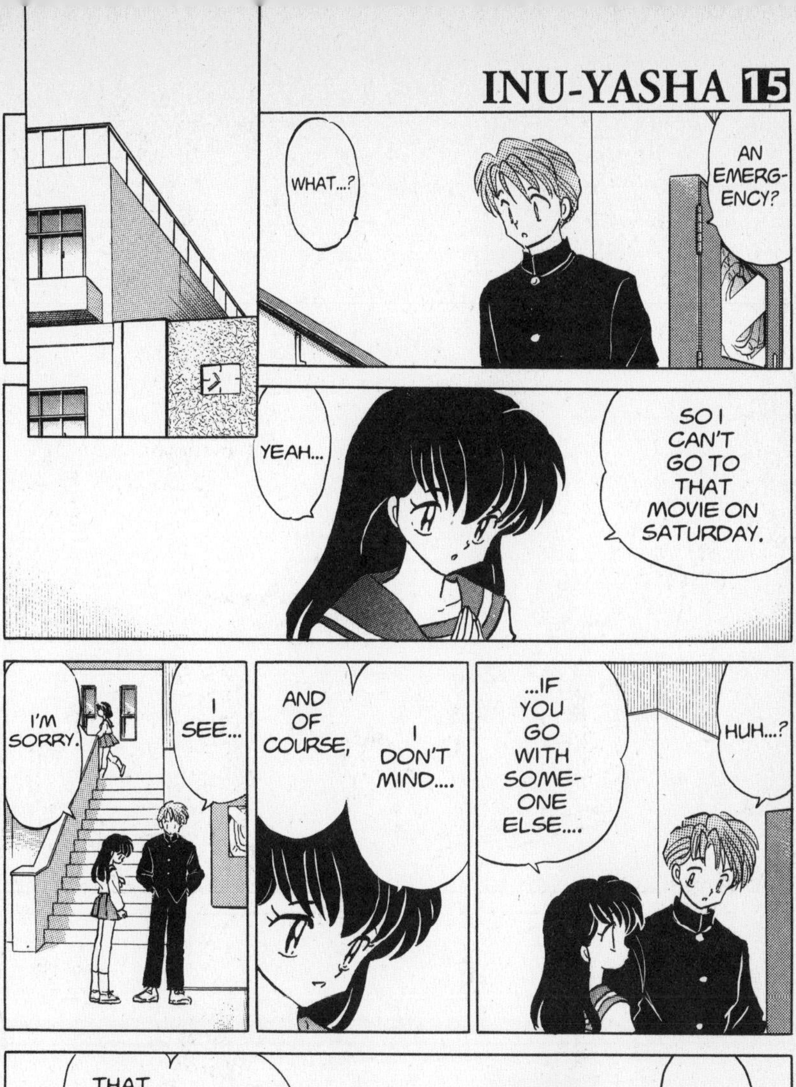
WHAT...?
AN EMERGENCY?
YEAH...
SO I CAN'T GO TO THAT MOVIE ON SATURDAY.
I'M SORRY.
I SEE...
AND OF COURSE,
I DON'T MIND....
...IF YOU GO WITH SOMEONE ELSE....
HUH...?
THAT FRESHMAN GIRL...
REALLY LIKES YOU, DOESN'T SHE...?
HIGURASHI...

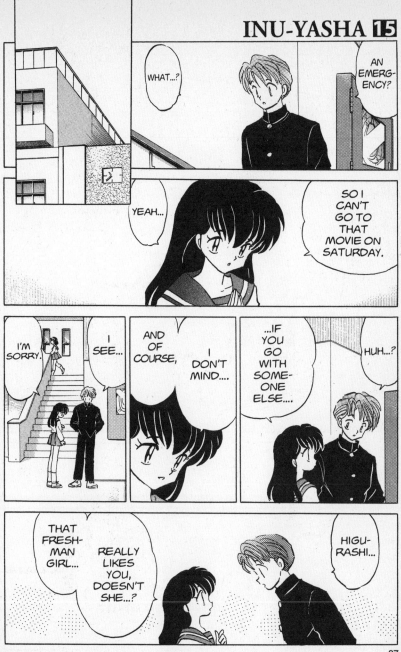

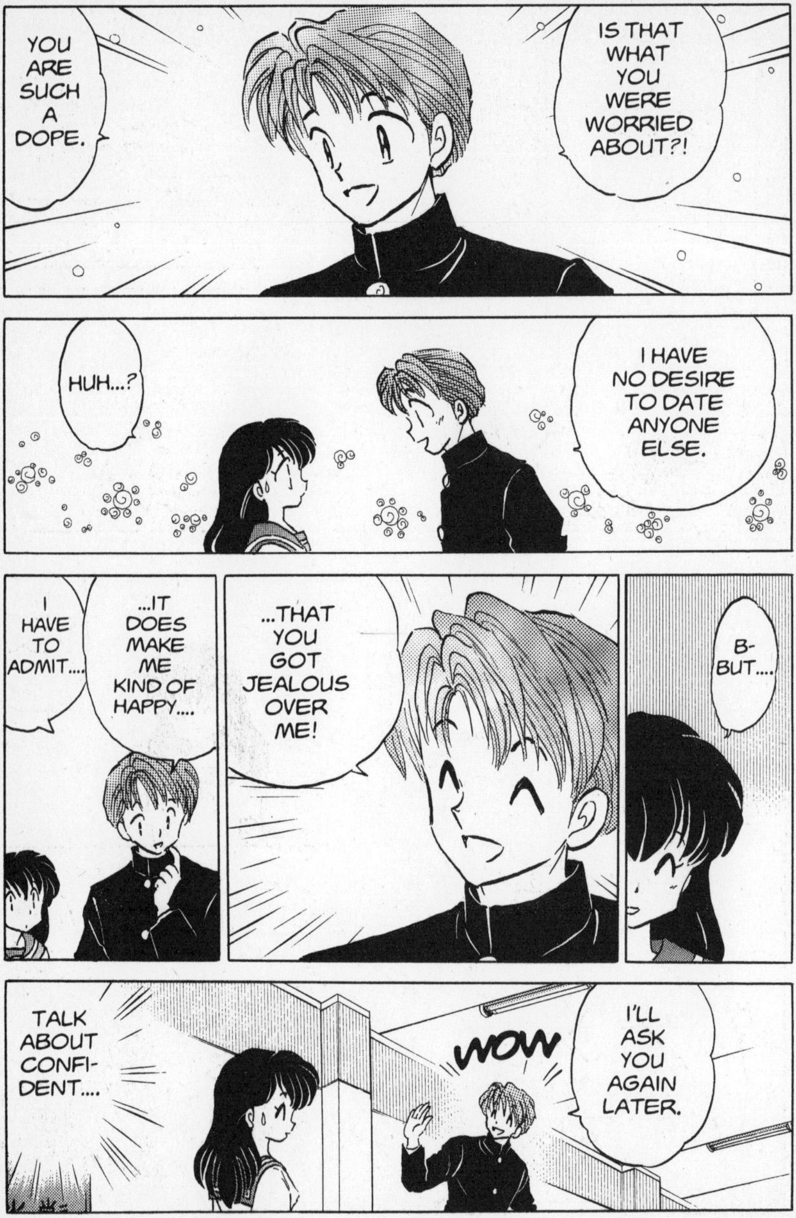
YOU ARE SUCH A DOPE.
IS THAT WHAT YOU WERE WORRIED ABOUT?!
HUH...?
I HAVE NO DESIRE TO DATE ANYONE ELSE.
I HAVE TO ADMIT....
...IT DOES MAKE ME KIND OF HAPPY....
...THAT YOU GOT JEALOUS OVER ME!
B-BUT....
TALK ABOUT CONFI-DENT....
WOW
I'LL ASK YOU AGAIN LATER.

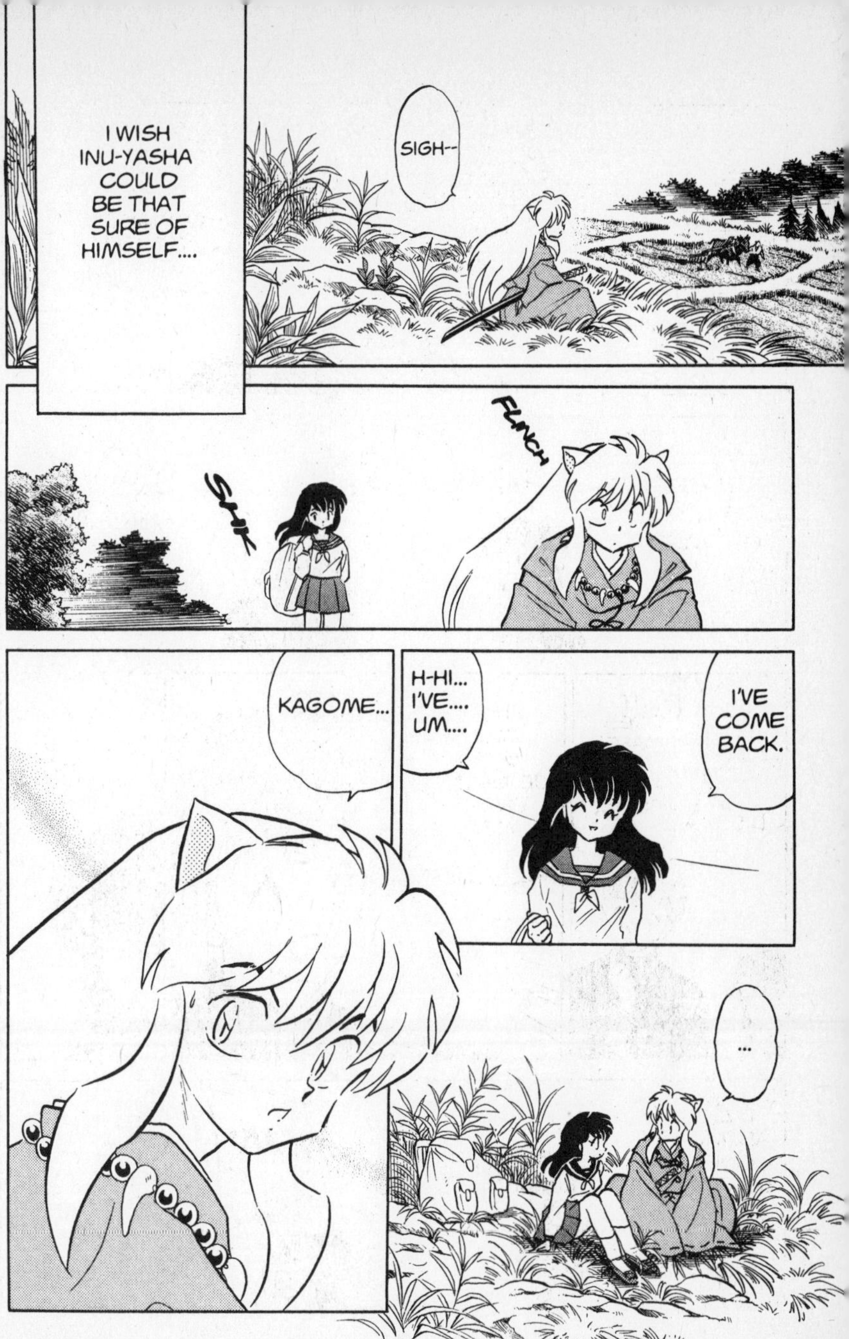
I WISH INU-YASHA COULD BE THAT SURE OF HIMSELF....
SIGH--
FLINCH
KAGOME...
H-HI... I'VE.... UM....
I'VE COME BACK.
...

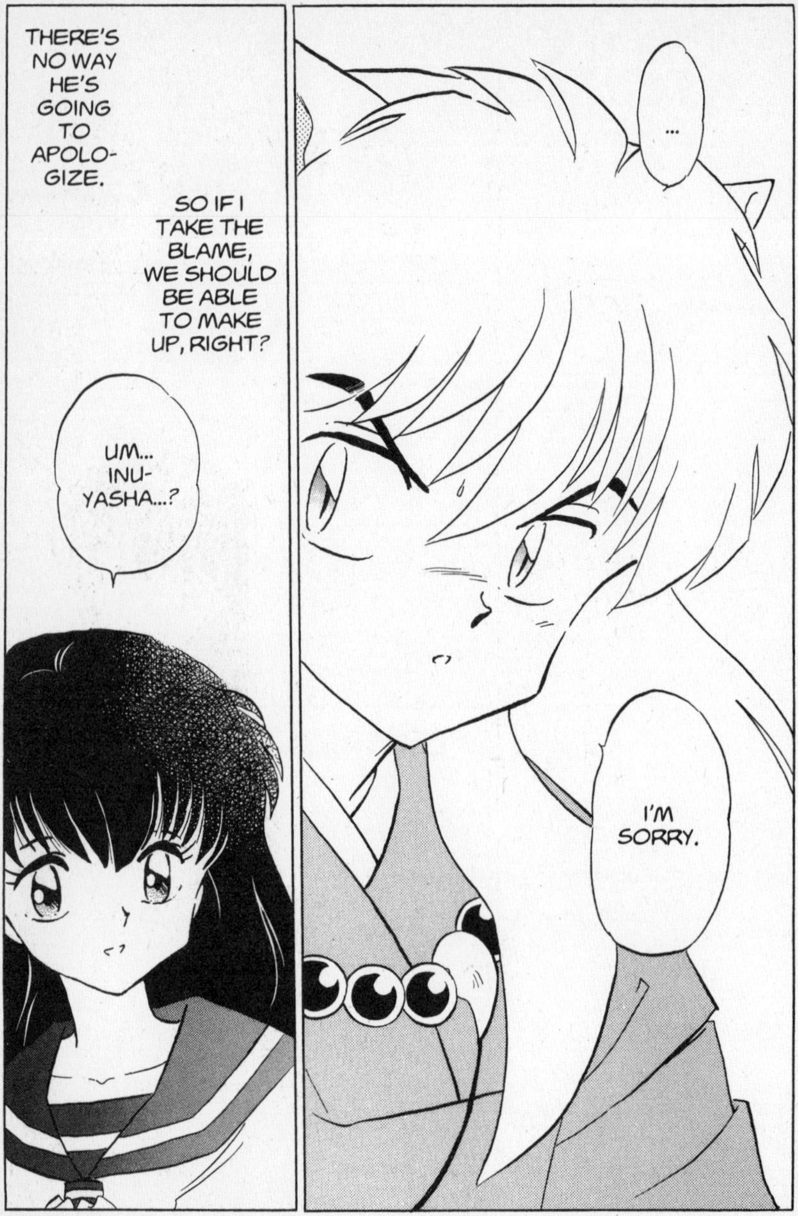
THERE'S NO WAY HE'S GOING TO APOLO-GIZE.
SO IF I TAKE THE BLAME, WE SHOULD BE ABLE TO MAKE UP, RIGHT?
UM... INU-YASHA...?
...
I'M SORRY.

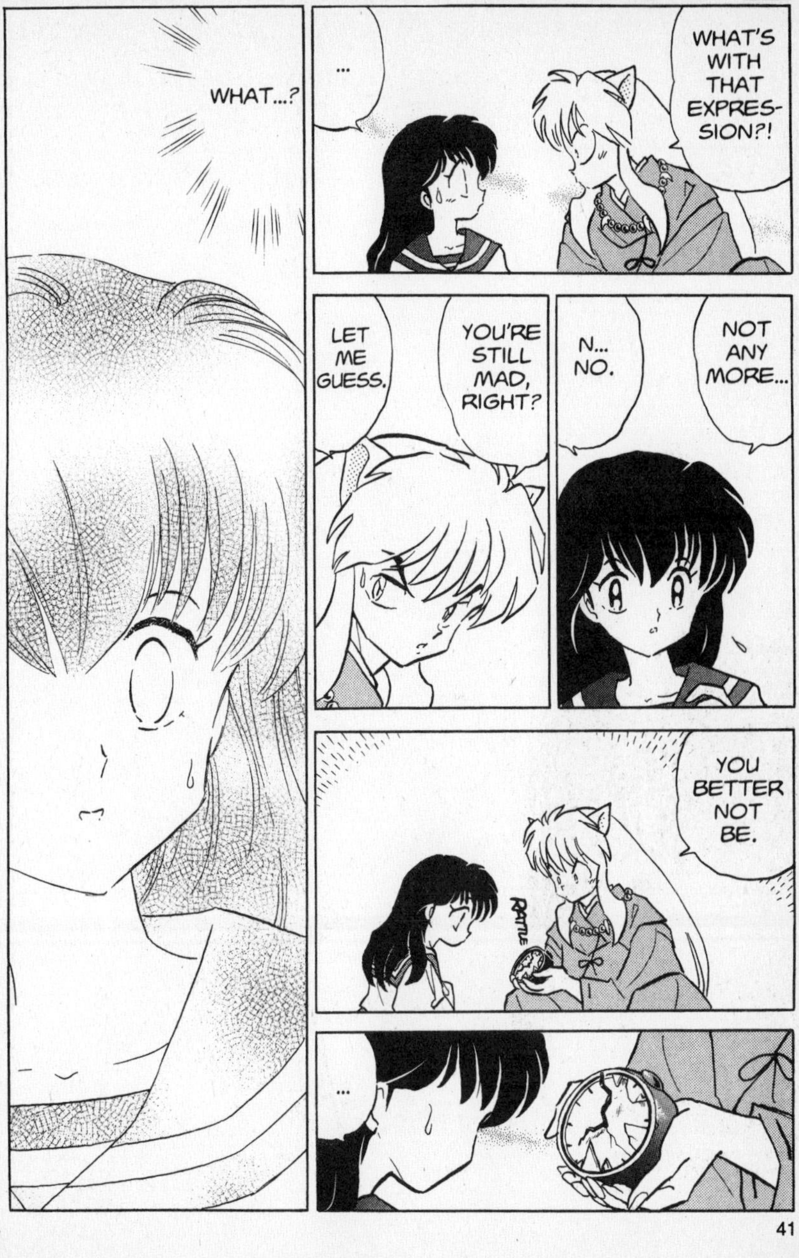
WHAT...?
...
WHAT'S WITH THAT EXPRES-SION?!
LET ME GUESS.
YOU'RE STILL MAD, RIGHT?
N... NO.
NOT ANY MORE...
RATTLE
YOU BETTER NOT BE.
...

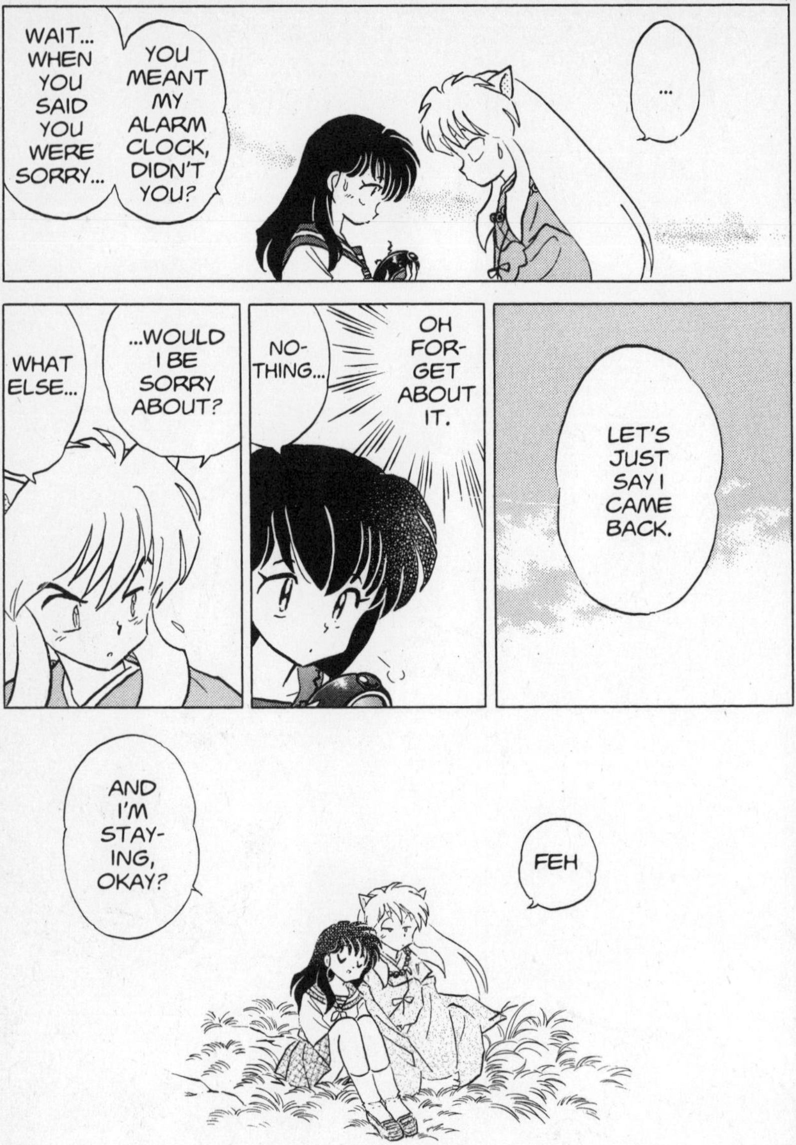
WAIT... WHEN YOU SAID YOU WERE SORRY...
YOU MEANT MY ALARM CLOCK, DIDN'T YOU?
...
WHAT ELSE...
...WOULD I BE SORRY ABOUT?
NO-THING...
OH FOR-GET ABOUT IT.
LET'S JUST SAY I CAME BACK.
AND I'M STAY-ING, OKAY?
FEH

SCROLL THREE
THE CHASE

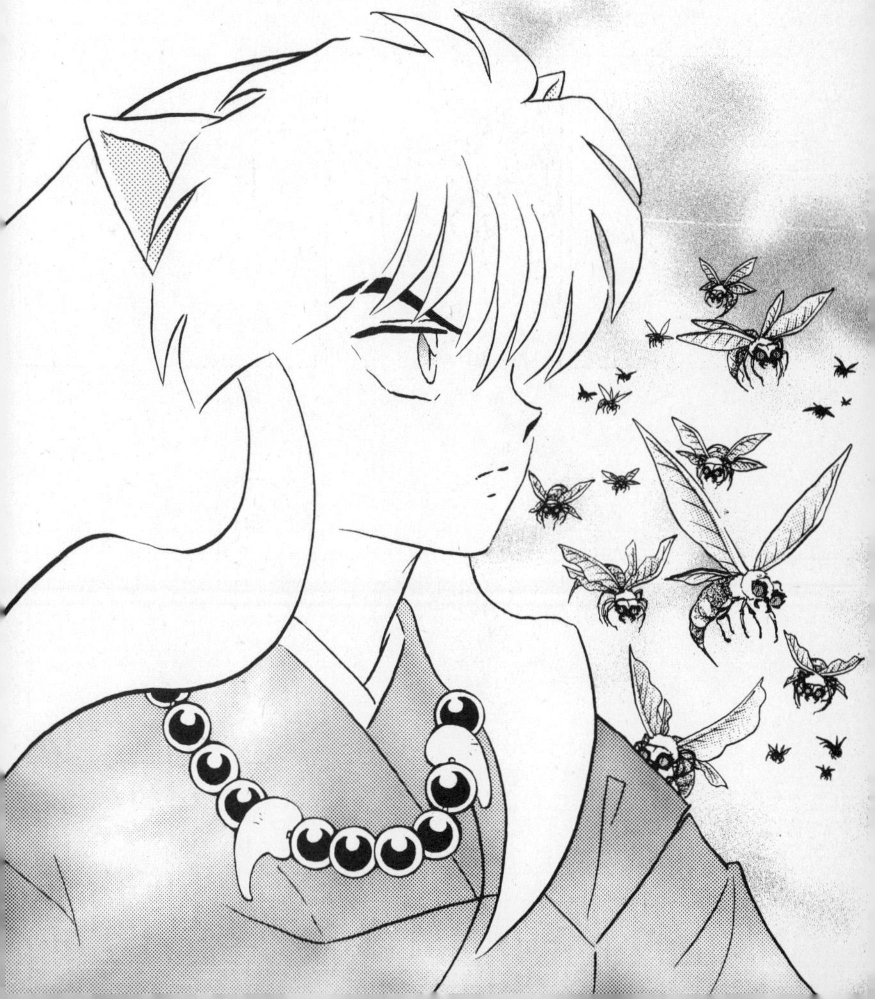

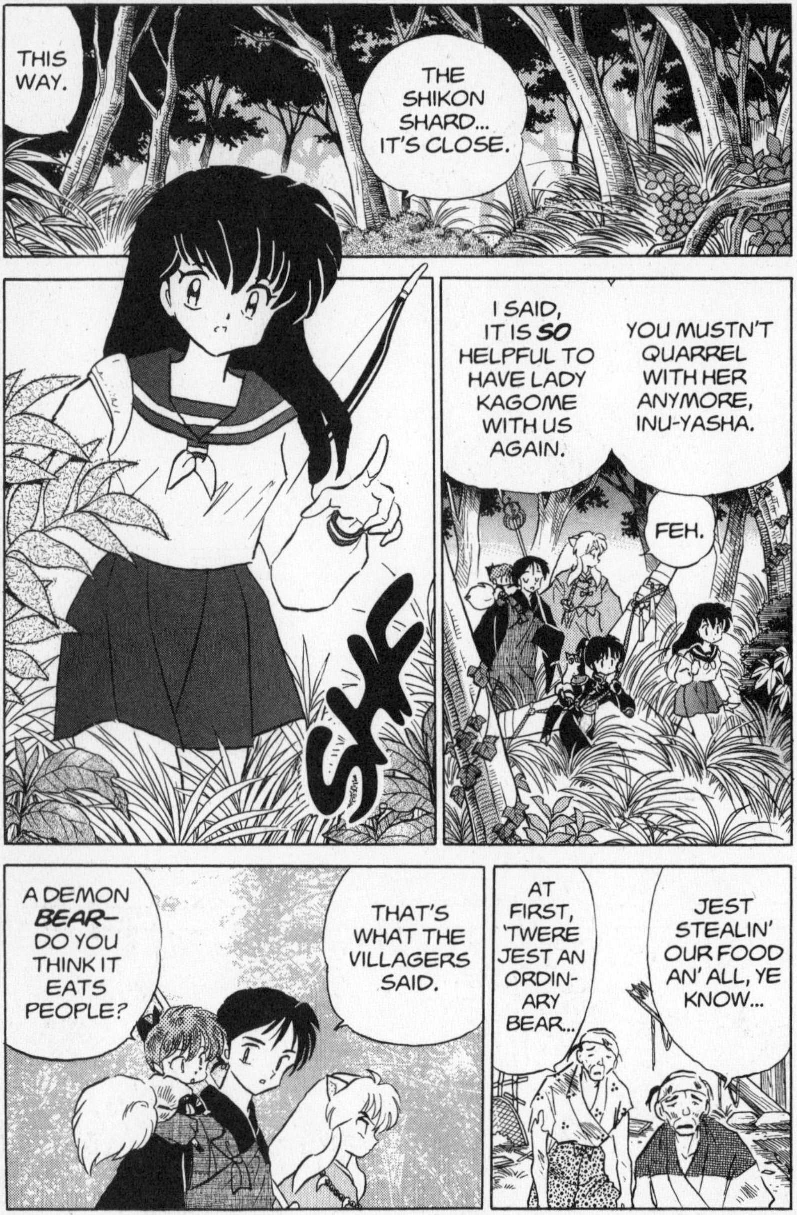
THIS WAY.
THE SHIKON SHARD... IT'S CLOSE.
SHF
I SAID, IT IS *SO* HELPFUL TO HAVE LADY KAGOME WITH US AGAIN.
YOU MUSTN'T QUARREL WITH HER ANYMORE, INU-YASHA.
FEH.
A DEMON *BEAR*– DO YOU THINK IT EATS PEOPLE?
THAT'S WHAT THE VILLAGERS SAID.
AT FIRST, 'TWERE JEST AN ORDIN-ARY BEAR...
JEST STEALIN' OUR FOOD AN' ALL, YE KNOW...

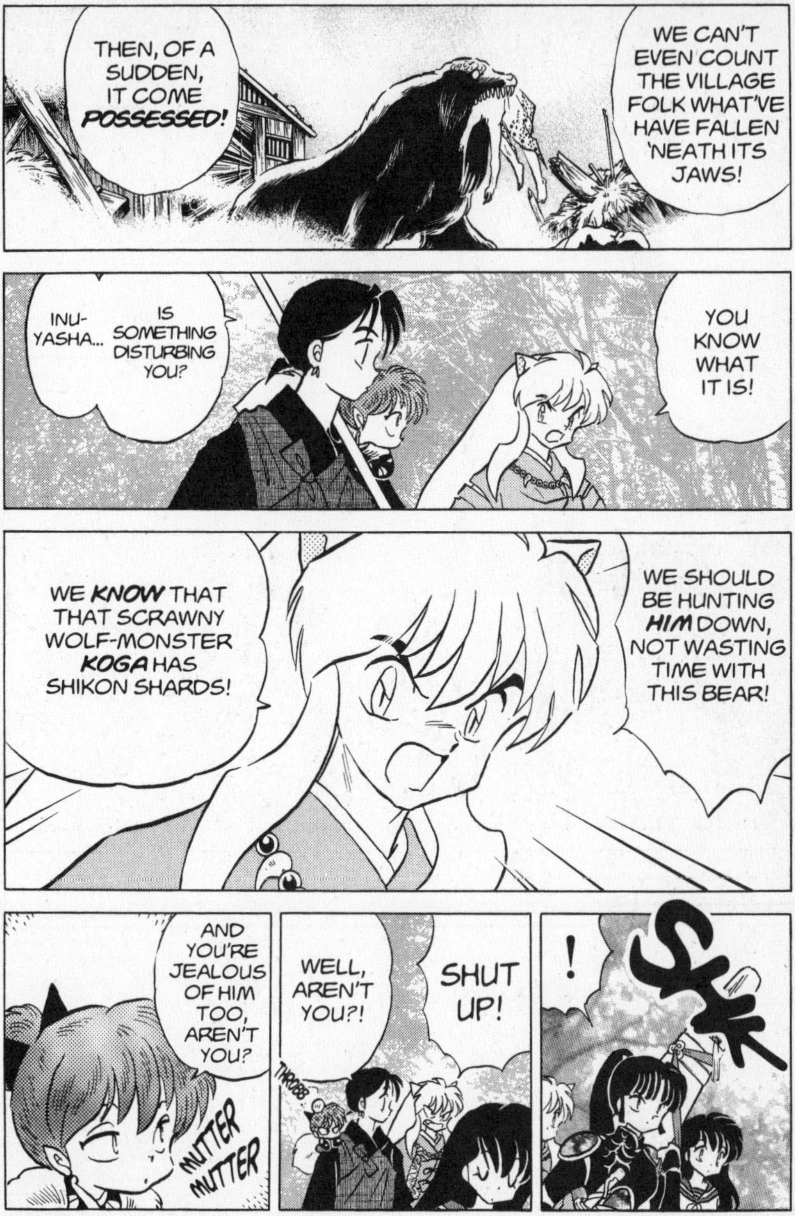
THEN, OF A SUDDEN, IT COME *POSSESSED!*
WE CAN'T EVEN COUNT THE VILLAGE FOLK WHAT'VE HAVE FALLEN 'NEATH ITS JAWS!
INU-YASHA... IS SOMETHING DISTURBING YOU?
YOU KNOW WHAT IT IS!
WE *KNOW* THAT THAT SCRAWNY WOLF-MONSTER *KOGA* HAS SHIKON SHARDS!
WE SHOULD BE HUNTING *HIM* DOWN, NOT WASTING TIME WITH THIS BEAR!
AND YOU'RE JEALOUS OF HIM TOO, AREN'T YOU?
MUTTER MUTTER
THROBB
WELL, AREN'T YOU?!
SHUT UP!
!
SHK

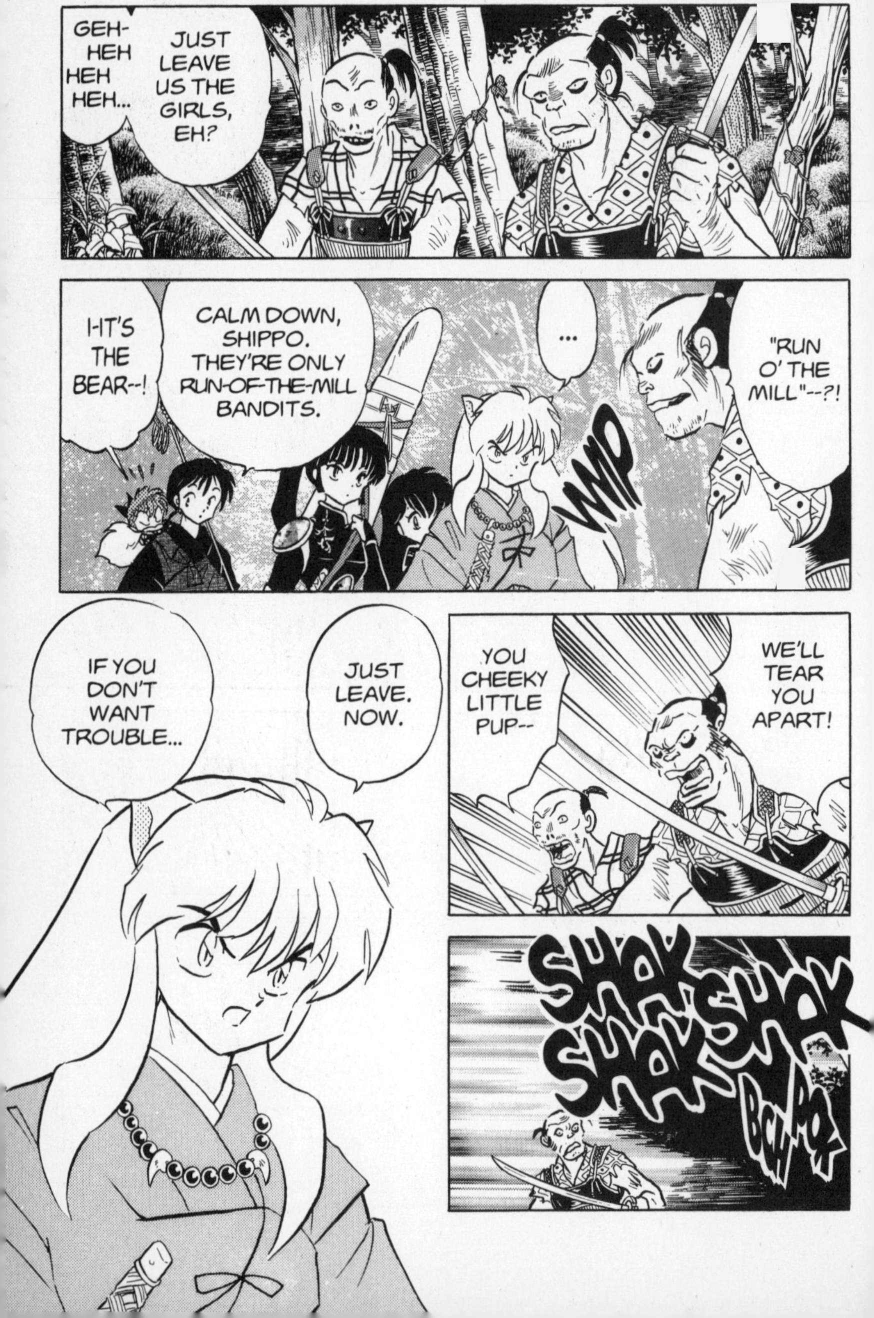
GEH-HEH HEH HEH...
JUST LEAVE US THE GIRLS, EH?
I-IT'S THE BEAR--!
CALM DOWN, SHIPPO. THEY'RE ONLY RUN-OF-THE-MILL BANDITS.
...
WMP
"RUN O' THE MILL"--?!
IF YOU DON'T WANT TROUBLE...
JUST LEAVE. NOW.
YOU CHEEKY LITTLE PUP--
WE'LL TEAR YOU APART!
SHAK SHAK SHAK SHAK SHAK
BCH POK

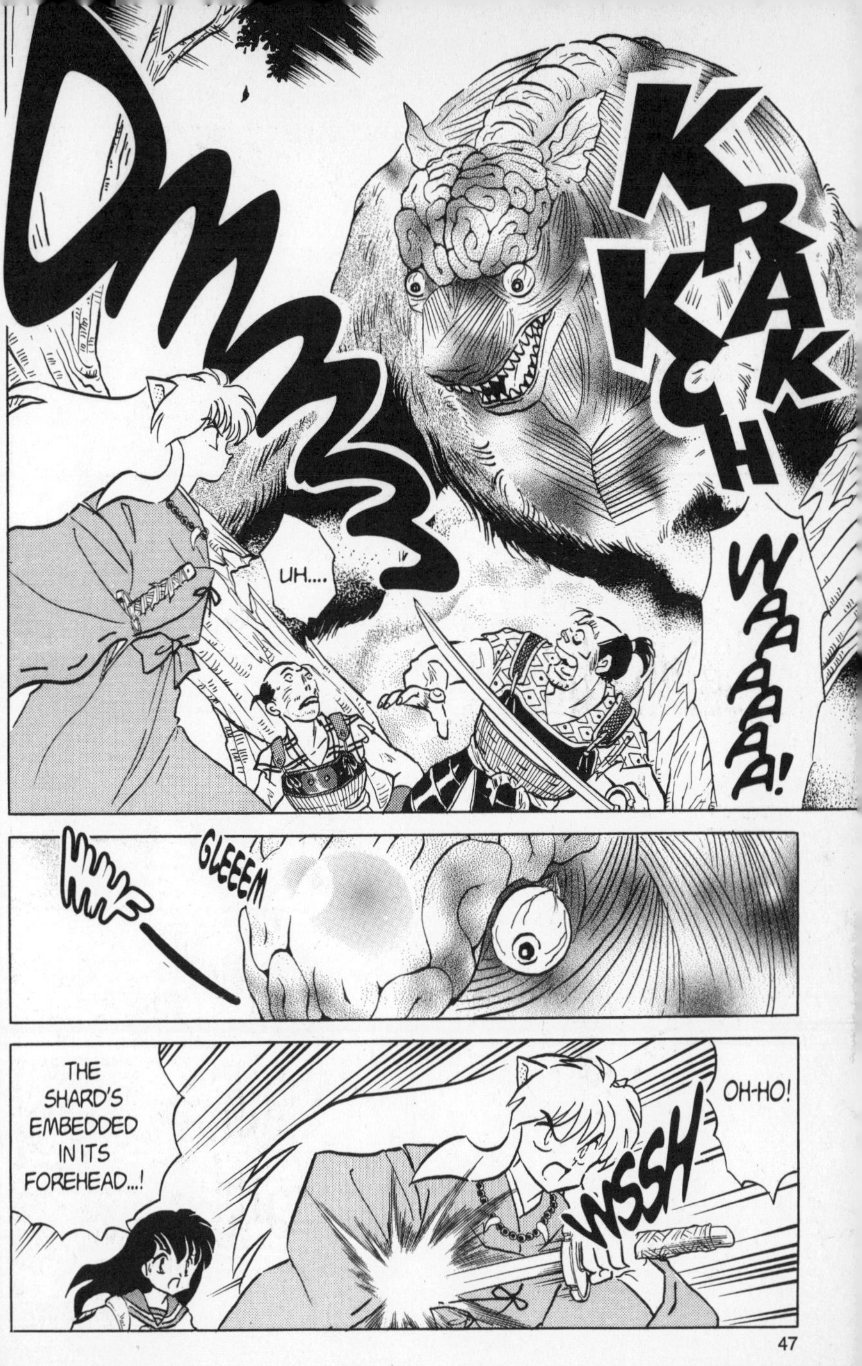
KRAKKCH
UH....
WAAAAA!
GLEEEM
THE SHARD'S EMBEDDED IN ITS FOREHEAD...!
WSSH
OH-HO!

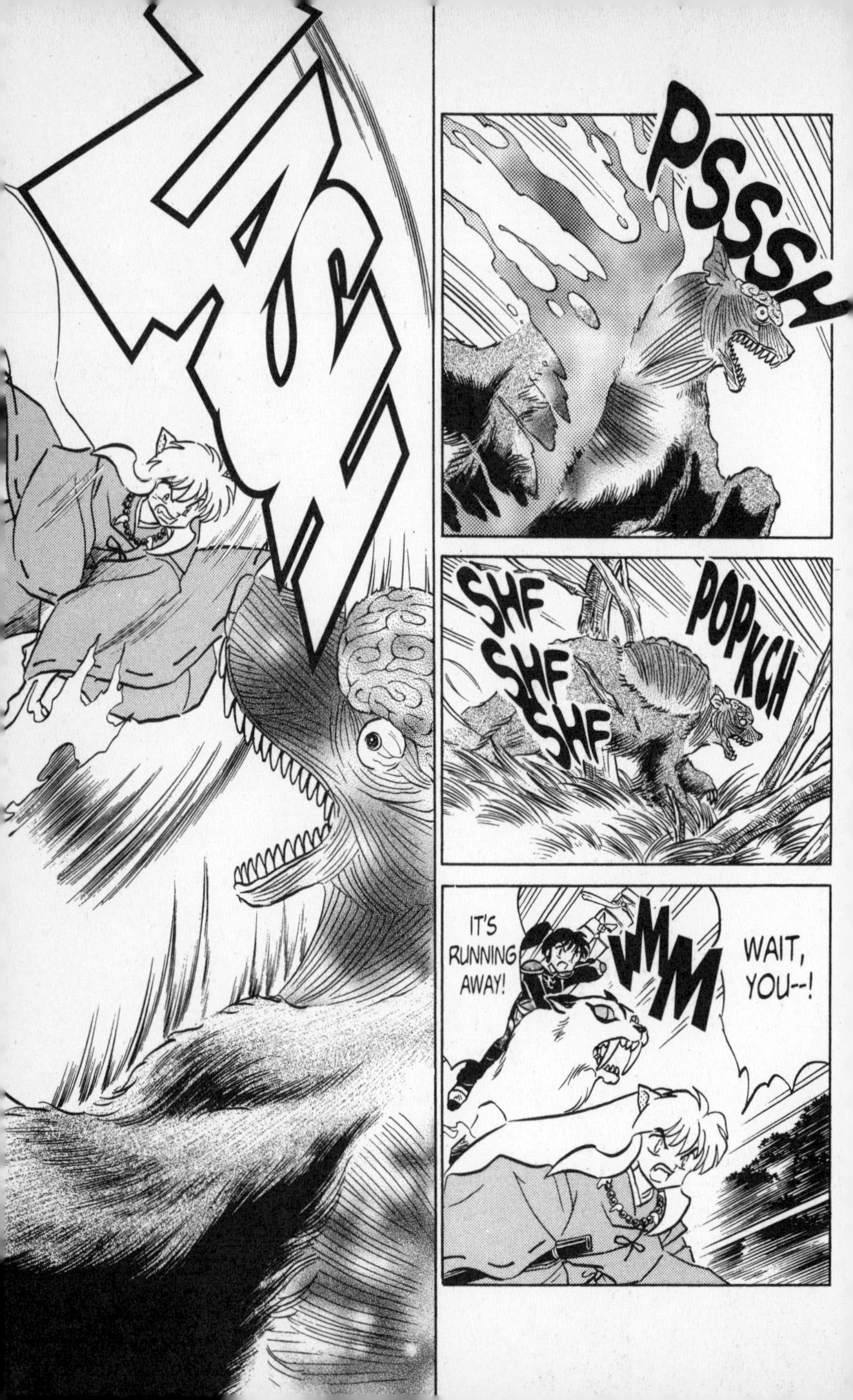
PSSSH
SHF SHF SHF
POPKCH
IT'S RUNNING AWAY!
VMM
WAIT, YOU--!

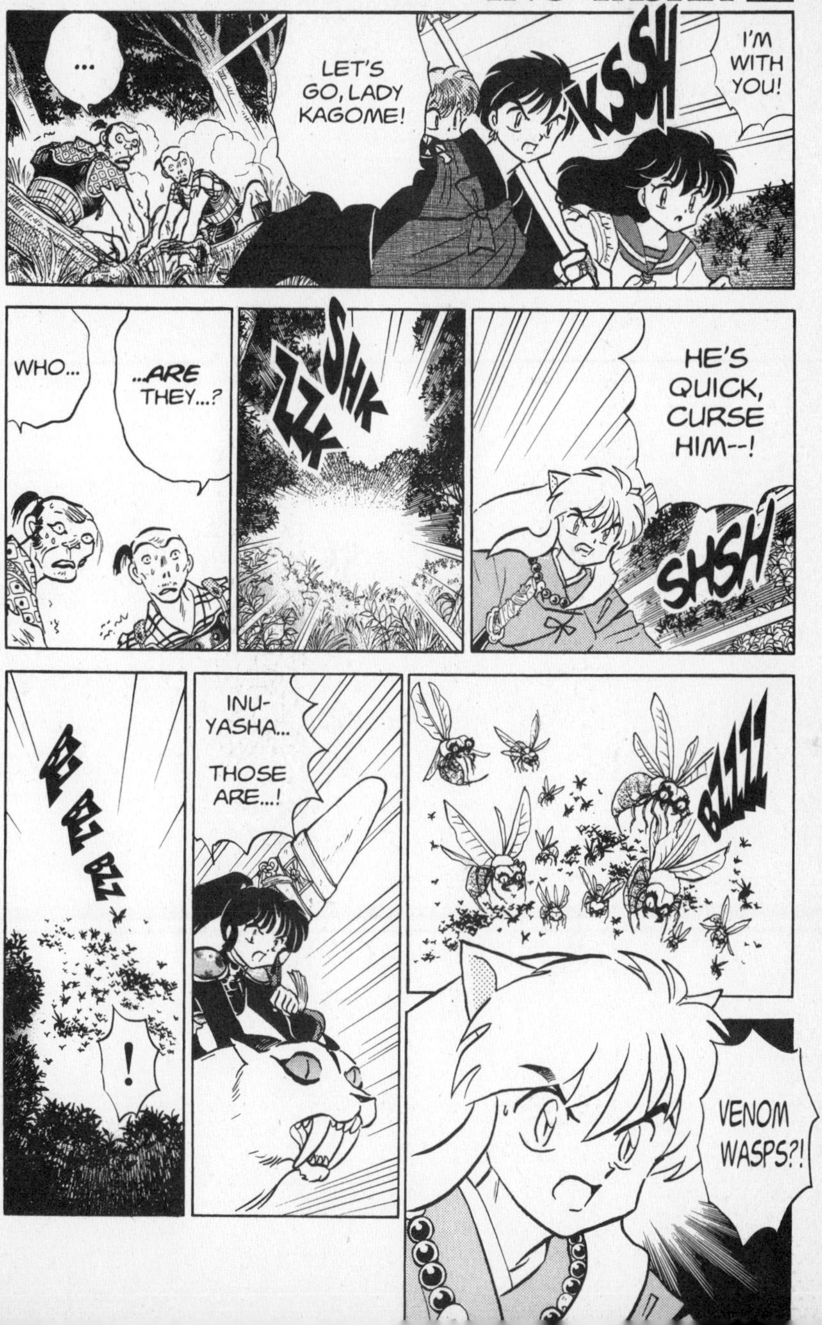
...
LET'S GO, LADY KAGOME!
KSSH
I'M WITH YOU!
WHO...
...ARE THEY...?
SHK
ZZK
HE'S QUICK, CURSE HIM--!
SHSH
BZZ BZZ BZZ
!
INU-YASHA... THOSE ARE...!
BZZZZZ
VENOM WASPS?!

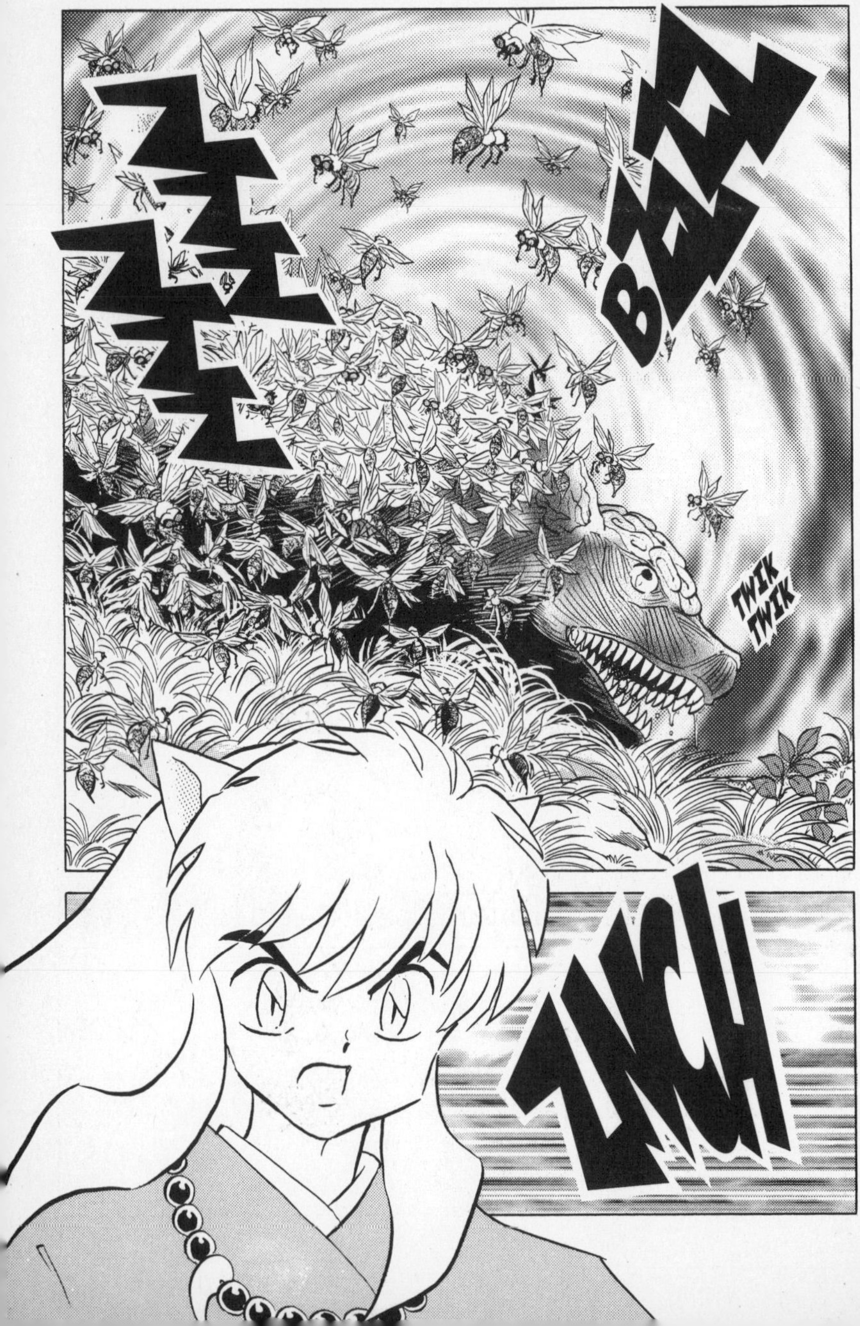
BZZZ
TWIK TWIK
TWICH

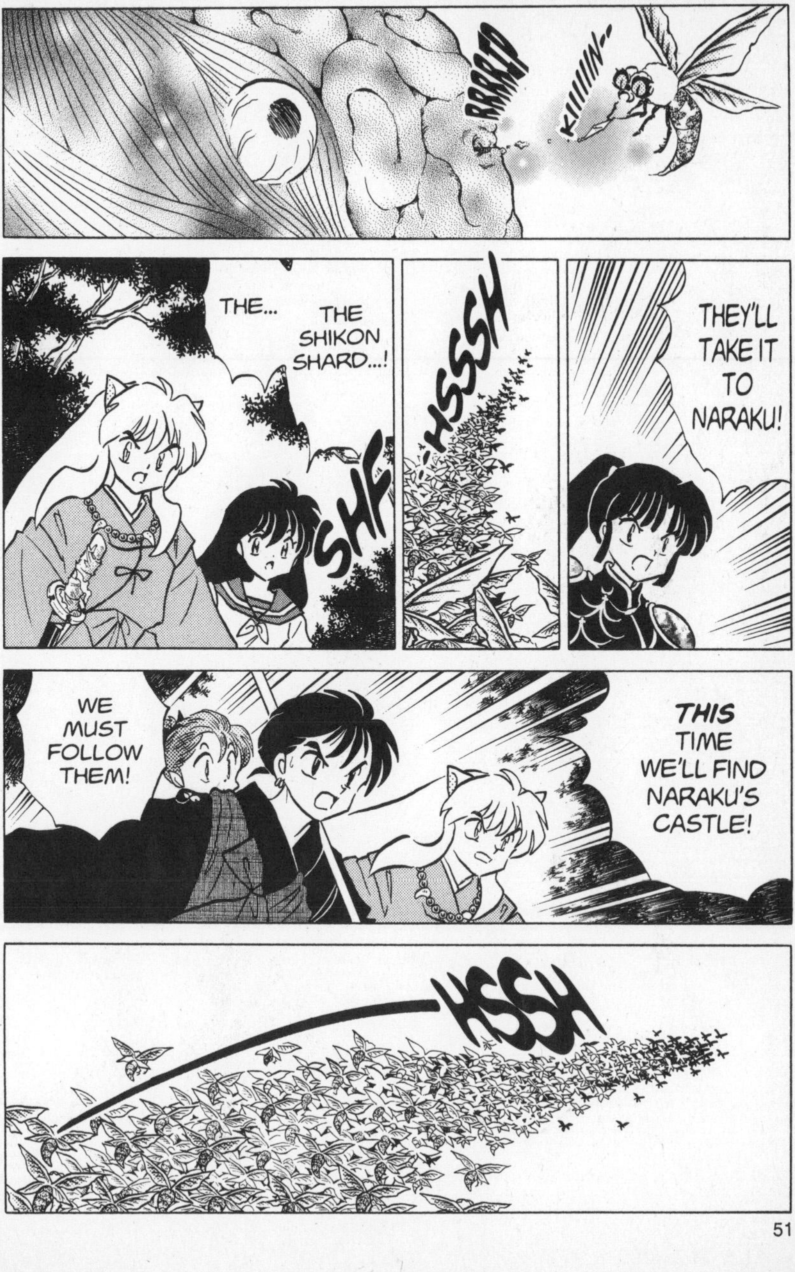
RRRRTP
KIIIIIIIN...
THE...
THE SHIKON SHARD...!
SHF
HSSSH
THEY'LL TAKE IT TO NARAKU!
WE MUST FOLLOW THEM!
THIS TIME WE'LL FIND NARAKU'S CASTLE!
HSSH

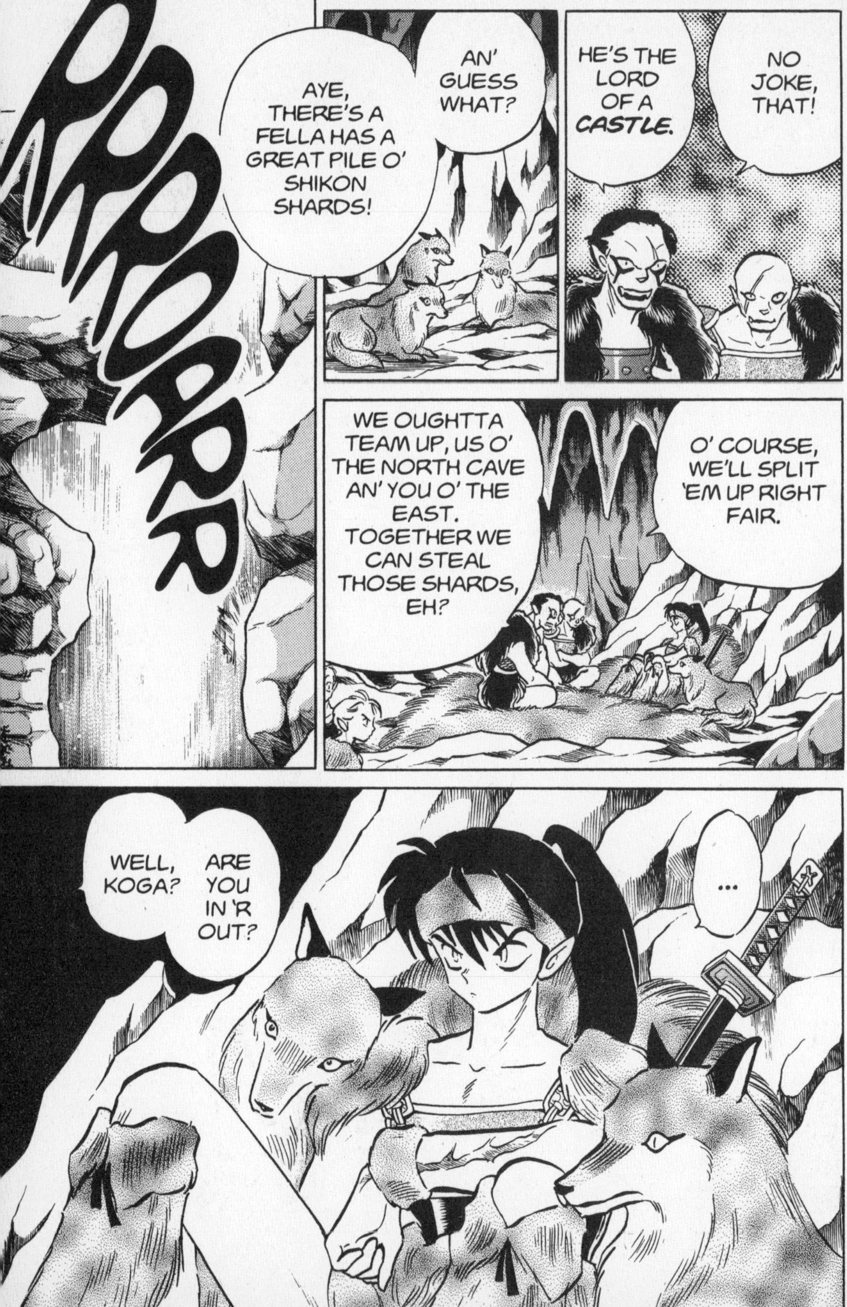
RRROARR
AYE, THERE'S A FELLA HAS A GREAT PILE O' SHIKON SHARDS!
AN' GUESS WHAT?
HE'S THE LORD OF A *CASTLE.*
NO JOKE, THAT!
WE OUGHTTA TEAM UP, US O' THE NORTH CAVE AN' YOU O' THE EAST. TOGETHER WE CAN STEAL THOSE SHARDS, EH?
O' COURSE, WE'LL SPLIT 'EM UP RIGHT FAIR.
WELL, KOGA?
ARE YOU IN 'R OUT?
...

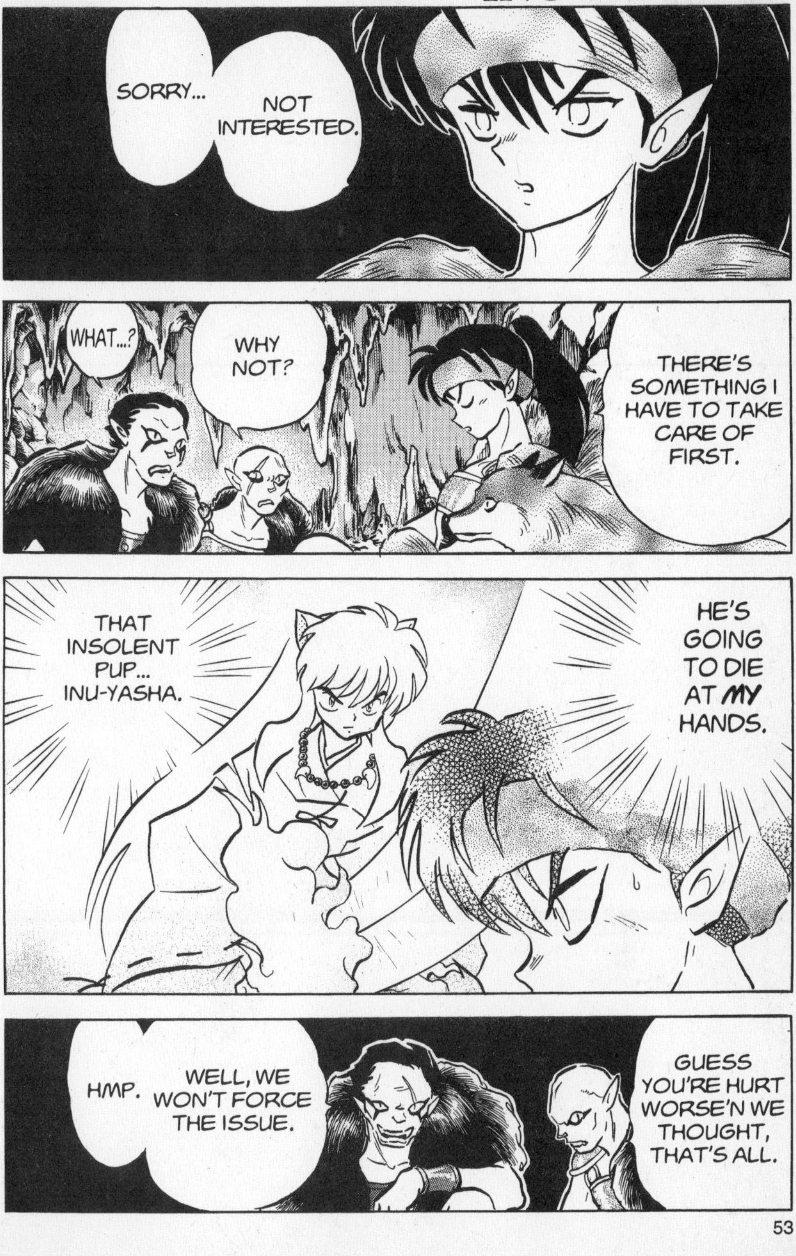
SORRY...
NOT INTERESTED.
WHAT...?
WHY NOT?
THERE'S SOMETHING I HAVE TO TAKE CARE OF FIRST.
THAT INSOLENT PUP... INU-YASHA.
HE'S GOING TO DIE AT *MY* HANDS.
HMP.
WELL, WE WON'T FORCE THE ISSUE.
GUESS YOU'RE HURT WORSE'N WE THOUGHT, THAT'S ALL.

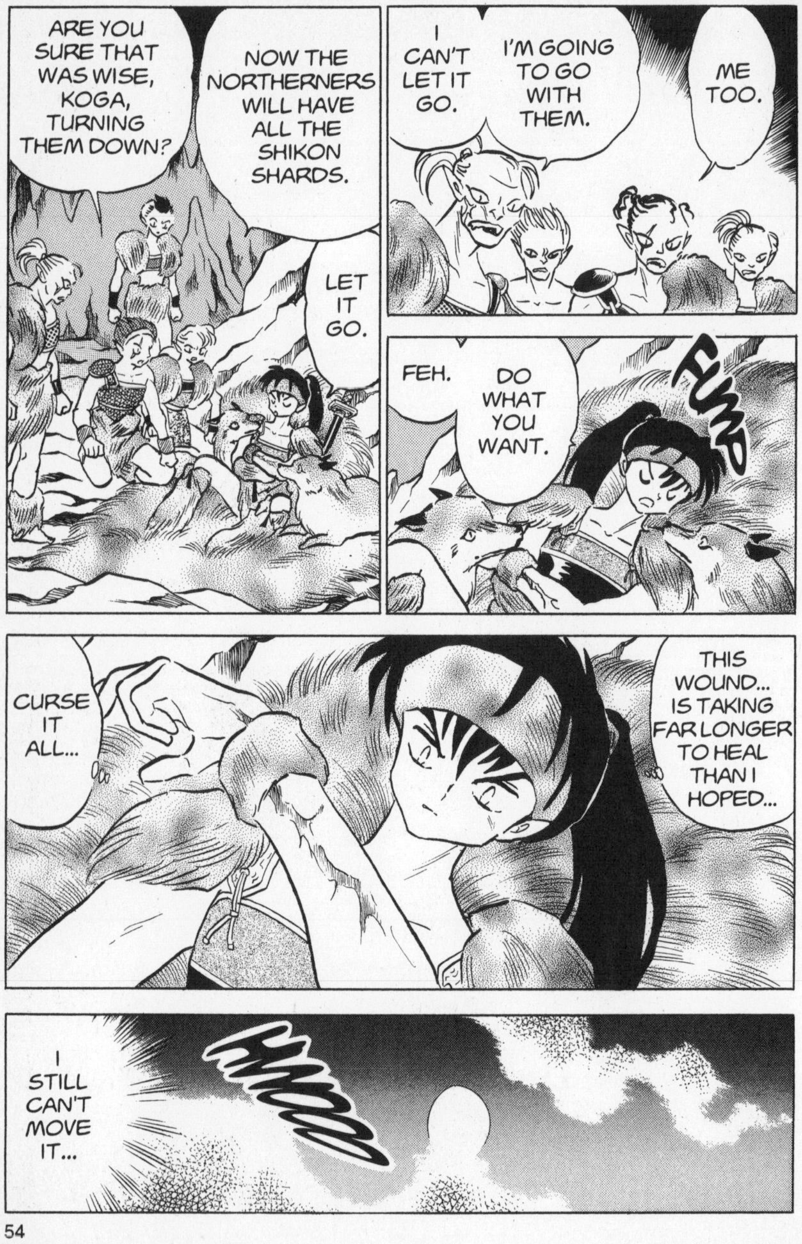
ARE YOU SURE THAT WAS WISE, KOGA, TURNING THEM DOWN?
NOW THE NORTHERNERS WILL HAVE ALL THE SHIKON SHARDS.
LET IT GO.
I CAN'T LET IT GO.
I'M GOING TO GO WITH THEM.
ME TOO.
FEH.
DO WHAT YOU WANT.
FUMP
CURSE IT ALL...
THIS WOUND... IS TAKING FAR LONGER TO HEAL THAN I HOPED...
I STILL CAN'T MOVE IT...

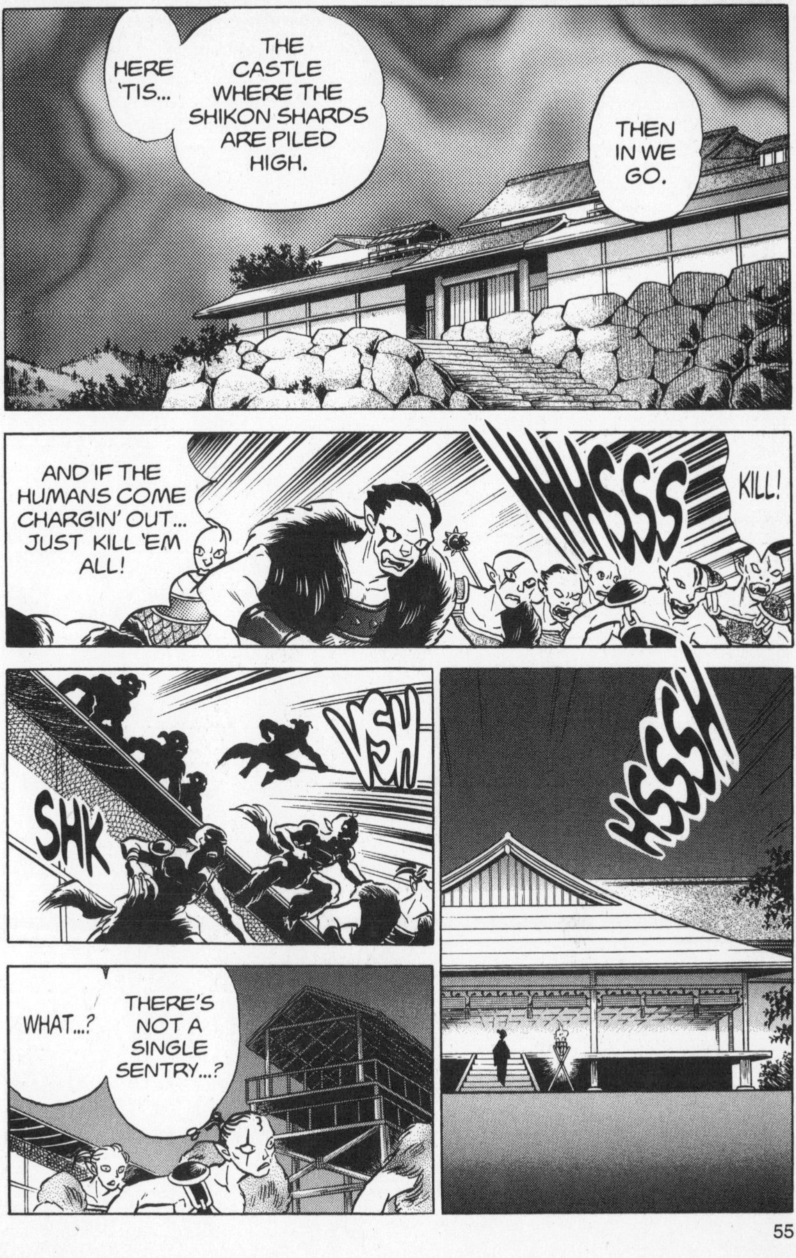
HERE 'TIS...
THE CASTLE WHERE THE SHIKON SHARDS ARE PILED HIGH.
THEN IN WE GO.
AND IF THE HUMANS COME CHARGIN' OUT... JUST KILL 'EM ALL!
HHHSSS
KILL!
VSH
SHK
HSSSH
WHAT...?
THERE'S NOT A SINGLE SENTRY...?

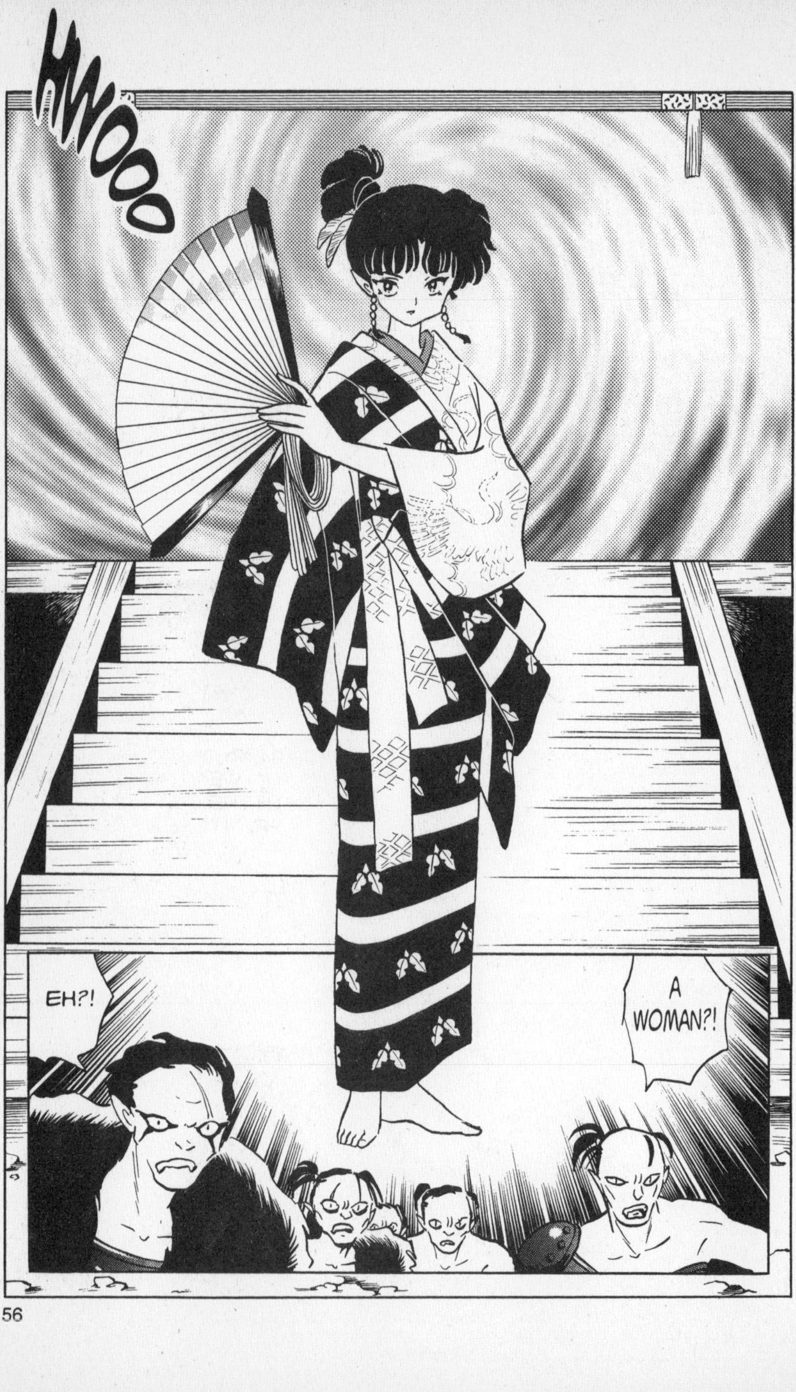
HWOOO
EH?!
A WOMAN?!

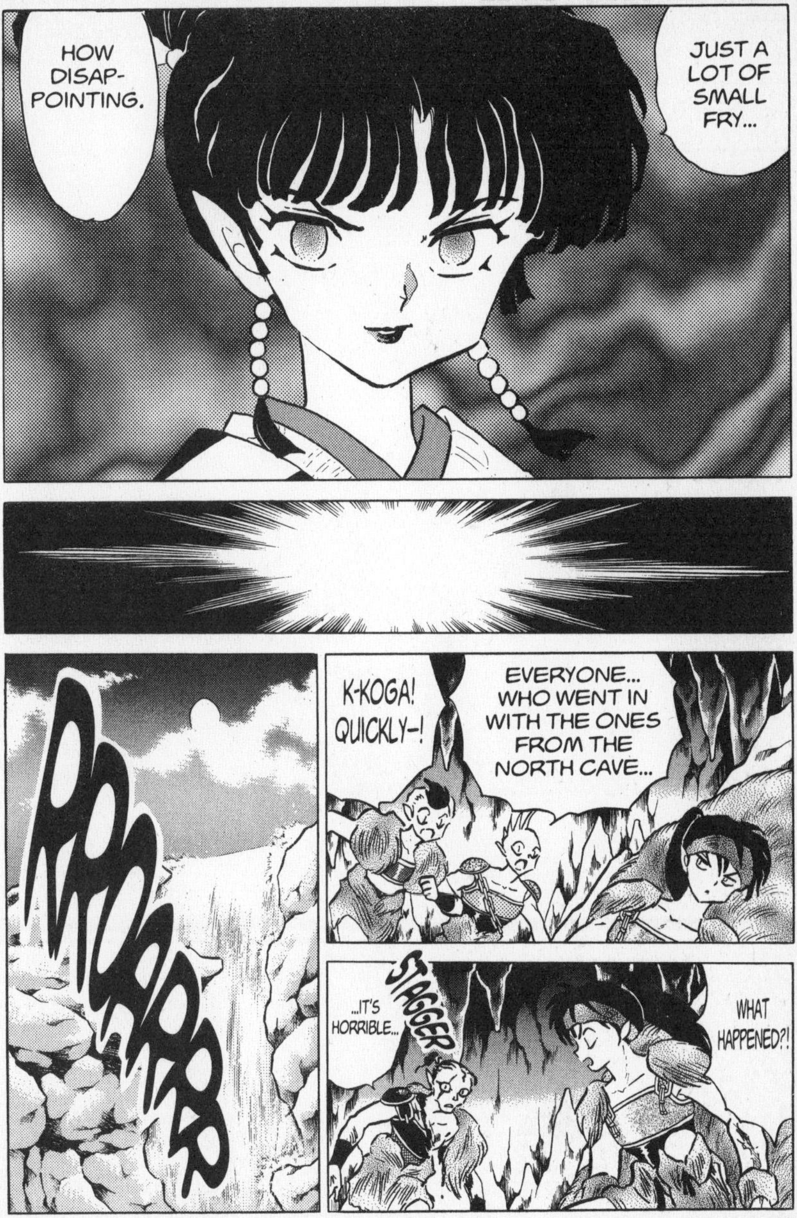
HOW DISAP-POINTING.
JUST A LOT OF SMALL FRY...
K-KOGA! QUICKLY-!
EVERYONE... WHO WENT IN WITH THE ONES FROM THE NORTH CAVE...
...IT'S HORRIBLE...
STAGGER
WHAT HAPPENED?!

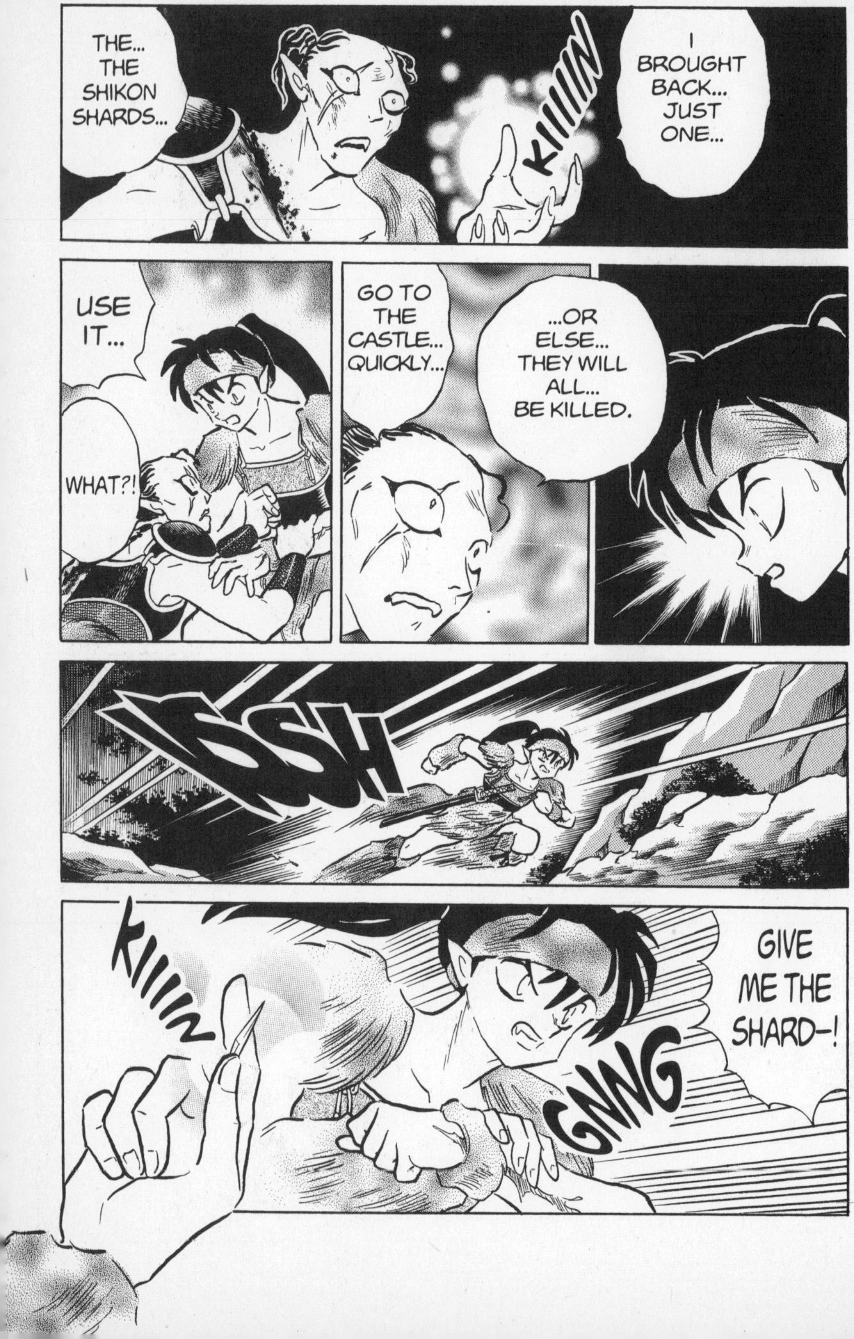
THE... THE SHIKON SHARDS...
KIIIIIN
I BROUGHT BACK... JUST ONE...
USE IT...
WHAT?!
GO TO THE CASTLE... QUICKLY...
...OR ELSE... THEY WILL ALL... BE KILLED.
FOSH
KIIIIIN
GNNG
GIVE ME THE SHARD-!

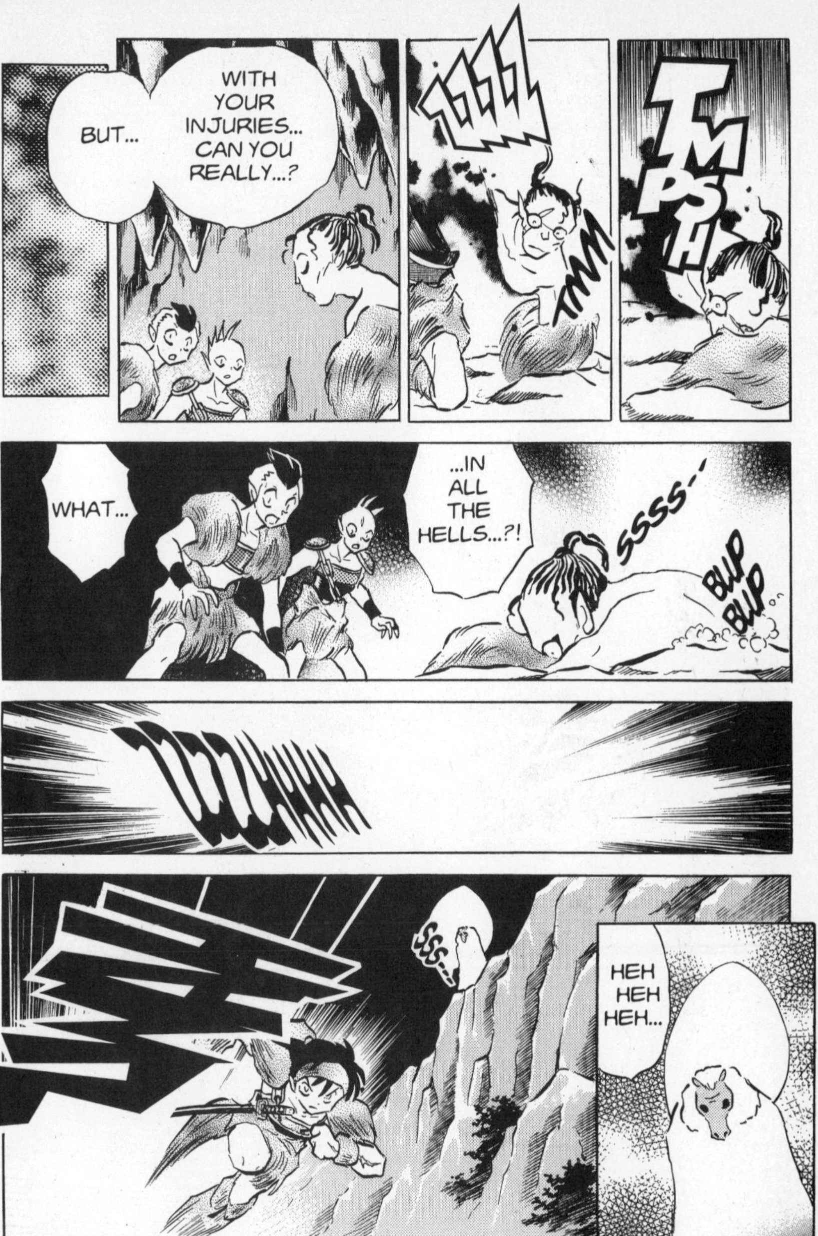
BUT...
WITH YOUR INJURIES... CAN YOU REALLY...?
WHAT...
...IN ALL THE HELLS...?!
SSSS
BLUP BLUP
HEH HEH HEH...

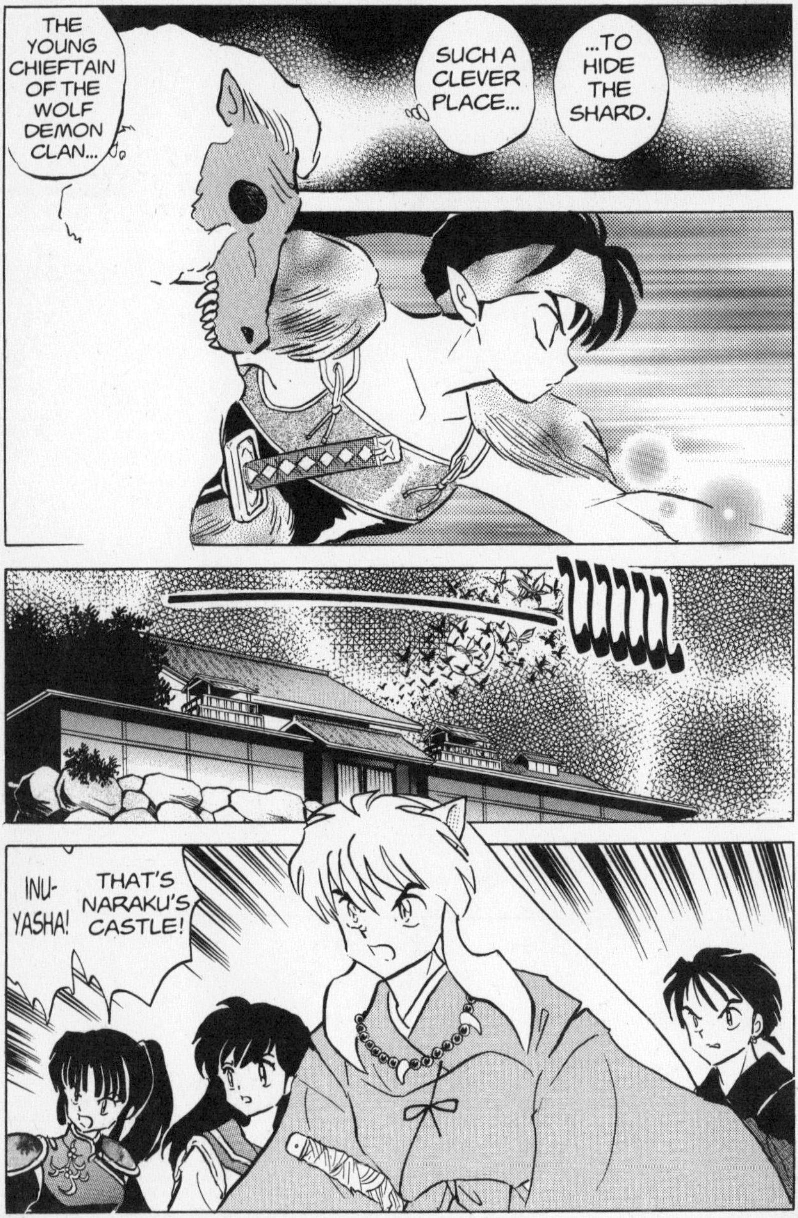
THE YOUNG CHIEFTAIN OF THE WOLF DEMON CLAN...
SUCH A CLEVER PLACE...
...TO HIDE THE SHARD.
ZZZZZZ
INU-YASHA!
THAT'S NARAKU'S CASTLE!

SCROLL FOUR

CORPSE DANCE

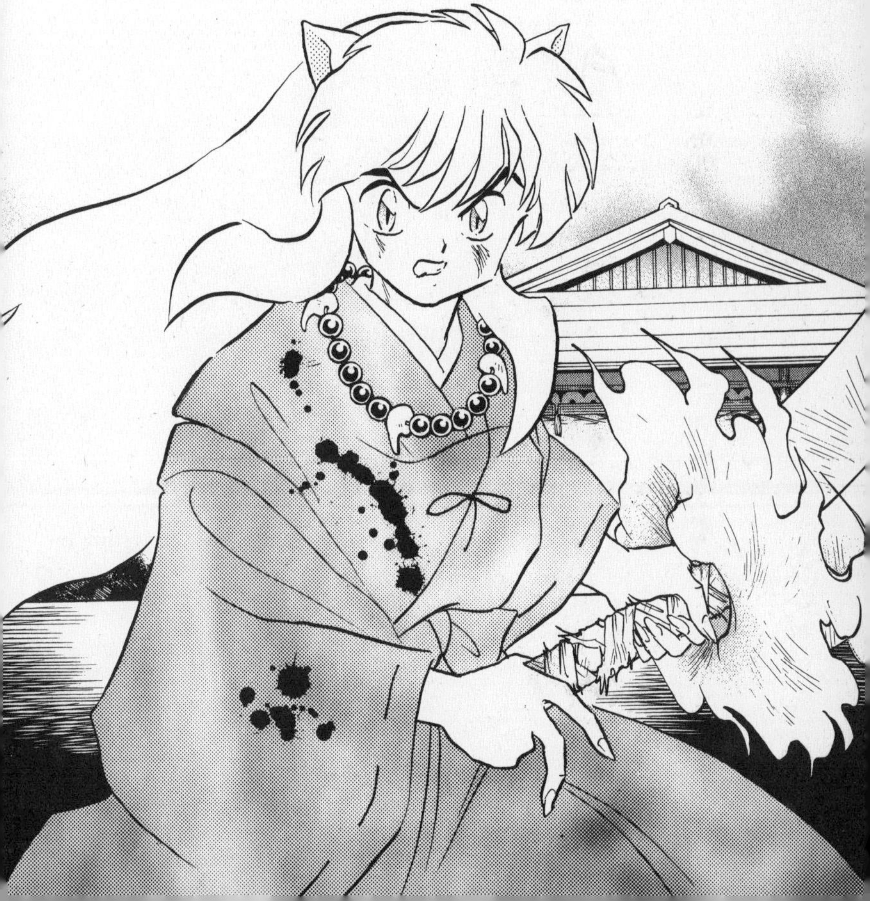

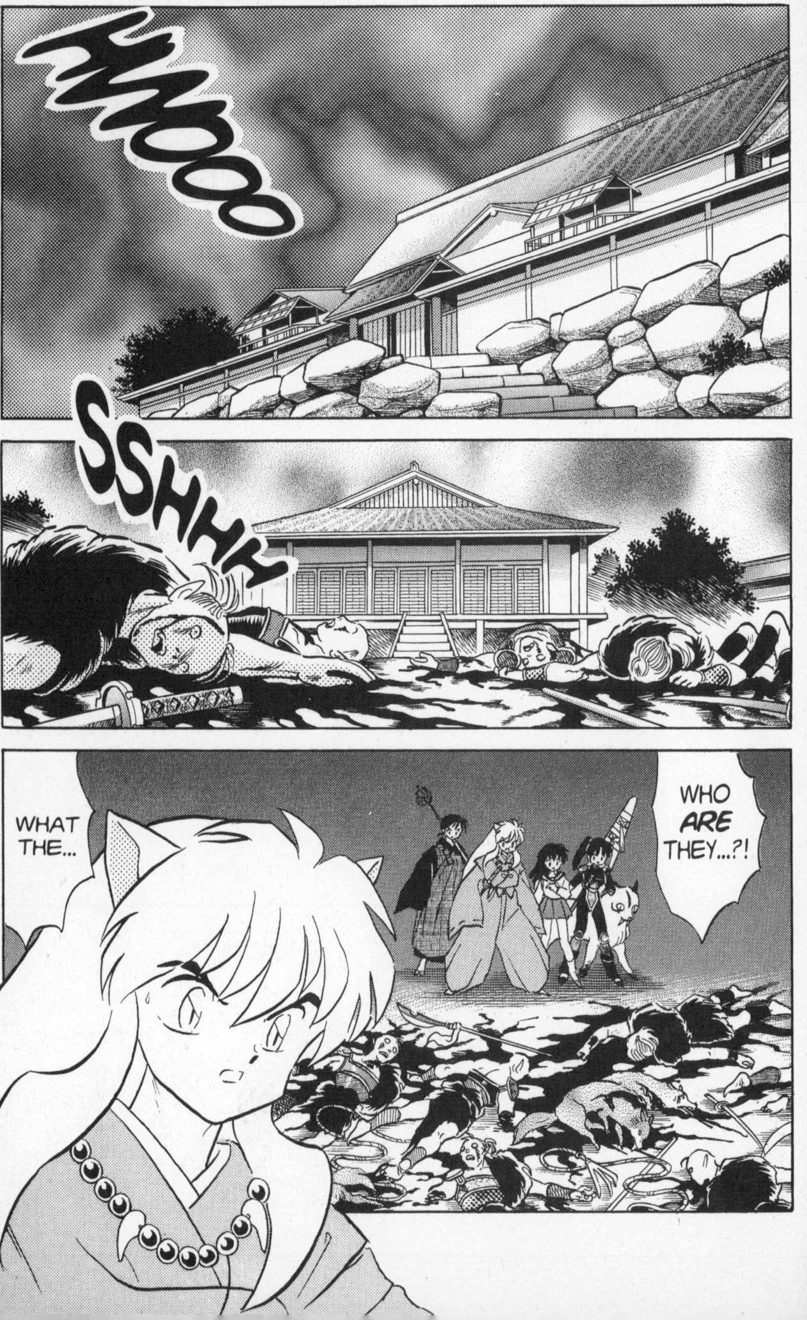
WHOOO
SSHHH
WHAT THE...
WHO ARE THEY...?!

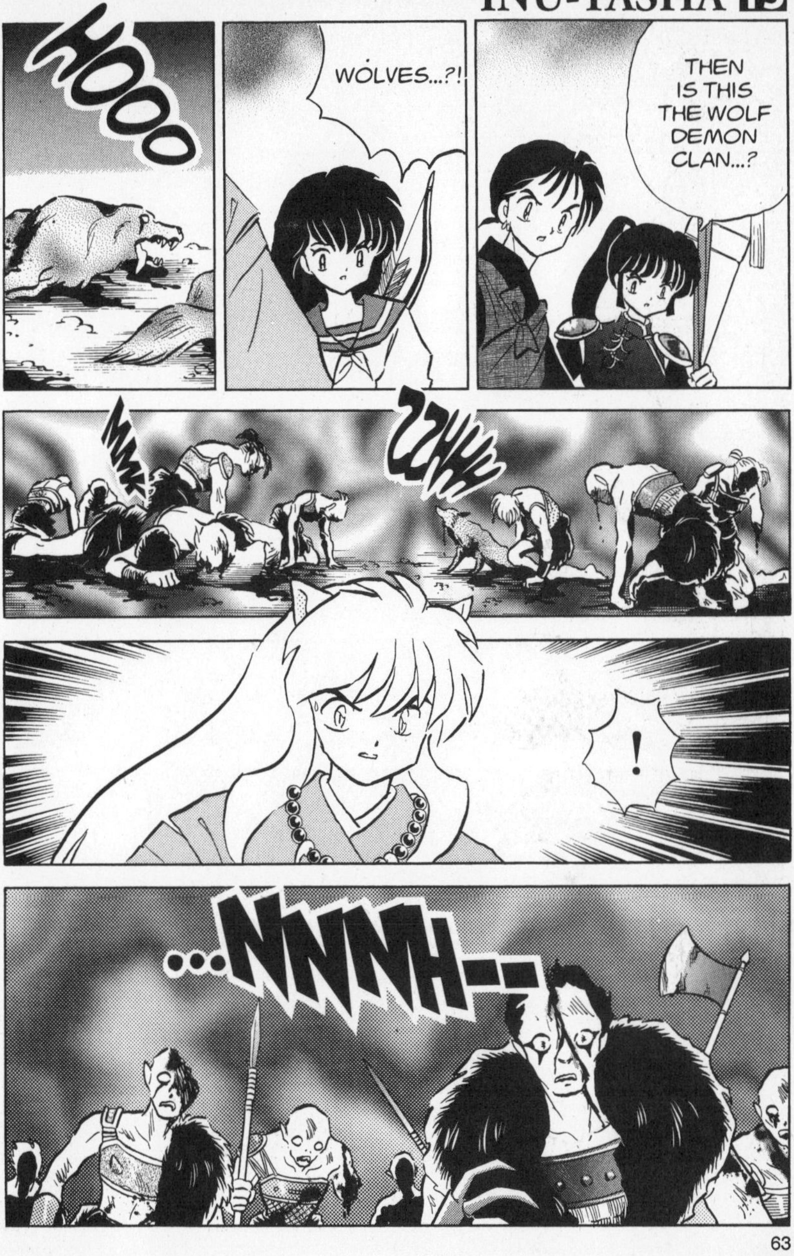
HOOO
WOLVES...?!
THEN IS THIS THE WOLF DEMON CLAN...?
MMK
ZZHK
!
...NNMH--

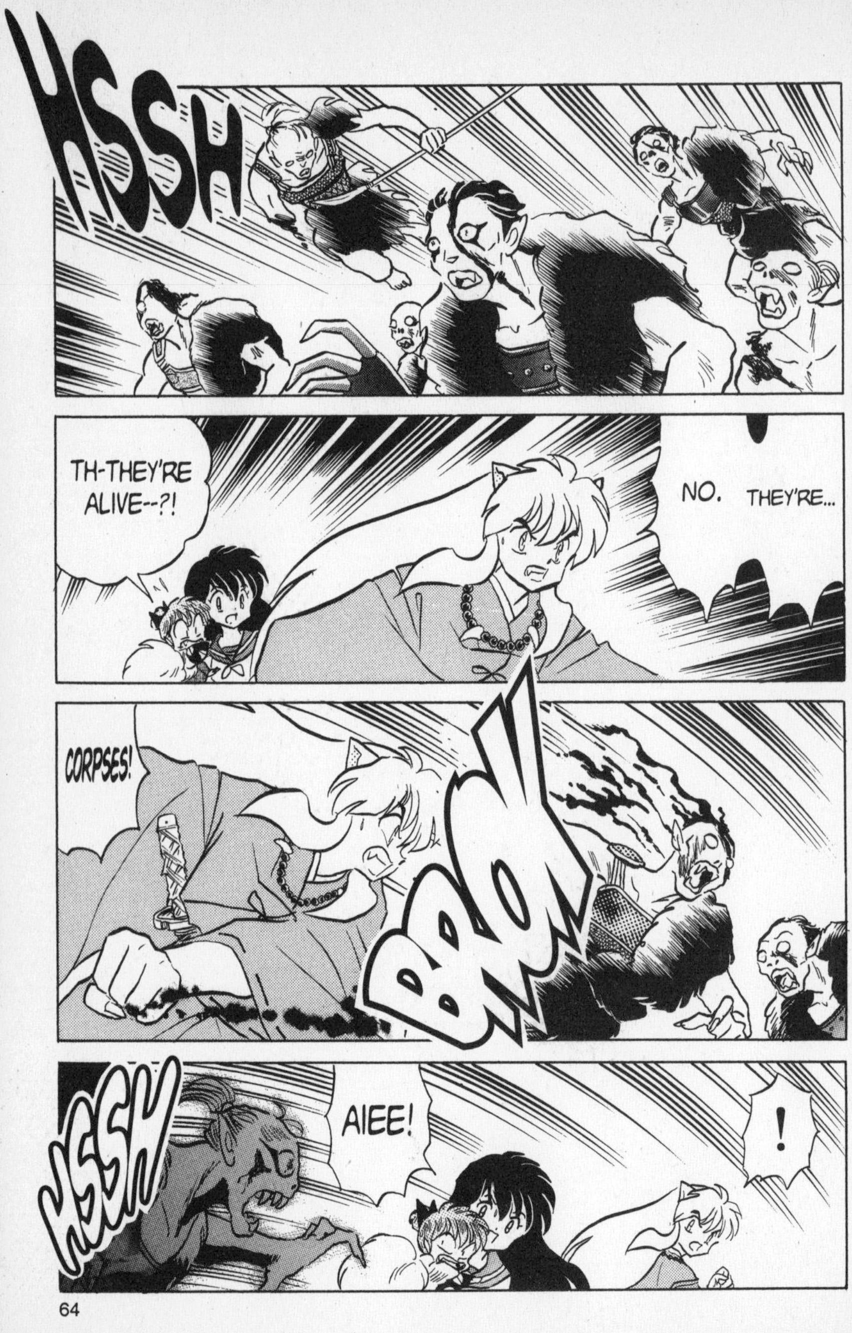
HSSH
TH-THEY'RE ALIVE--?!
NO.
THEY'RE...
CORPSES!
BAM
HSSH
AIEE!
!

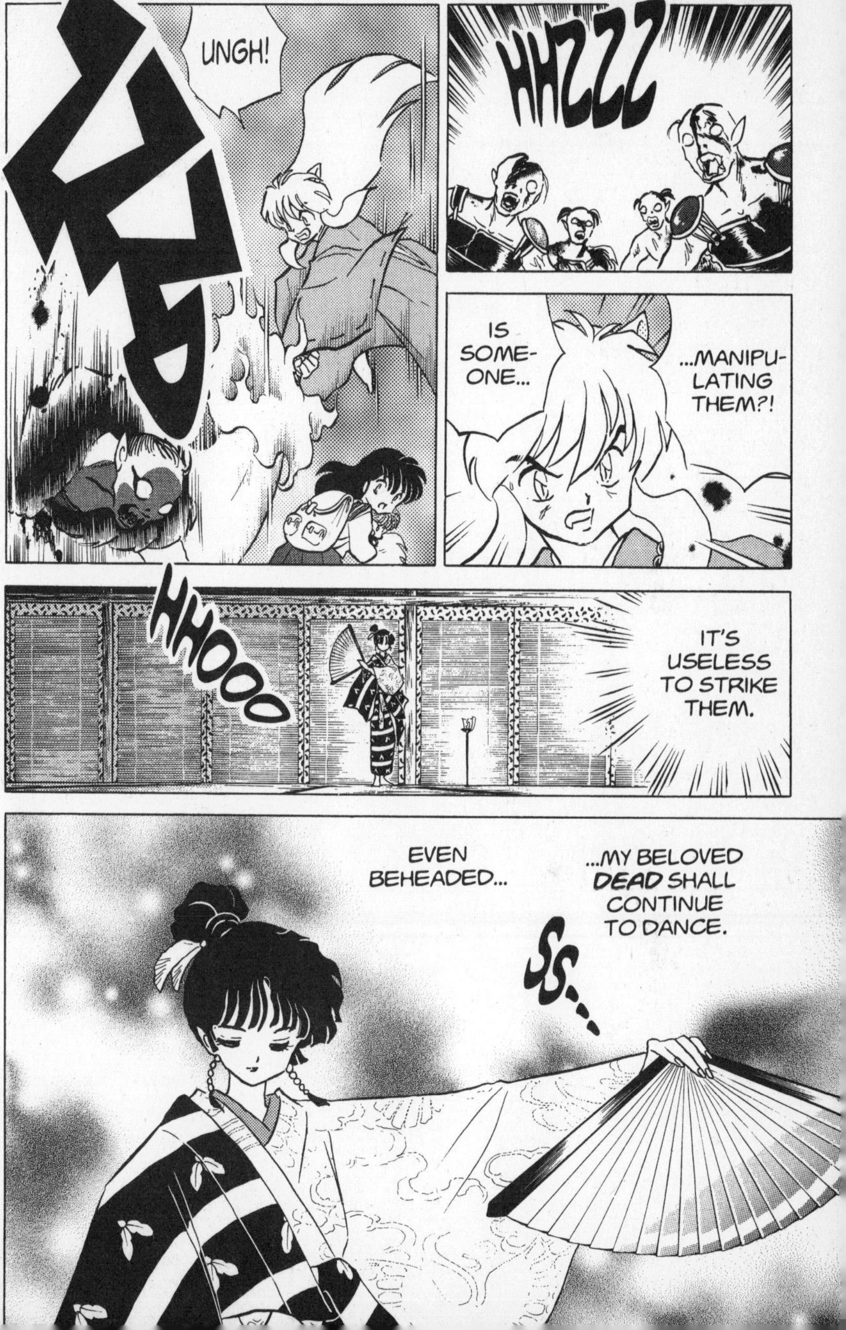
UNGH!
HHZZZ
IS SOMEONE...
...MANIPULATING THEM?!
HHOOO
IT'S USELESS TO STRIKE THEM.
EVEN BEHEADED...
...MY BELOVED **DEAD** SHALL CONTINUE TO DANCE.
SS...

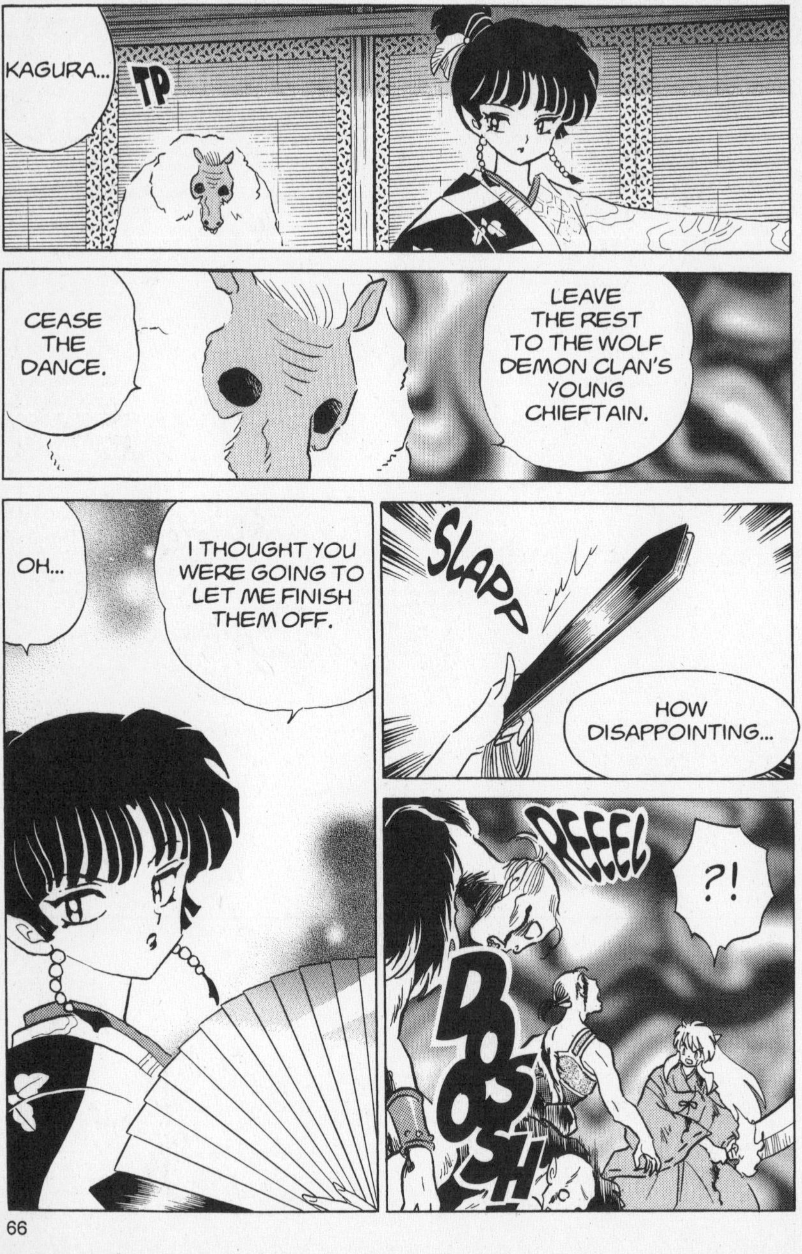
KAGURA...
TP
CEASE THE DANCE.
LEAVE THE REST TO THE WOLF DEMON CLAN'S YOUNG CHIEFTAIN.
OH...
I THOUGHT YOU WERE GOING TO LET ME FINISH THEM OFF.
SLAPP
HOW DISAPPOINTING...
REEEL
?!
DOOSH

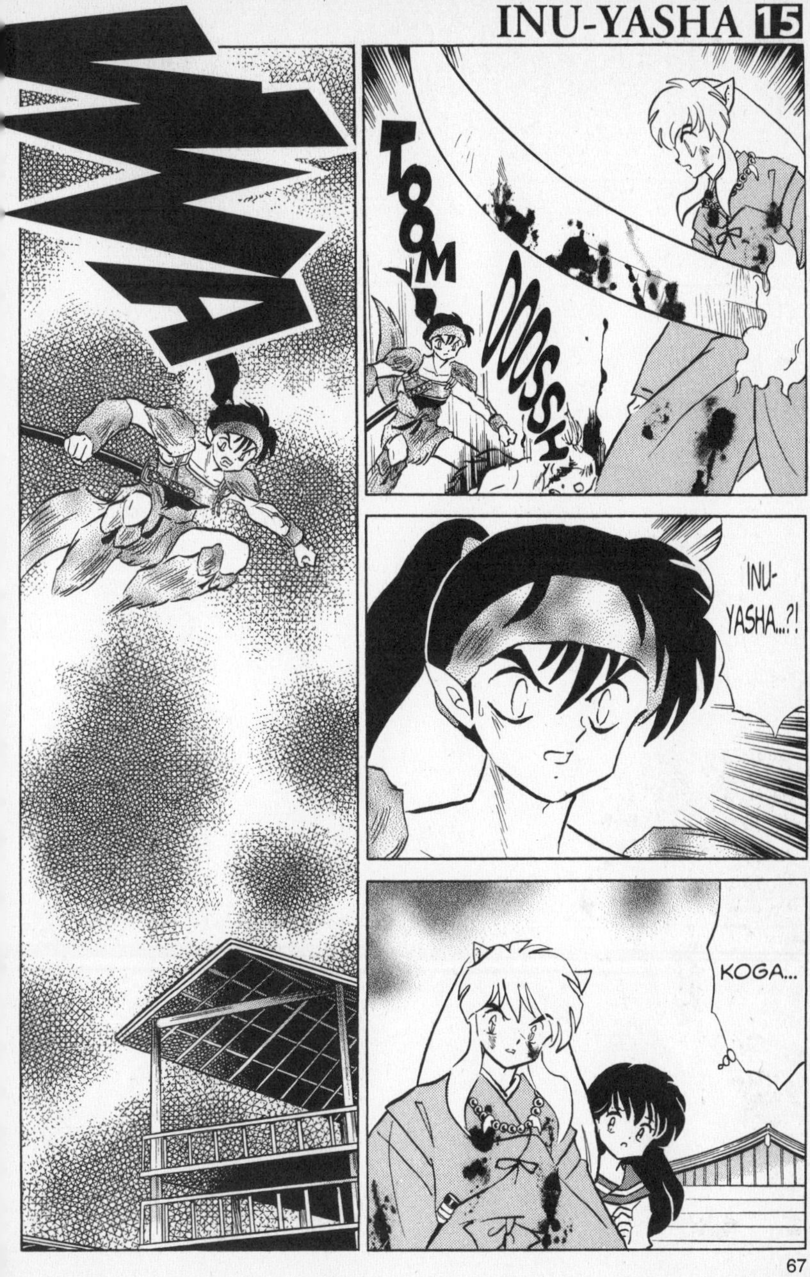
TOOM
DOOSH
INU-YASHA...?!
KOGA...

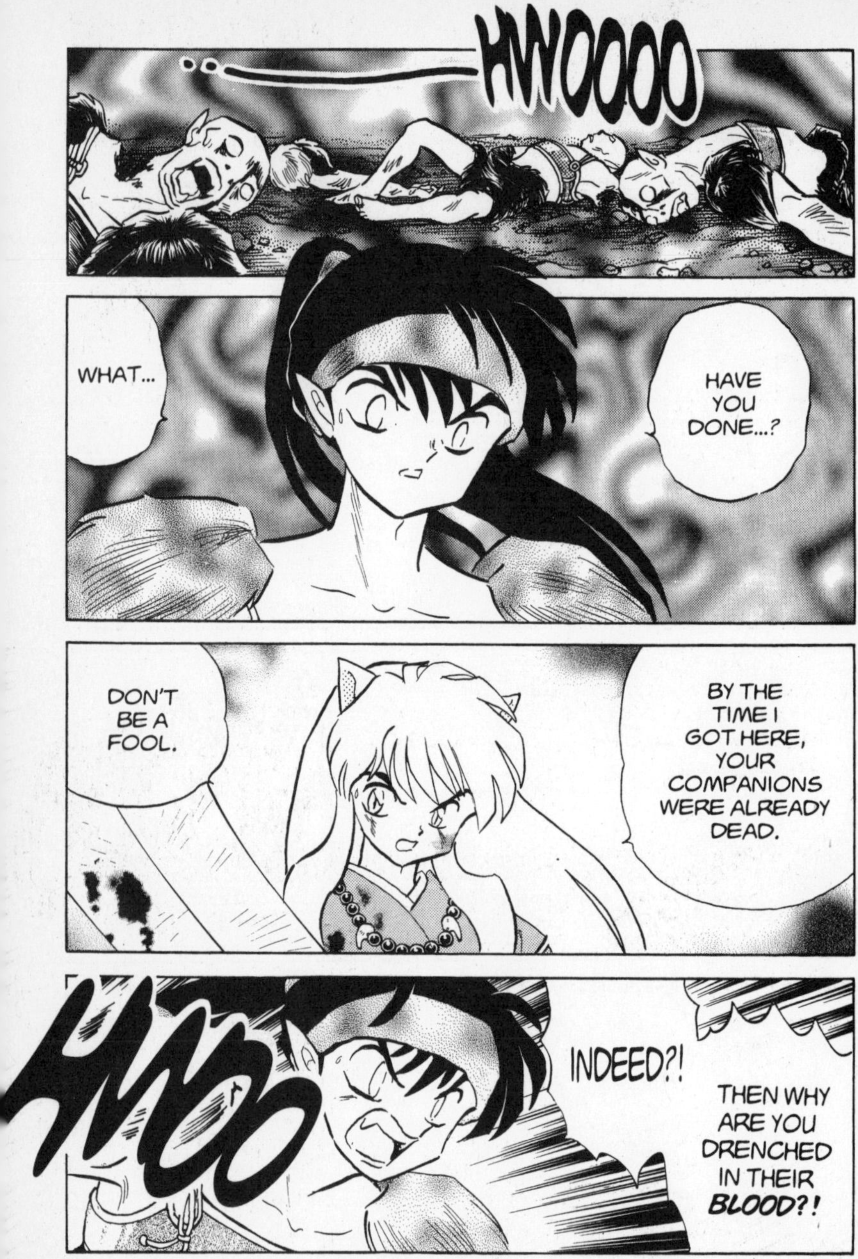
HWOOOO
WHAT...
HAVE YOU DONE...?
DON'T BE A FOOL.
BY THE TIME I GOT HERE, YOUR COMPANIONS WERE ALREADY DEAD.
HWOO
INDEED?!
THEN WHY ARE YOU DRENCHED IN THEIR BLOOD?!

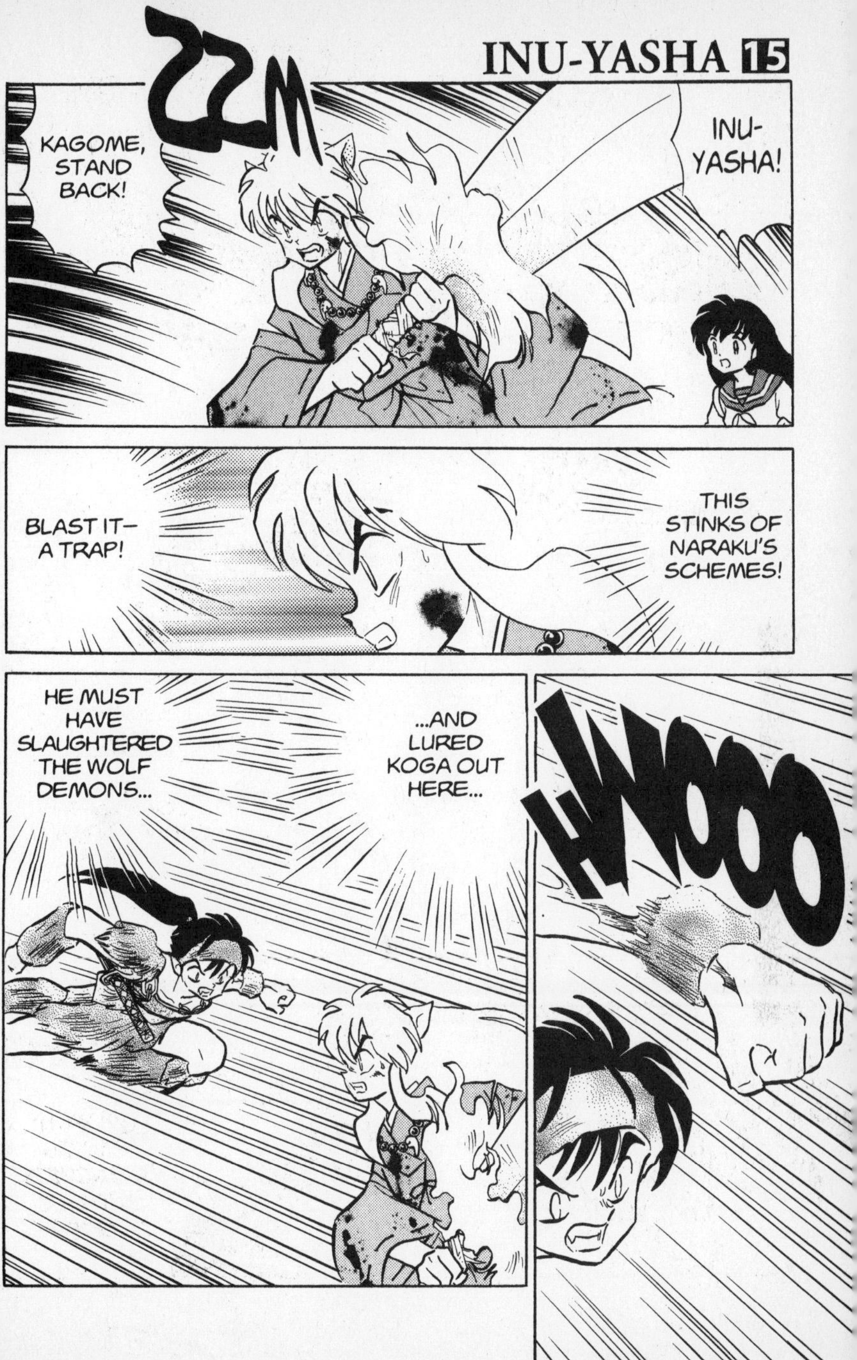
ZZM
KAGOME, STAND BACK!
INU-YASHA!
BLAST IT— A TRAP!
THIS STINKS OF NARAKU'S SCHEMES!
HE MUST HAVE SLAUGHTERED THE WOLF DEMONS...
...AND LURED KOGA OUT HERE...
HWOOO

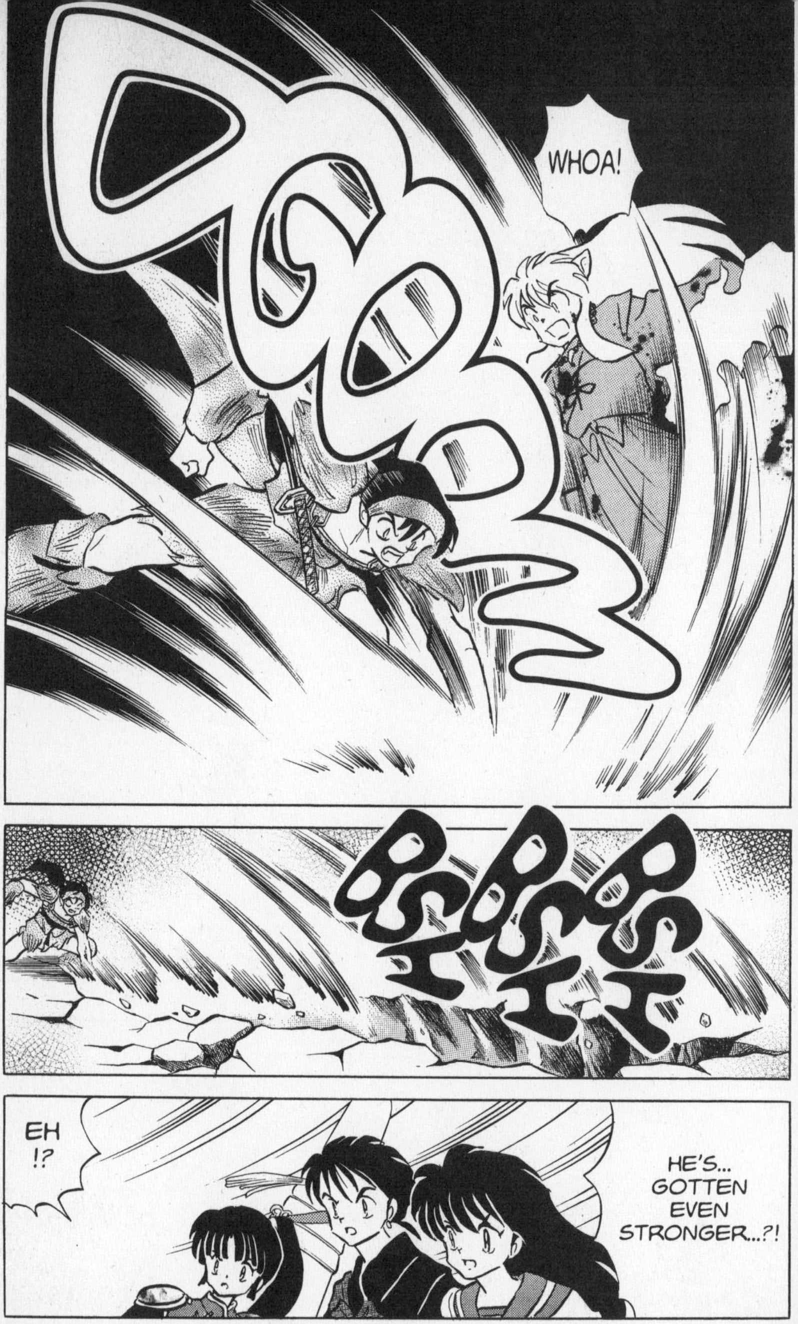
WHOA!
EH !?
HE'S... GOTTEN EVEN STRONGER...?!

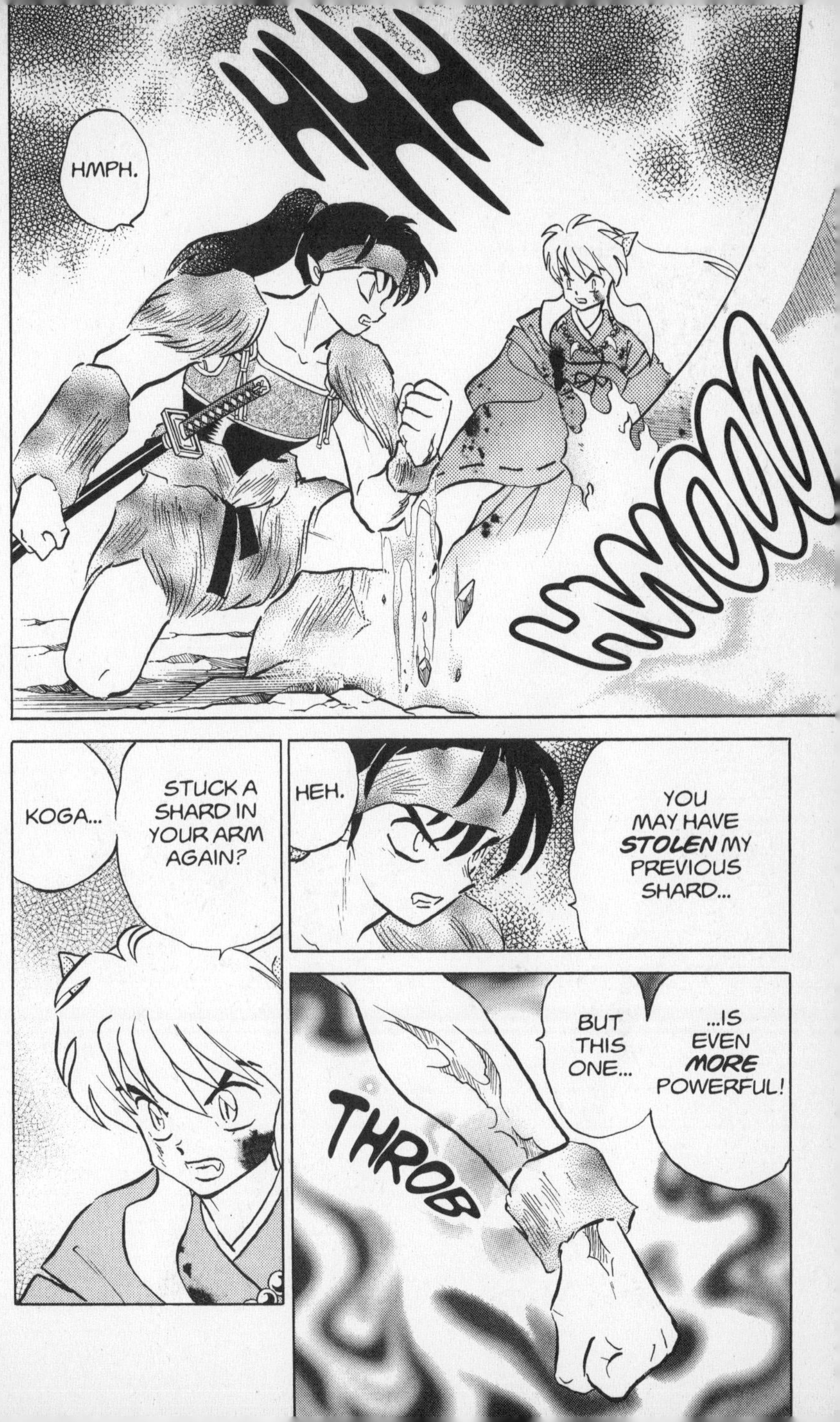
HMPH.
KOGA...
STUCK A SHARD IN YOUR ARM AGAIN?
HEH.
YOU MAY HAVE **STOLEN** MY PREVIOUS SHARD...
BUT THIS ONE...
...IS EVEN **MORE** POWERFUL!
THROB

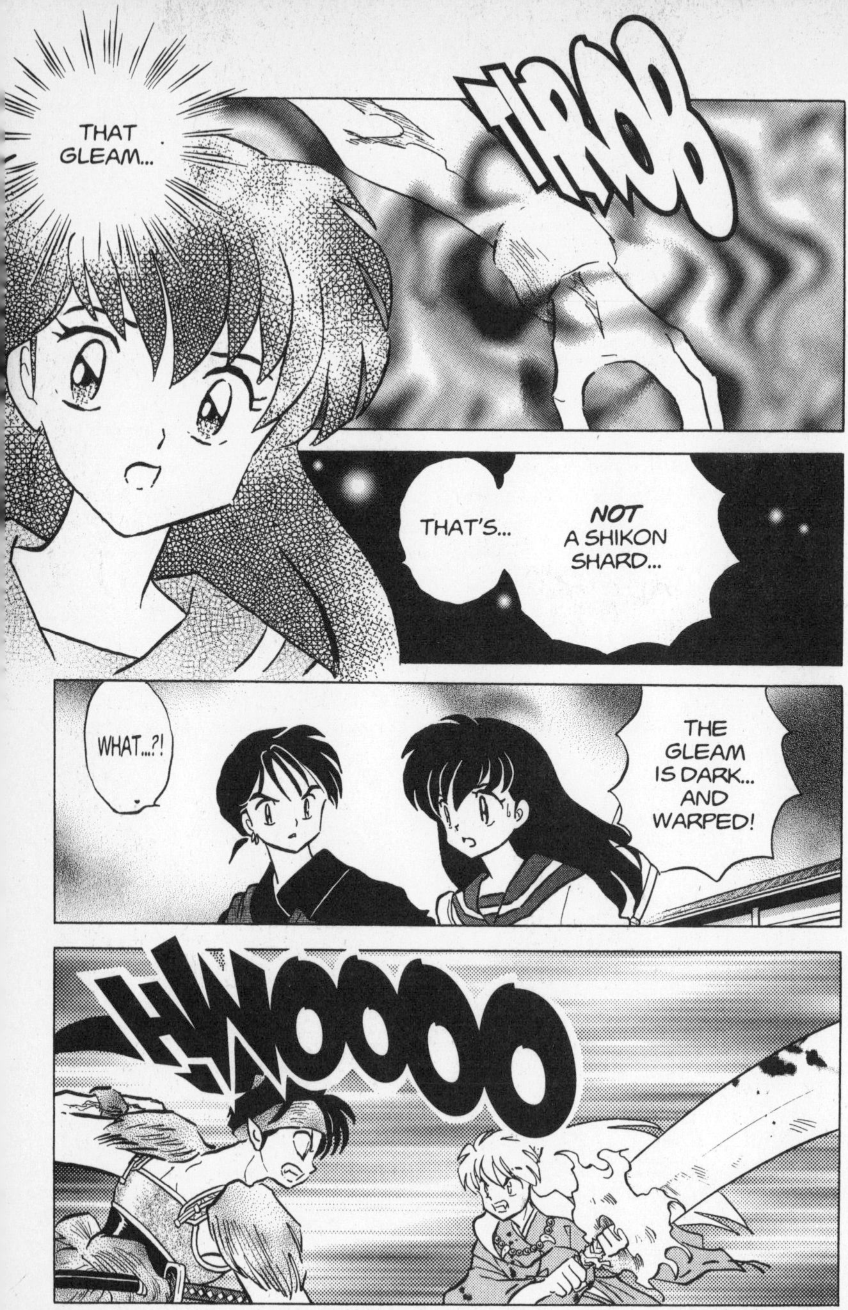
THAT GLEAM...
THROB
THAT'S...
NOT A SHIKON SHARD...
WHAT...?!
THE GLEAM IS DARK... AND WARPED!
HWOOOO

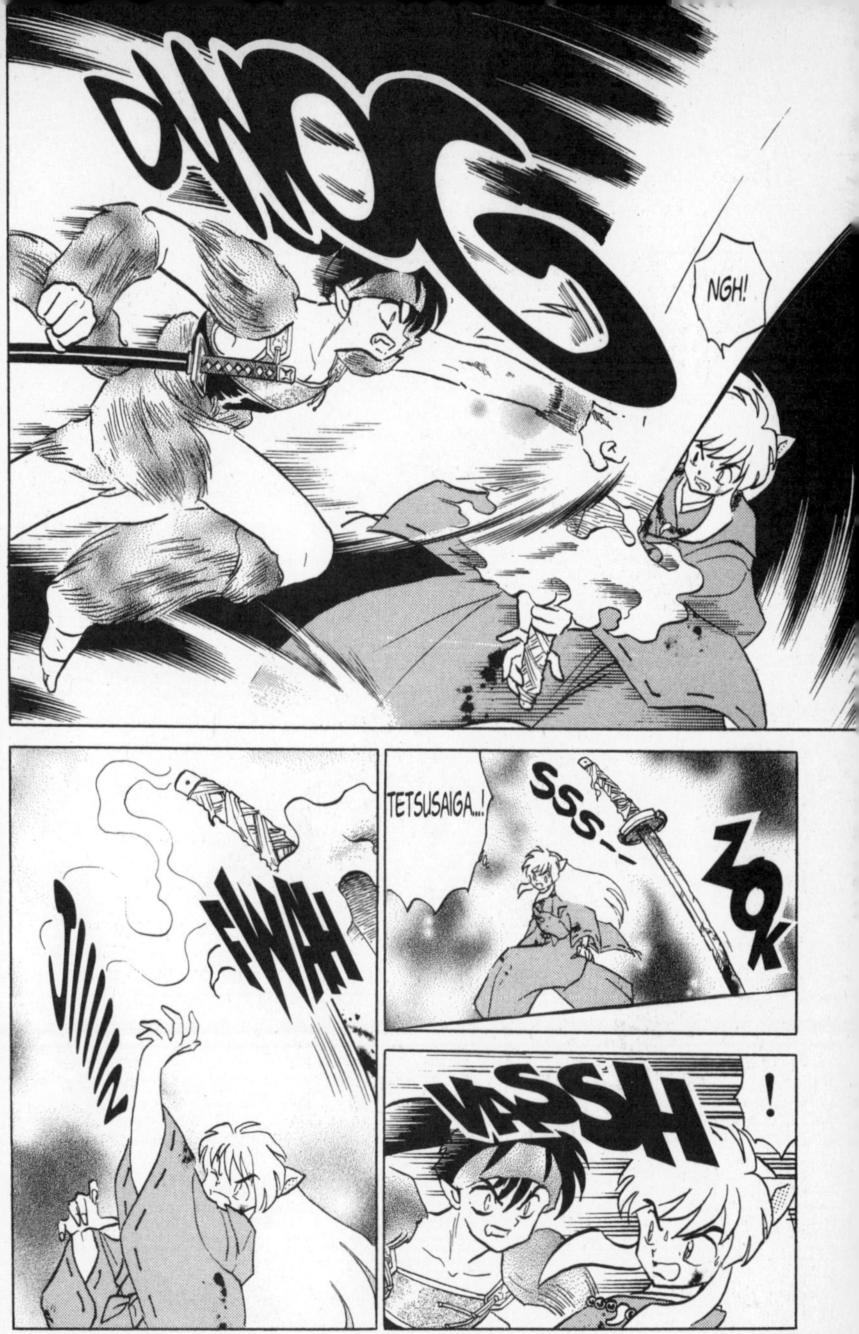
NGH!
FWAH
TETSUSAIGA..!
SSS--
ZOK
VASSH
!

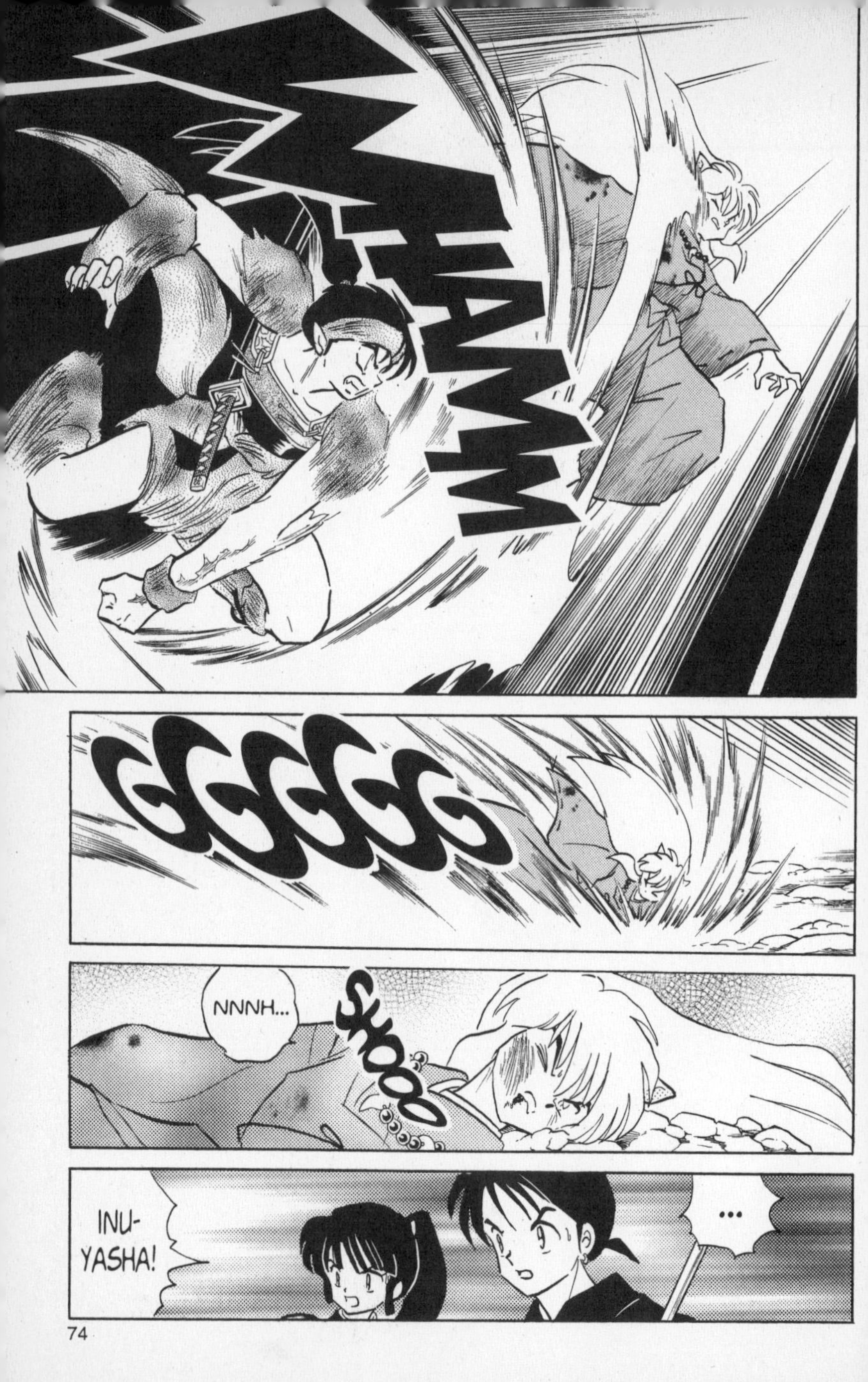
WHAMMM!
GGGGG
NNNH...
SHOOOO
INU-YASHA!
...

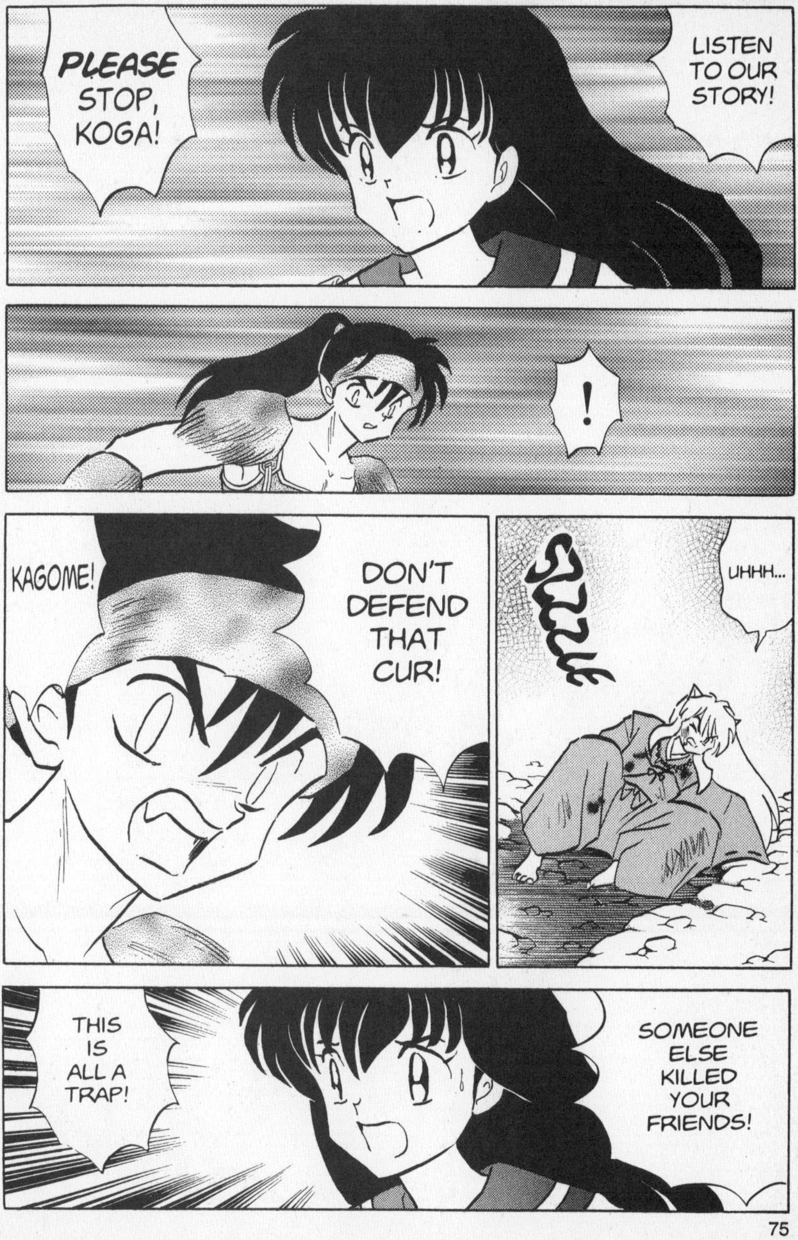
PLEASE STOP, KOGA!
LISTEN TO OUR STORY!
!
KAGOME!
DON'T DEFEND THAT CUR!
UHHH...
THIS IS ALL A TRAP!
SOMEONE ELSE KILLED YOUR FRIENDS!

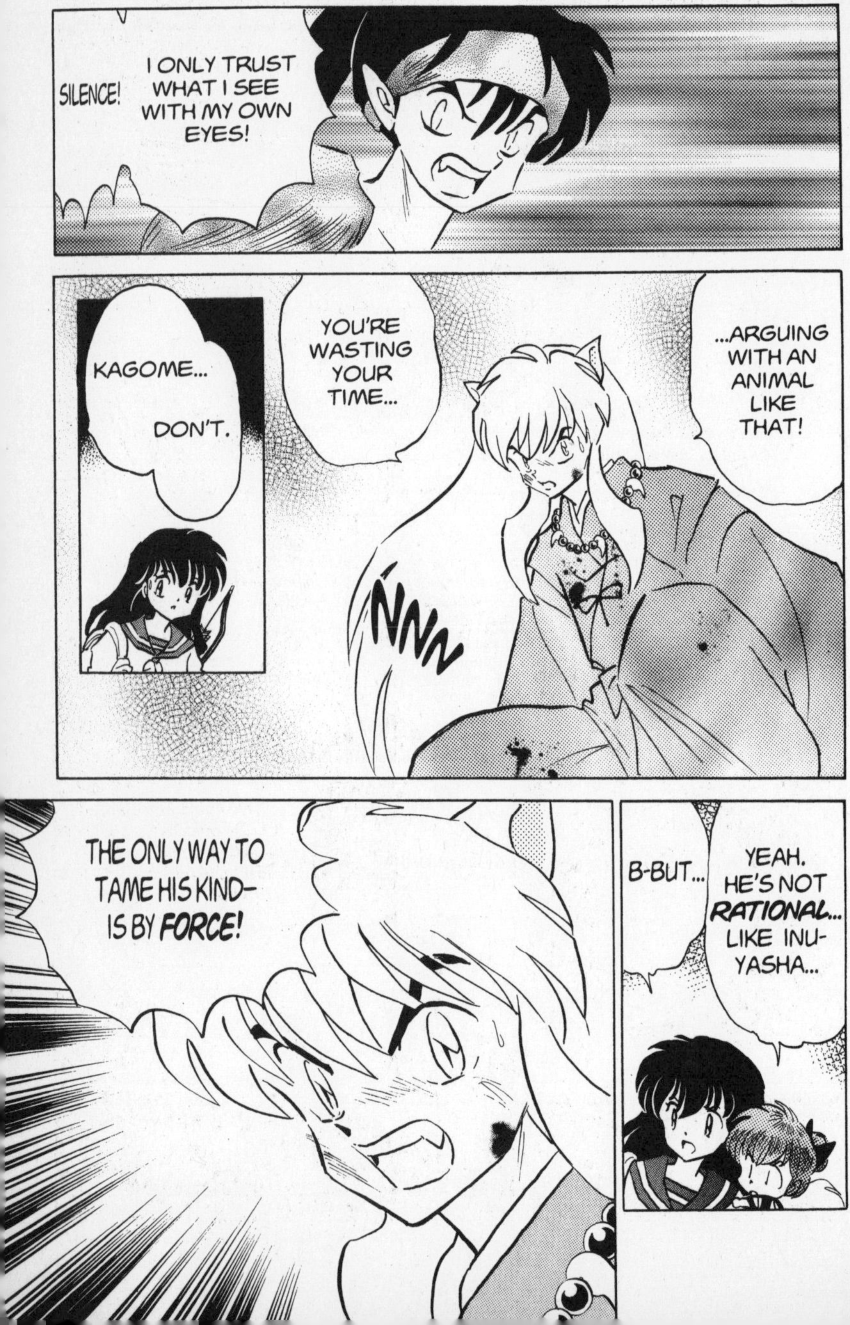
SILENCE!
I ONLY TRUST WHAT I SEE WITH MY OWN EYES!
KAGOME... DON'T.
YOU'RE WASTING YOUR TIME...
...ARGUING WITH AN ANIMAL LIKE THAT!
NNN
THE ONLY WAY TO TAME HIS KIND-IS BY FORCE!
B-BUT...
YEAH. HE'S NOT RATIONAL... LIKE INU-YASHA...

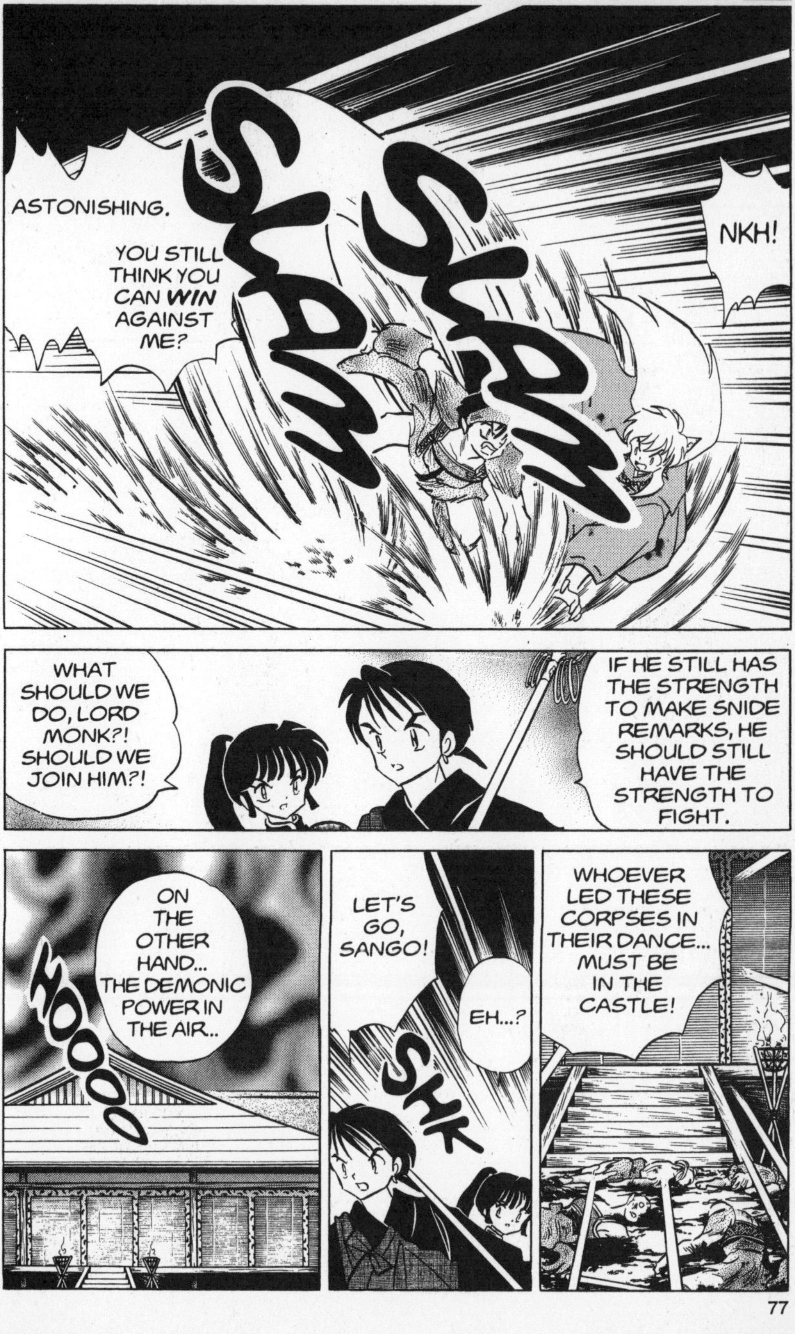
ASTONISHING.
YOU STILL THINK YOU CAN WIN AGAINST ME?
SLAM
NKH!
WHAT SHOULD WE DO, LORD MONK?! SHOULD WE JOIN HIM?!
IF HE STILL HAS THE STRENGTH TO MAKE SNIDE REMARKS, HE SHOULD STILL HAVE THE STRENGTH TO FIGHT.
HOOOO
ON THE OTHER HAND... THE DEMONIC POWER IN THE AIR..
LET'S GO, SANGO!
EH...?
SHK
WHOEVER LED THESE CORPSES IN THEIR DANCE... MUST BE IN THE CASTLE!

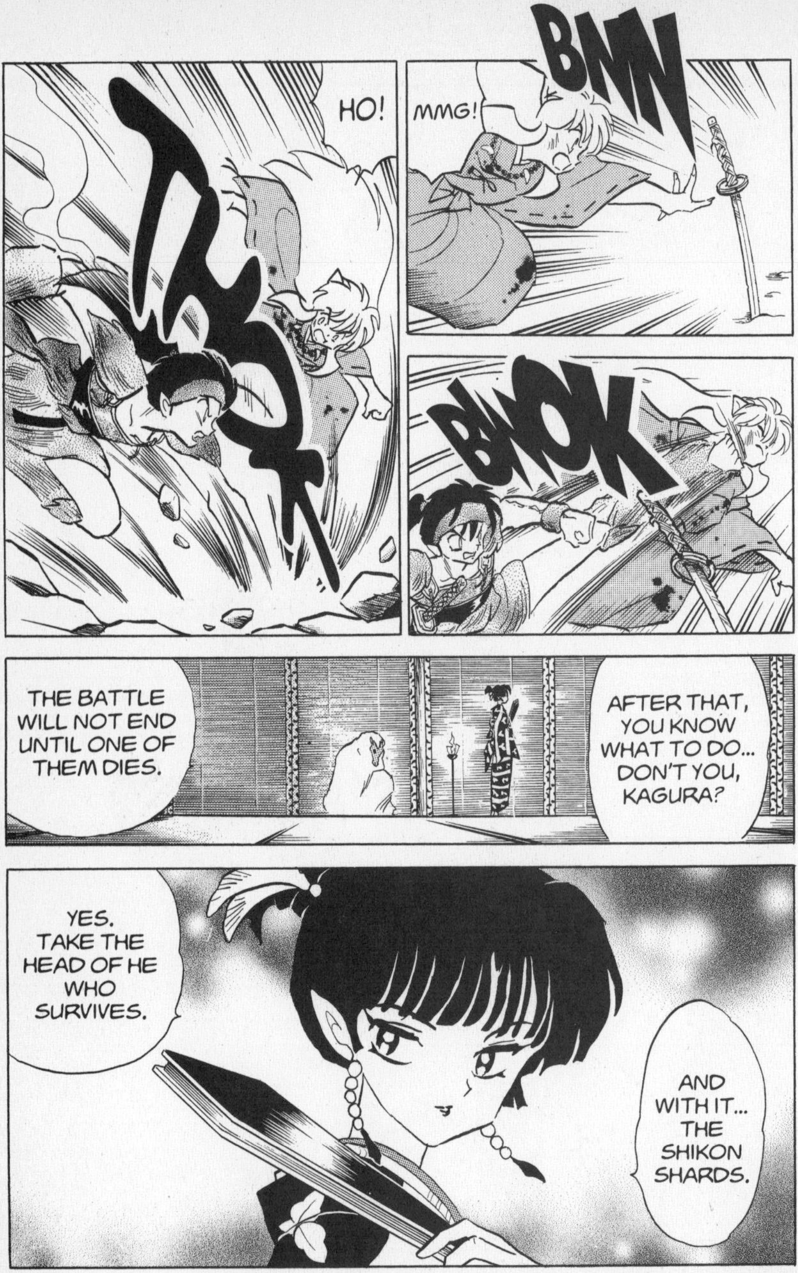
HO!
MMG!
BWOK
THE BATTLE WILL NOT END UNTIL ONE OF THEM DIES.
AFTER THAT, YOU KNOW WHAT TO DO... DON'T YOU, KAGURA?
YES. TAKE THE HEAD OF HE WHO SURVIVES.
AND WITH IT... THE SHIKON SHARDS.

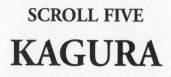

SCROLL FIVE

KAGURA

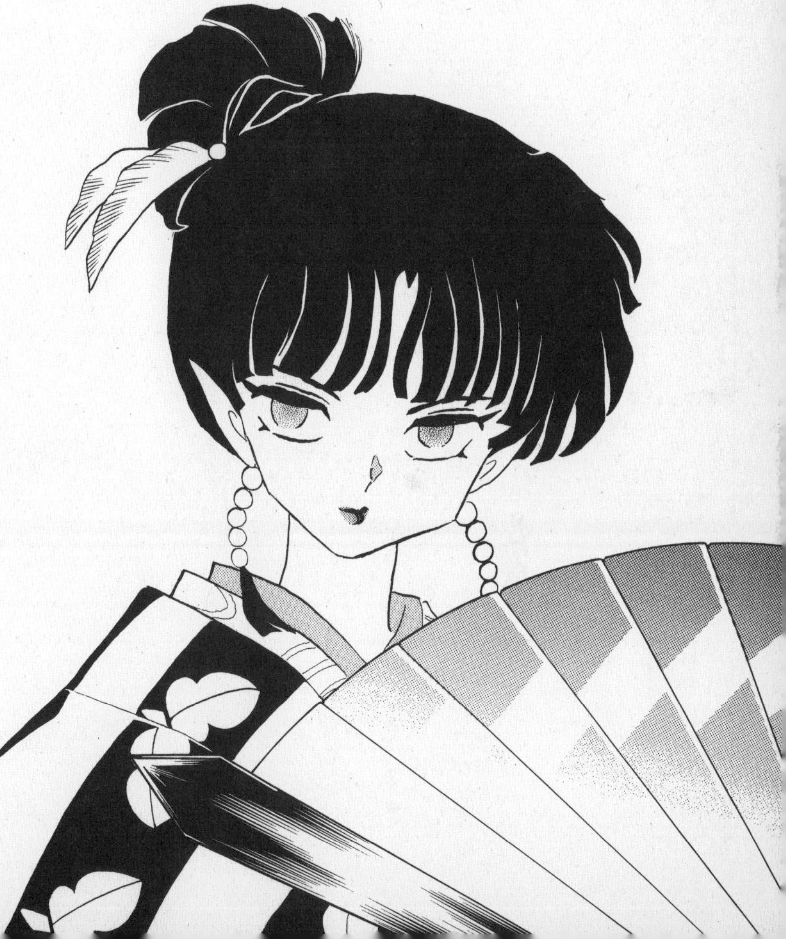

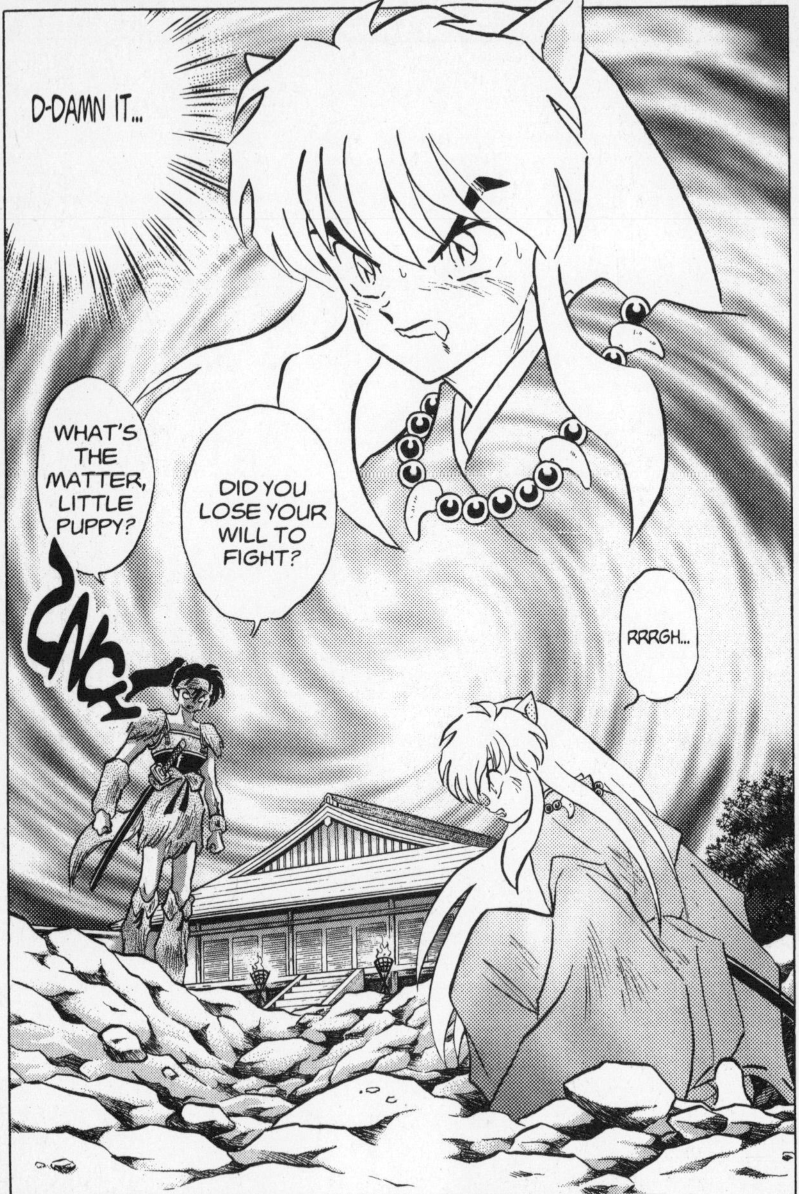
D-DAMN IT...
WHAT'S THE MATTER, LITTLE PUPPY?
DID YOU LOSE YOUR WILL TO FIGHT?
RRRGH...

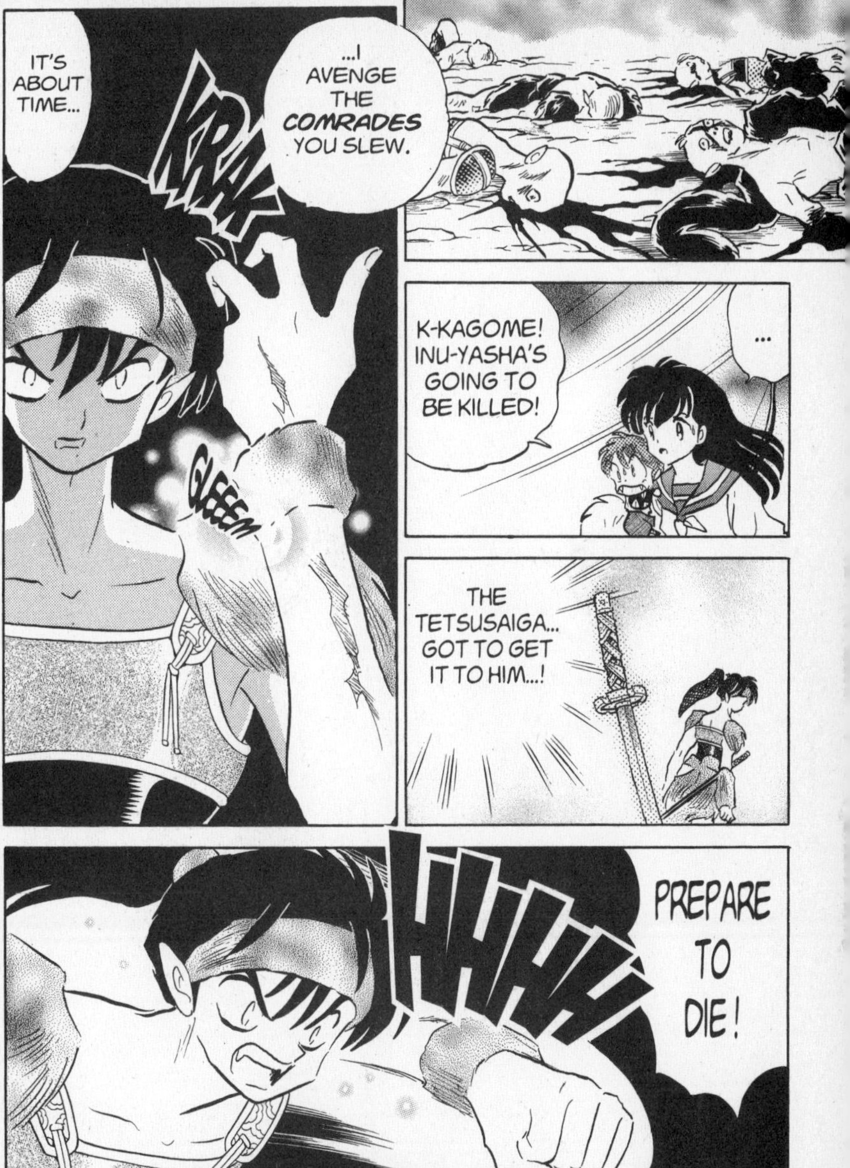
IT'S ABOUT TIME...
...I AVENGE THE COMRADES YOU SLEW.
KRAK
GLEEEM
K-KAGOME! INU-YASHA'S GOING TO BE KILLED!
...
THE TETSUSAIGA... GOT TO GET IT TO HIM...!
PREPARE TO DIE!

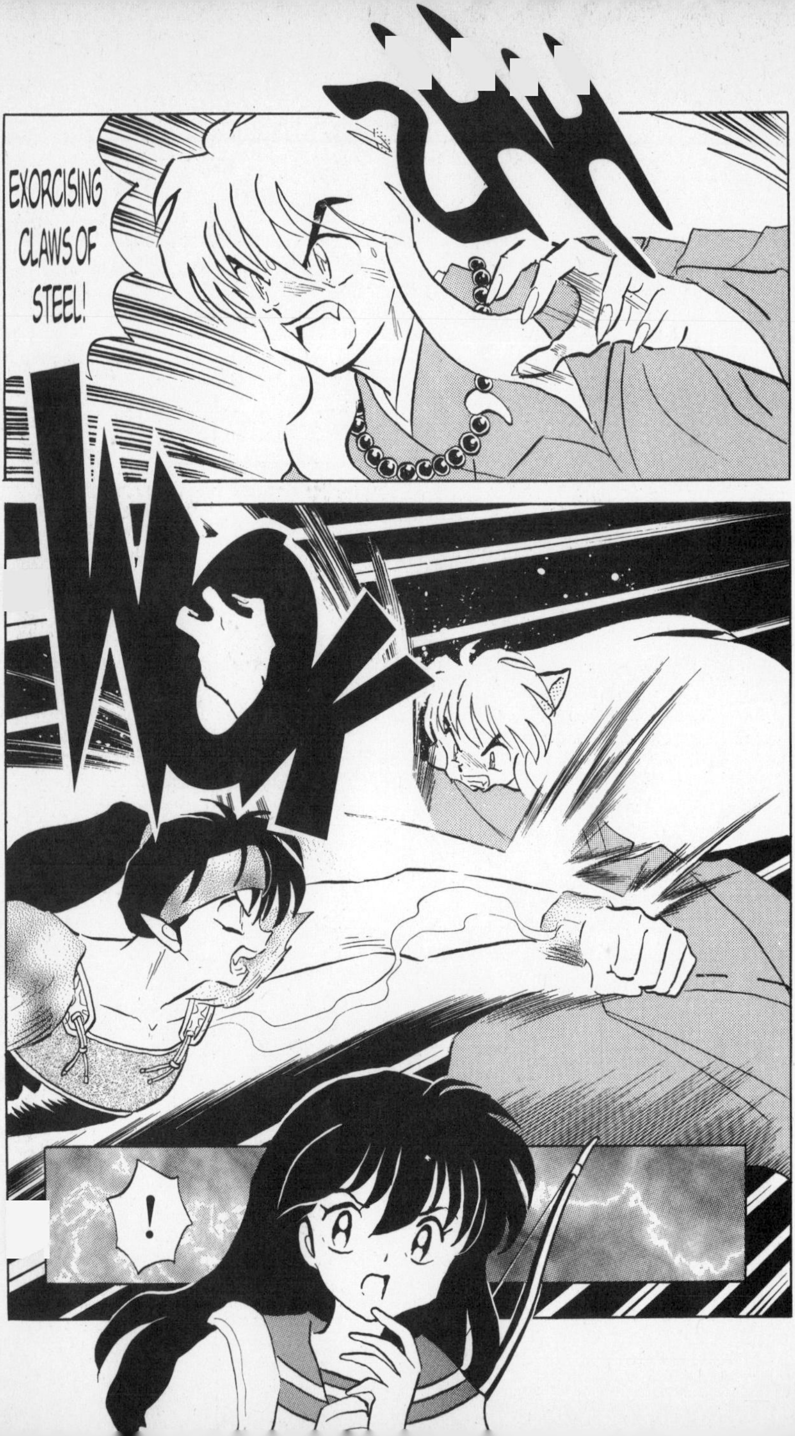
EXORCISING CLAWS OF STEEL!
!

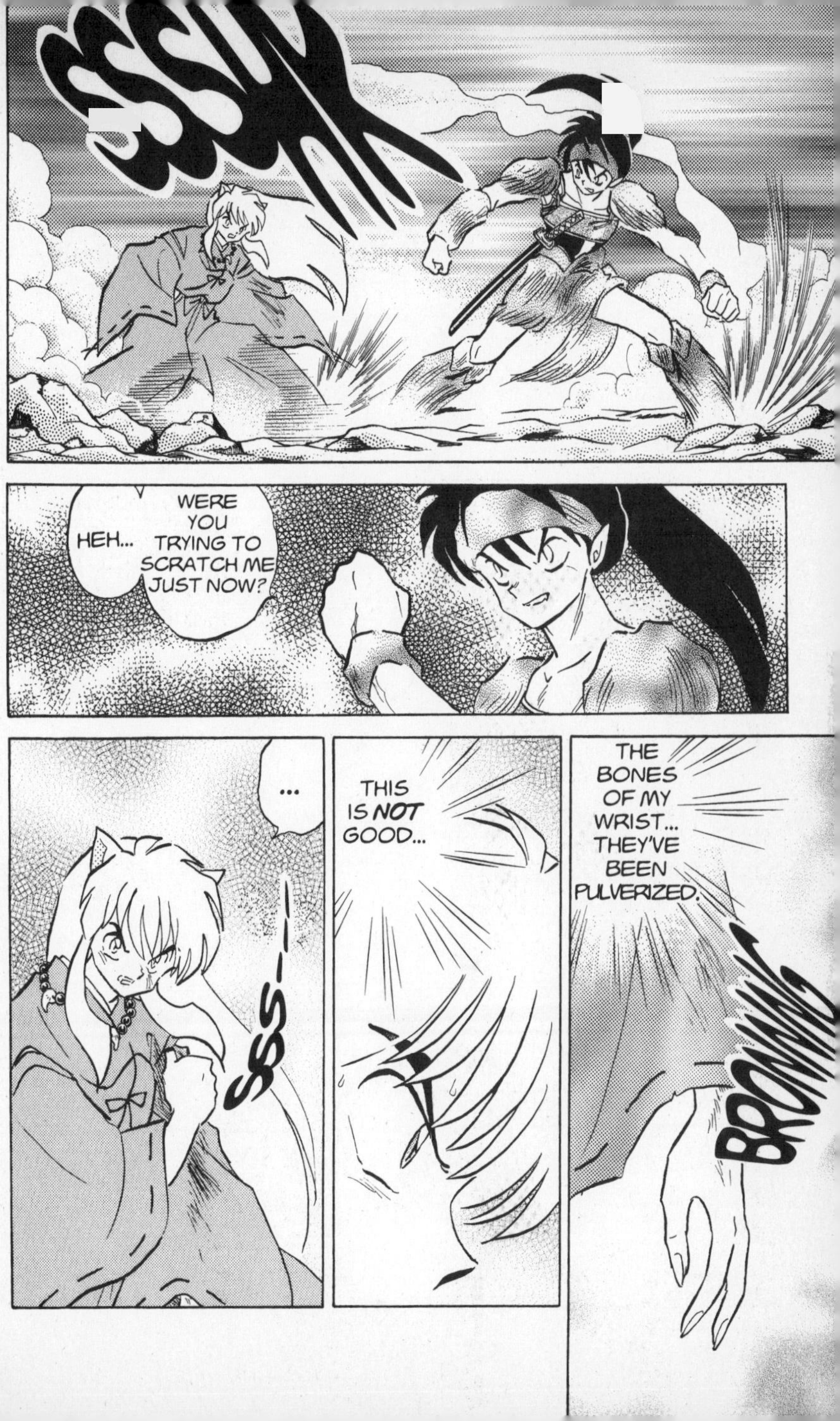
HEH...
WERE YOU TRYING TO SCRATCH ME JUST NOW?
...
THIS IS *NOT* GOOD...
THE BONES OF MY WRIST... THEY'VE BEEN PULVERIZED.

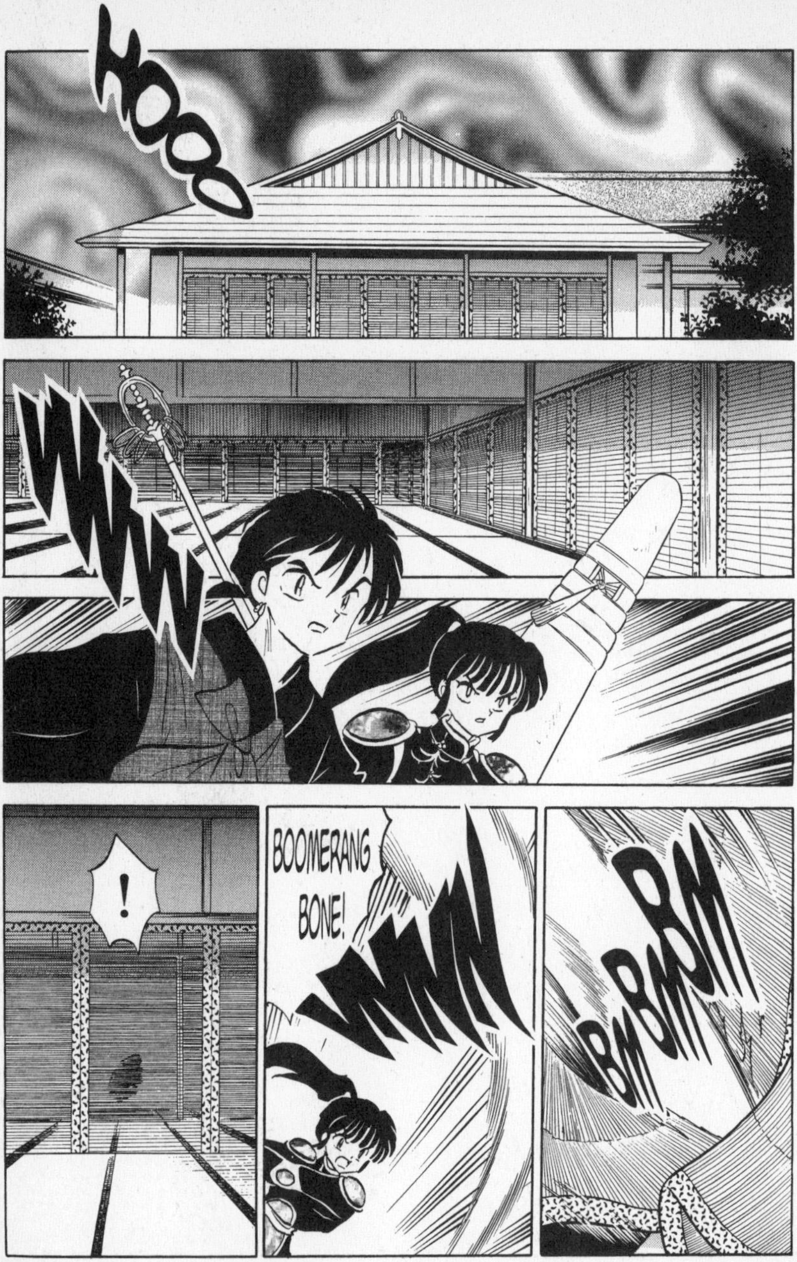
HOOO
VWWW
!
BOOMERANG BONE!
VWWM
BMBMBM

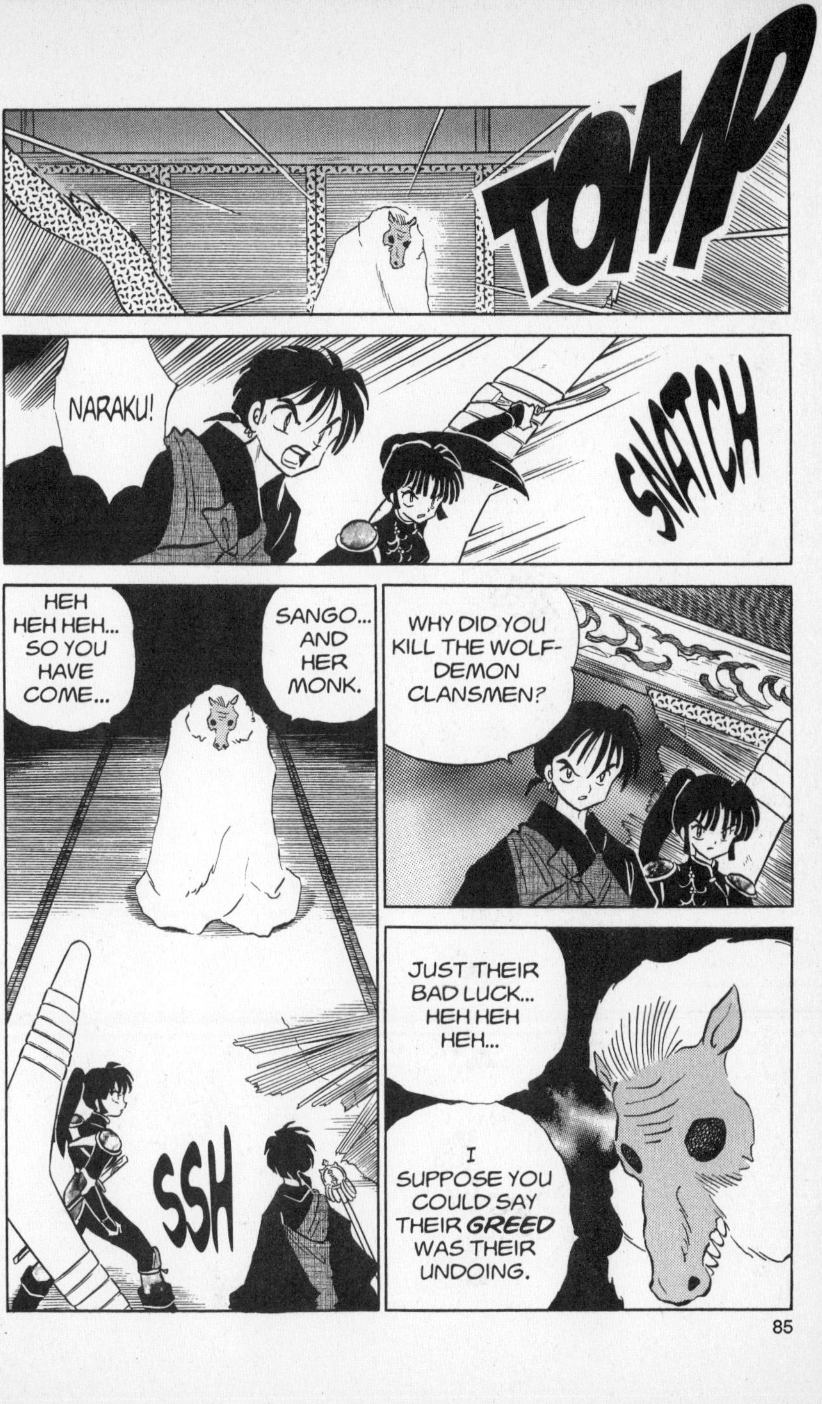
TOMP
NARAKU!
SNATCH
HEH HEH HEH... SO YOU HAVE COME...
SANGO... AND HER MONK.
SSH
WHY DID YOU KILL THE WOLF-DEMON CLANSMEN?
JUST THEIR BAD LUCK... HEH HEH HEH...
I SUPPOSE YOU COULD SAY THEIR ***GREED*** WAS THEIR UNDOING.

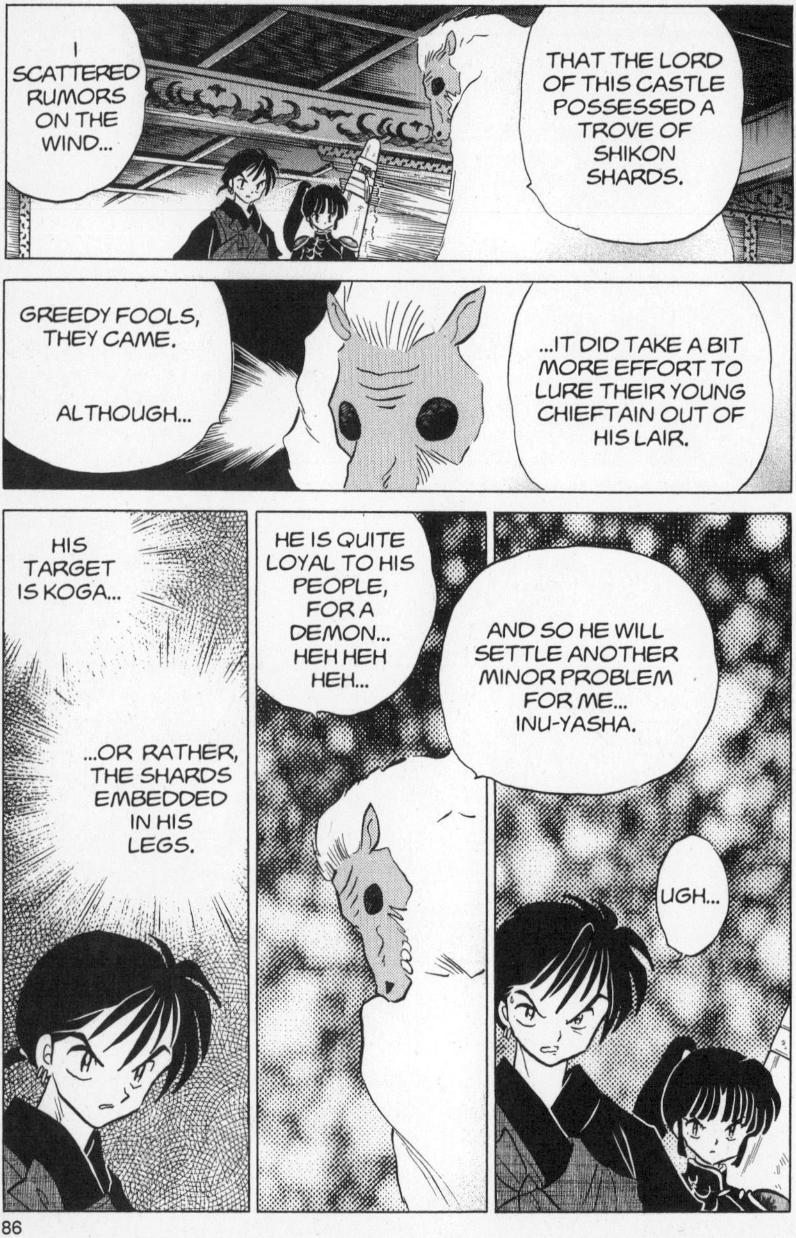
I SCATTERED RUMORS ON THE WIND...
THAT THE LORD OF THIS CASTLE POSSESSED A TROVE OF SHIKON SHARDS.
GREEDY FOOLS, THEY CAME.
ALTHOUGH...
...IT DID TAKE A BIT MORE EFFORT TO LURE THEIR YOUNG CHIEFTAIN OUT OF HIS LAIR.
HIS TARGET IS KOGA...
...OR RATHER, THE SHARDS EMBEDDED IN HIS LEGS.
HE IS QUITE LOYAL TO HIS PEOPLE, FOR A DEMON... HEH HEH HEH...
AND SO HE WILL SETTLE ANOTHER MINOR PROBLEM FOR ME... INU-YASHA.
UGH...

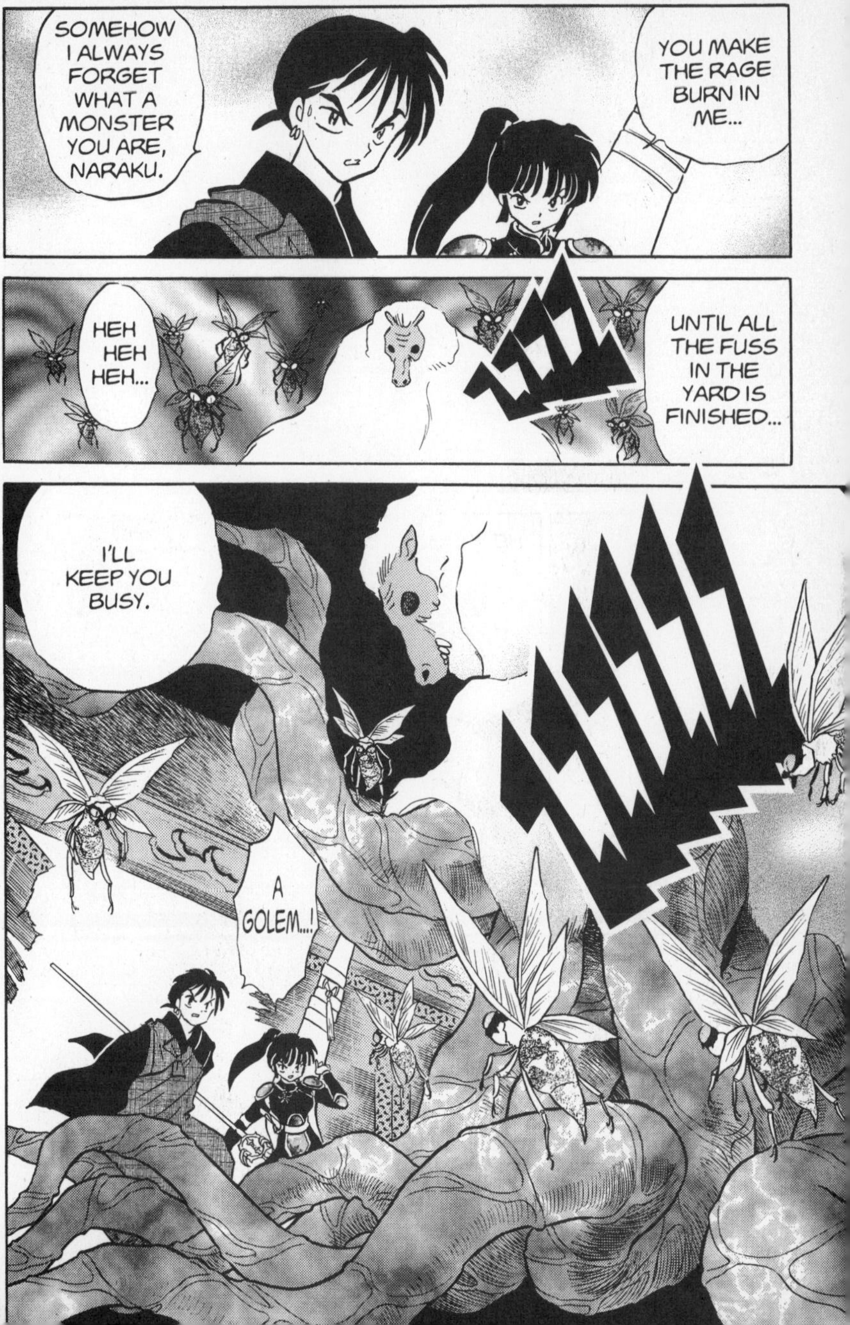
SOMEHOW I ALWAYS FORGET WHAT A MONSTER YOU ARE, NARAKU.
YOU MAKE THE RAGE BURN IN ME...
HEH HEH HEH...
UNTIL ALL THE FUSS IN THE YARD IS FINISHED...
I'LL KEEP YOU BUSY.
A GOLEM...!

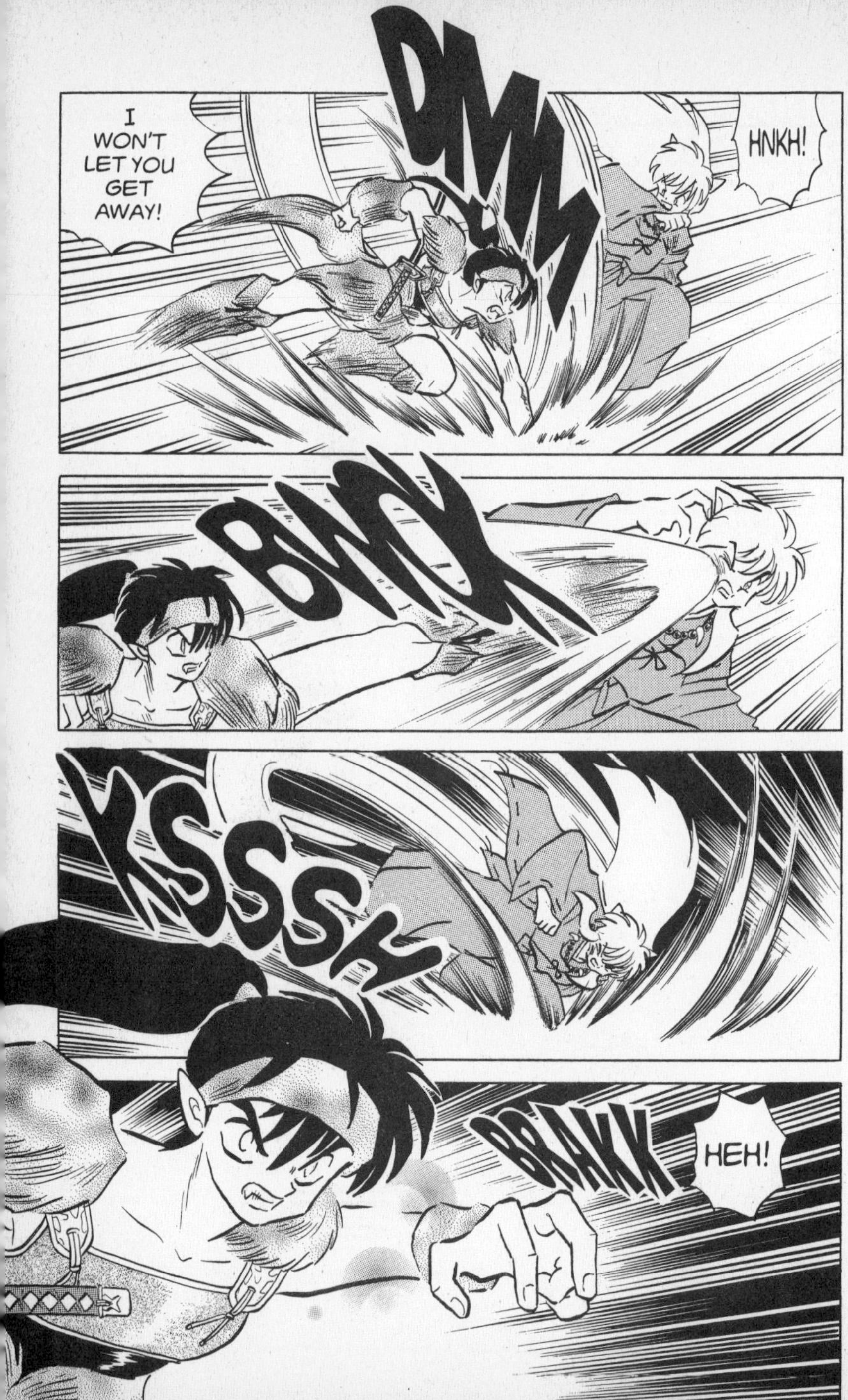
I WON'T LET YOU GET AWAY!
DMM
HNKH!
BWOK
KSSSH
BRAKK
HEH!

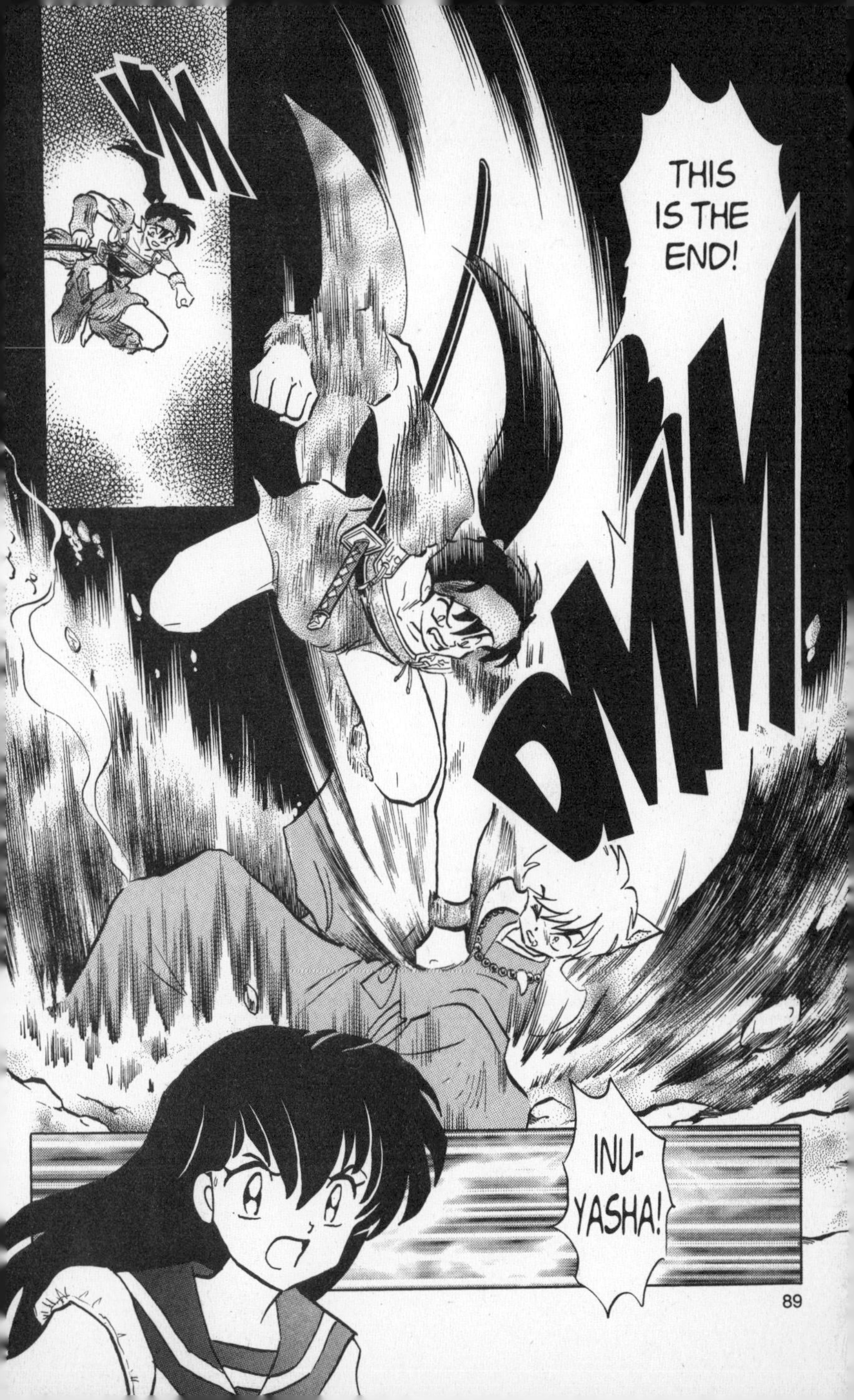

WM
THIS IS THE END!
DMM!
INU-YASHA!

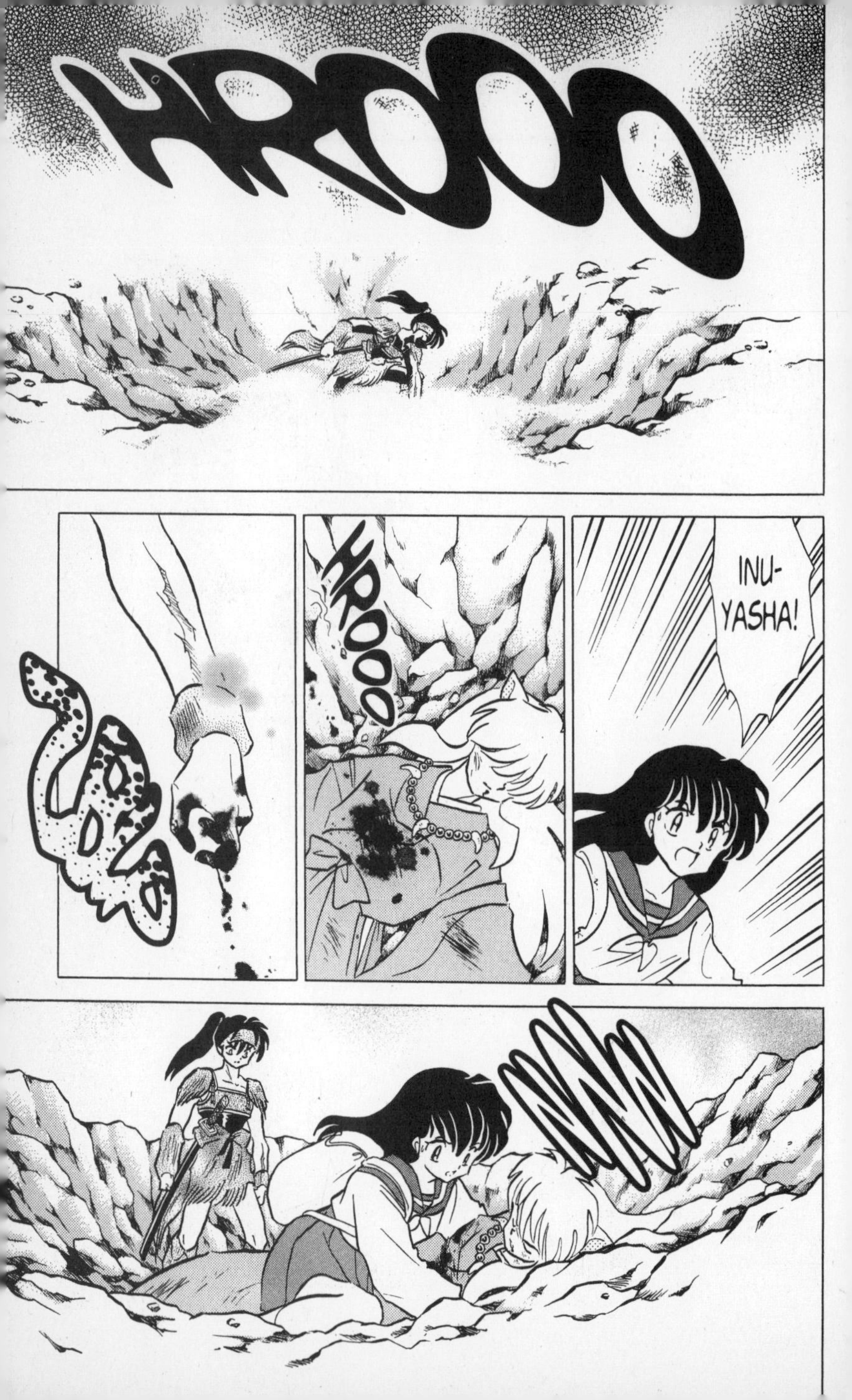
HROOO
HROOO
INU-YASHA!

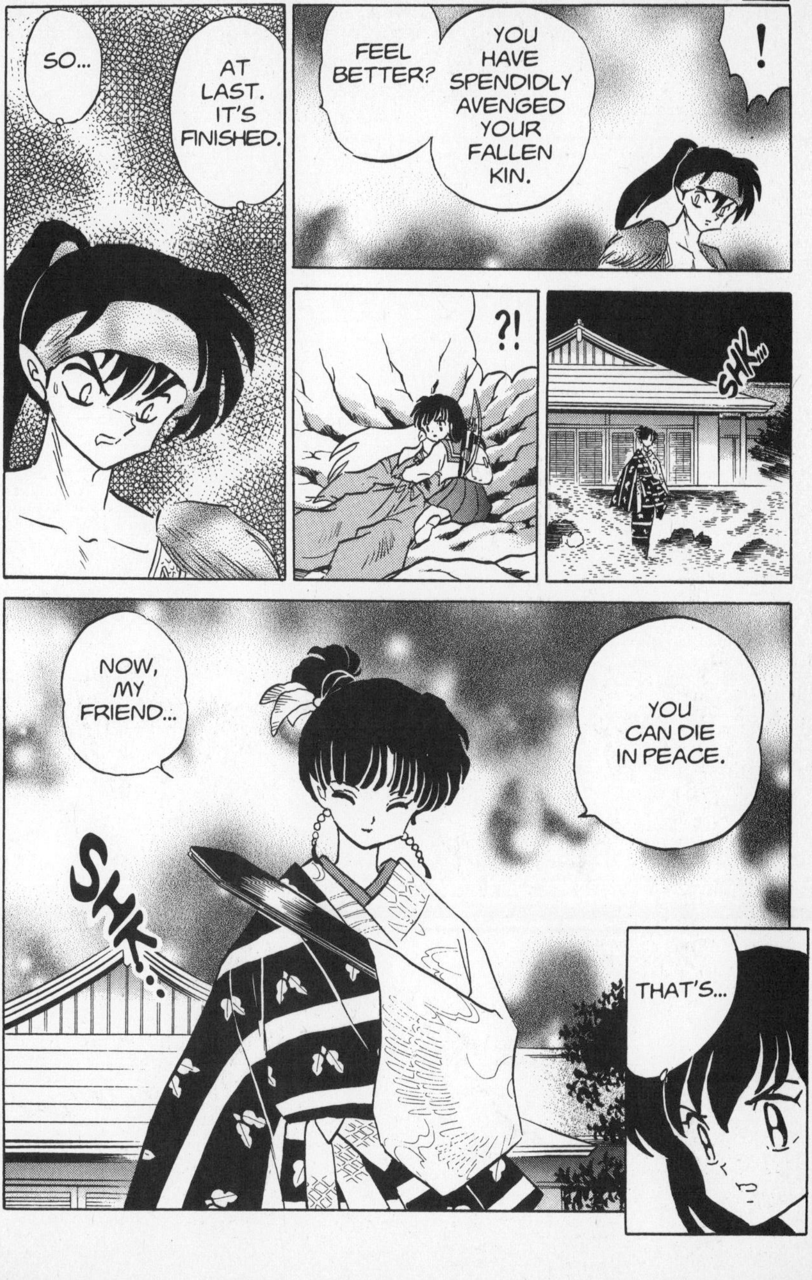
SO...
AT LAST. IT'S FINISHED.
FEEL BETTER?
YOU HAVE SPENDIDLY AVENGED YOUR FALLEN KIN.
!
?!
SHK...
NOW, MY FRIEND...
YOU CAN DIE IN PEACE.
SHK...
THAT'S...

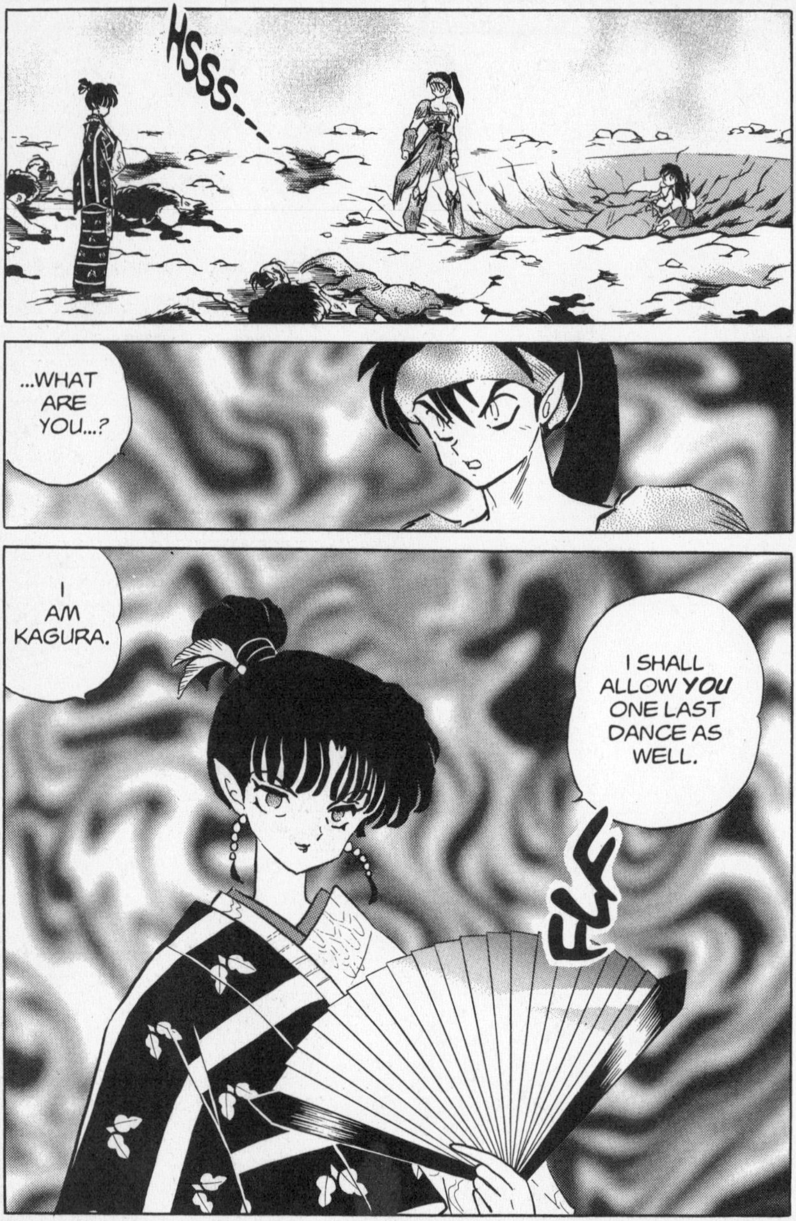
HSSS---
...WHAT ARE YOU...?
I AM KAGURA.
I SHALL ALLOW *YOU* ONE LAST DANCE AS WELL.

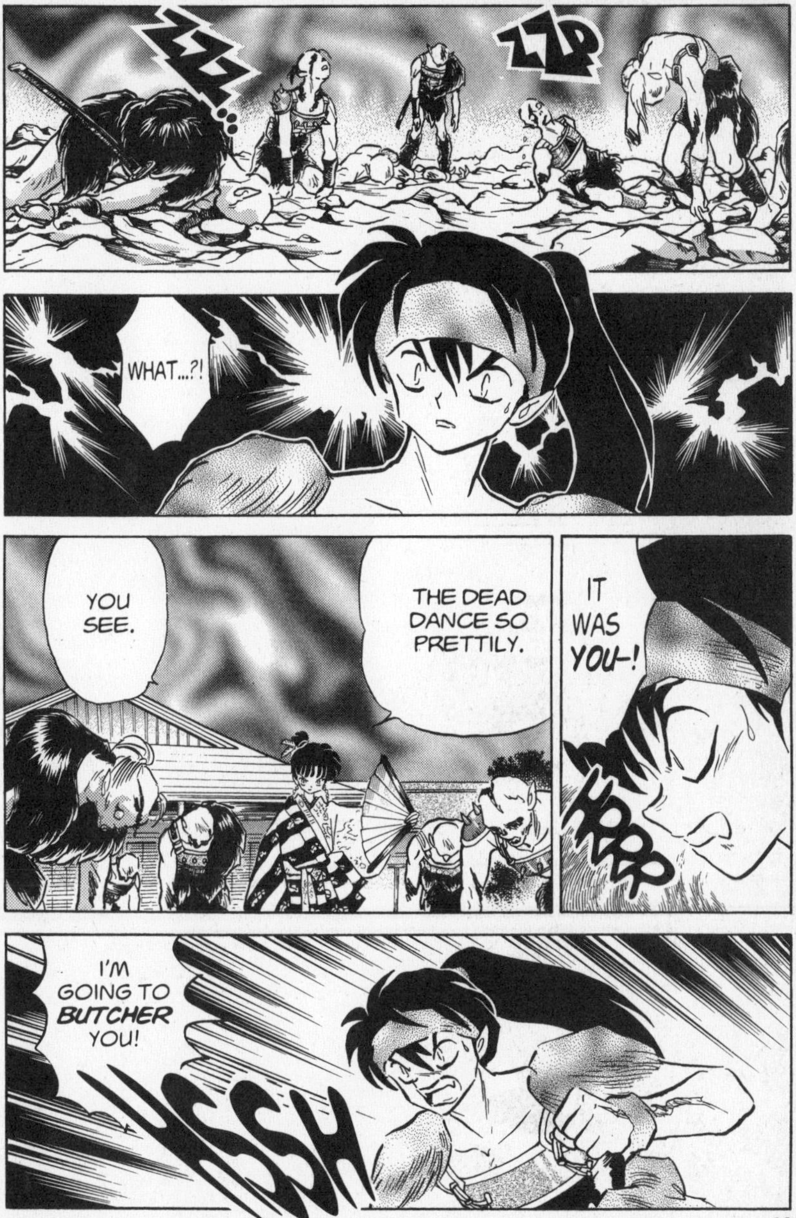
ZZZ...
ZZZ
WHAT...?!
YOU SEE.
THE DEAD DANCE SO PRETTILY.
IT WAS YOU-!
HRRRR
I'M GOING TO BUTCHER YOU!
WSSH

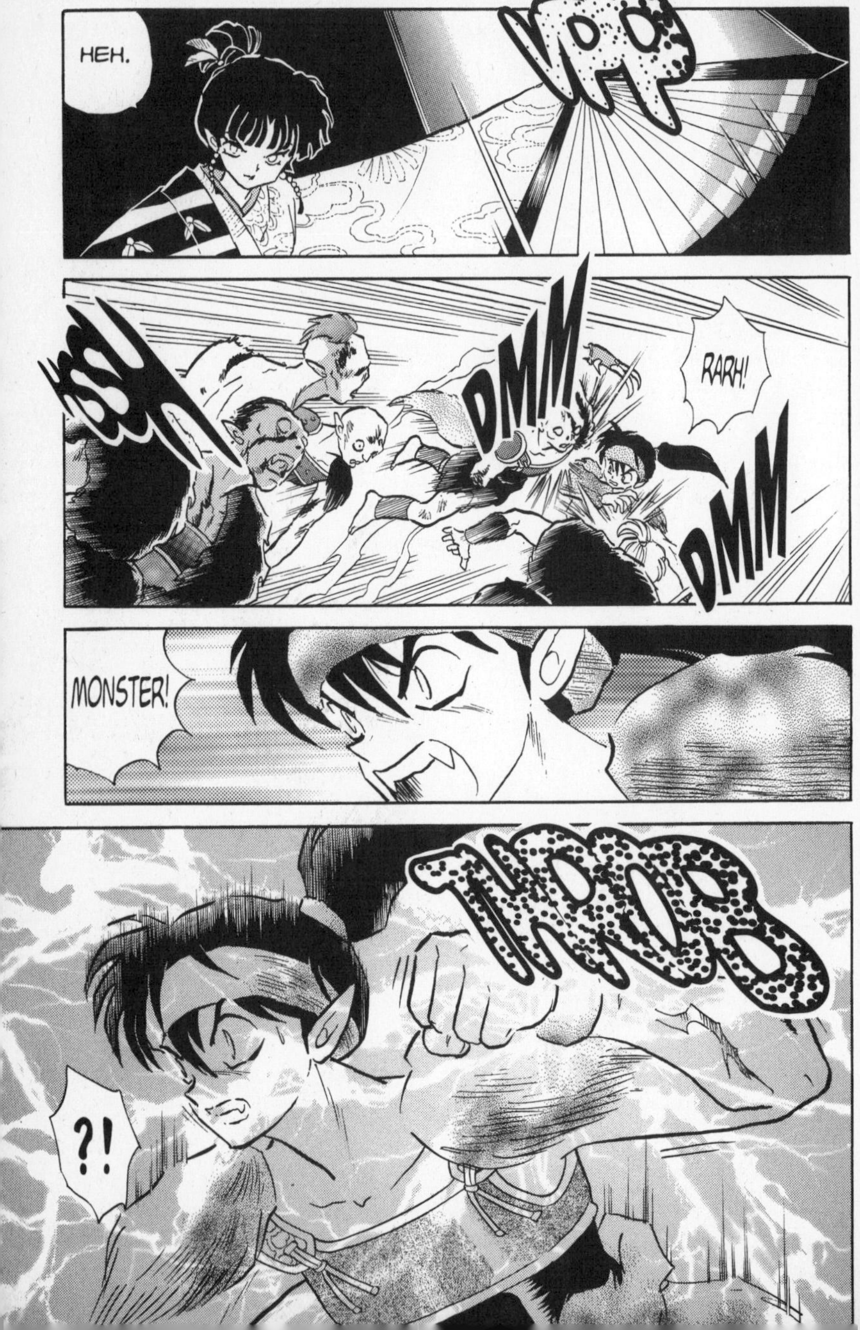
HEH.
VOOP
WOSH
DMM
RARH!
DMM
MONSTER!
THROB
?!

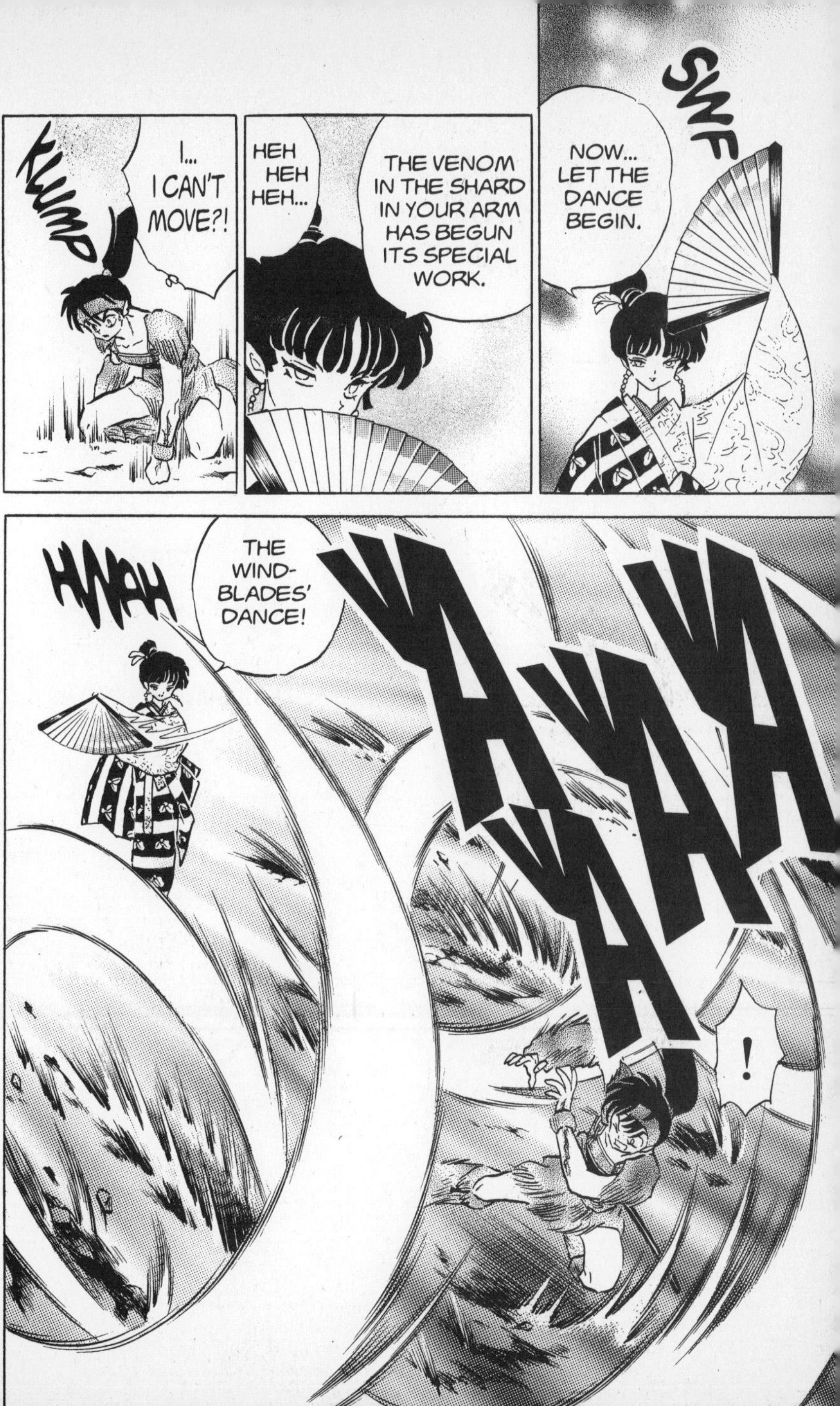
KLUMP
I... I CAN'T MOVE?!
HEH HEH HEH...
THE VENOM IN THE SHARD IN YOUR ARM HAS BEGUN ITS SPECIAL WORK.
SWF
NOW... LET THE DANCE BEGIN.
HWAH
THE WIND-BLADES' DANCE!
YAAAAAAA
!

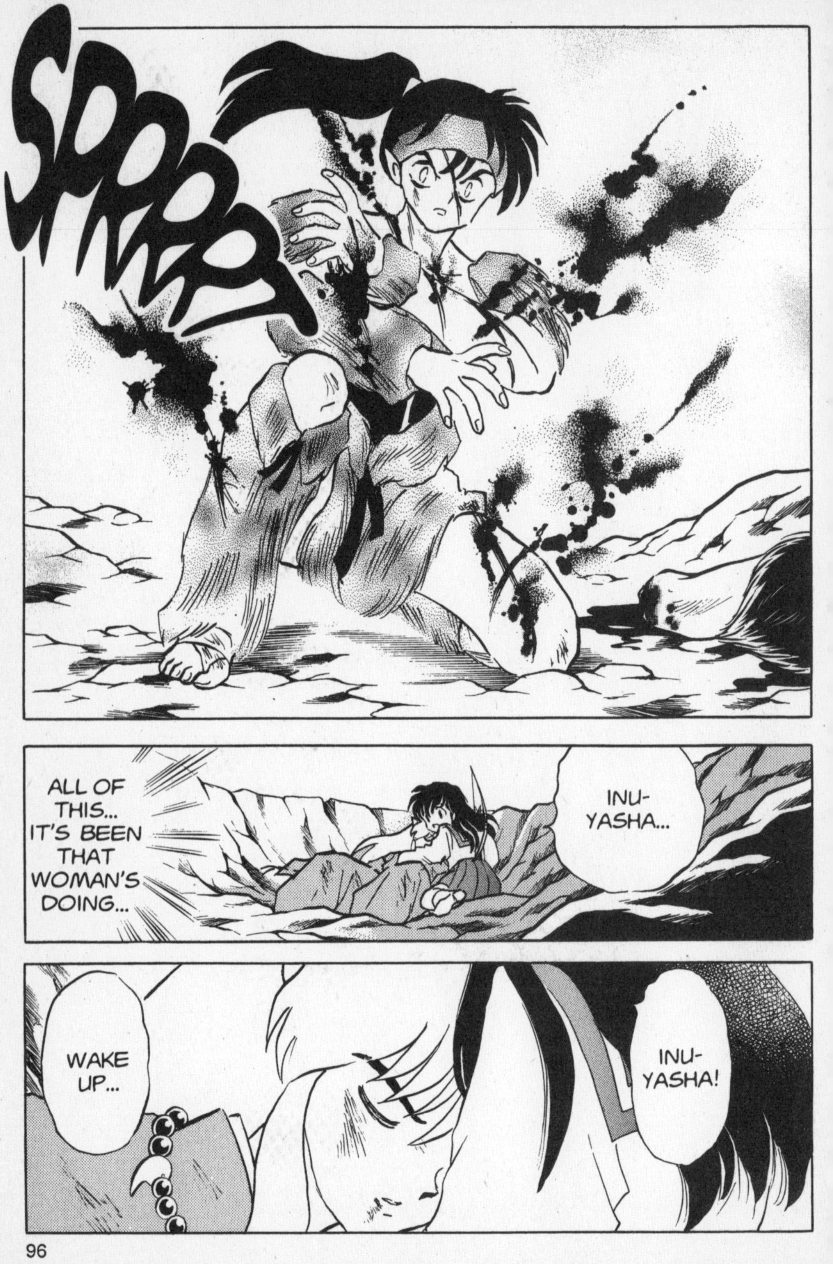
SPRRT
ALL OF THIS... IT'S BEEN THAT WOMAN'S DOING...
INU-YASHA...
WAKE UP...
INU-YASHA!

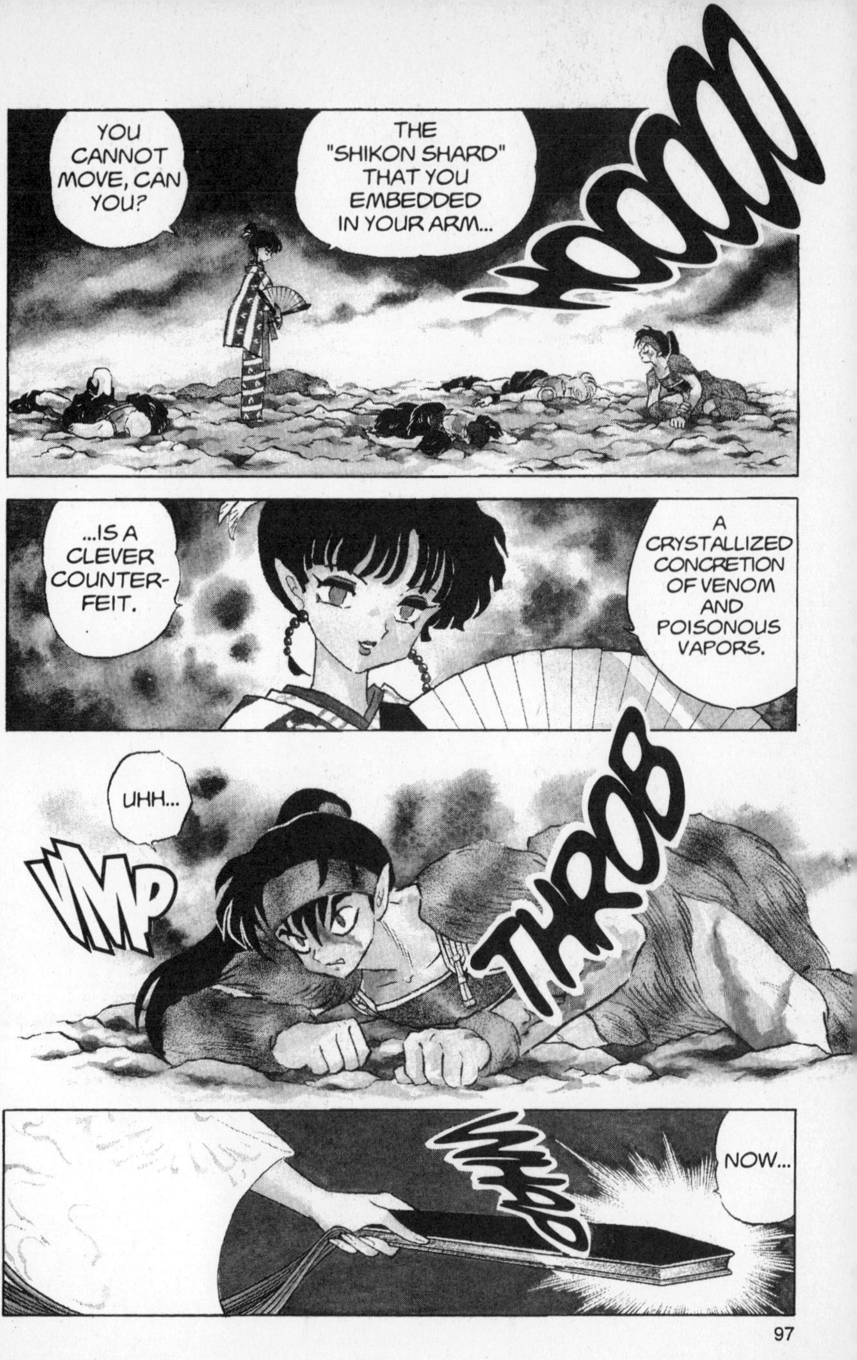
YOU CANNOT MOVE, CAN YOU?
THE "SHIKON SHARD" THAT YOU EMBEDDED IN YOUR ARM...
...IS A CLEVER COUNTER-FEIT.
A CRYSTALLIZED CONCRETION OF VENOM AND POISONOUS VAPORS.
UHH...
VMP
THROB
NOW...

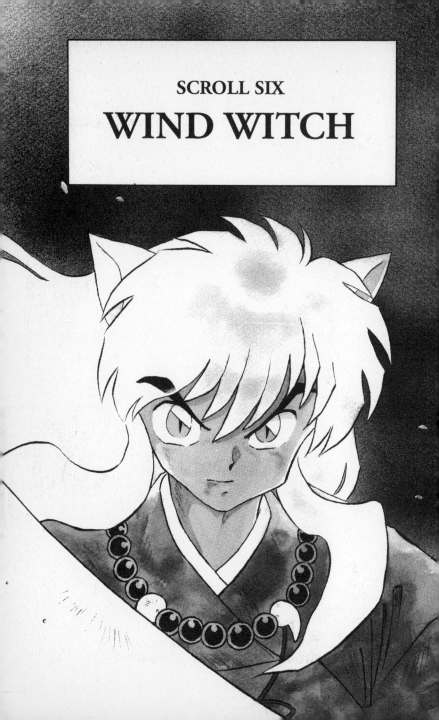

SCROLL SIX
WIND WITCH

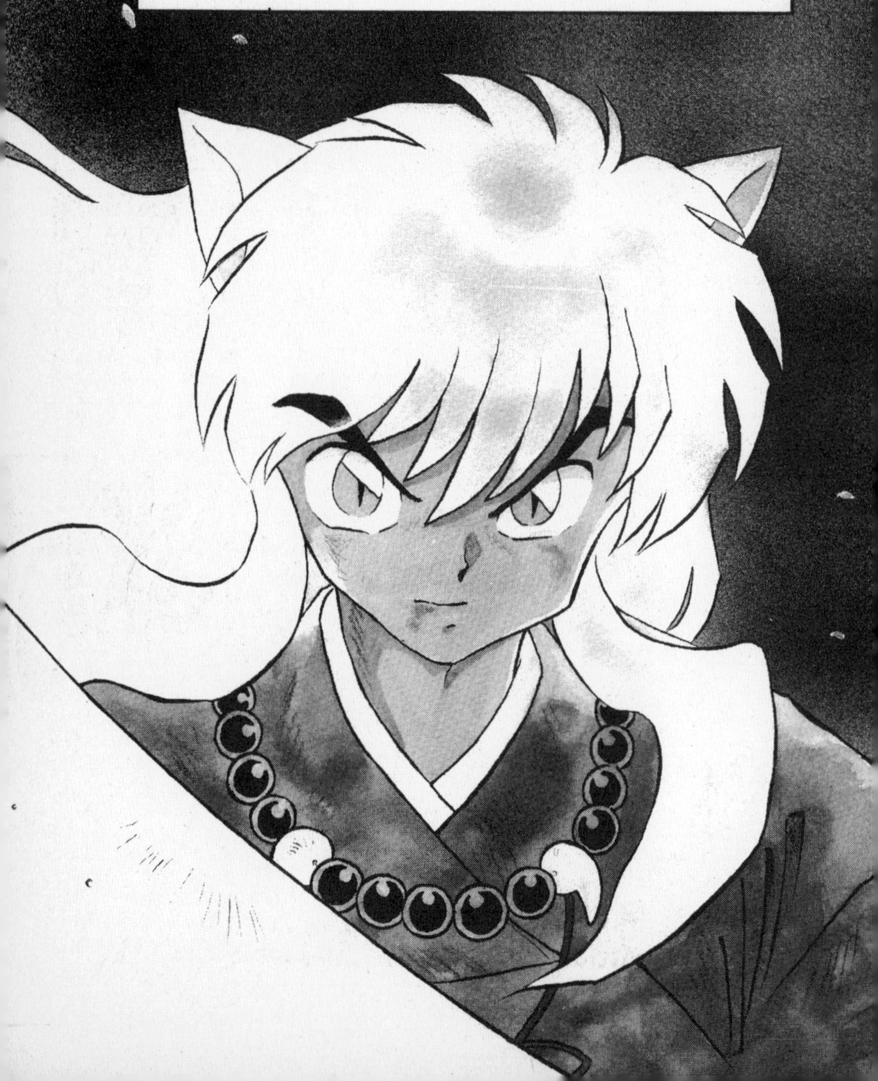

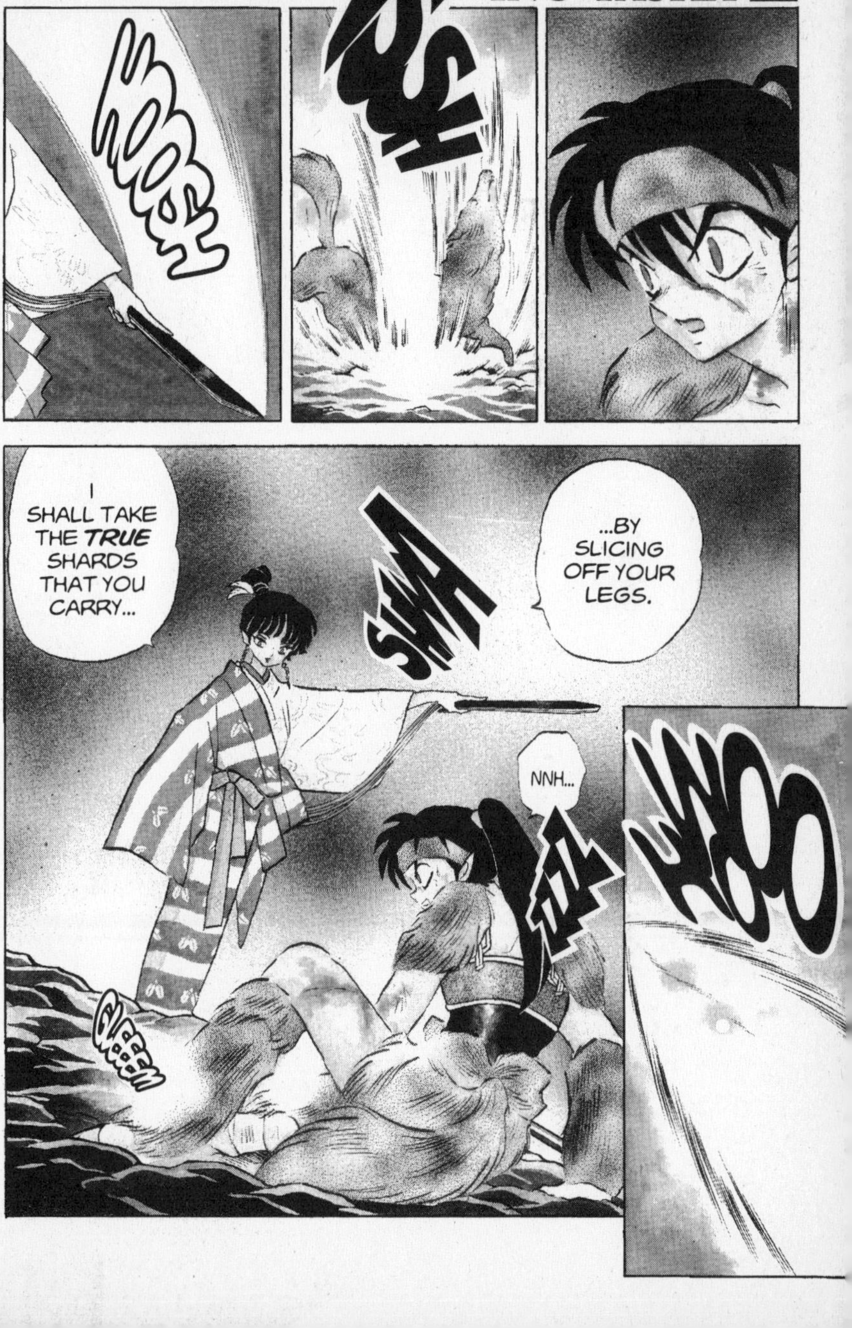
WOOSH
VSSH
I SHALL TAKE THE *TRUE* SHARDS THAT YOU CARRY...
SHWA
...BY SLICING OFF YOUR LEGS.
NNH...
FZZT
WHOO
GLEEEEM

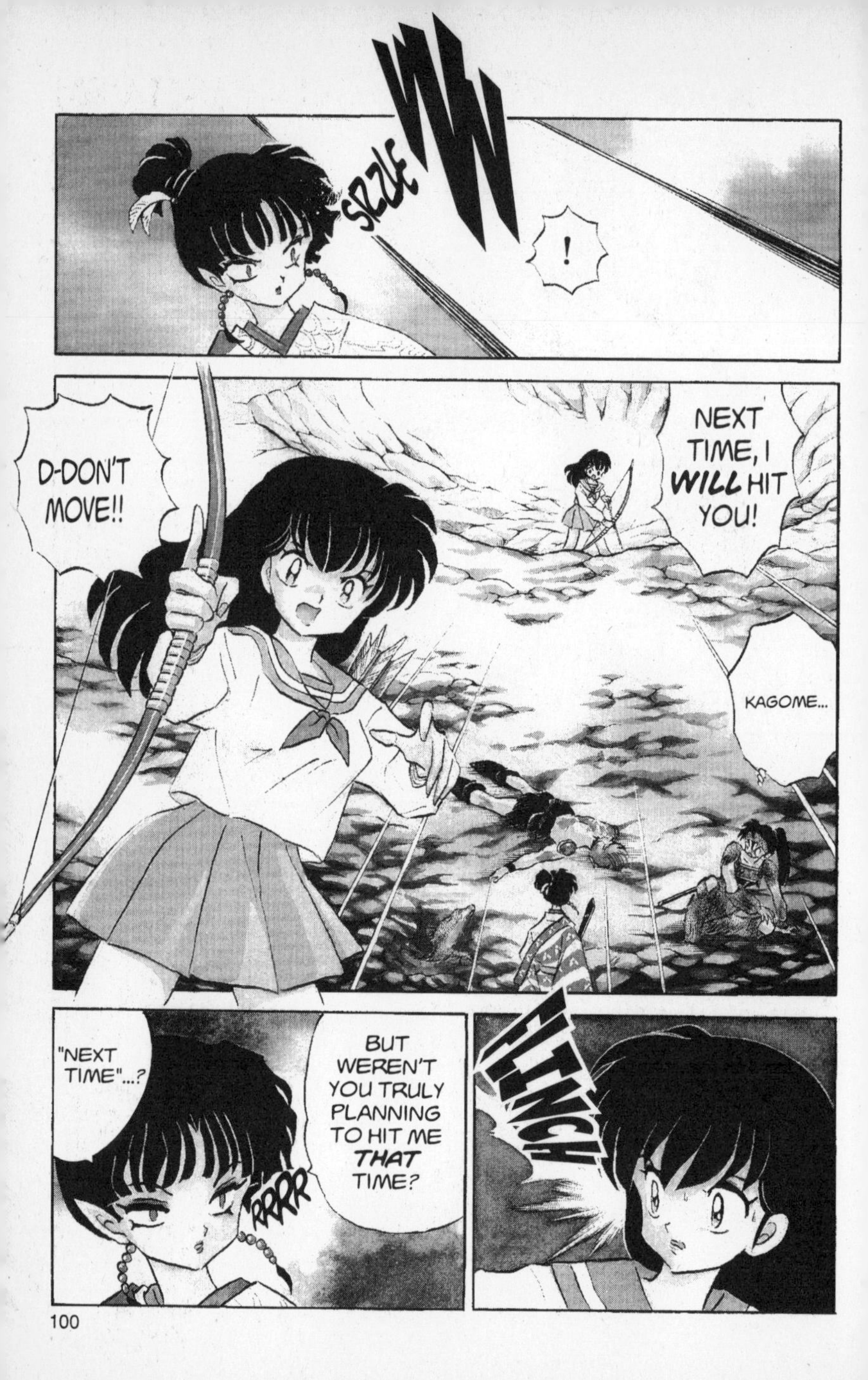
SIZZLE
VWW
!
D-DON'T MOVE!!
NEXT TIME, I **WILL** HIT YOU!
KAGOME...
"NEXT TIME"...?
BUT WEREN'T YOU TRULY PLANNING TO HIT ME **THAT** TIME?
RRRR
FLINCH

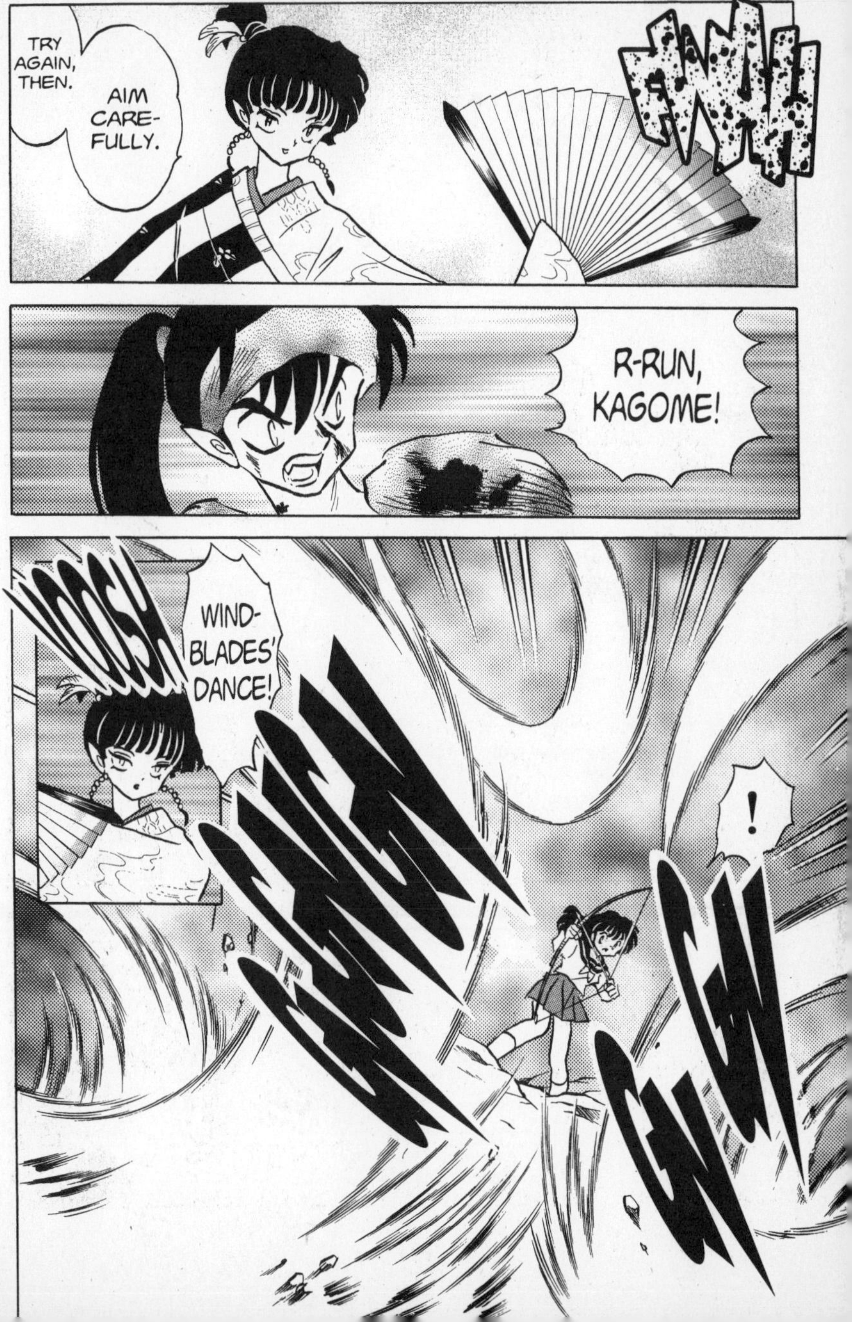
TRY AGAIN, THEN.
AIM CAREFULLY.
FWAH
R-RUN, KAGOME!
WOOSH!
WIND-BLADES' DANCE!
!

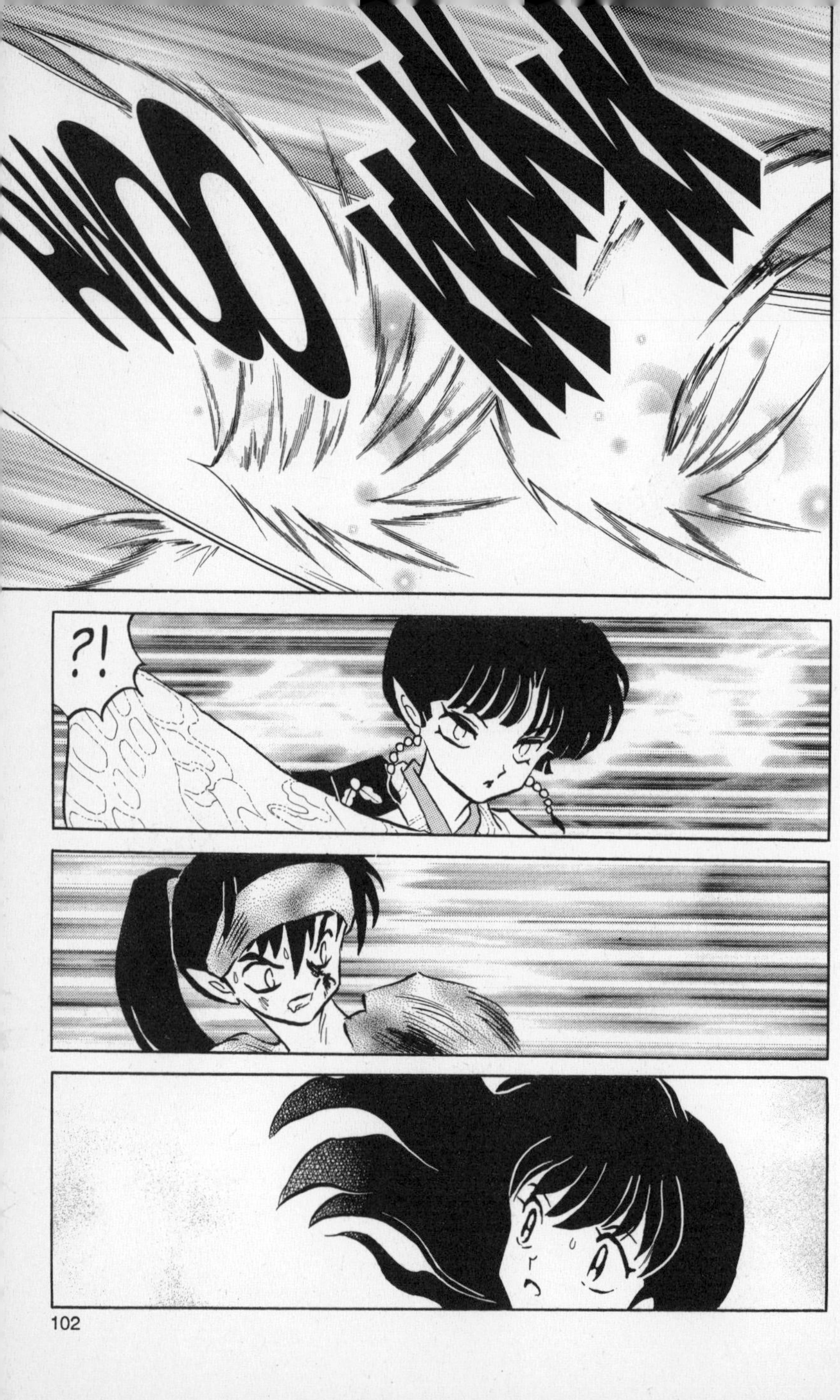
?!

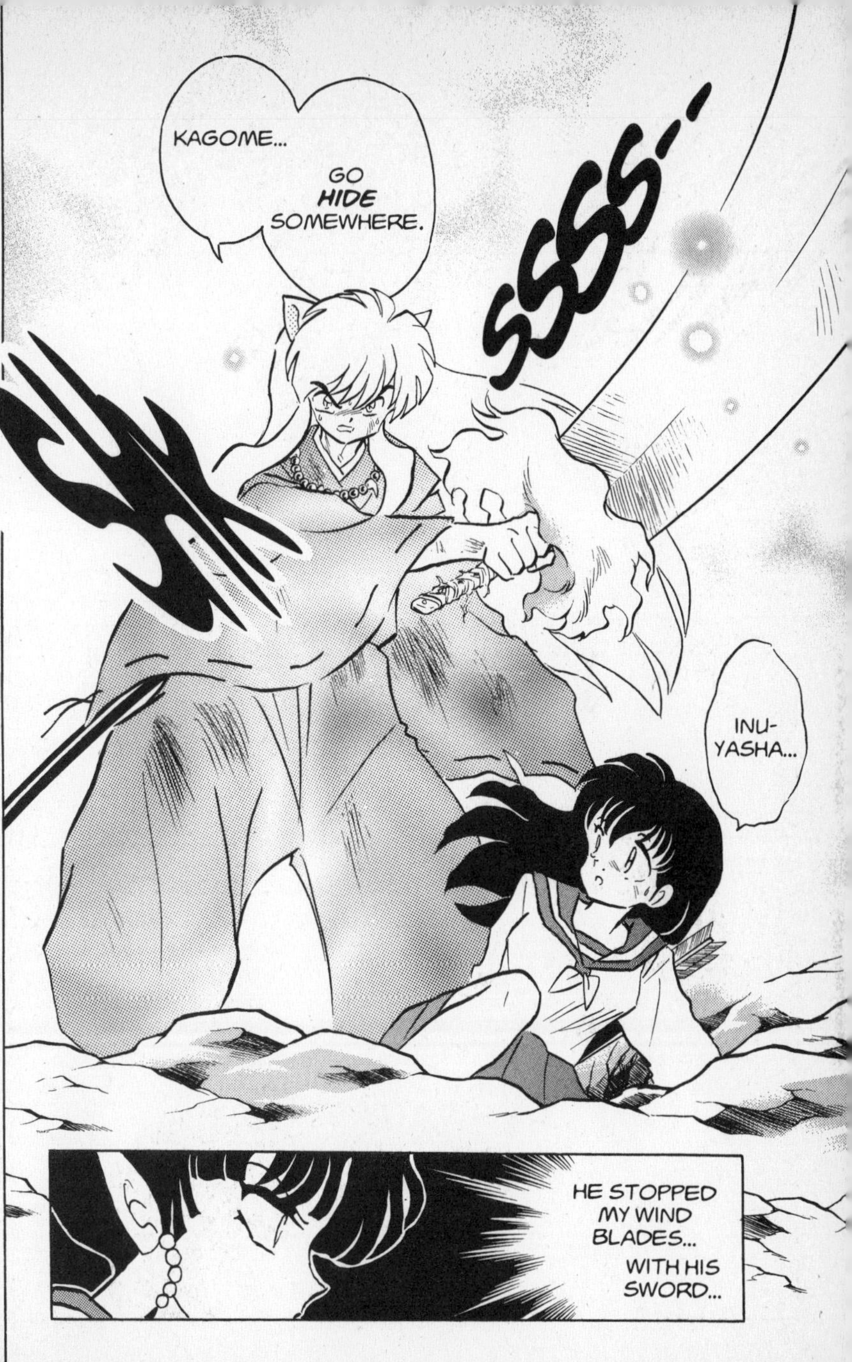
KAGOME... GO **HIDE** SOMEWHERE.
SSSS--
SH
INU-YASHA...
HE STOPPED MY WIND BLADES... WITH HIS SWORD...

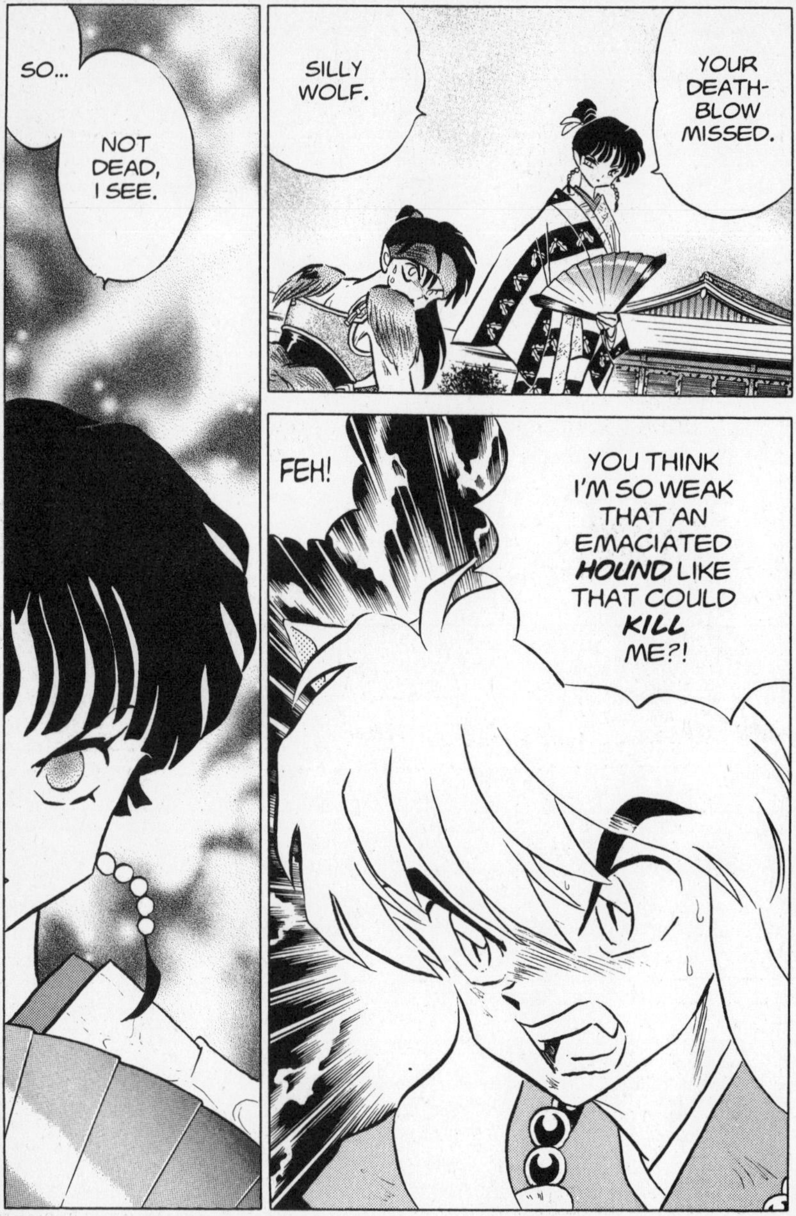
SO...
NOT DEAD, I SEE.
SILLY WOLF.
YOUR DEATH-BLOW MISSED.
FEH!
YOU THINK I'M SO WEAK THAT AN EMACIATED HOUND LIKE THAT COULD KILL ME?!

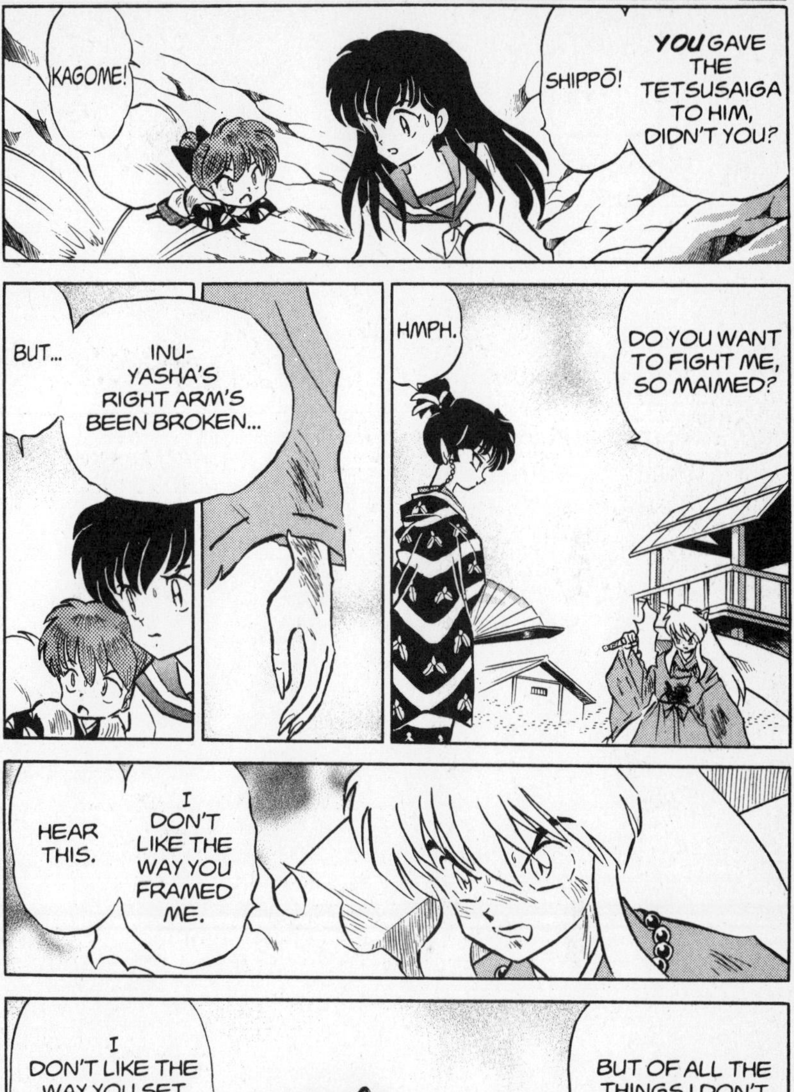
KAGOME!
SHIPPŌ!
YOU GAVE THE TETSUSAIGA TO HIM, DIDN'T YOU?
BUT...
INU-YASHA'S RIGHT ARM'S BEEN BROKEN...
HMPH.
DO YOU WANT TO FIGHT ME, SO MAIMED?
HEAR THIS.
I DON'T LIKE THE WAY YOU FRAMED ME.
I DON'T LIKE THE WAY YOU SET THAT IDIOT ON ME.
BUT OF ALL THE THINGS I DON'T LIKE ABOUT YOU, THE WORST IS...

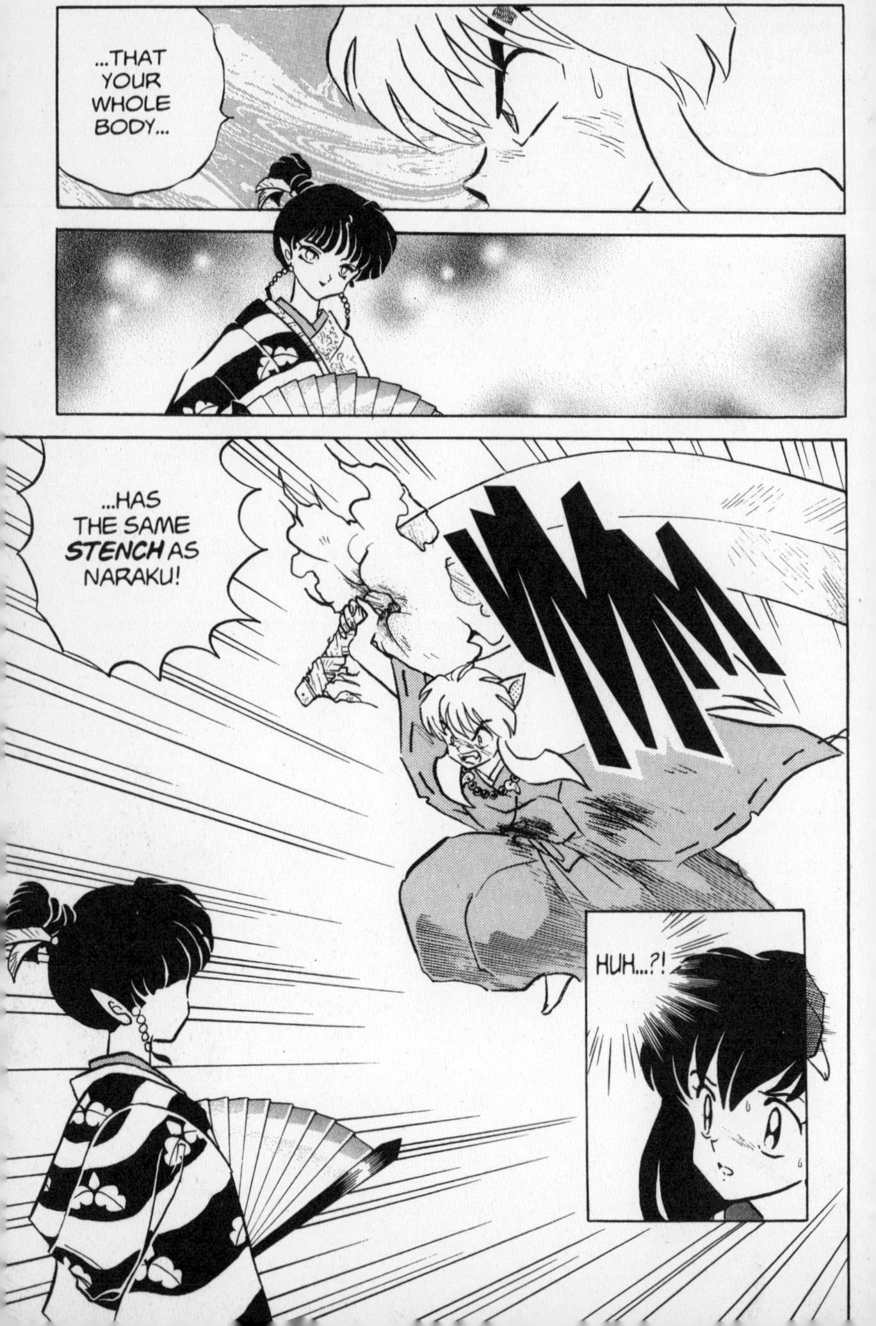
...THAT YOUR WHOLE BODY...
...HAS THE SAME **STENCH** AS NARAKU!
HUH...?!

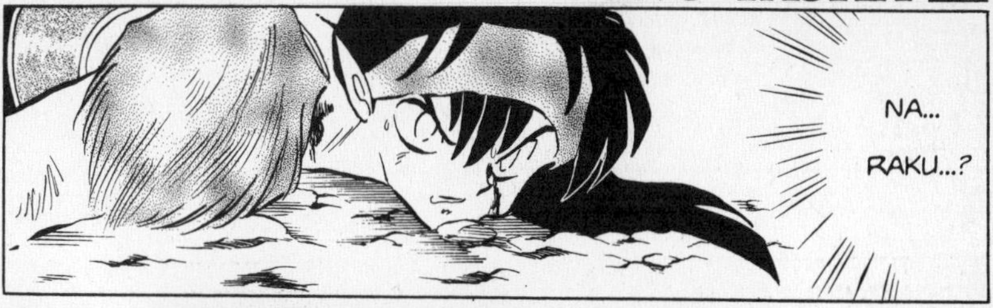
NA...
RAKU...?

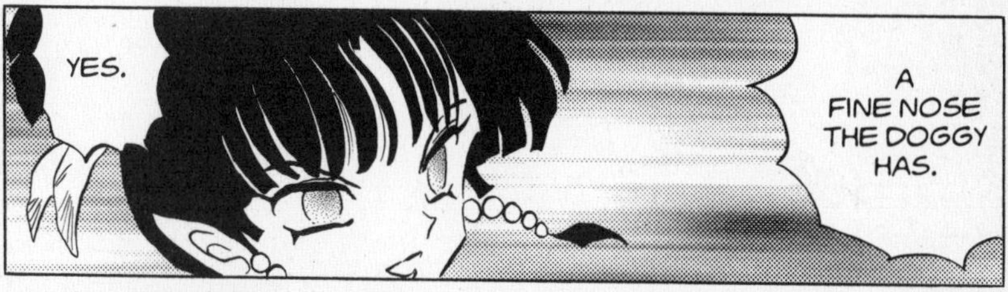
YES.
A FINE NOSE THE DOGGY HAS.

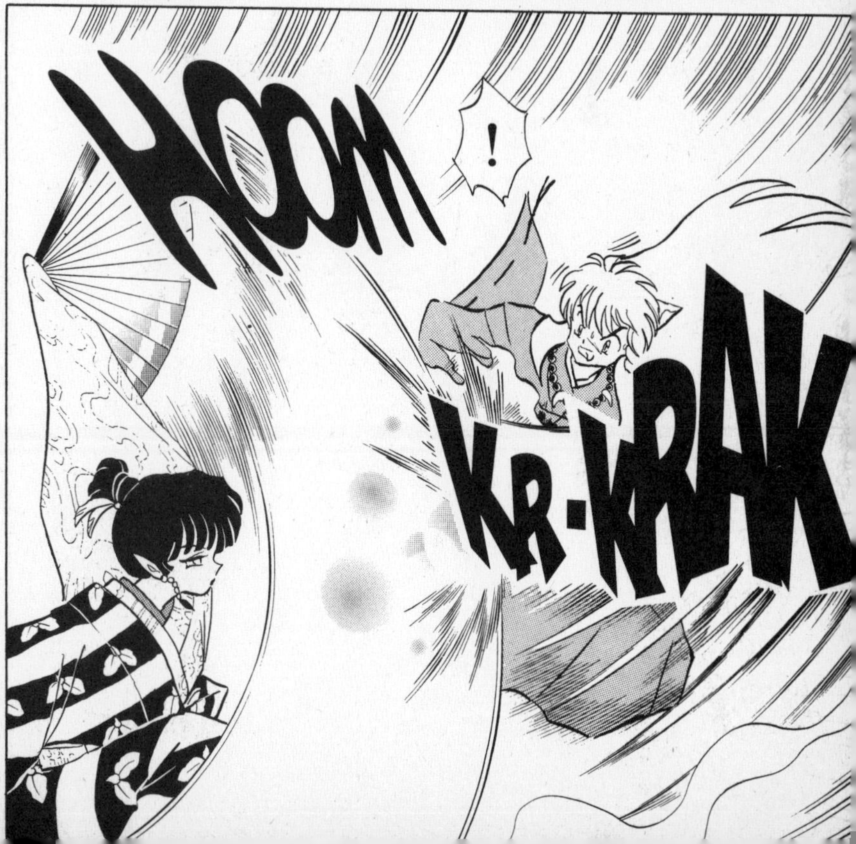
HOOM
!
KR-KRAK

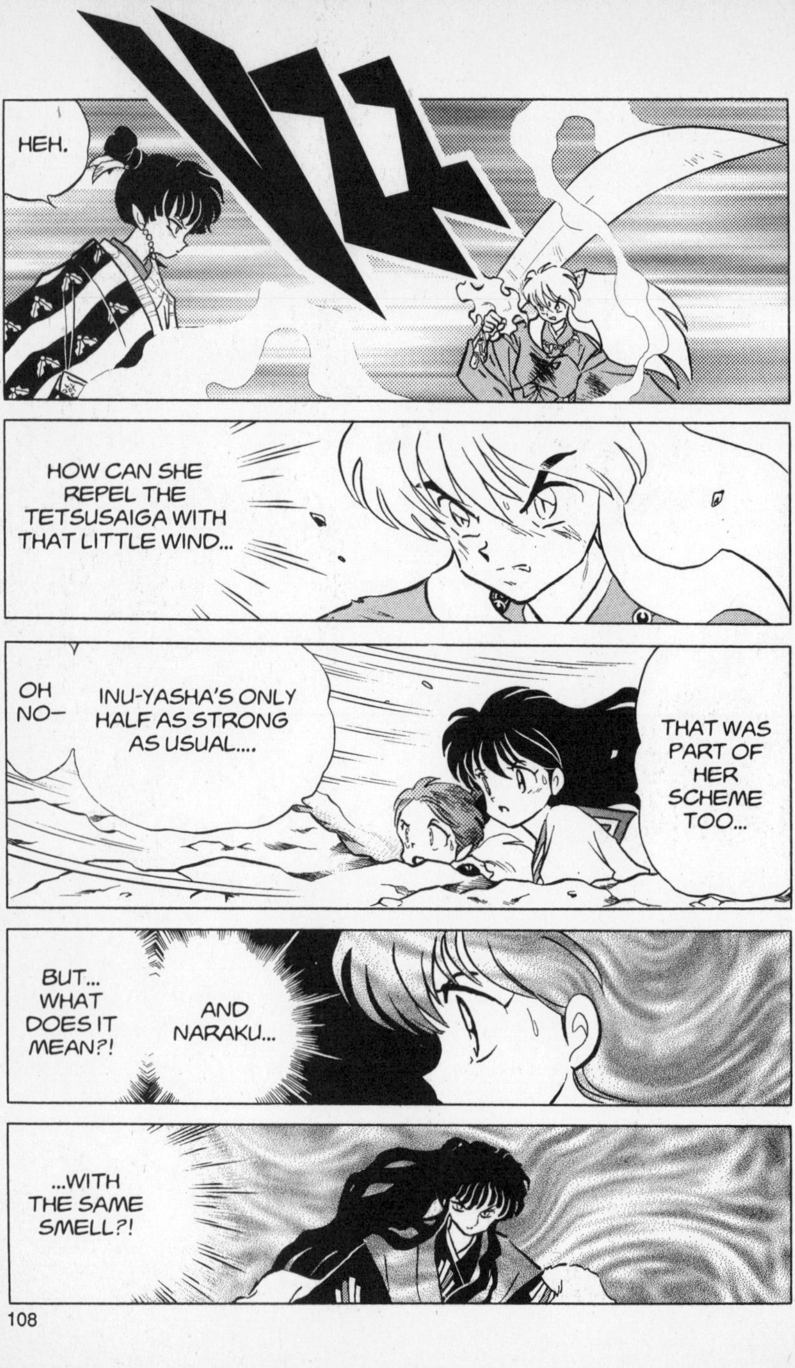
HEH.
HOW CAN SHE REPEL THE TETSUSAIGA WITH THAT LITTLE WIND...
OH NO—
INU-YASHA'S ONLY HALF AS STRONG AS USUAL....
THAT WAS PART OF HER SCHEME TOO...
BUT... WHAT DOES IT MEAN?!
AND NARAKU...
...WITH THE SAME SMELL?!

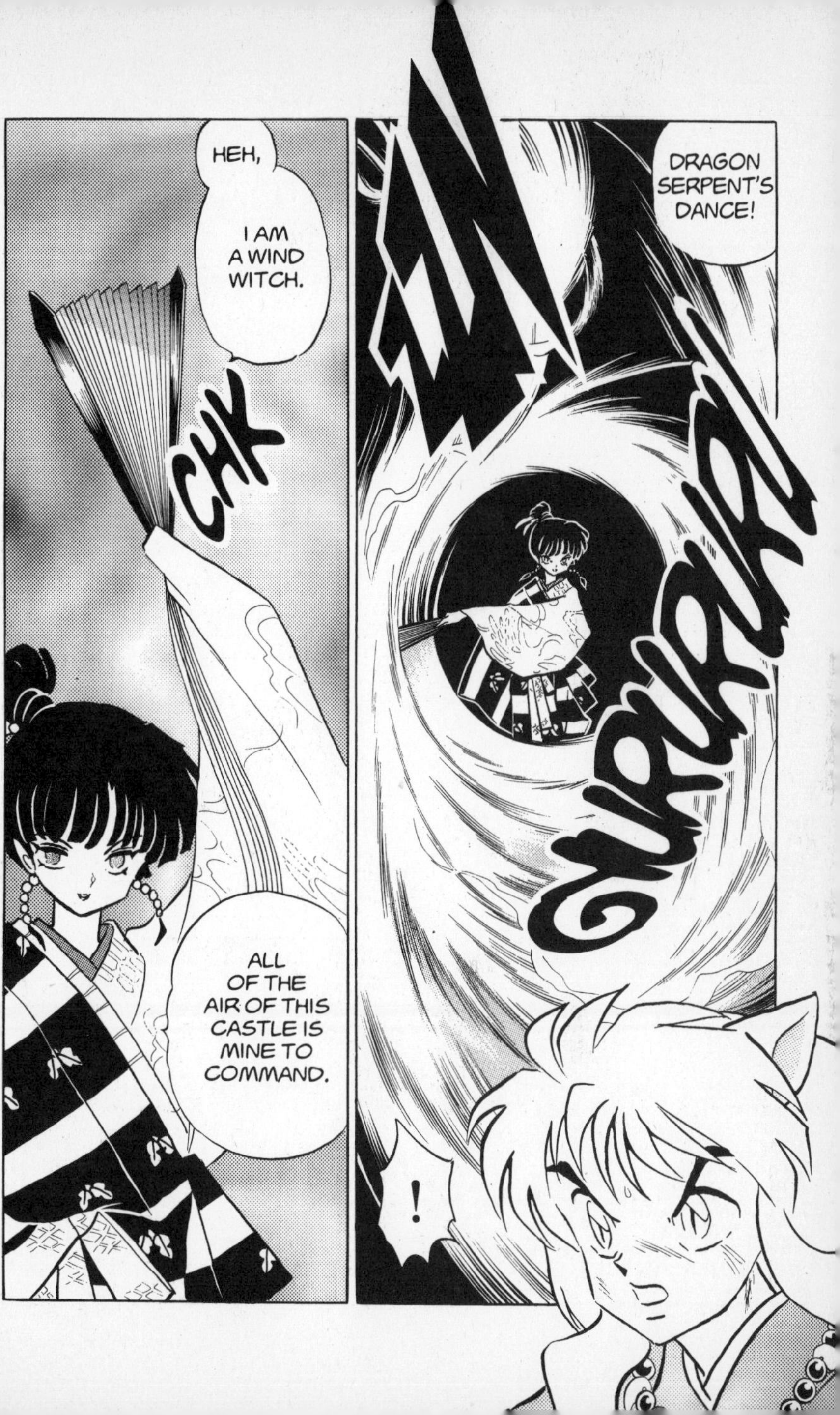
DRAGON SERPENT'S DANCE!
GWURURU!
!
HEH,
I AM A WIND WITCH.
CHK
ALL OF THE AIR OF THIS CASTLE IS MINE TO COMMAND.

GYURURURU

WHOA!

WAAH!

ZAZAZA

T-TWISTERS?!

SHE'S GOING TO IMPALE THEM—!

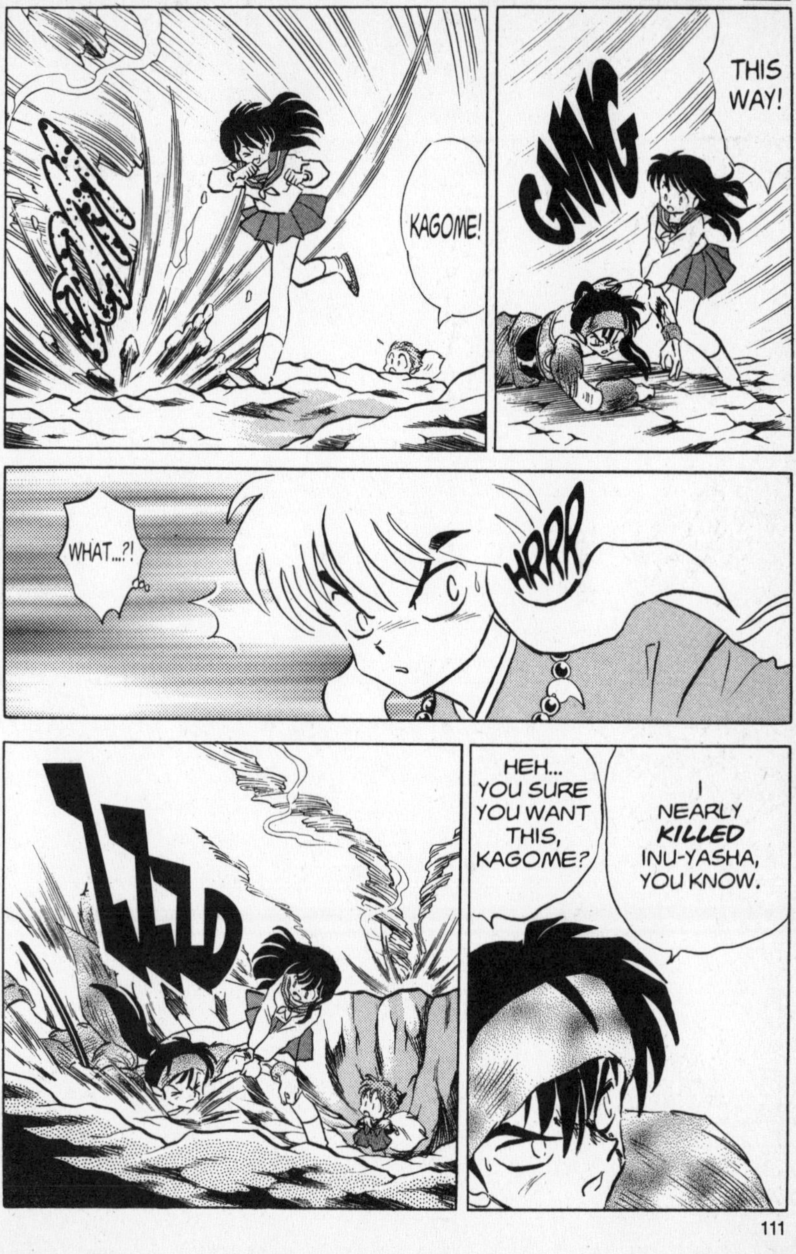
KAGOME!
THIS WAY!
WHAT...?!
HRRR
HEH... YOU SURE YOU WANT THIS, KAGOME?
I NEARLY **KILLED** INU-YASHA, YOU KNOW.

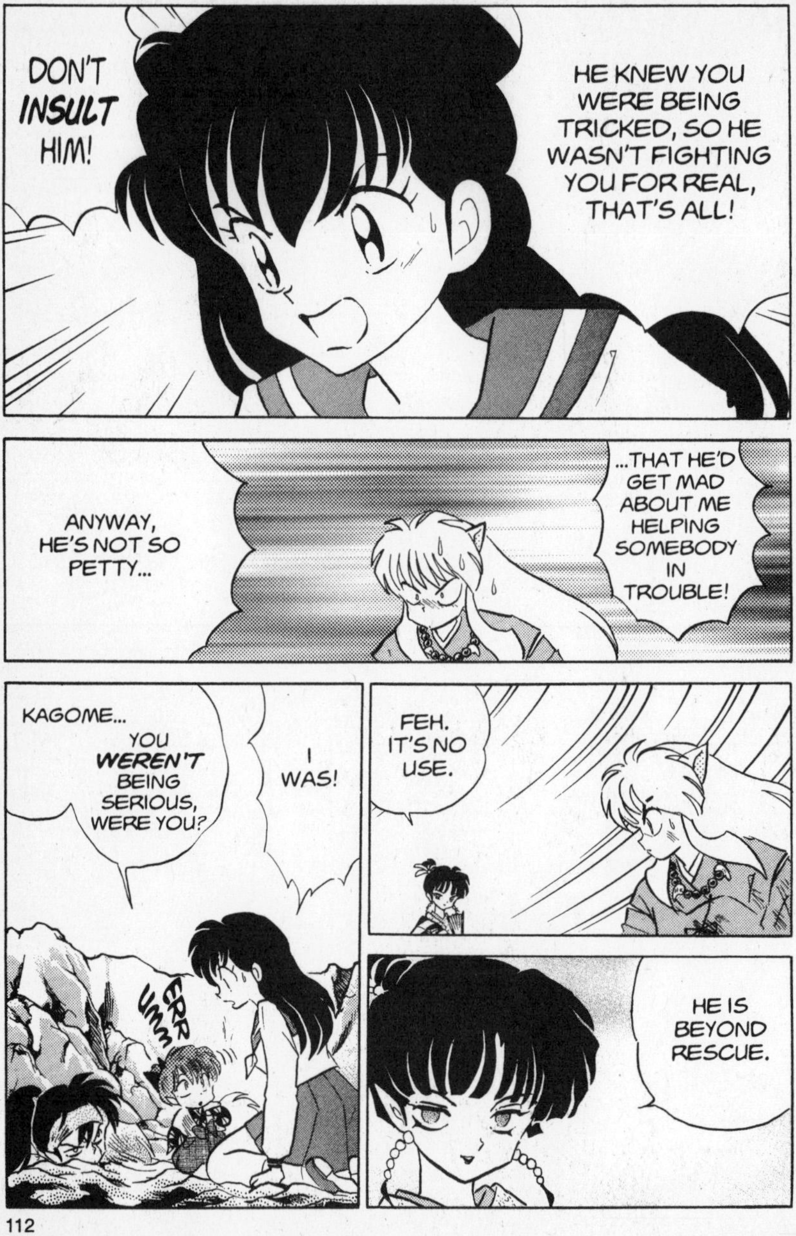
DON'T **INSULT** HIM!
HE KNEW YOU WERE BEING TRICKED, SO HE WASN'T FIGHTING YOU FOR REAL, THAT'S ALL!
ANYWAY, HE'S NOT SO PETTY...
...THAT HE'D GET MAD ABOUT ME HELPING SOMEBODY IN TROUBLE!
KAGOME... YOU **WEREN'T** BEING SERIOUS, WERE YOU?
I WAS!
ERR UMM
FEH. IT'S NO USE.
HE IS BEYOND RESCUE.

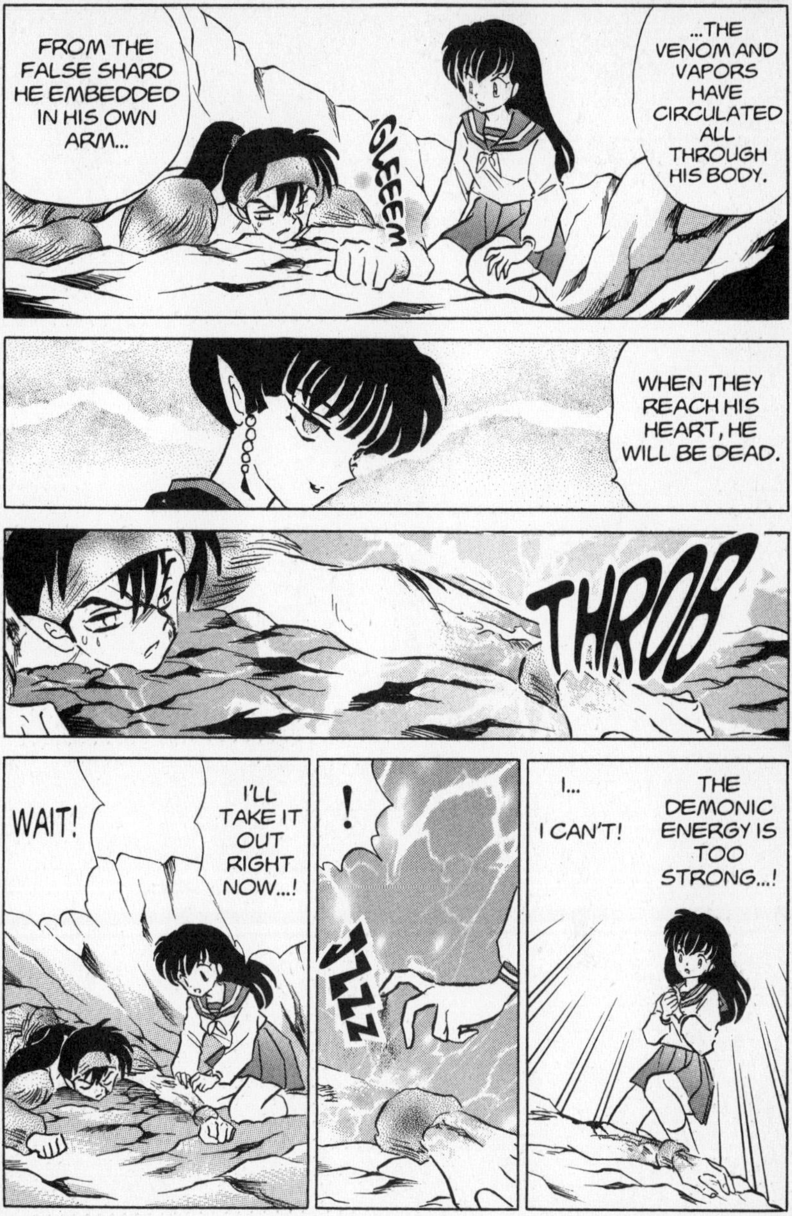
FROM THE FALSE SHARD HE EMBEDDED IN HIS OWN ARM...
GLEEEM
...THE VENOM AND VAPORS HAVE CIRCULATED ALL THROUGH HIS BODY.
WHEN THEY REACH HIS HEART, HE WILL BE DEAD.
THROB
WAIT!
I'LL TAKE IT OUT RIGHT NOW...!
!
ZZZT
I...
I CAN'T!
THE DEMONIC ENERGY IS TOO STRONG...!

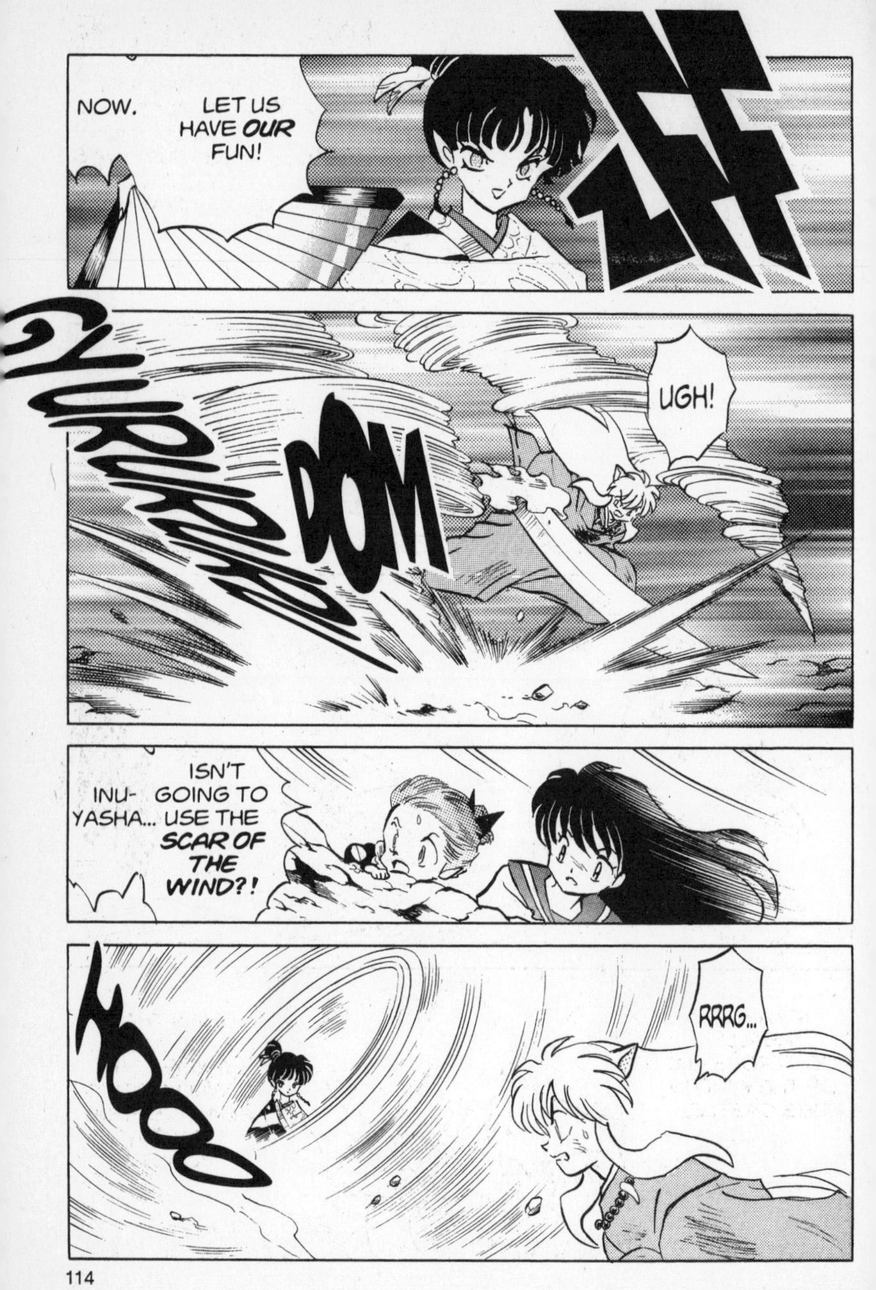
NOW.
LET US HAVE ***OUR*** FUN!
DOM
UGH!
INU-YASHA...
ISN'T GOING TO USE THE ***SCAR OF THE WIND?!***
HOOOO
RRRG...

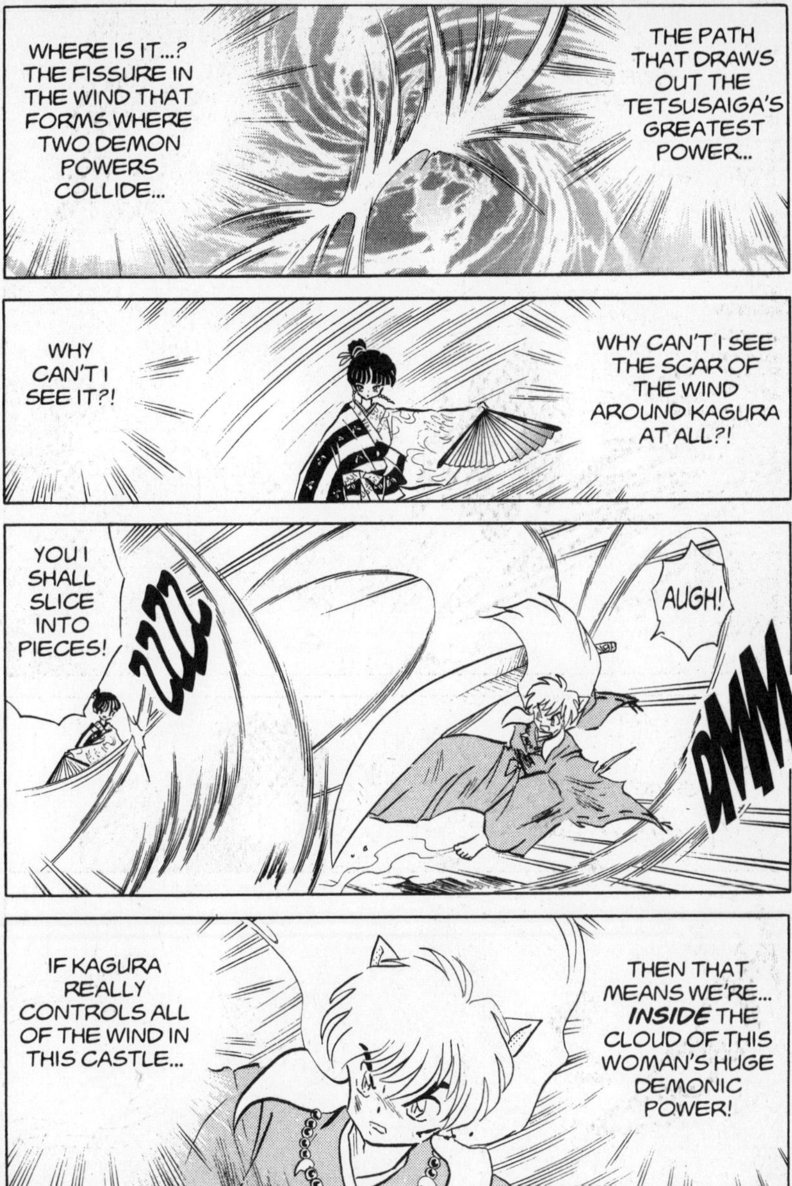
WHERE IS IT...? THE FISSURE IN THE WIND THAT FORMS WHERE TWO DEMON POWERS COLLIDE...
THE PATH THAT DRAWS OUT THE TETSUSAIGA'S GREATEST POWER...
WHY CAN'T I SEE IT?!
WHY CAN'T I SEE THE SCAR OF THE WIND AROUND KAGURA AT ALL?!
YOU I SHALL SLICE INTO PIECES!
AUGH!
IF KAGURA REALLY CONTROLS ALL OF THE WIND IN THIS CASTLE...
THEN THAT MEANS WE'RE... ***INSIDE*** THE CLOUD OF THIS WOMAN'S HUGE DEMONIC POWER!

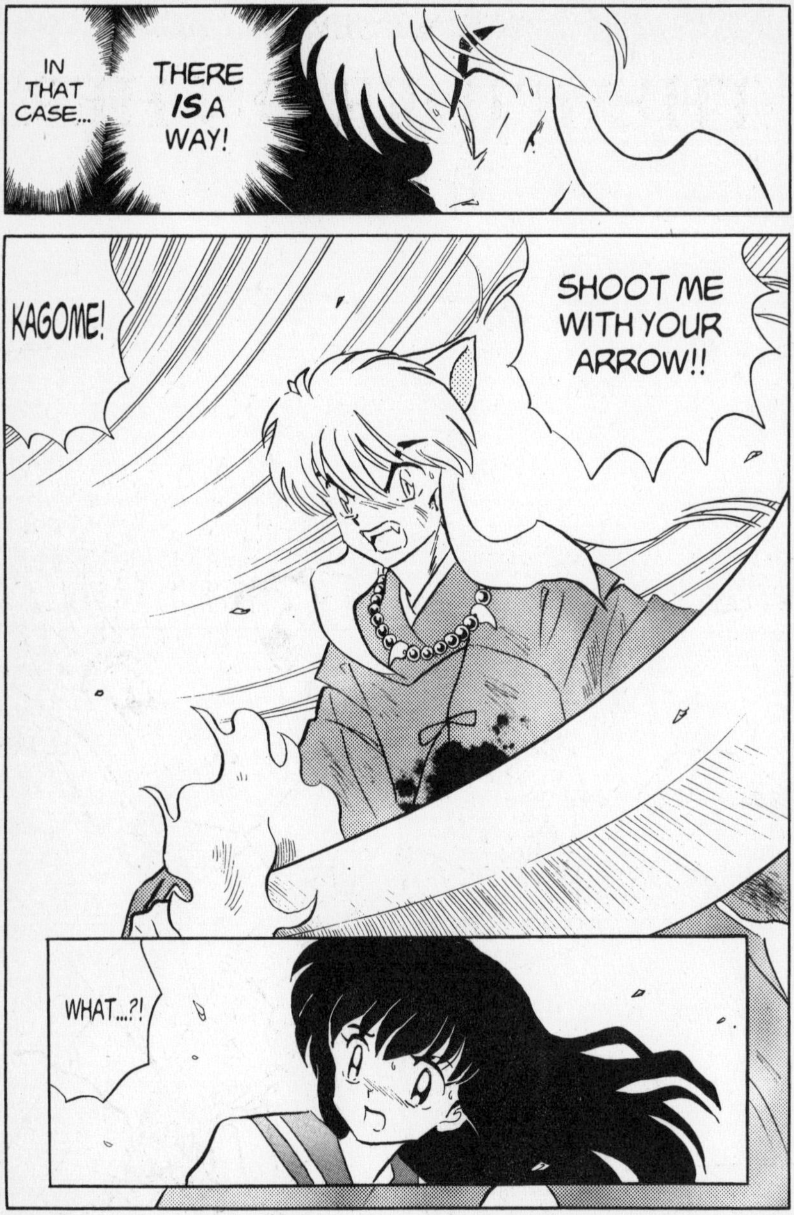
IN THAT CASE...
THERE IS A WAY!
KAGOME!
SHOOT ME WITH YOUR ARROW!!
WHAT...?!

SCROLL SEVEN

THE SPIDER ON HER BACK

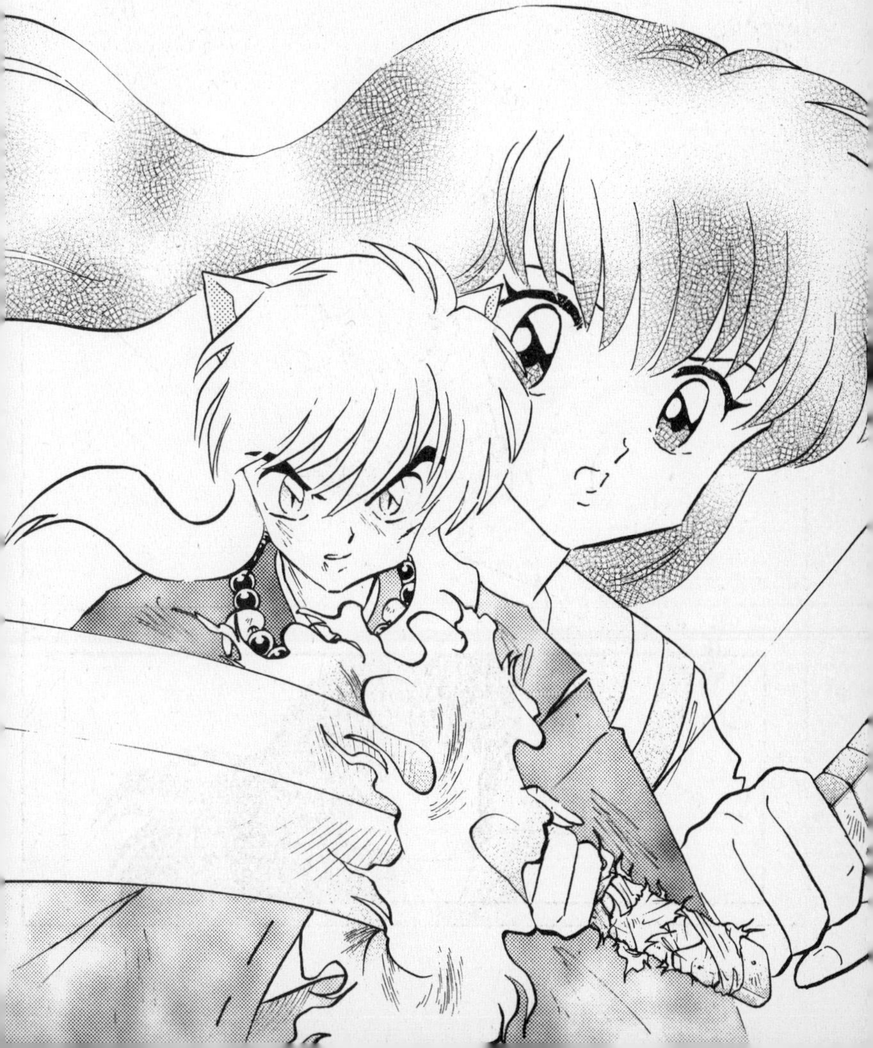

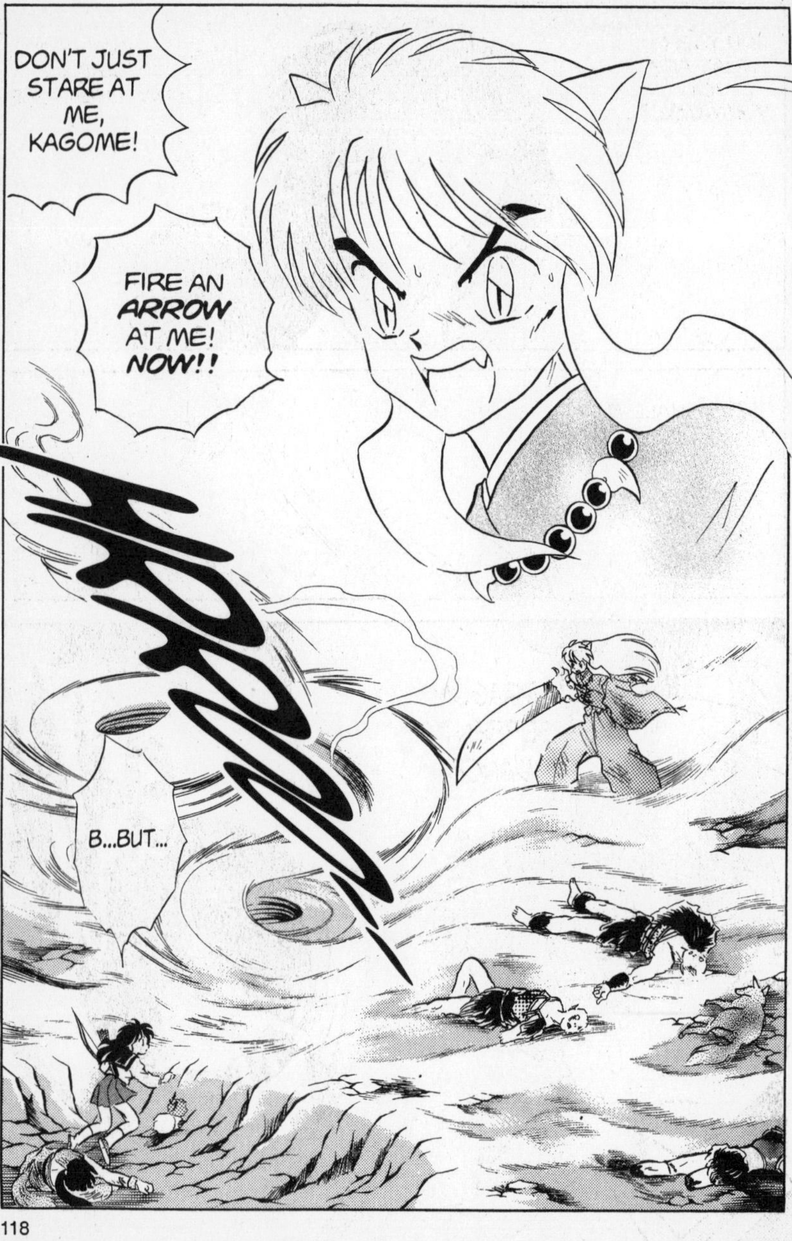
DON'T JUST STARE AT ME, KAGOME!
FIRE AN ARROW AT ME! NOW!!
B...BUT...

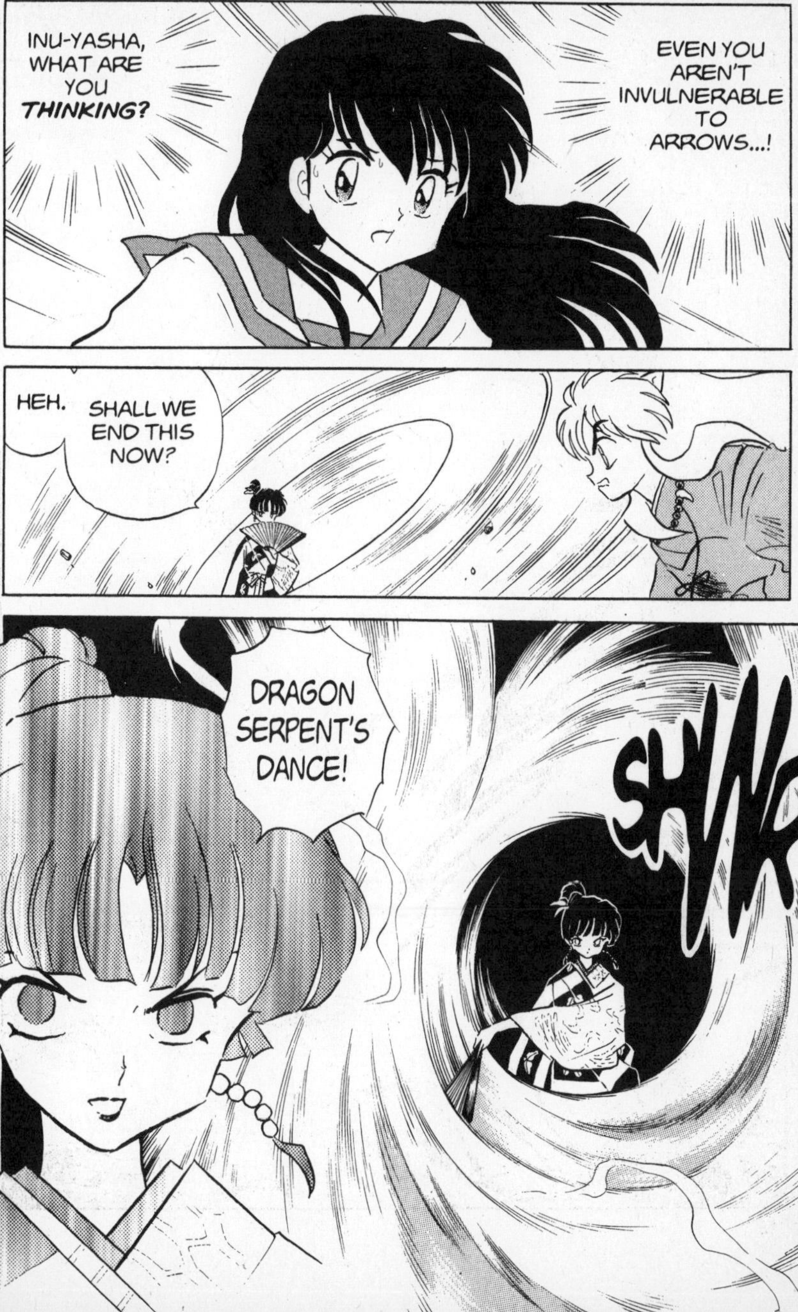
INU-YASHA, WHAT ARE YOU *THINKING?*
EVEN YOU AREN'T INVULNERABLE TO ARROWS...!
HEH.
SHALL WE END THIS NOW?
DRAGON SERPENT'S DANCE!
SHING

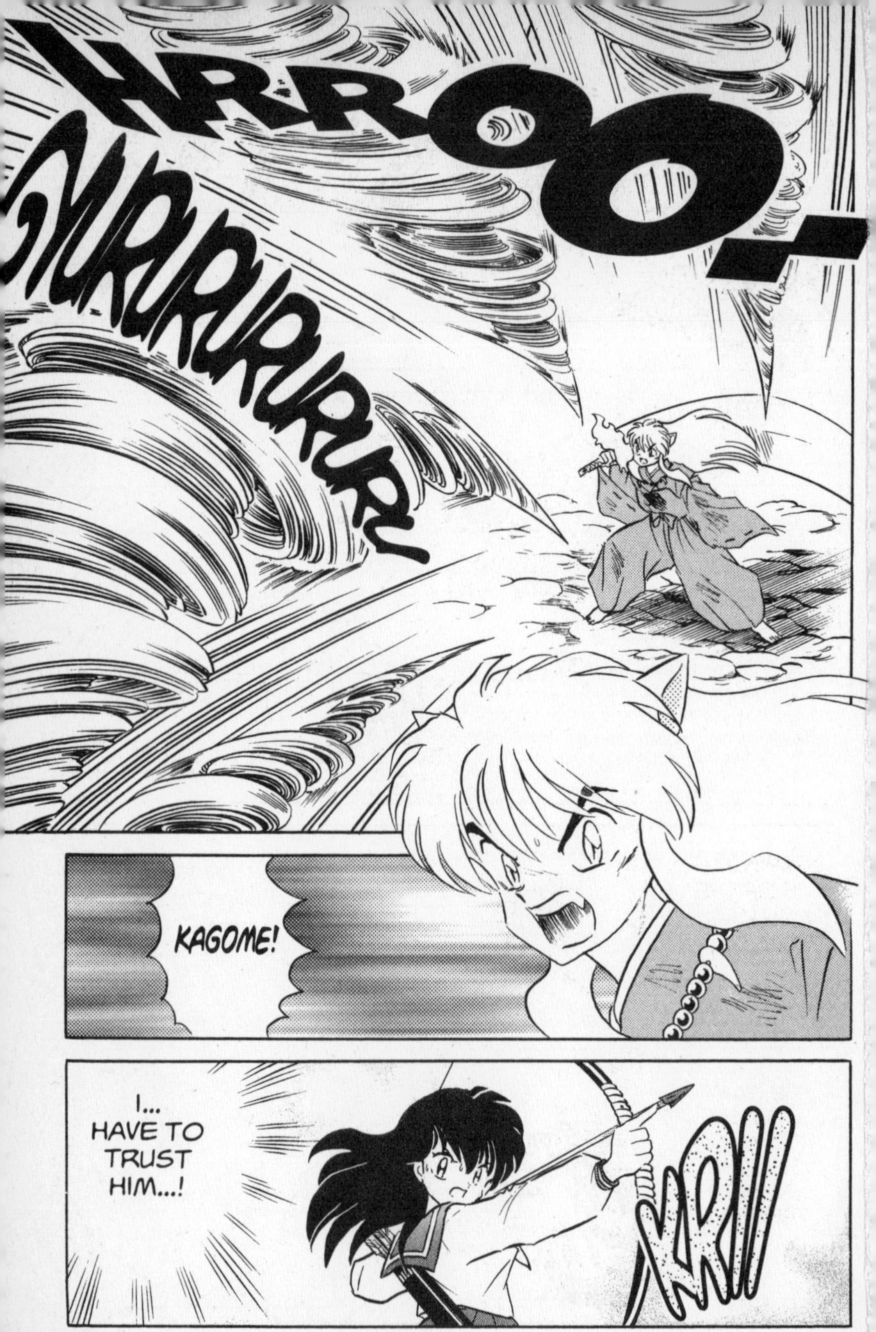
HRROOO
GYURURURURURURU
KAGOME!
I... HAVE TO TRUST HIM...!
KRII

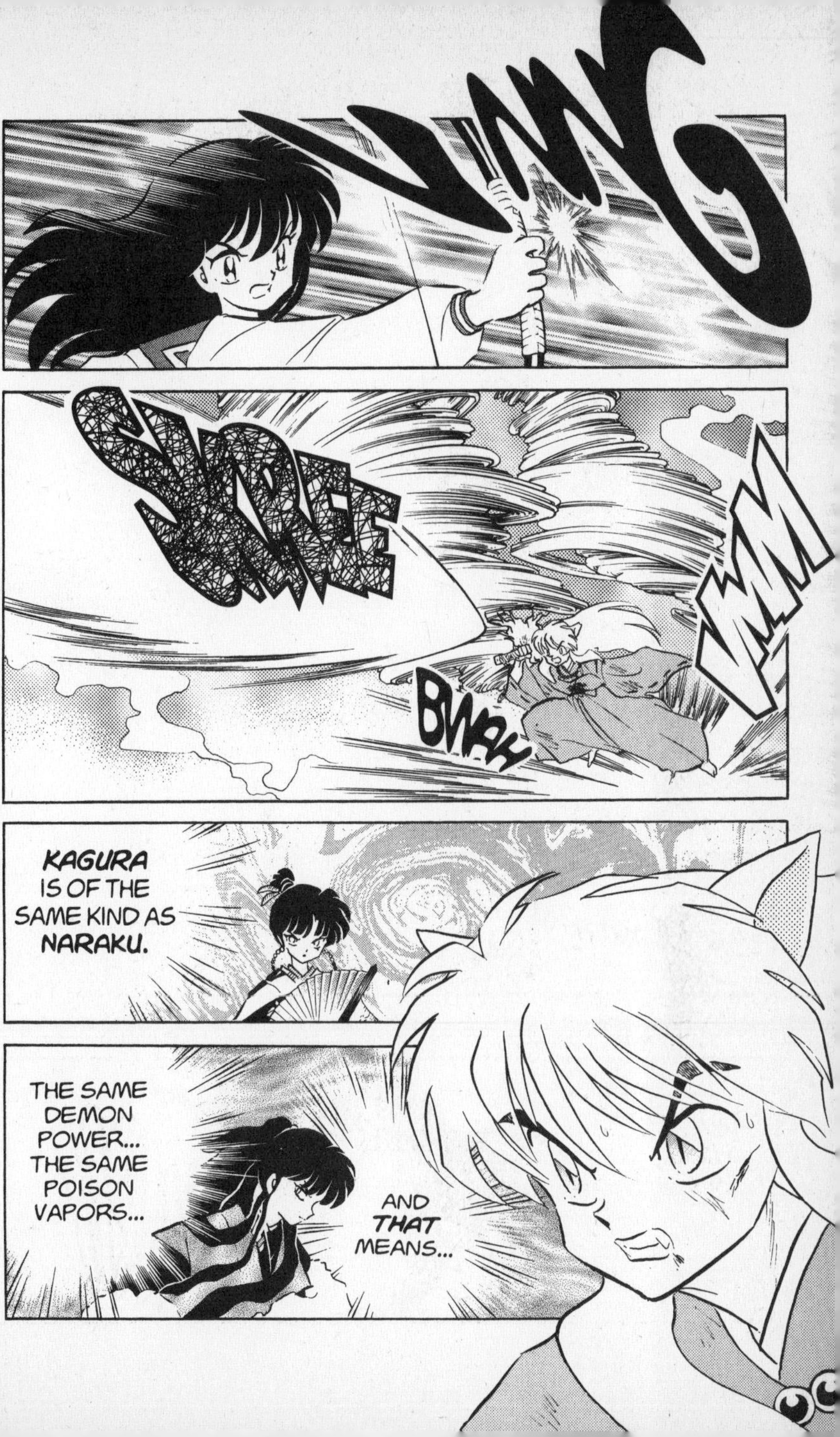
BWAH
KAGURA IS OF THE SAME KIND AS NARAKU.
THE SAME DEMON POWER... THE SAME POISON VAPORS...
AND THAT MEANS...

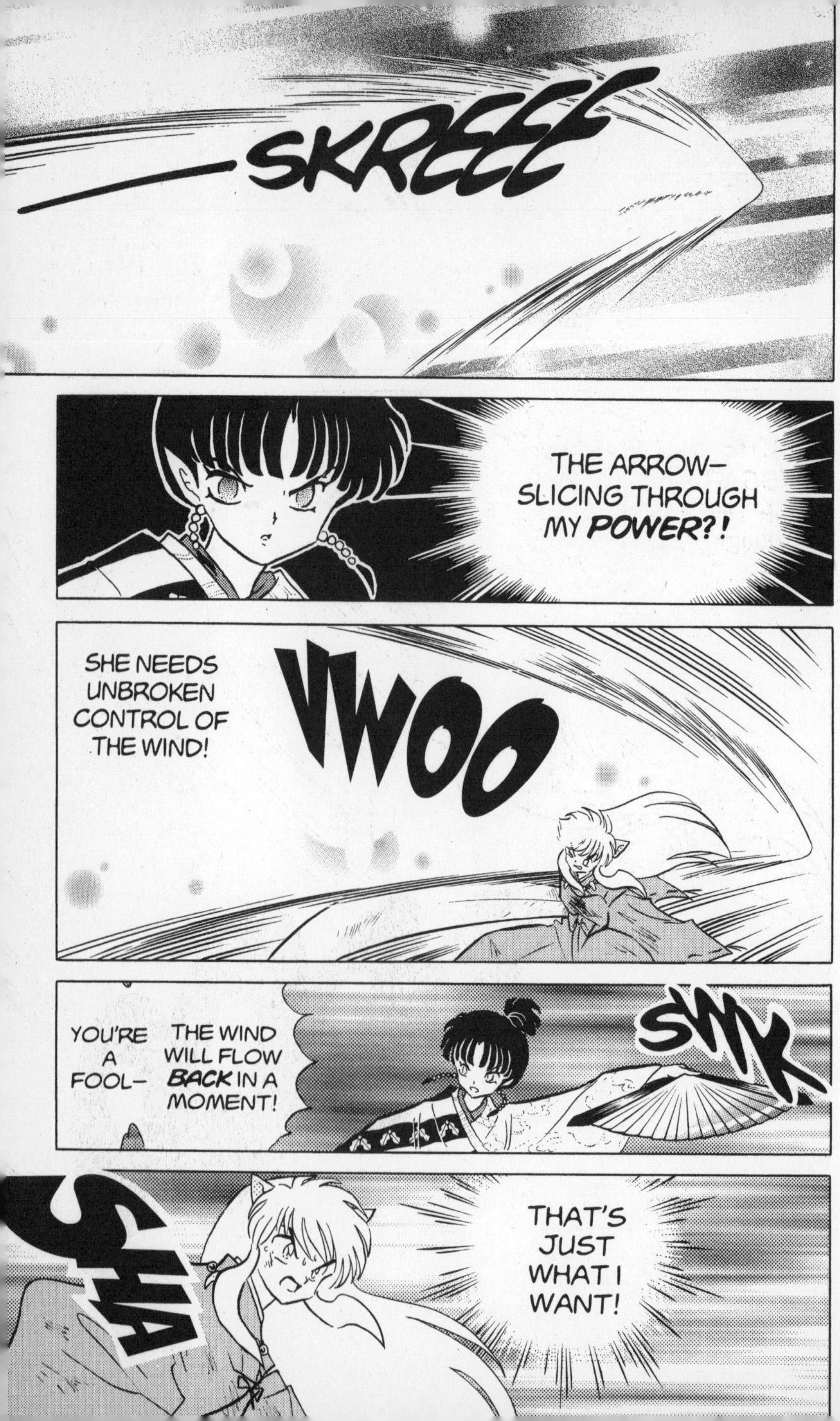
SKREEE
THE ARROW— SLICING THROUGH MY POWER?!
SHE NEEDS UNBROKEN CONTROL OF THE WIND!
VWOO
YOU'RE A FOOL—
THE WIND WILL FLOW BACK IN A MOMENT!
SWK
SHA
THAT'S JUST WHAT I WANT!

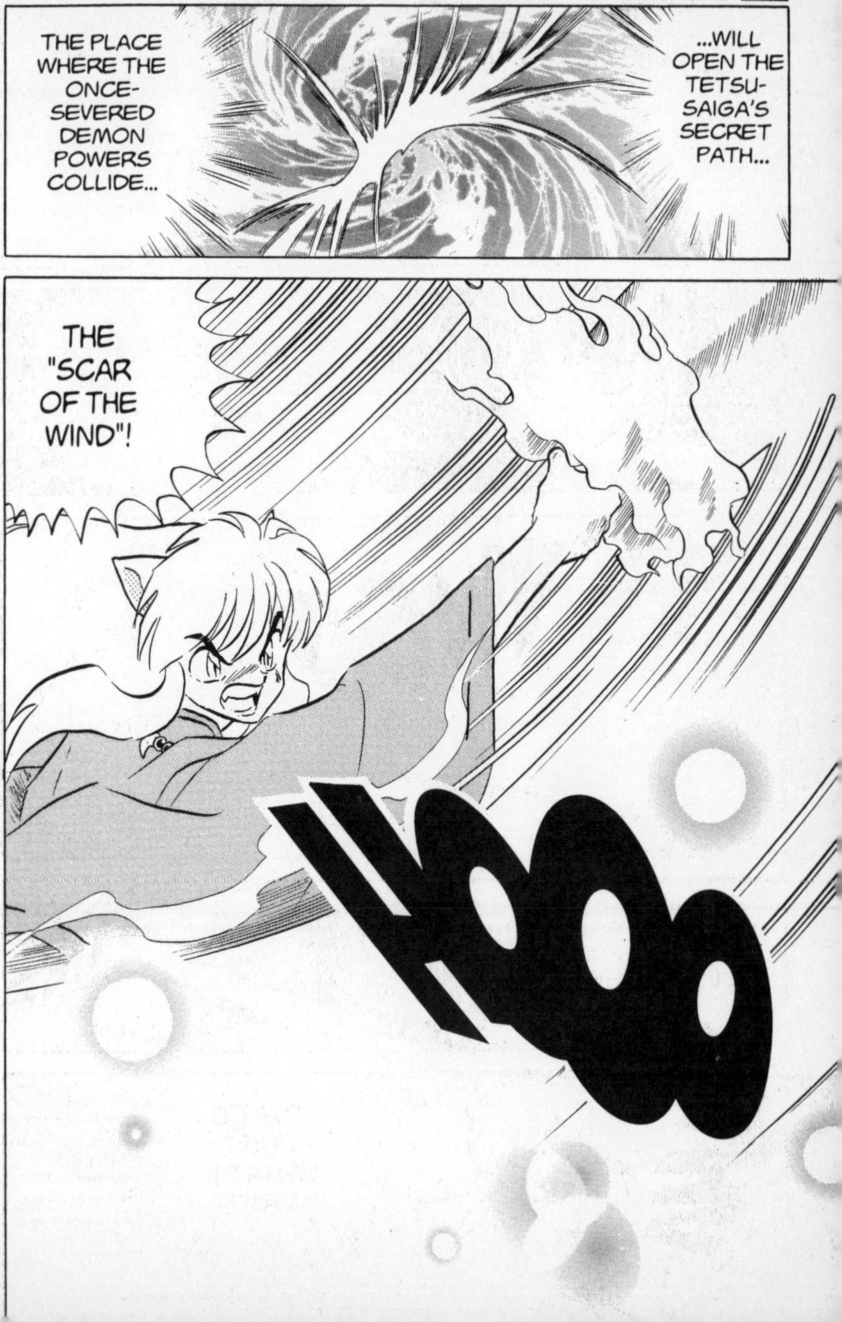
THE PLACE WHERE THE ONCE-SEVERED DEMON POWERS COLLIDE...
...WILL OPEN THE TETSU-SAIGA'S SECRET PATH...
THE "SCAR OF THE WIND"!
WOOO

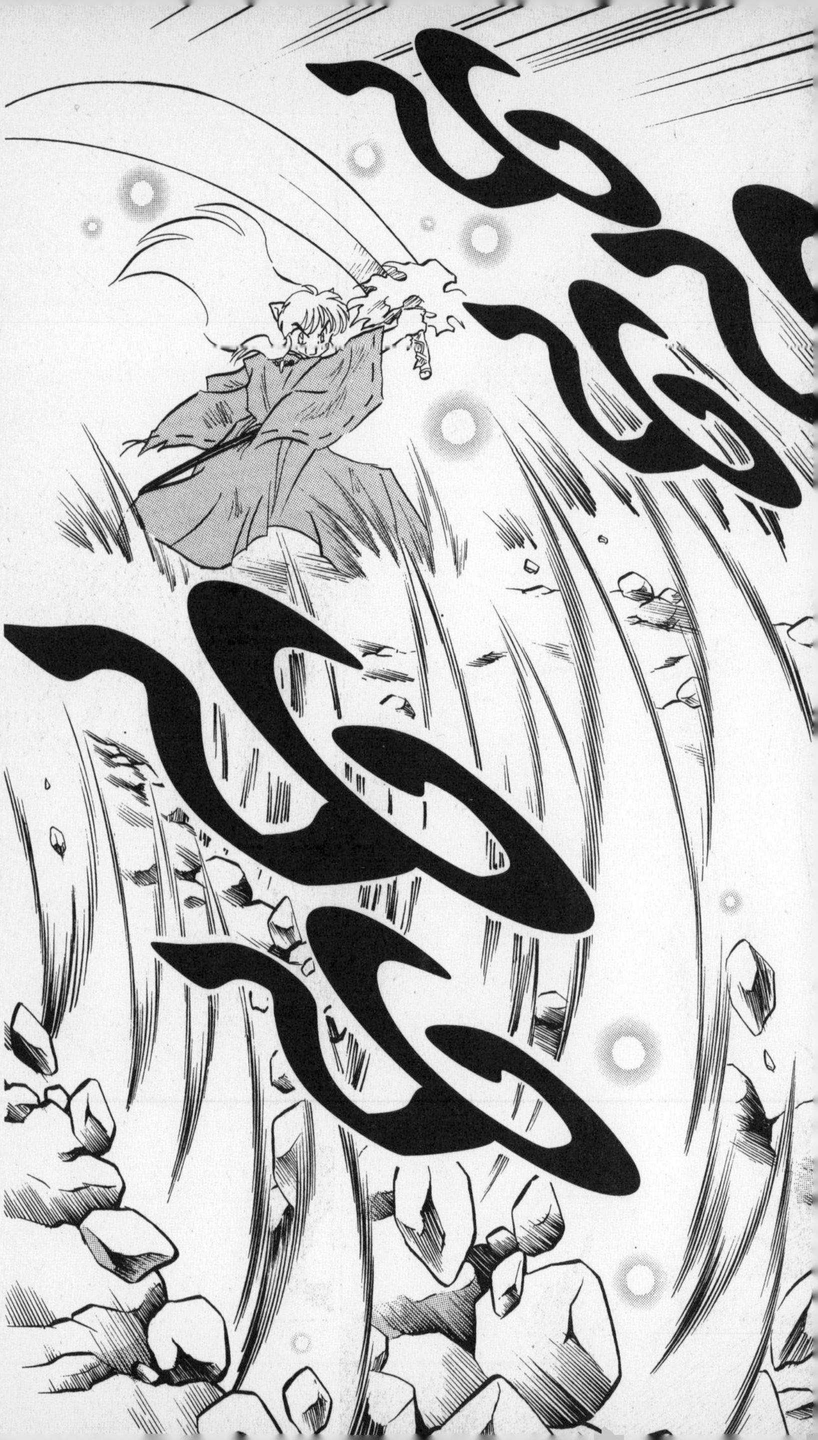

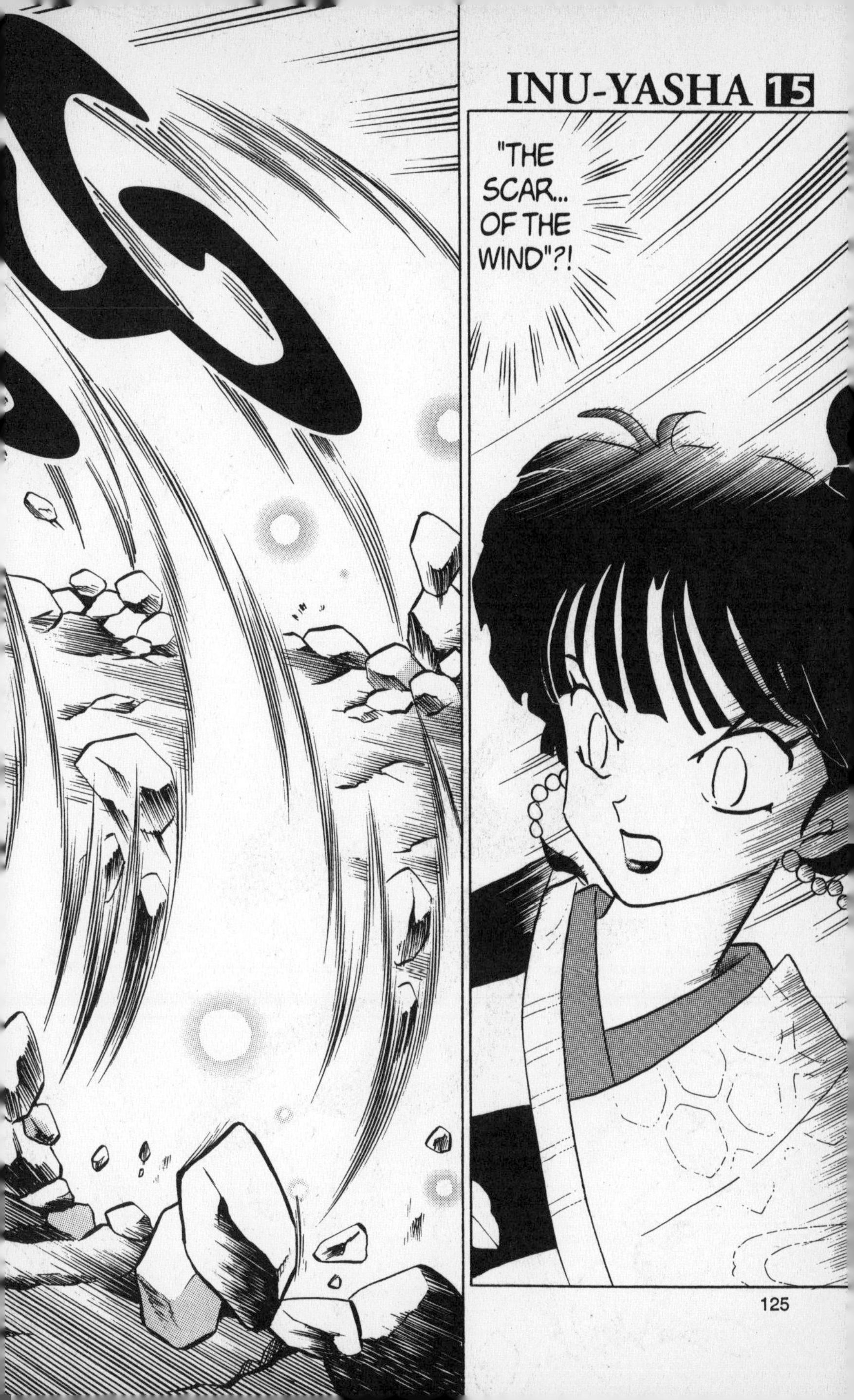
"THE SCAR... OF THE WIND"?!

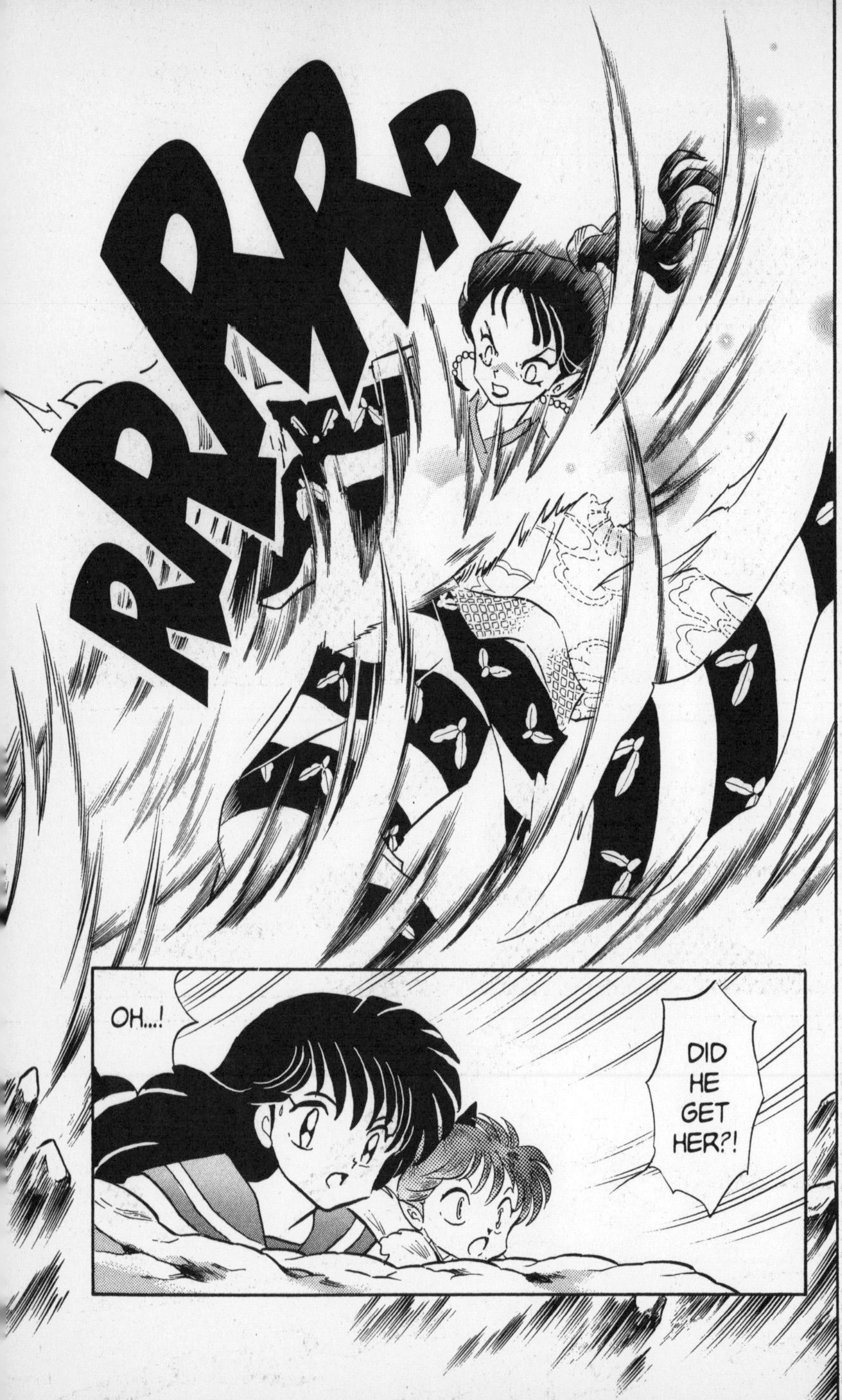
RRRRR
OH...!
DID HE GET HER?!

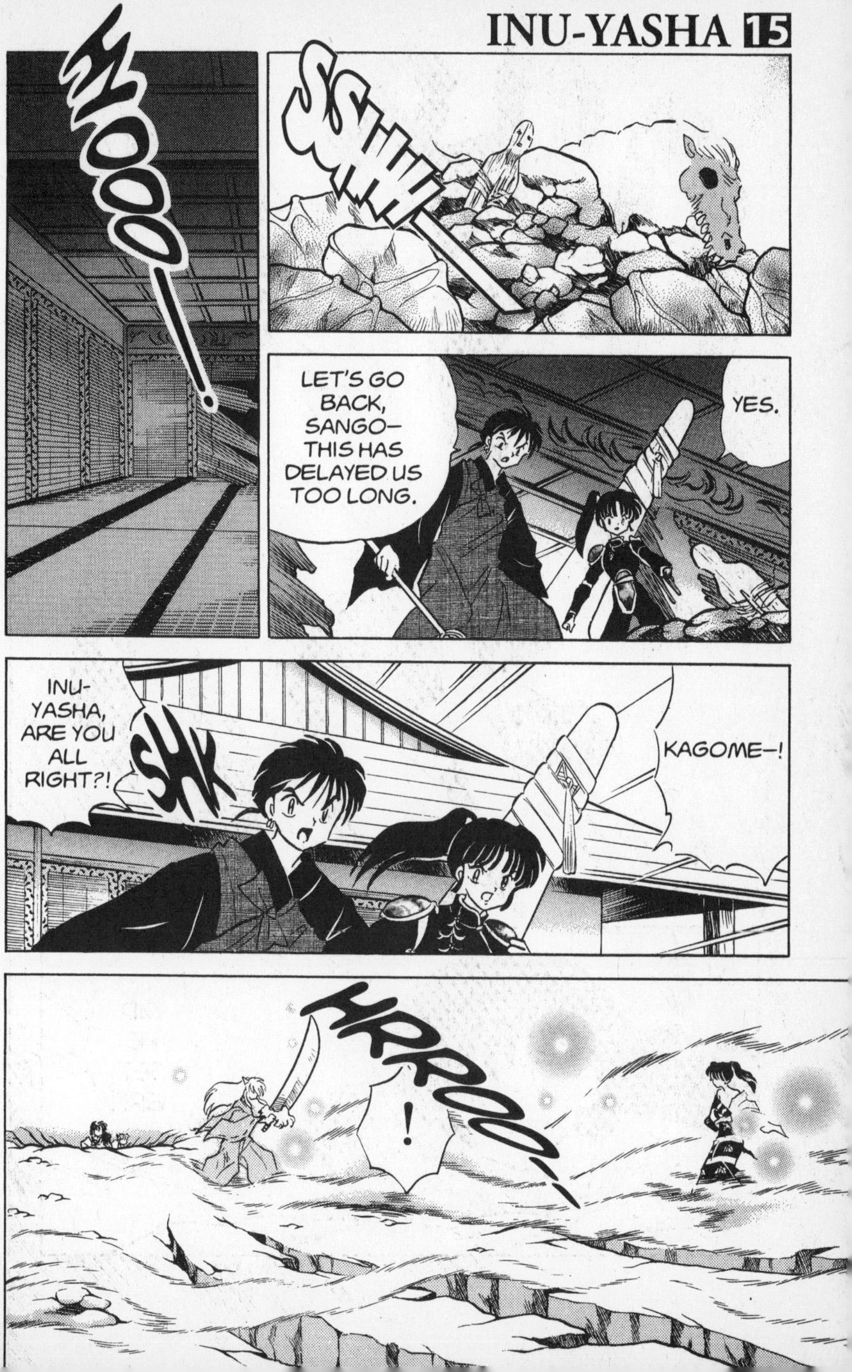
HYOOO-!
SSHH
LET'S GO BACK, SANGO— THIS HAS DELAYED US TOO LONG.
YES.
INU-YASHA, ARE YOU ALL RIGHT?!
SHK
KAGOME—!
HRROO-!

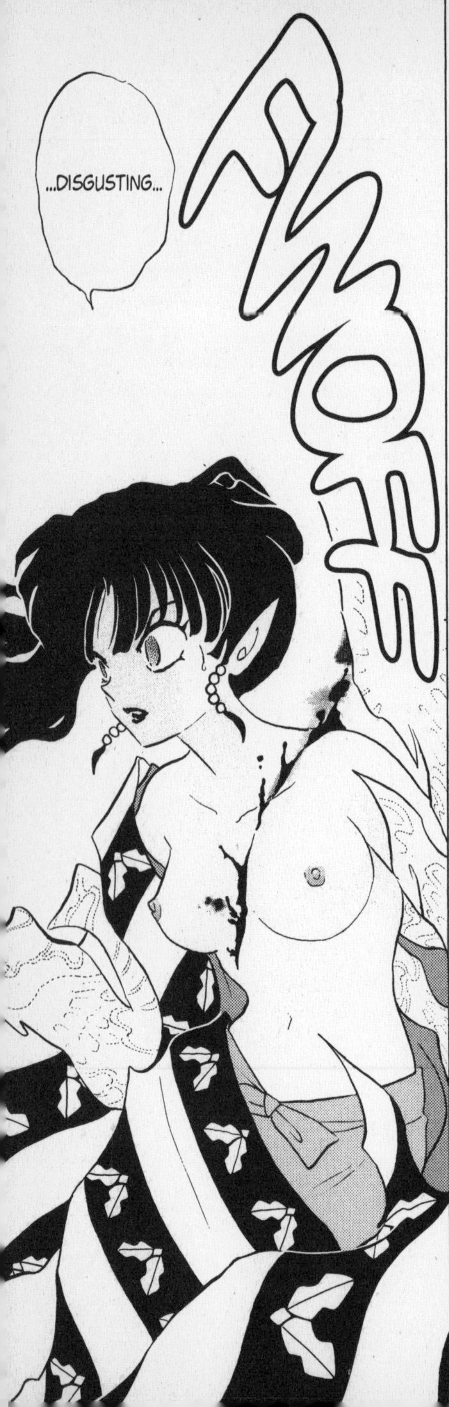
...DISGUSTING...
GWOFF
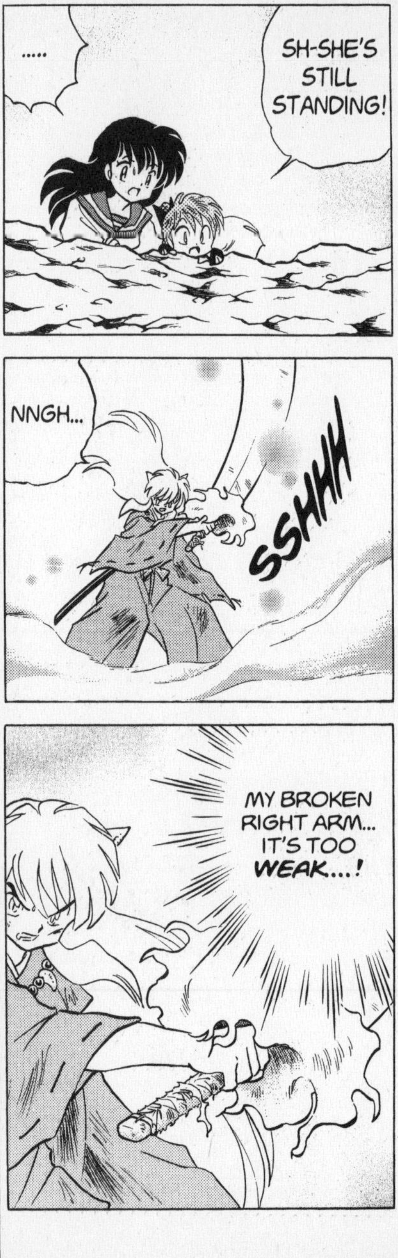
.....
SH-SHE'S STILL STANDING!
NNGH...
SSHHH
MY BROKEN RIGHT ARM... IT'S TOO **WEAK...!**

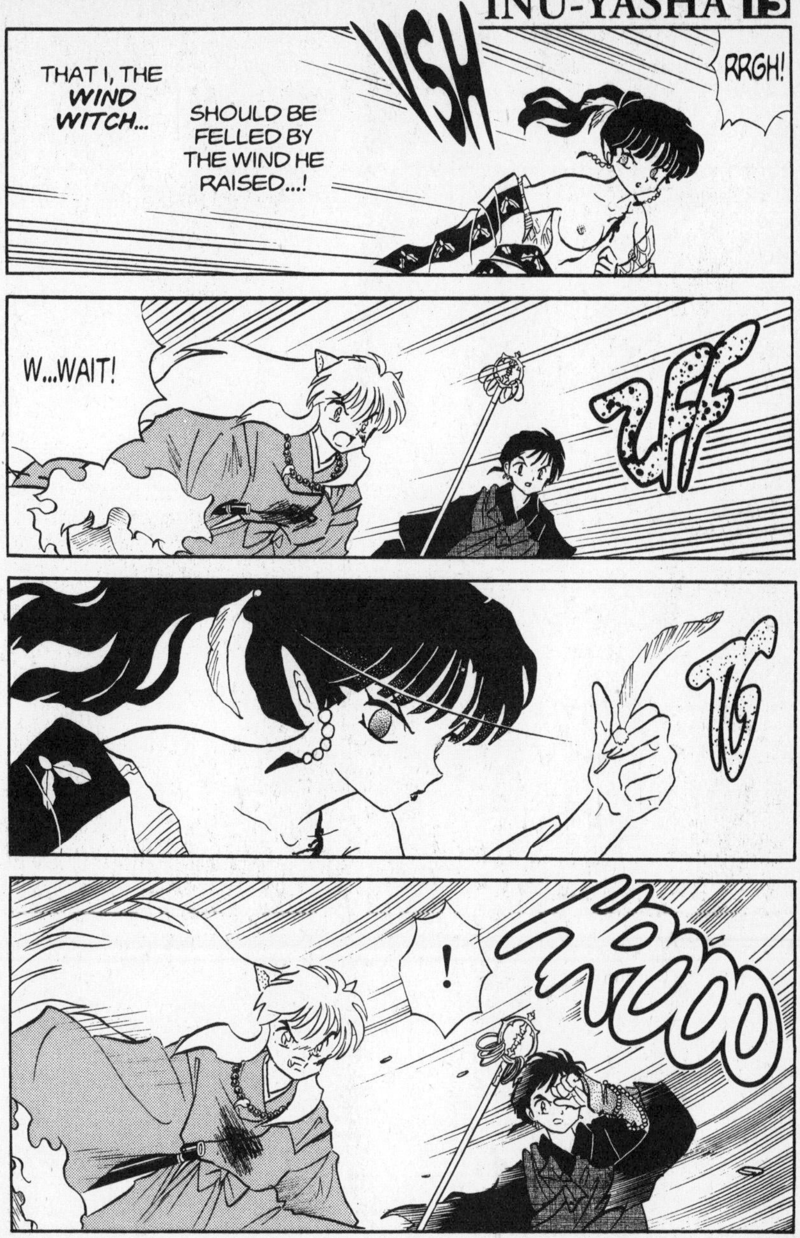
THAT I, THE WIND WITCH...
SHOULD BE FELLED BY THE WIND HE RAISED...!
VSH
RRGH!
W...WAIT!
UFF
TG
!
HOOOO

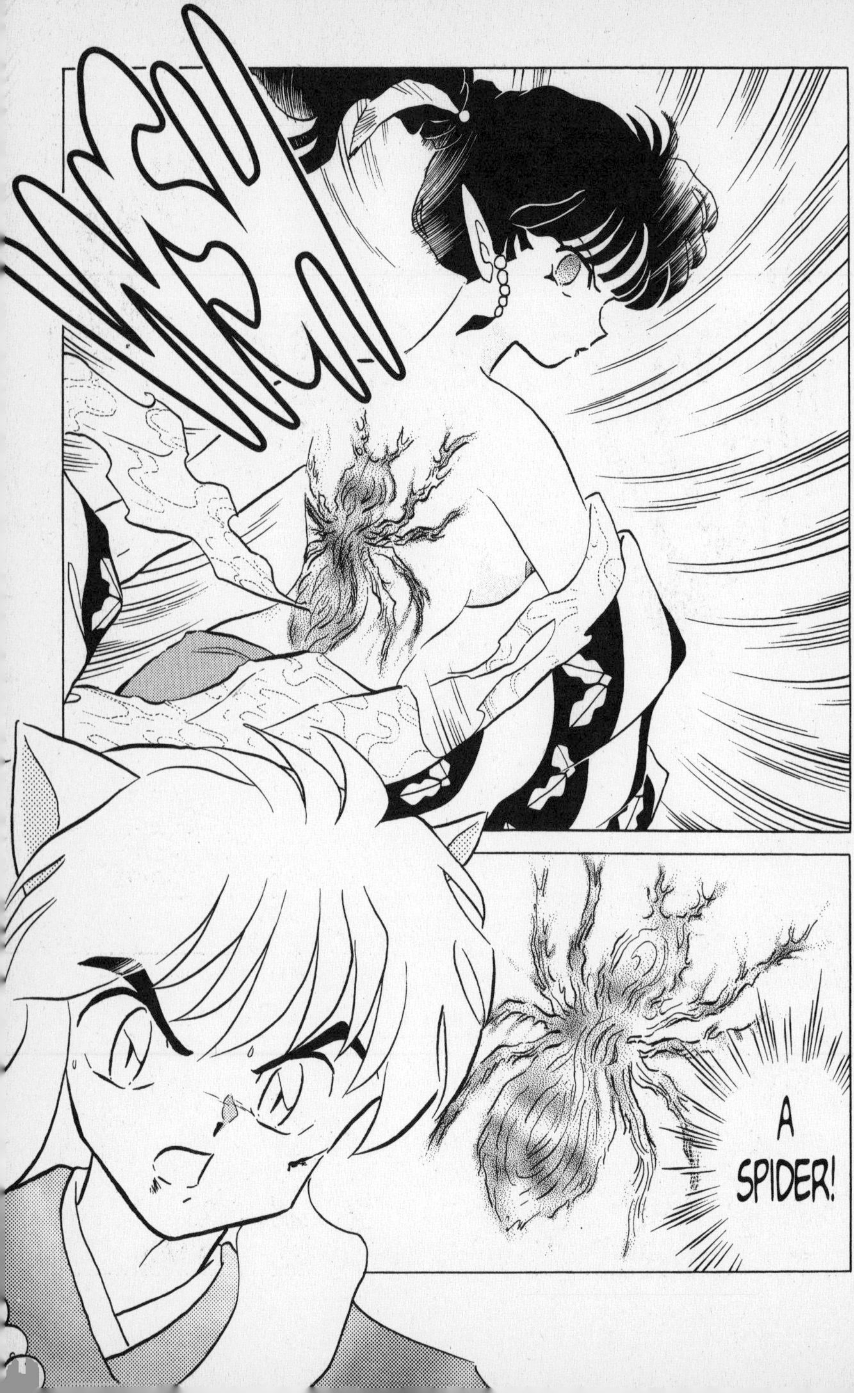
WOSH
A SPIDER!

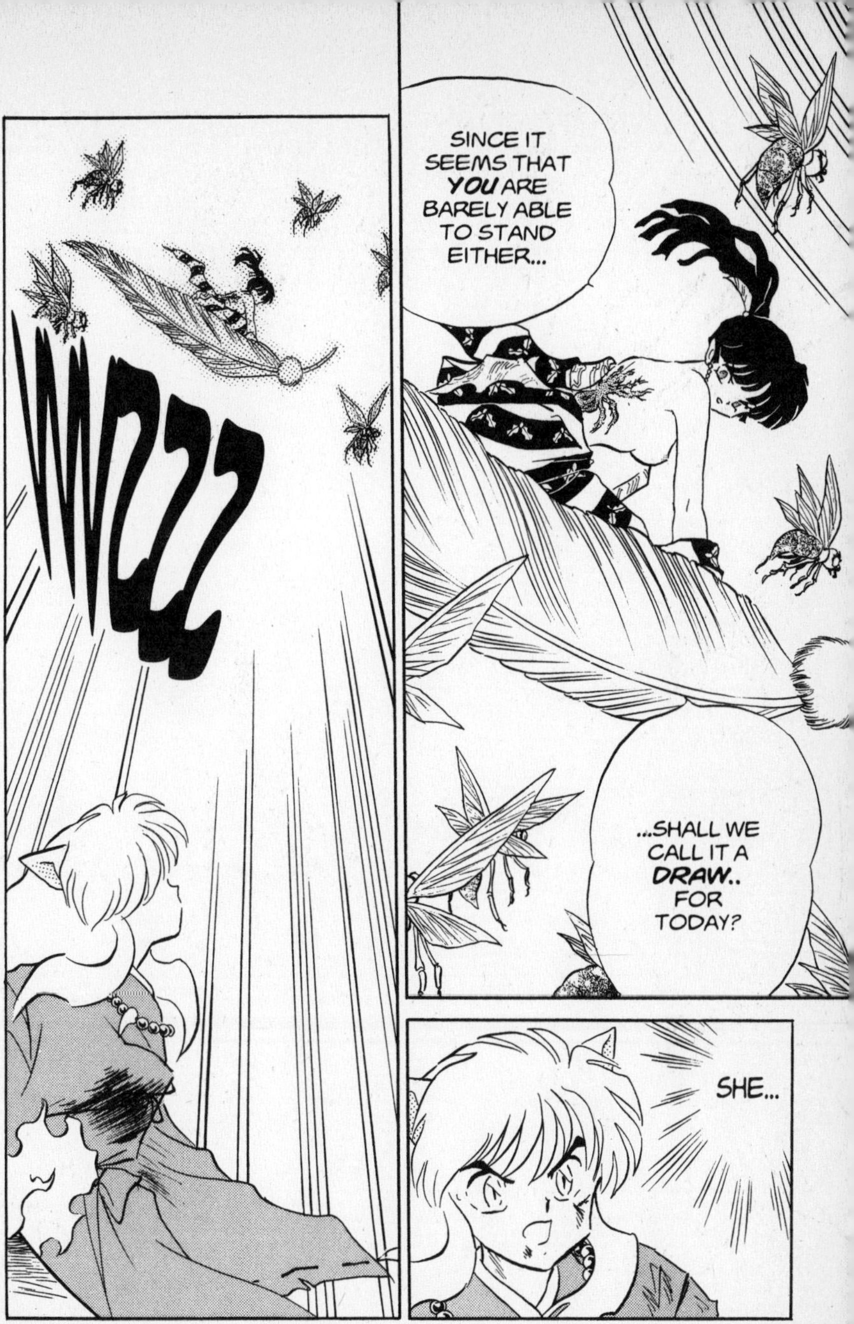
VVZZZ
SINCE IT SEEMS THAT *YOU* ARE BARELY ABLE TO STAND EITHER...
...SHALL WE CALL IT A *DRAW*.. FOR TODAY?
SHE...

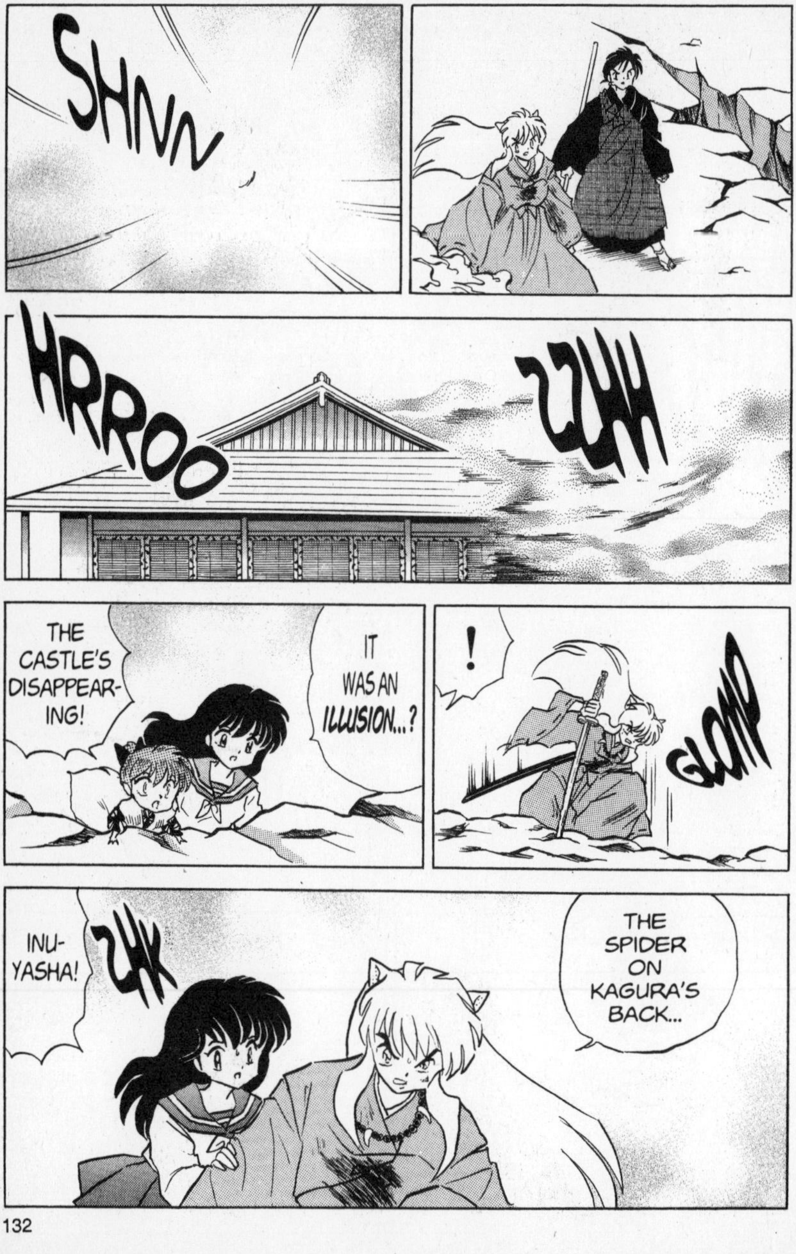
SHNN
HRROO
ZZUHH
THE CASTLE'S DISAPPEARING!
IT WAS AN ILLUSION...?
!
GLOMP
INU-YASHA!
ZHK
THE SPIDER ON KAGURA'S BACK...

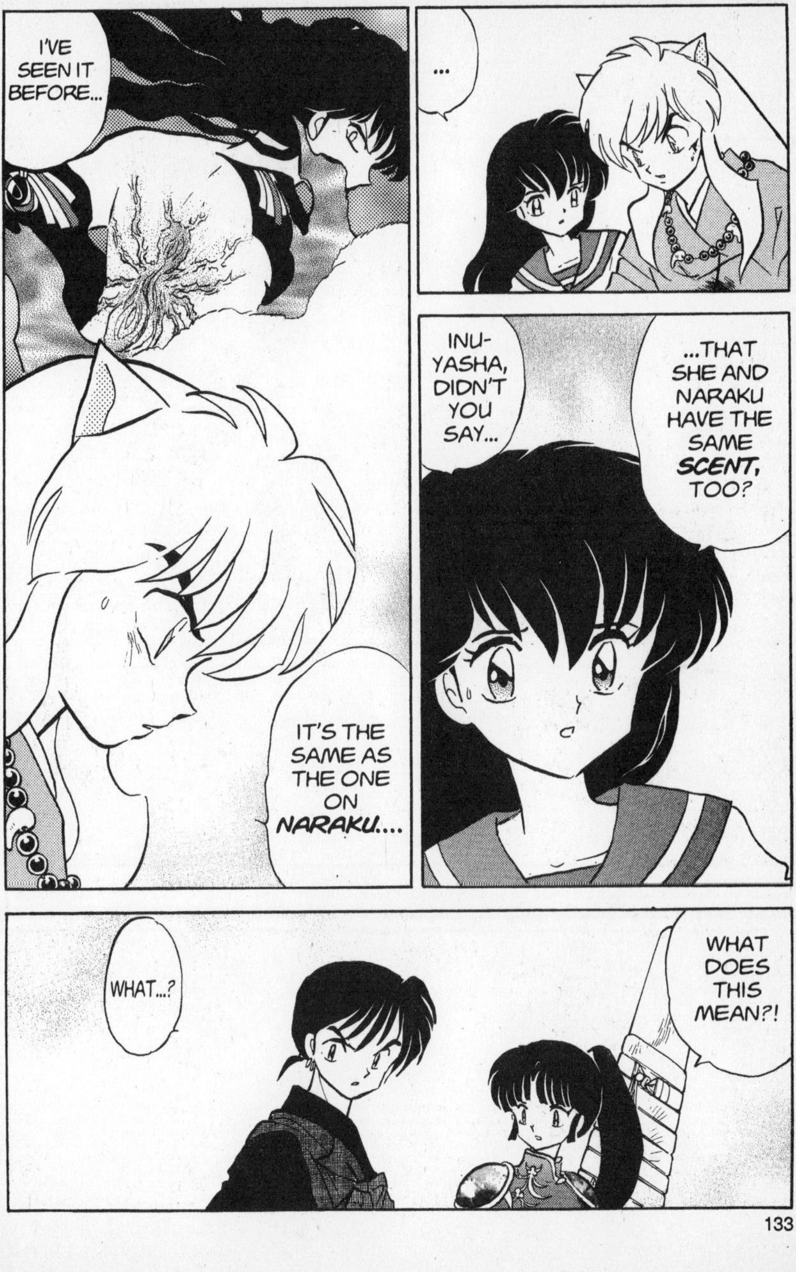
I'VE SEEN IT BEFORE...
IT'S THE SAME AS THE ONE ON NARAKU....
...
INU-YASHA, DIDN'T YOU SAY...
...THAT SHE AND NARAKU HAVE THE SAME SCENT, TOO?
WHAT...?
WHAT DOES THIS MEAN?!

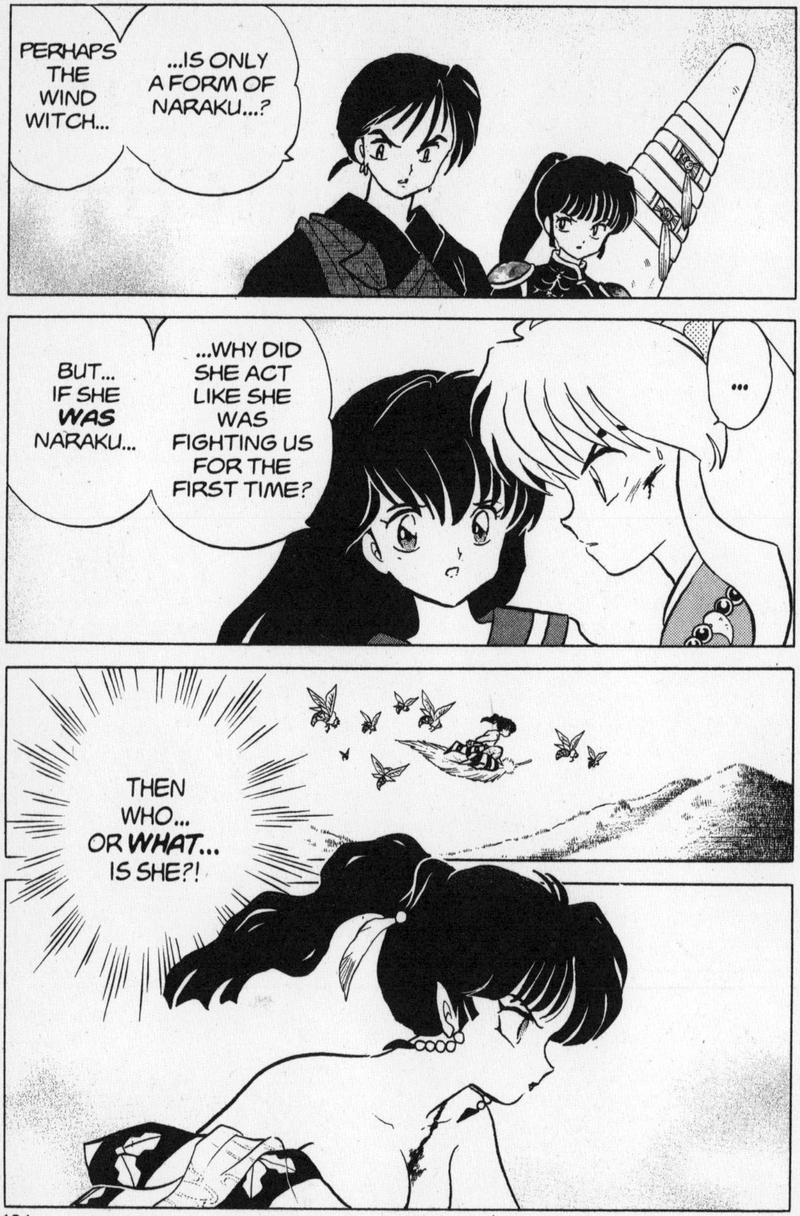
PERHAPS THE WIND WITCH...
...IS ONLY A FORM OF NARAKU...?
BUT... IF SHE **WAS** NARAKU...
...WHY DID SHE ACT LIKE SHE WAS FIGHTING US FOR THE FIRST TIME?
...
THEN WHO... OR **WHAT**... IS SHE?!

SCROLL EIGHT

MYSTERY OF THE WIND WITCH

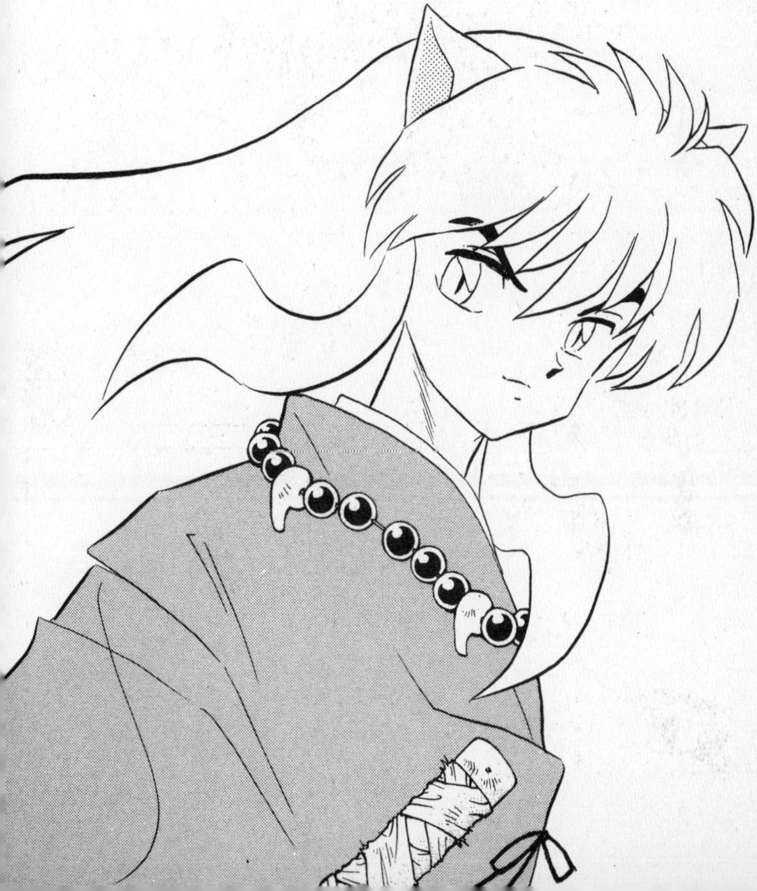

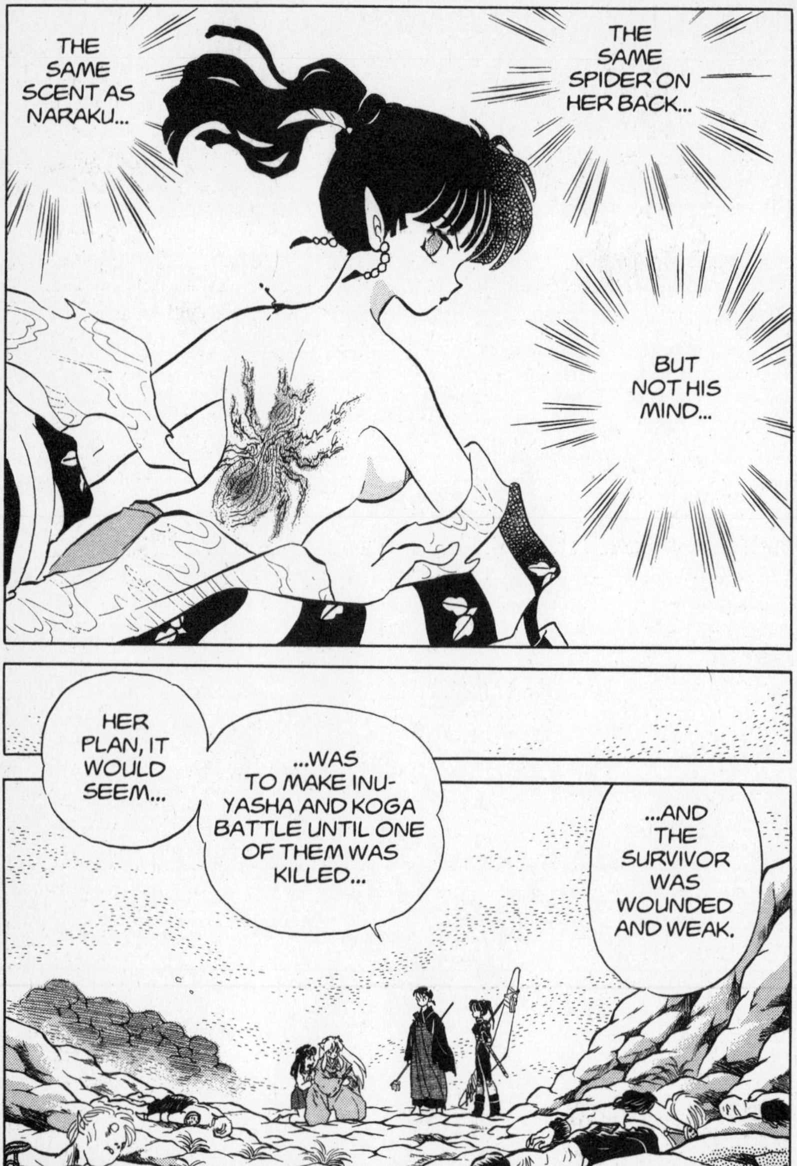
THE SAME SCENT AS NARAKU...
THE SAME SPIDER ON HER BACK...
BUT NOT HIS MIND...
HER PLAN, IT WOULD SEEM...
...WAS TO MAKE INU-YASHA AND KOGA BATTLE UNTIL ONE OF THEM WAS KILLED...
...AND THE SURVIVOR WAS WOUNDED AND WEAK.

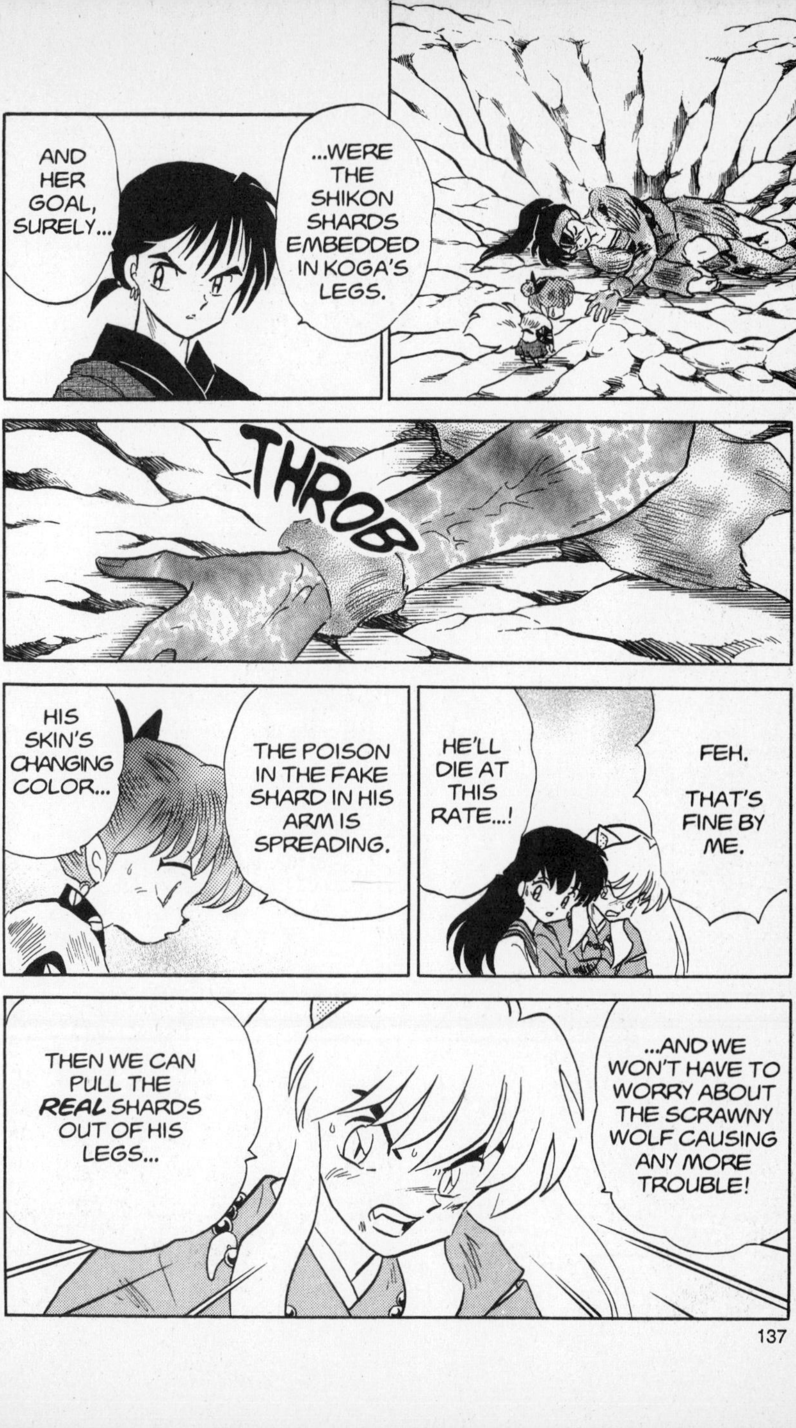
AND HER GOAL, SURELY...
...WERE THE SHIKON SHARDS EMBEDDED IN KOGA'S LEGS.
THROB
HIS SKIN'S CHANGING COLOR...
THE POISON IN THE FAKE SHARD IN HIS ARM IS SPREADING.
HE'LL DIE AT THIS RATE...!
FEH.
THAT'S FINE BY ME.
THEN WE CAN PULL THE *REAL* SHARDS OUT OF HIS LEGS...
...AND WE WON'T HAVE TO WORRY ABOUT THE SCRAWNY WOLF CAUSING ANY MORE TROUBLE!

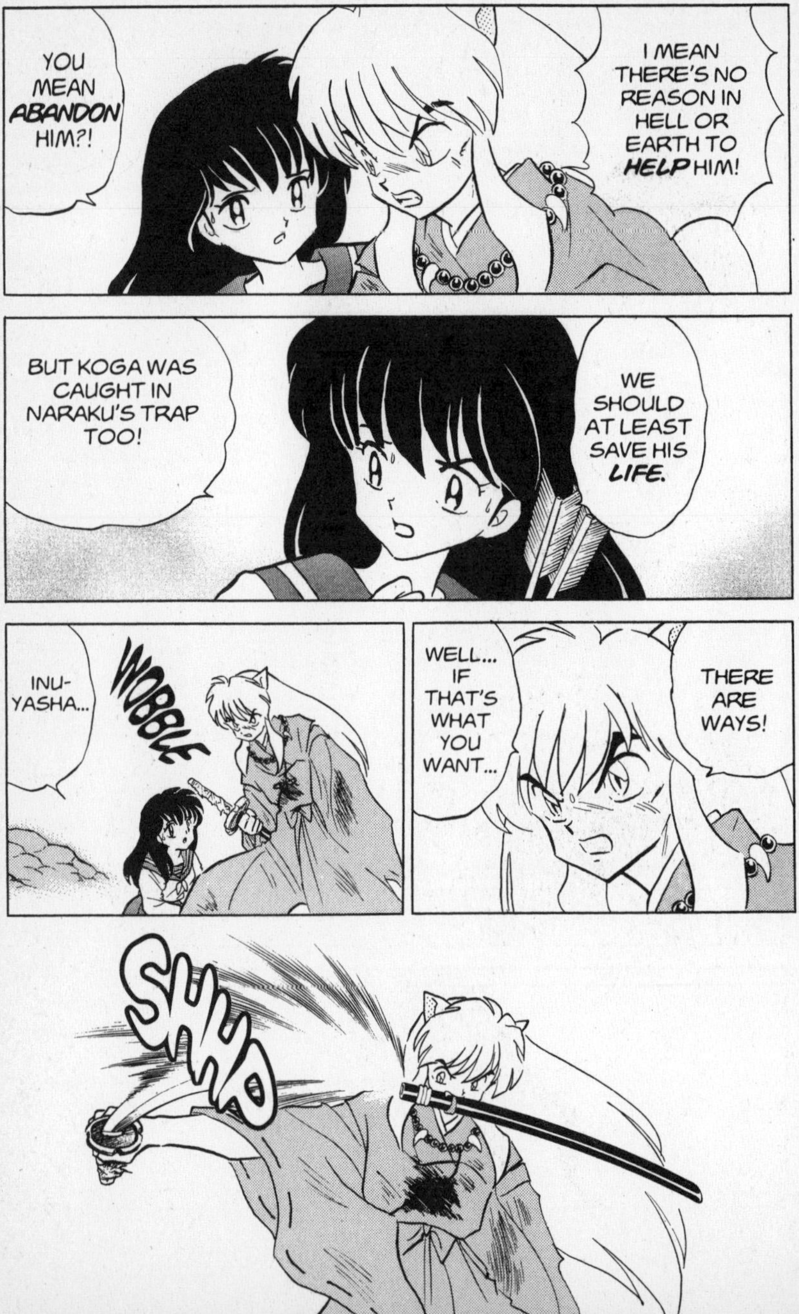
YOU MEAN ABANDON HIM?!
I MEAN THERE'S NO REASON IN HELL OR EARTH TO HELP HIM!
BUT KOGA WAS CAUGHT IN NARAKU'S TRAP TOO!
WE SHOULD AT LEAST SAVE HIS LIFE.
INU-YASHA...
WOBBLE
WELL... IF THAT'S WHAT YOU WANT...
THERE ARE WAYS!
SHWP

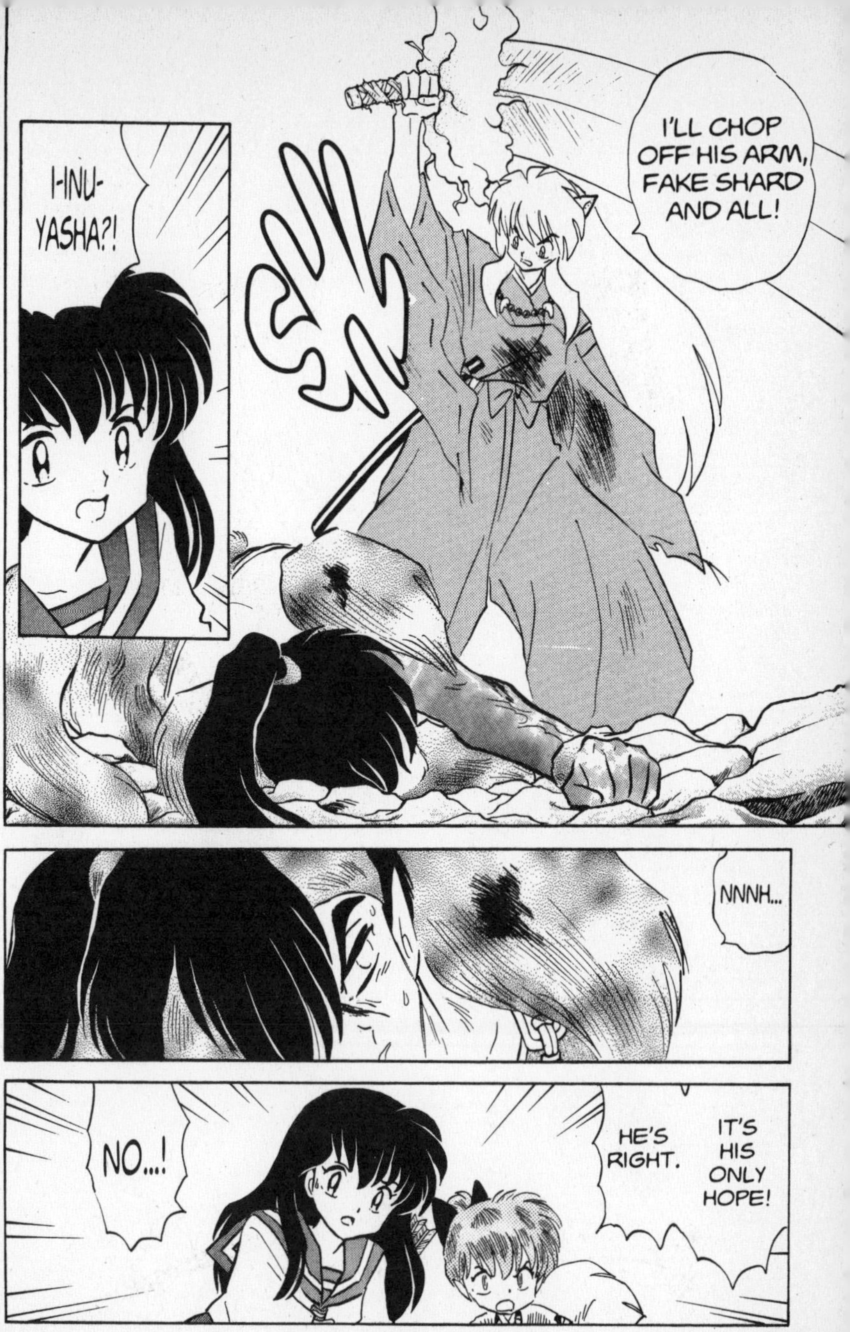
I-INU-YASHA?!
I'LL CHOP OFF HIS ARM, FAKE SHARD AND ALL!
NNNH...
NO...!
HE'S RIGHT.
IT'S HIS ONLY HOPE!

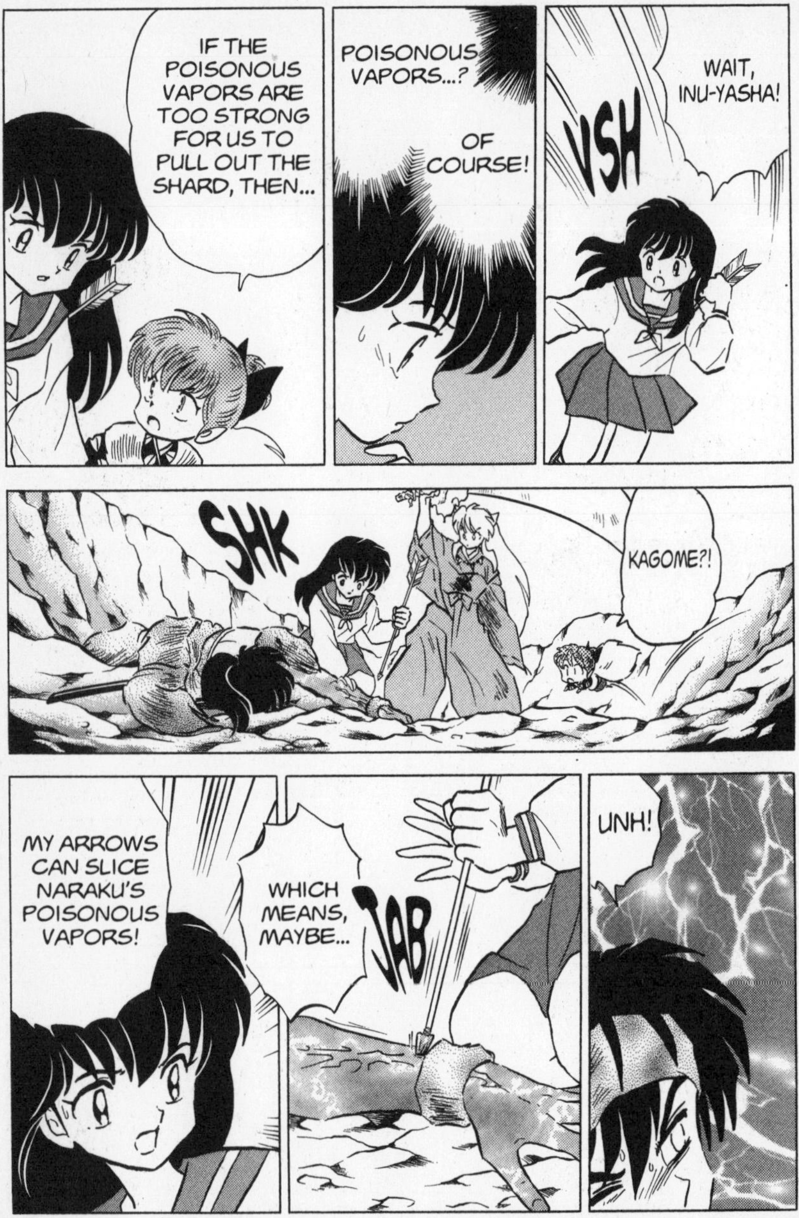
WAIT, INU-YASHA!
VSH
POISONOUS VAPORS...?
OF COURSE!
IF THE POISONOUS VAPORS ARE TOO STRONG FOR US TO PULL OUT THE SHARD, THEN...
KAGOME?!
SHK
UNH!
WHICH MEANS, MAYBE...
JAB
MY ARROWS CAN SLICE NARAKU'S POISONOUS VAPORS!

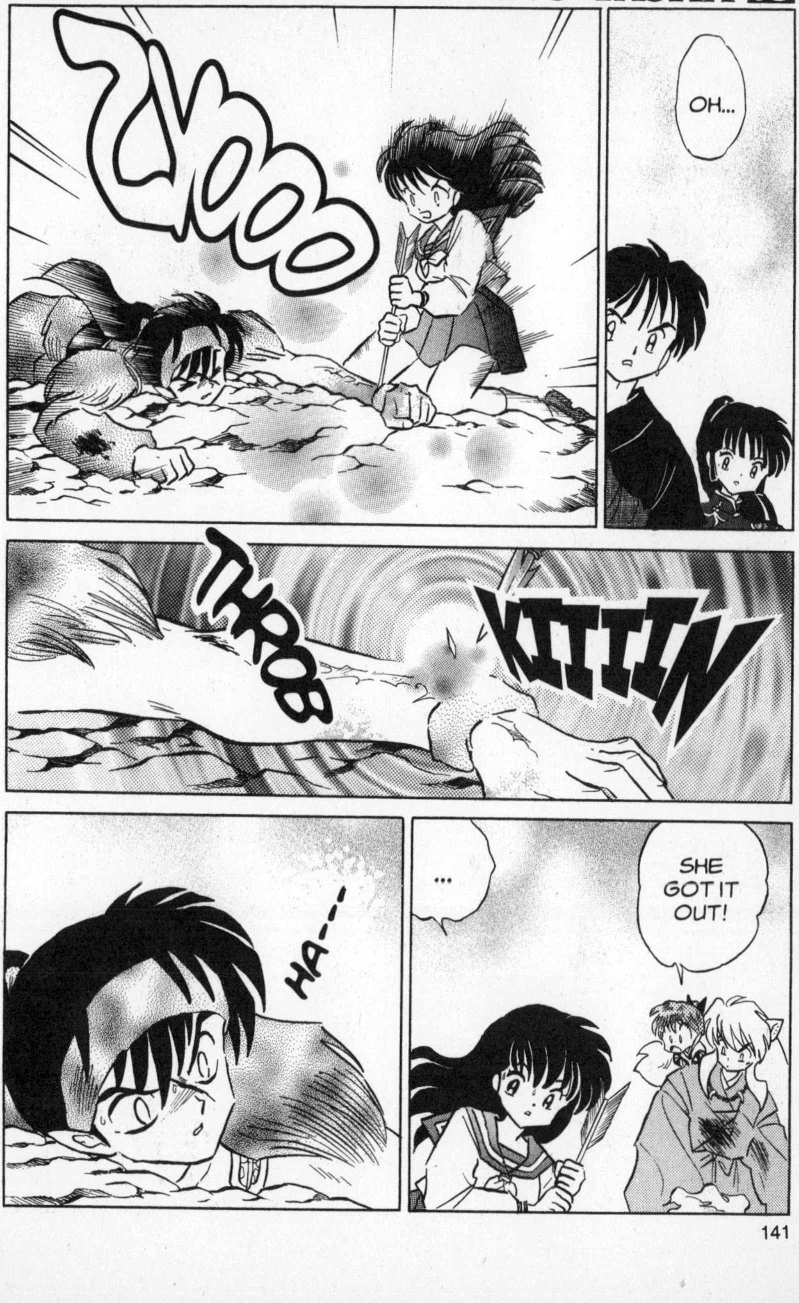
ZWOOO
OH...
THROB
KITIIN
HA---
...
SHE GOT IT OUT!

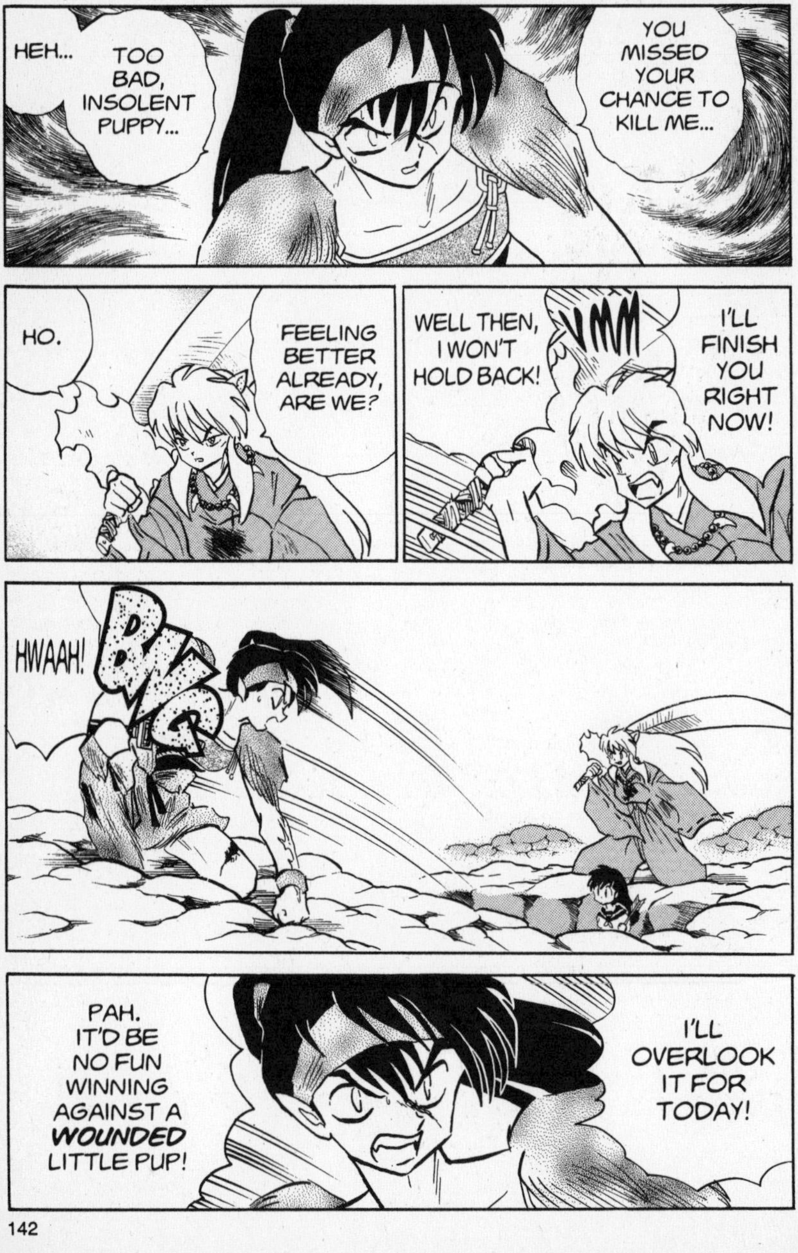
HEH...
TOO BAD, INSOLENT PUPPY...
YOU MISSED YOUR CHANCE TO KILL ME...
HO.
FEELING BETTER ALREADY, ARE WE?
WELL THEN, I WON'T HOLD BACK!
VMM
I'LL FINISH YOU RIGHT NOW!
HWAAH!
PAH. IT'D BE NO FUN WINNING AGAINST A WOUNDED LITTLE PUP!
I'LL OVERLOOK IT FOR TODAY!

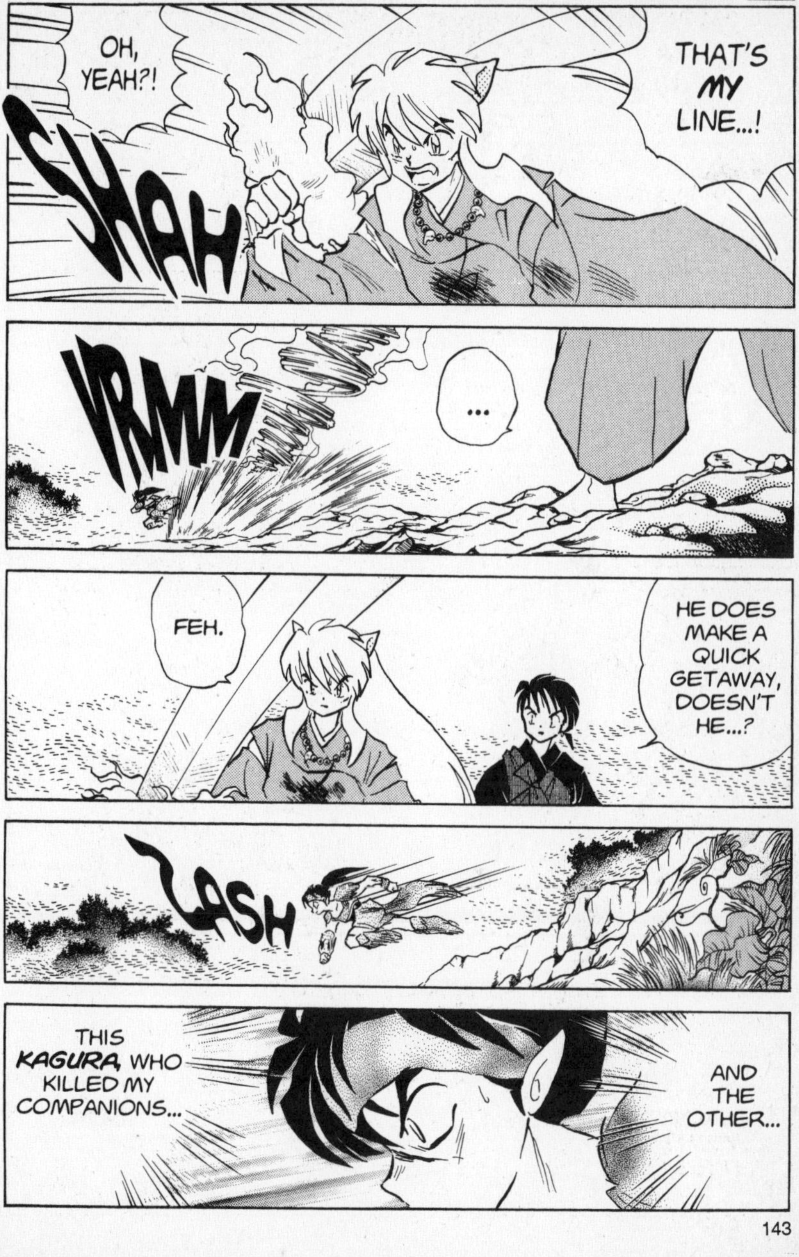
OH, YEAH?!
SHAH
THAT'S MY LINE...!
VRMM
...
FEH.
HE DOES MAKE A QUICK GETAWAY, DOESN'T HE...?
LASH
THIS KAGURA, WHO KILLED MY COMPANIONS...
AND THE OTHER...

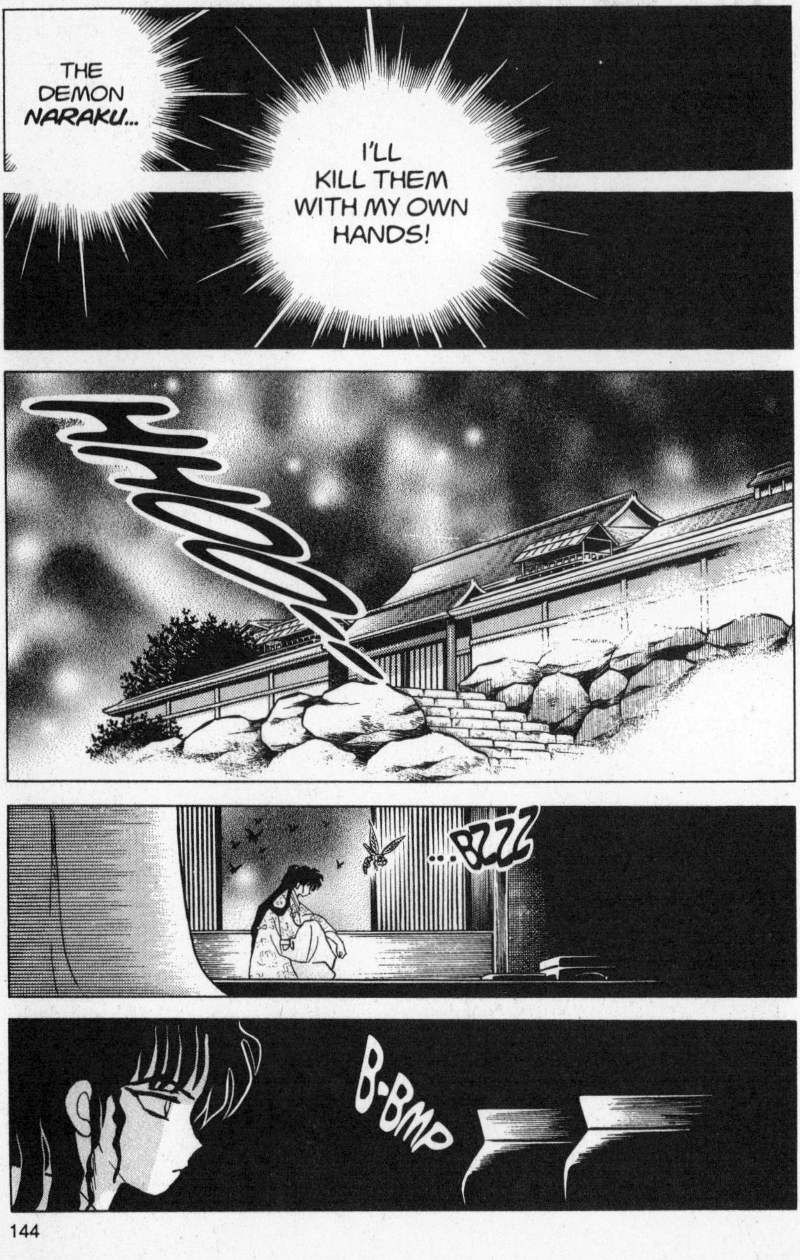
THE DEMON NARAKU...
I'LL KILL THEM WITH MY OWN HANDS!
...BZZZ
B-BMP

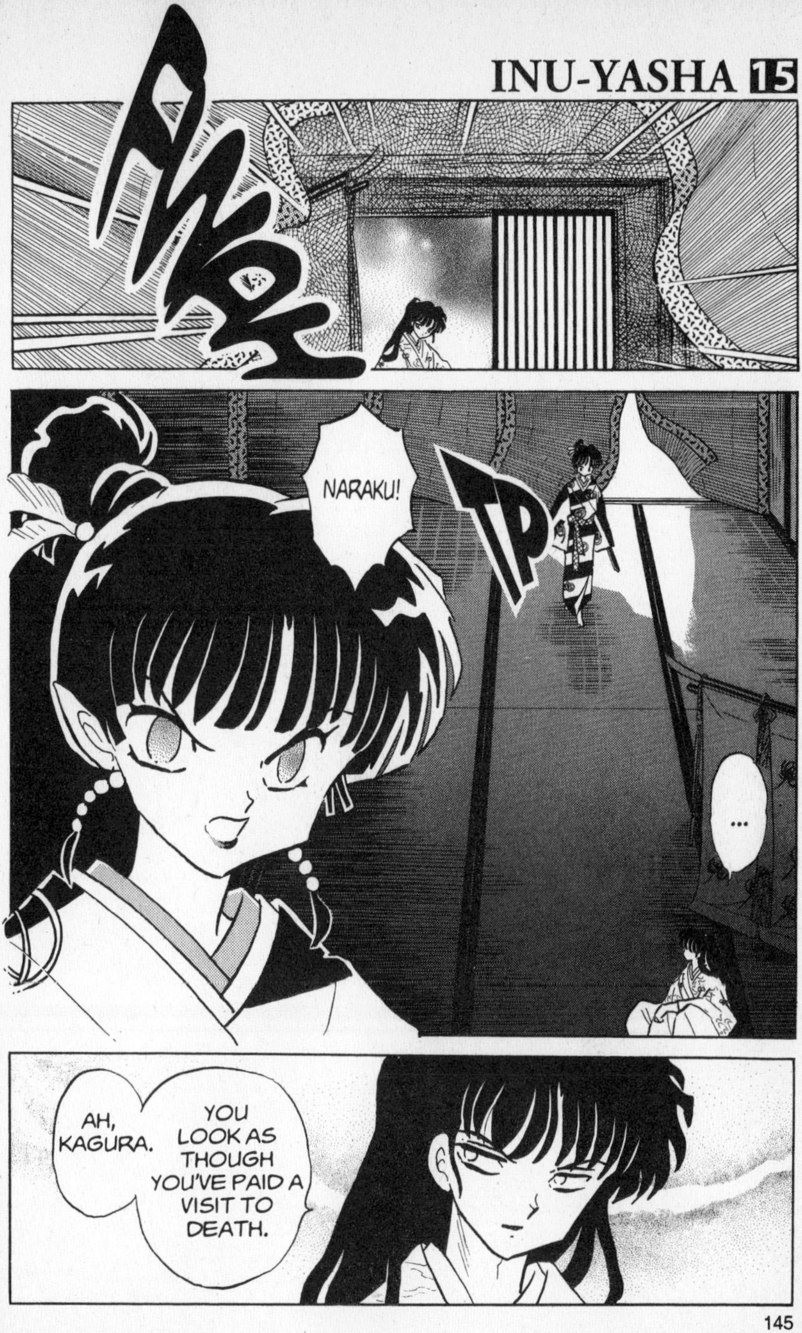
NARAKU!
TIP
...
AH, KAGURA.
YOU LOOK AS THOUGH YOU'VE PAID A VISIT TO DEATH.

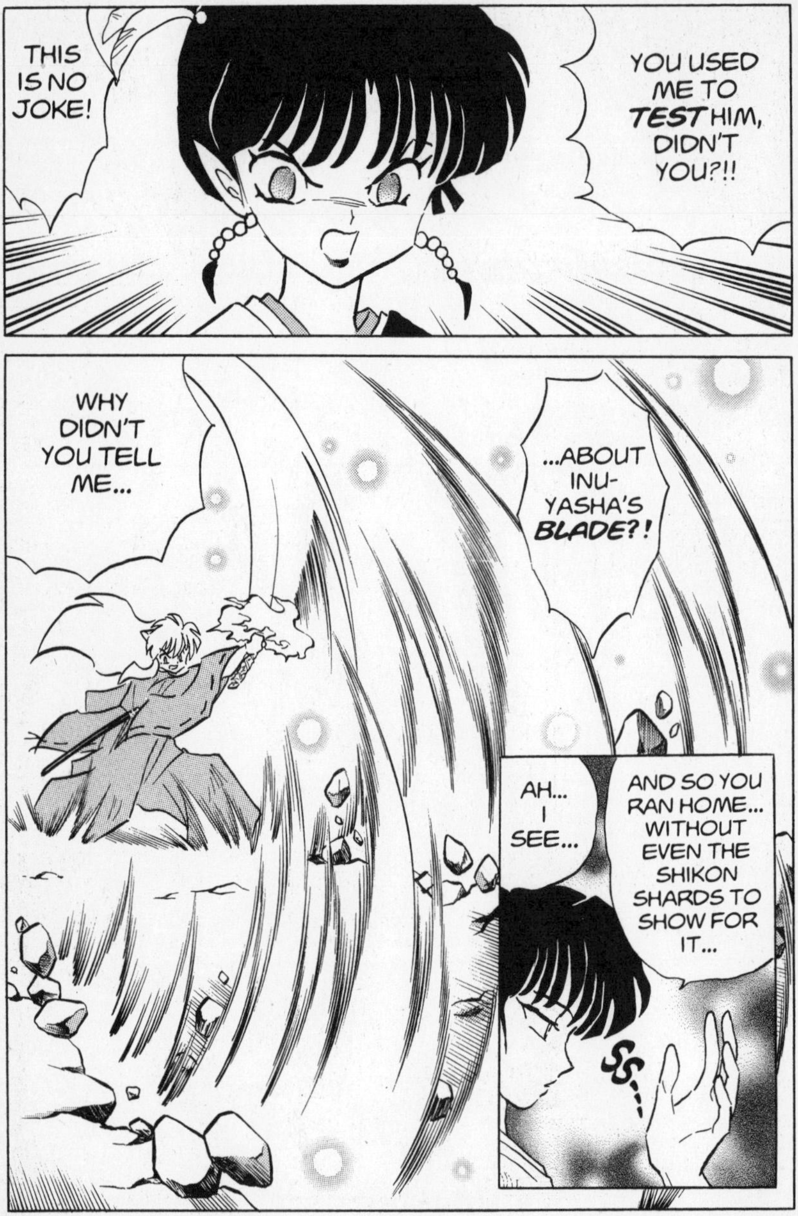
THIS IS NO JOKE!
YOU USED ME TO TEST HIM, DIDN'T YOU?!!
WHY DIDN'T YOU TELL ME...
...ABOUT INU-YASHA'S BLADE?!
AH... I SEE...
AND SO YOU RAN HOME... WITHOUT EVEN THE SHIKON SHARDS TO SHOW FOR IT...
SS...

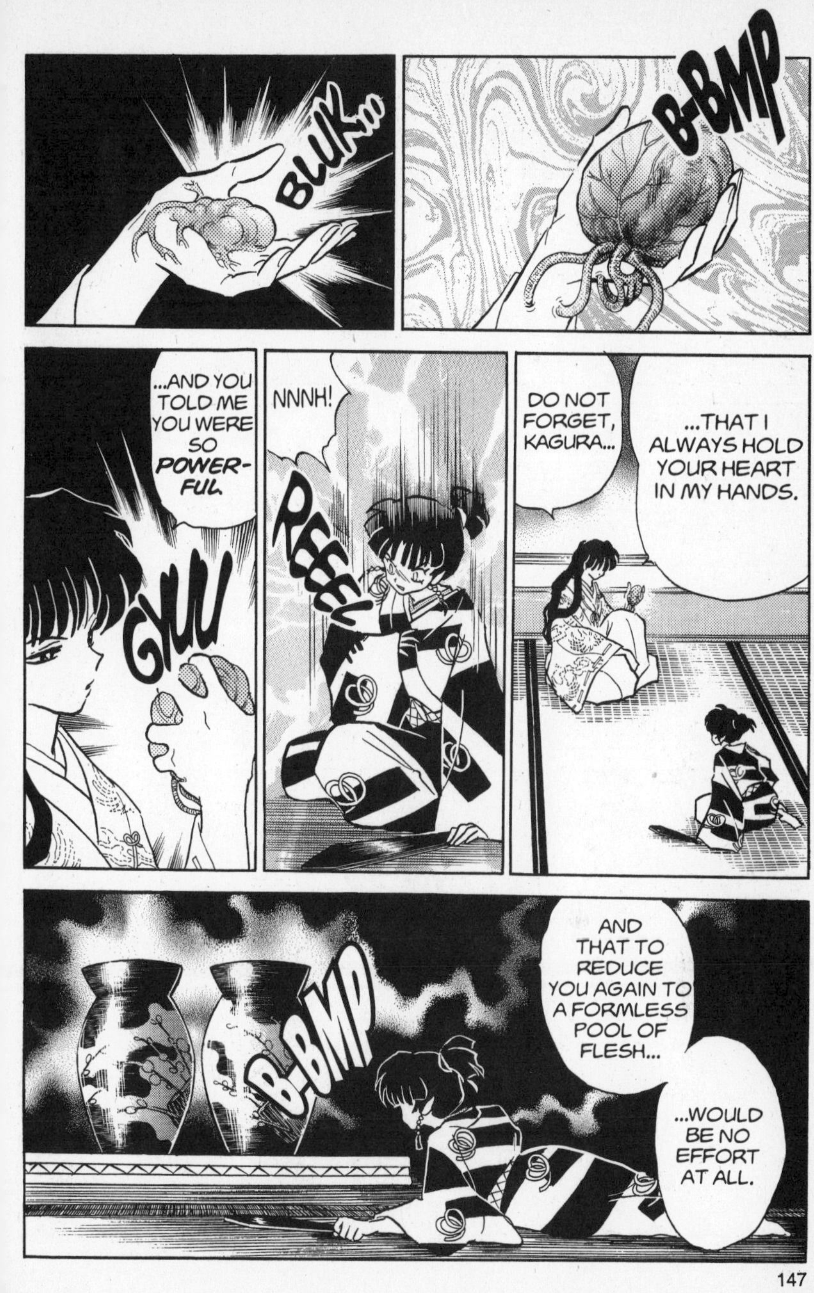
BLUK
B-BMP
...AND YOU TOLD ME YOU WERE SO *POWER-FUL.*
GYUU
NNNH!
REEEL
DO NOT FORGET, KAGURA...
...THAT I ALWAYS HOLD YOUR HEART IN MY HANDS.
B-BMP
AND THAT TO REDUCE YOU AGAIN TO A FORMLESS POOL OF FLESH...
...WOULD BE NO EFFORT AT ALL.

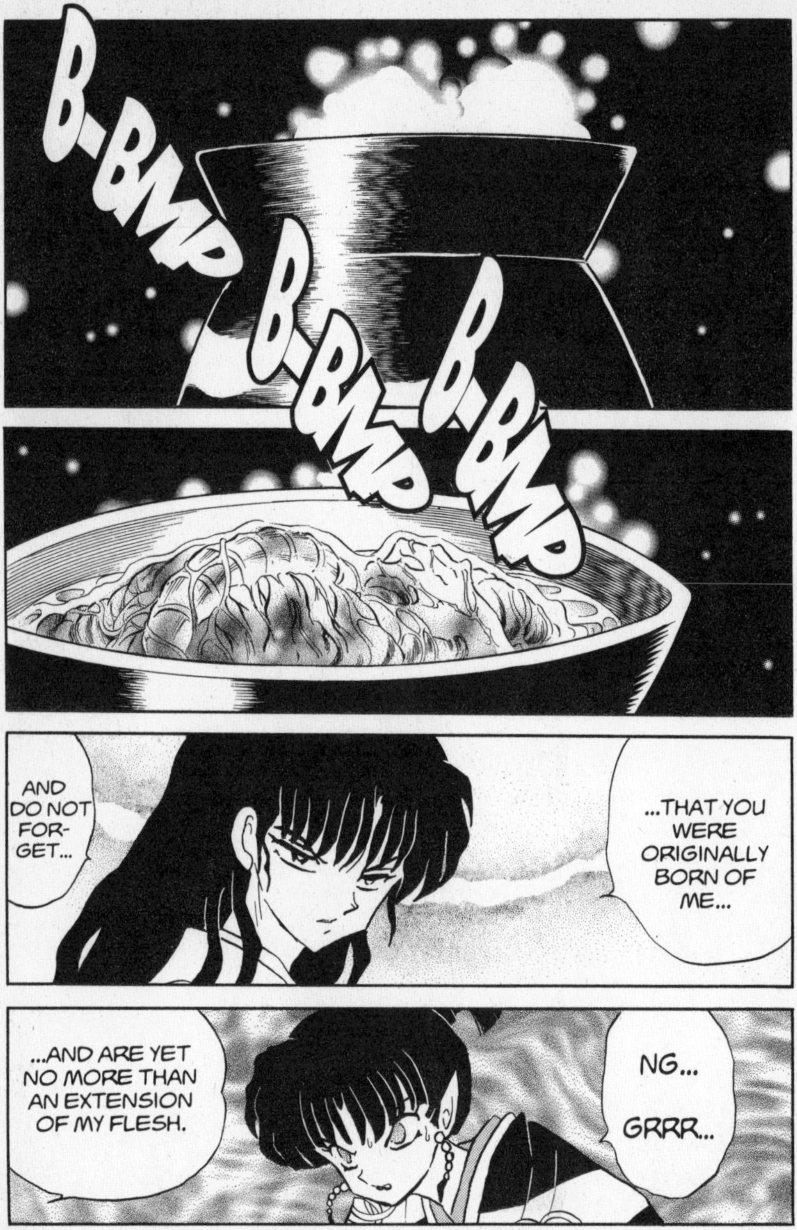
B-BMP
B-BMP
B-BMP
B-BMP
AND DO NOT FOR-GET...
...THAT YOU WERE ORIGINALLY BORN OF ME...
...AND ARE YET NO MORE THAN AN EXTENSION OF MY FLESH.
NG...
GRRR...

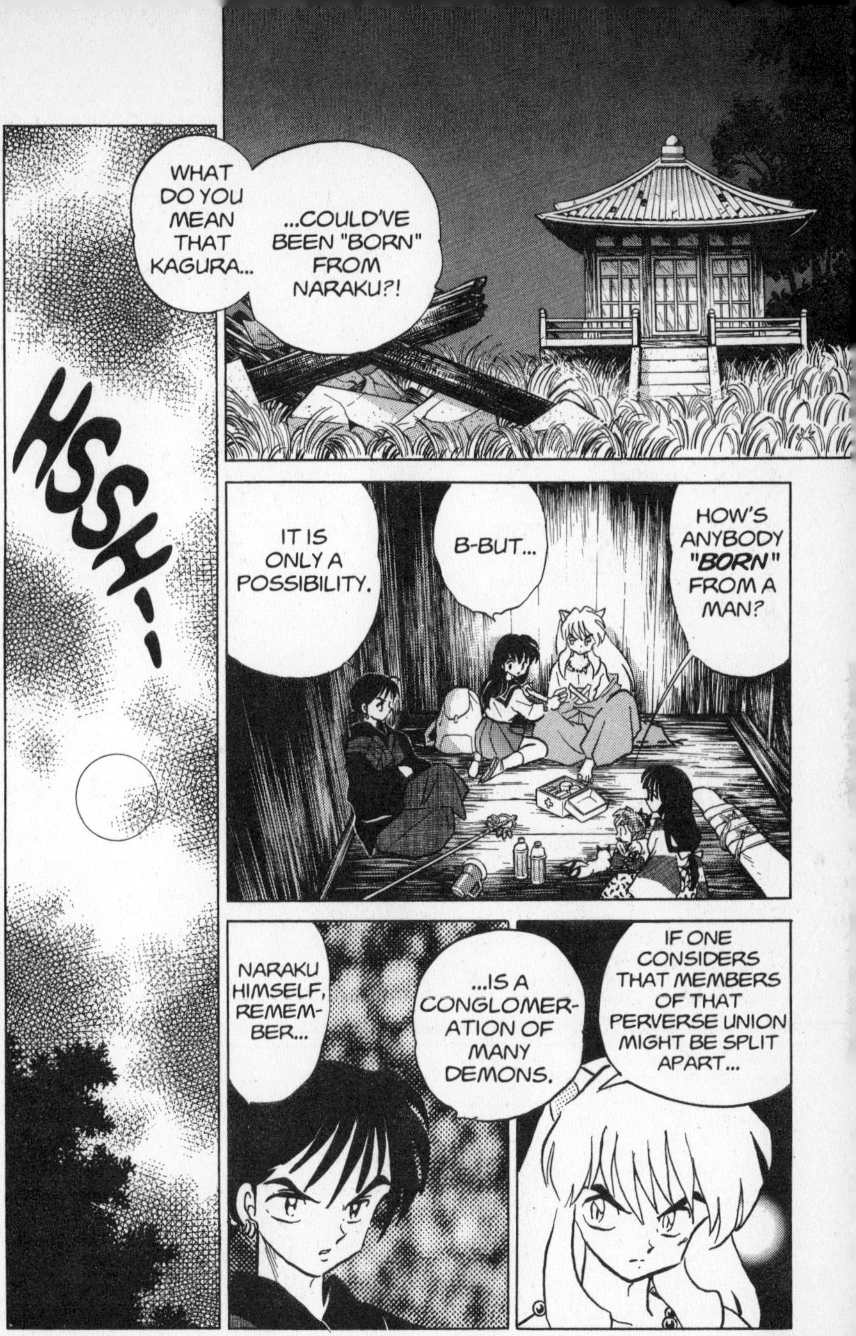
HSSH
WHAT DO YOU MEAN THAT KAGURA...
...COULD'VE BEEN "BORN" FROM NARAKU?!
IT IS ONLY A POSSIBILITY.
B-BUT...
HOW'S ANYBODY "**BORN**" FROM A MAN?
NARAKU HIMSELF, REMEM-BER...
...IS A CONGLOMER-ATION OF MANY DEMONS.
IF ONE CONSIDERS THAT MEMBERS OF THAT PERVERSE UNION MIGHT BE SPLIT APART...

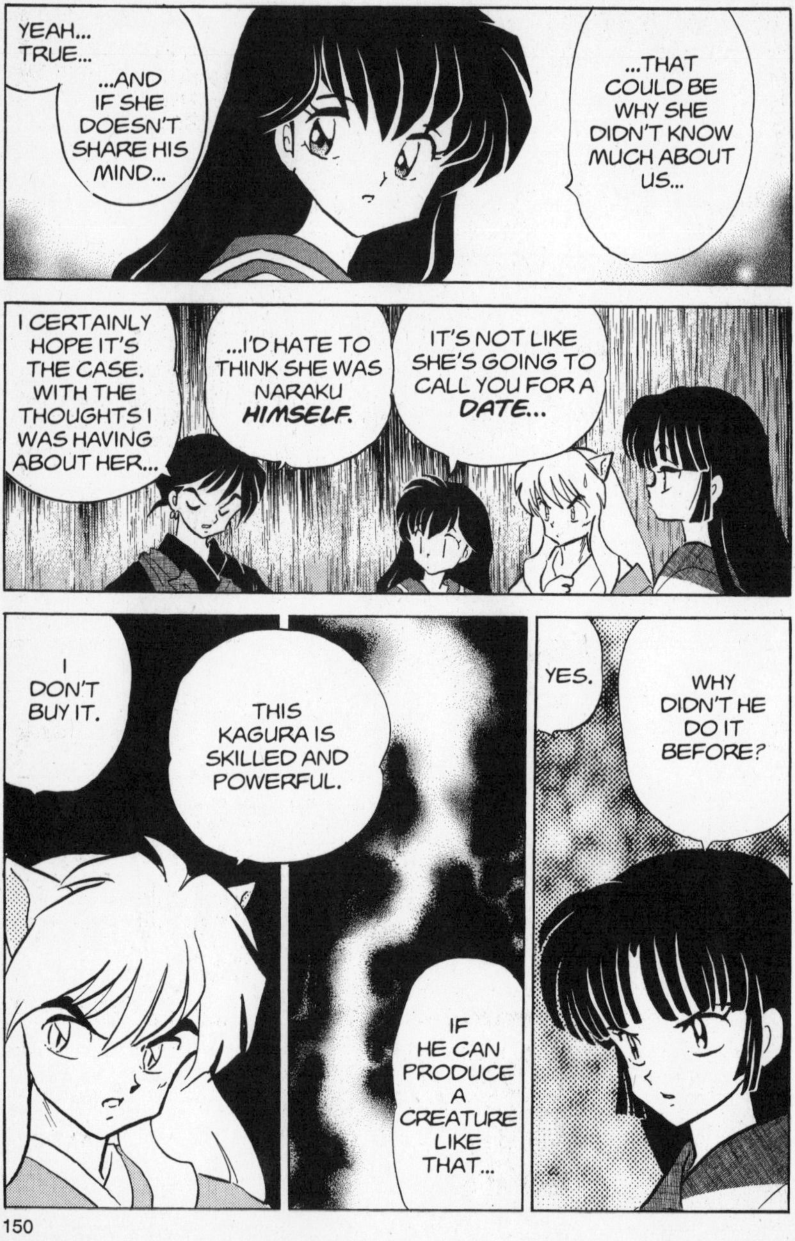
YEAH... TRUE...
...AND IF SHE DOESN'T SHARE HIS MIND...
...THAT COULD BE WHY SHE DIDN'T KNOW MUCH ABOUT US...
I CERTAINLY HOPE IT'S THE CASE. WITH THE THOUGHTS I WAS HAVING ABOUT HER...
...I'D HATE TO THINK SHE WAS NARAKU *HIMSELF*.
IT'S NOT LIKE SHE'S GOING TO CALL YOU FOR A *DATE*...
I DON'T BUY IT.
THIS KAGURA IS SKILLED AND POWERFUL.
IF HE CAN PRODUCE A CREATURE LIKE THAT...
YES.
WHY DIDN'T HE DO IT BEFORE?

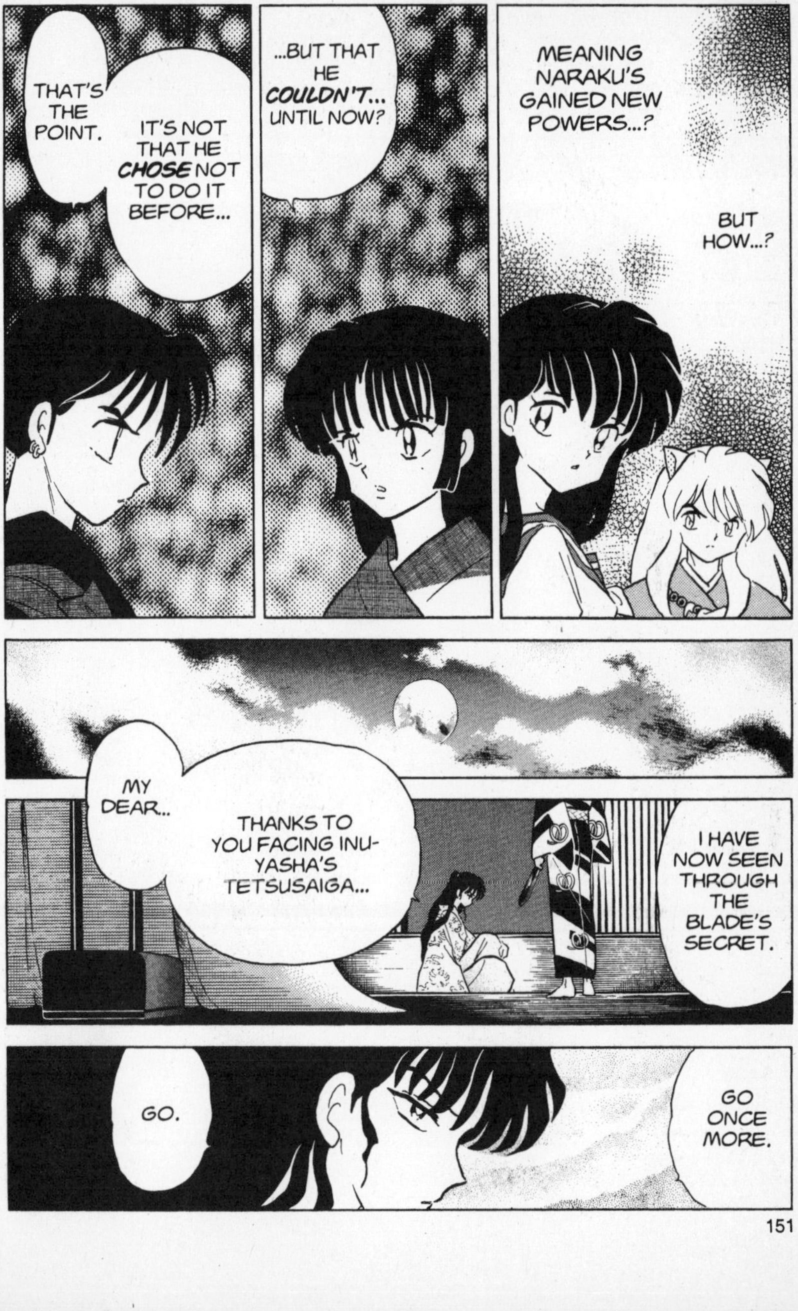
THAT'S THE POINT.
IT'S NOT THAT HE CHOSE NOT TO DO IT BEFORE...
...BUT THAT HE COULDN'T... UNTIL NOW?
MEANING NARAKU'S GAINED NEW POWERS...?
BUT HOW...?
MY DEAR...
THANKS TO YOU FACING INU-YASHA'S TETSUSAIGA...
I HAVE NOW SEEN THROUGH THE BLADE'S SECRET.
GO.
GO ONCE MORE.

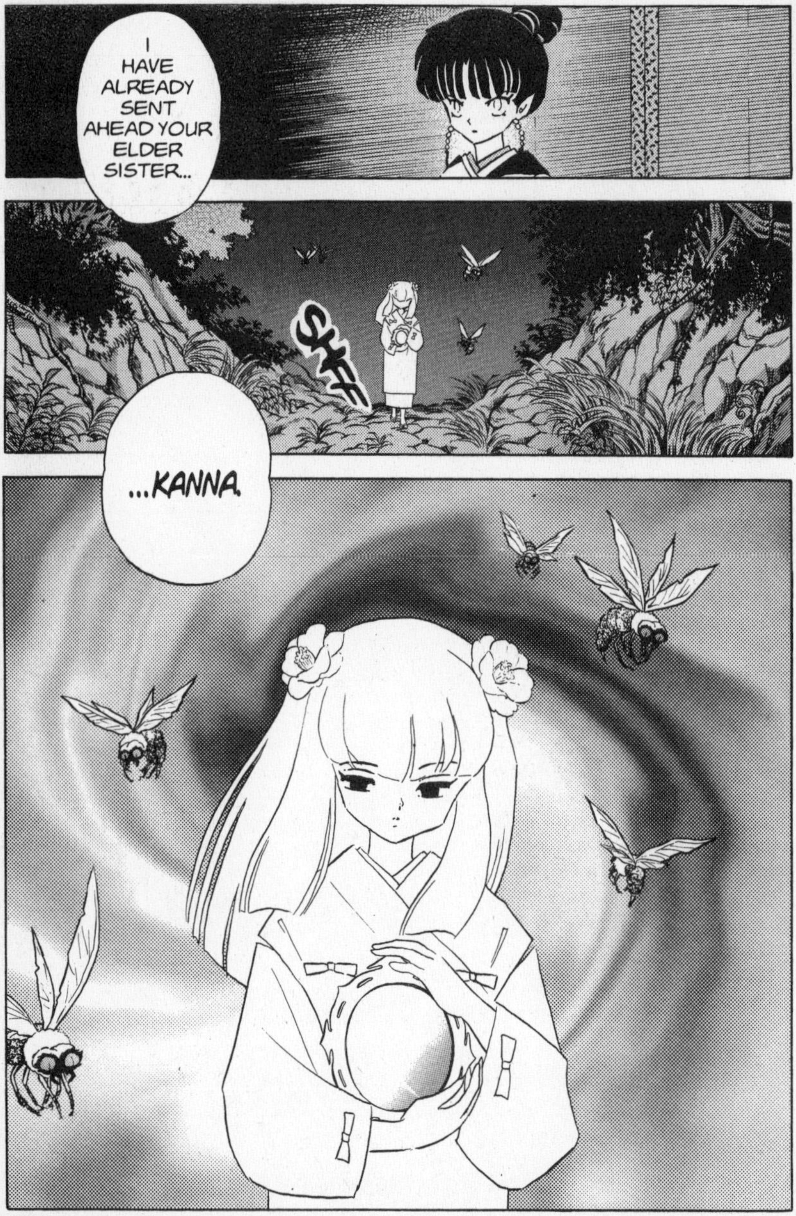
I HAVE ALREADY SENT AHEAD YOUR ELDER SISTER...
SHFF
...KANNA.

SCROLL NINE

KOHARU

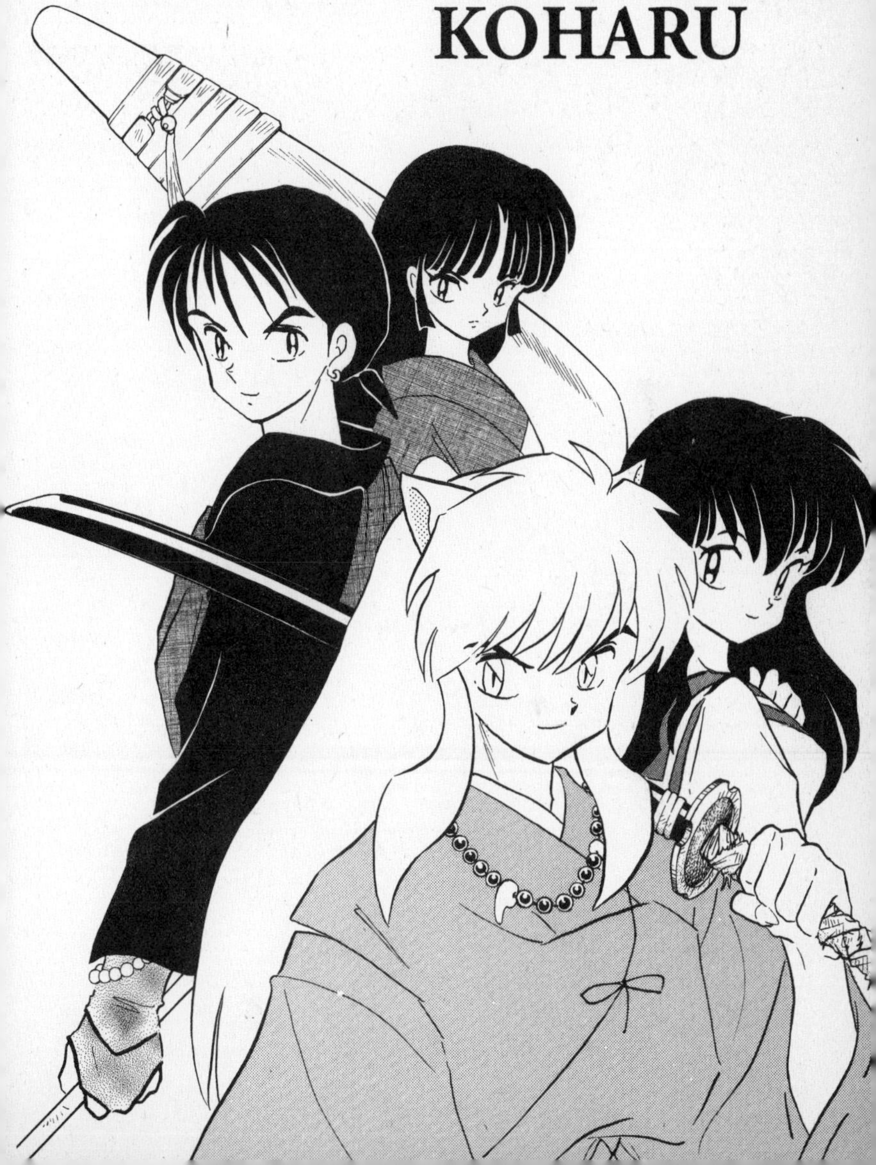

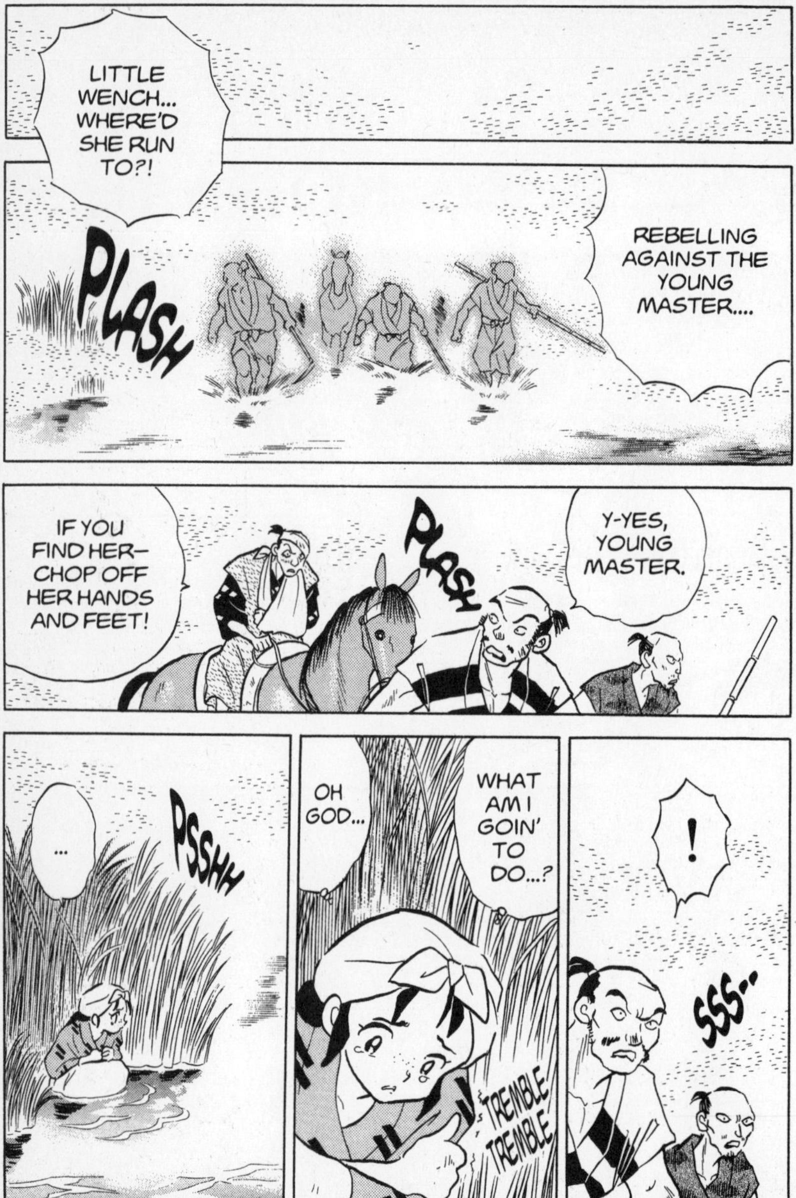
LITTLE WENCH... WHERE'D SHE RUN TO?!
PLASH
REBELLING AGAINST THE YOUNG MASTER....
IF YOU FIND HER—CHOP OFF HER HANDS AND FEET!
PLASH
Y-YES, YOUNG MASTER.
...
PSSHH
OH GOD...
WHAT AM I GOIN' TO DO...?
TREMBLE TREMBLE
!
SSS..

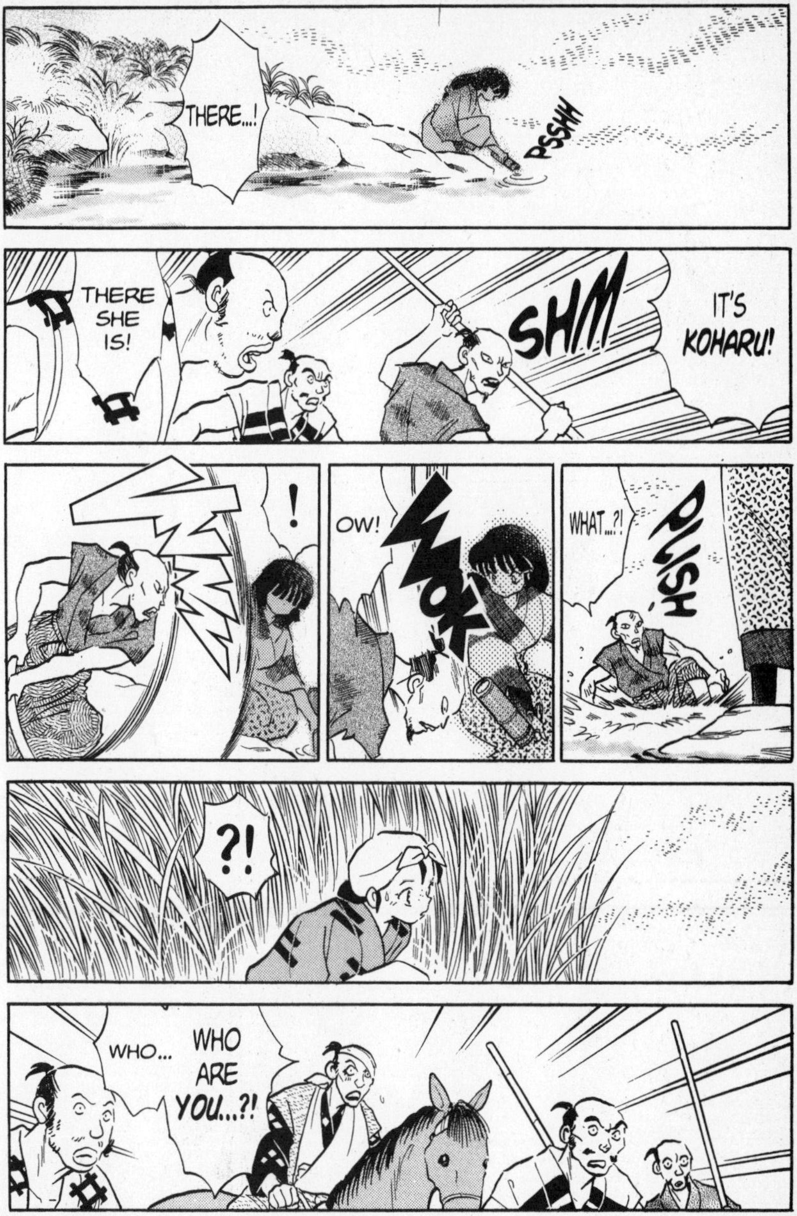
THERE...!
PSSHH
THERE SHE IS!
SHM
IT'S KOHARU!
!
OW!
WOK
WHAT...?!
PUSH
?!
WHO...
WHO ARE YOU...?!

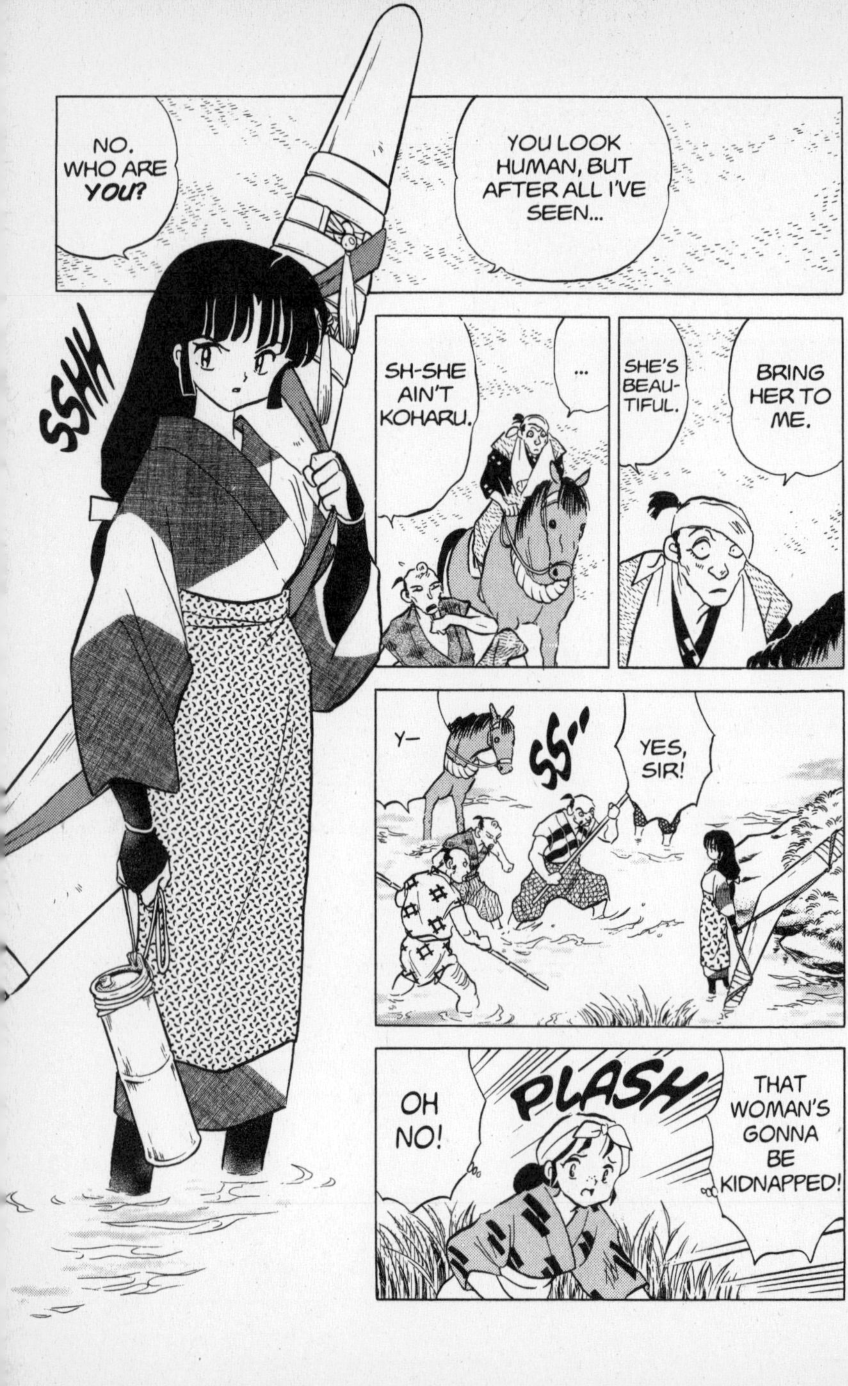
NO. WHO ARE YOU?
YOU LOOK HUMAN, BUT AFTER ALL I'VE SEEN...
SSHH
SH-SHE AIN'T KOHARU.
...
SHE'S BEAU-TIFUL.
BRING HER TO ME.
Y—
SS...
YES, SIR!
OH NO!
PLASH
THAT WOMAN'S GONNA BE KIDNAPPED!

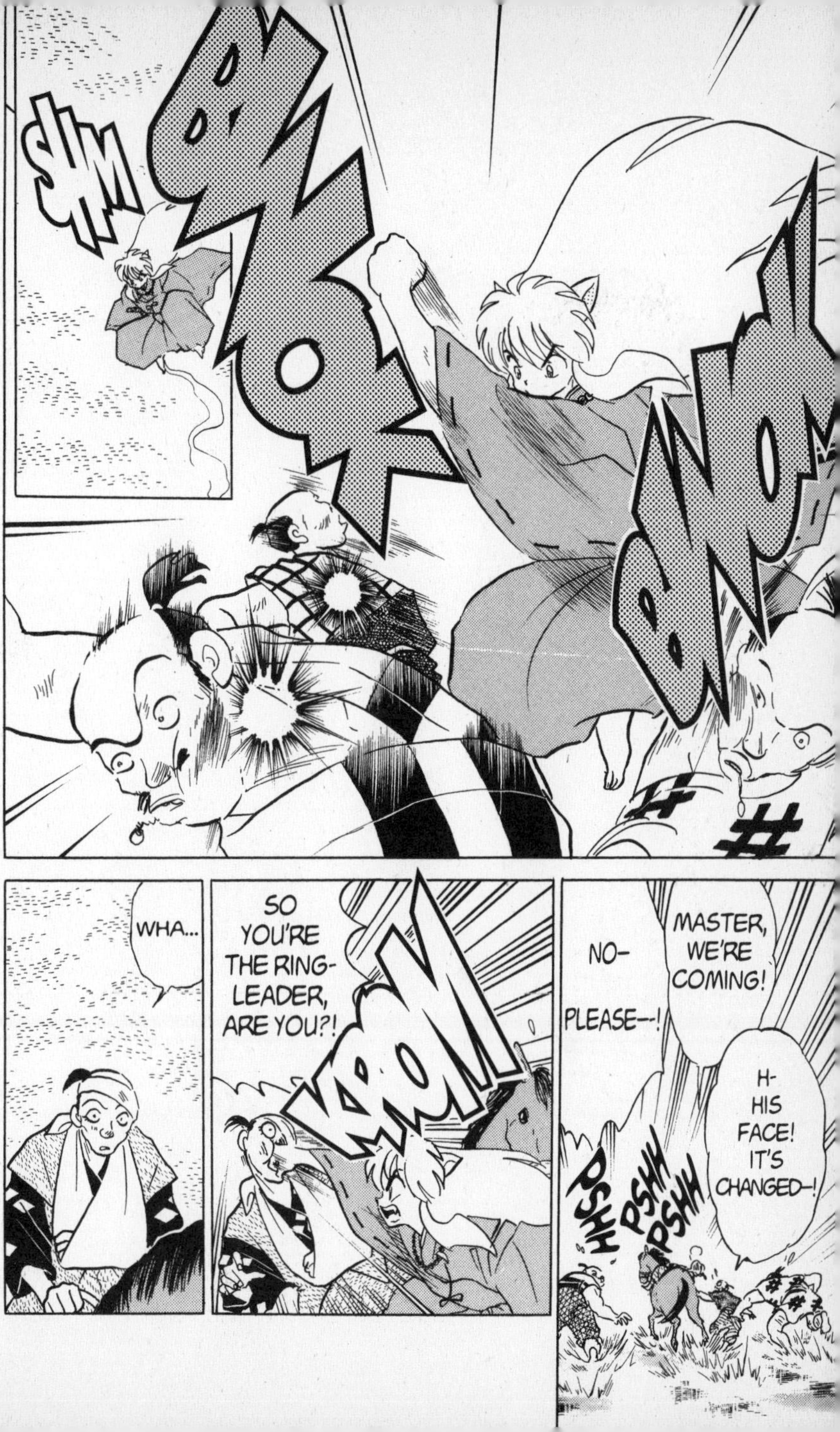
WHA...
SO YOU'RE THE RING-LEADER, ARE YOU?!
NO- PLEASE--!
MASTER, WE'RE COMING!
H-HIS FACE! IT'S CHANGED--!
PSHH PSHH PSHH

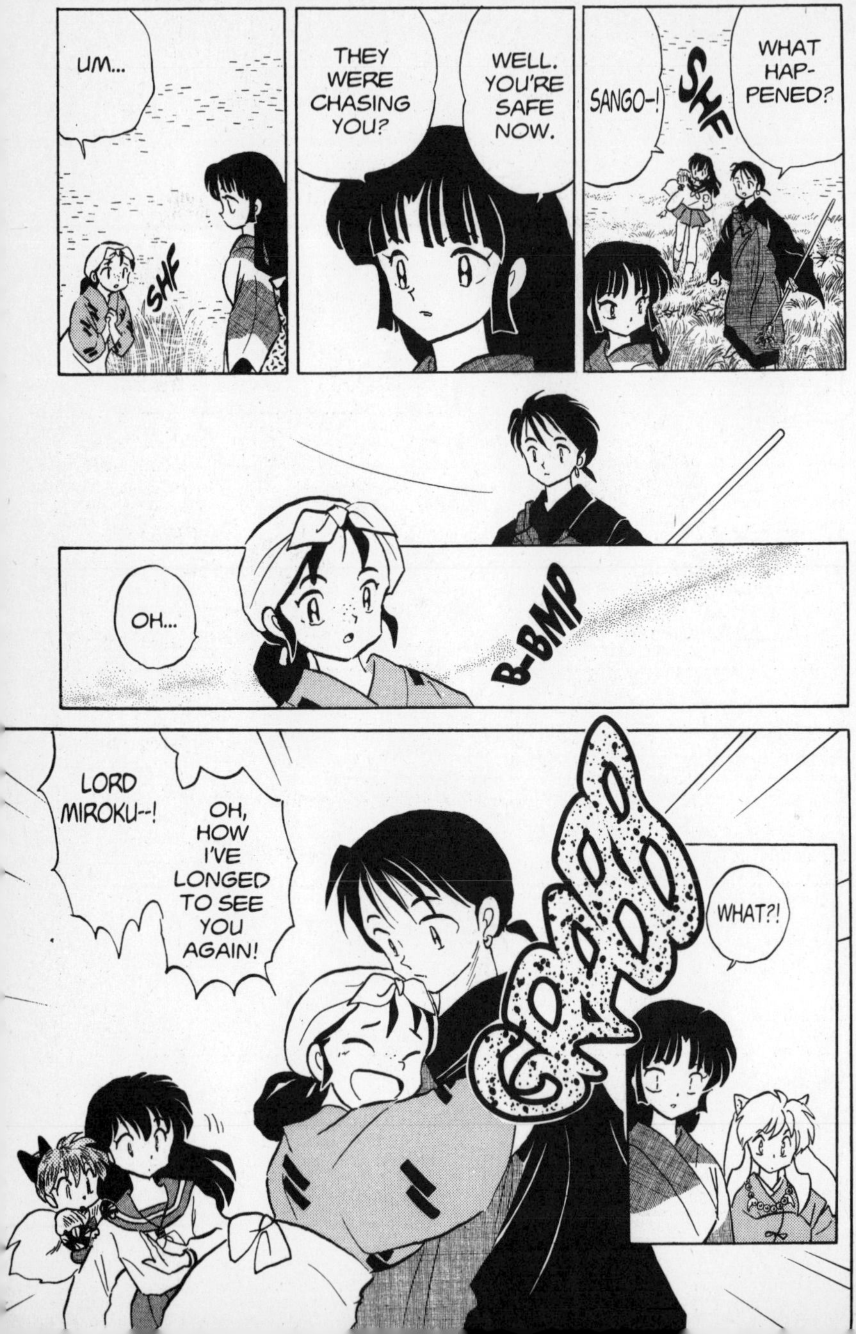
UM...
SHF
THEY WERE CHASING YOU?
WELL. YOU'RE SAFE NOW.
SANGO-!
SHF
WHAT HAP-PENED?
OH...
B-BMP
LORD MIROKU--!
OH, HOW I'VE LONGED TO SEE YOU AGAIN!
WHAT?!

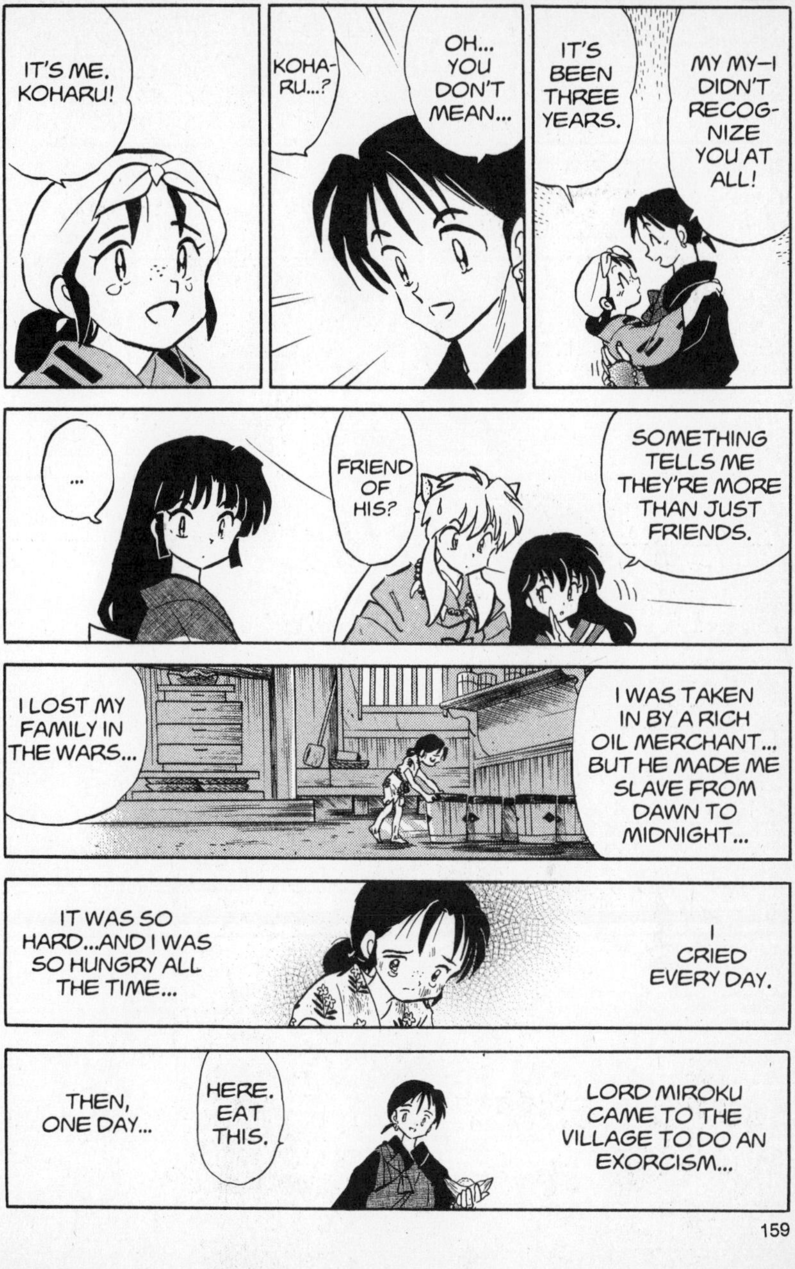
IT'S ME. KOHARU!
KOHA-RU...?
OH... YOU DON'T MEAN...
IT'S BEEN THREE YEARS.
MY MY—I DIDN'T RECOG-NIZE YOU AT ALL!
...
FRIEND OF HIS?
SOMETHING TELLS ME THEY'RE MORE THAN JUST FRIENDS.
I LOST MY FAMILY IN THE WARS...
I WAS TAKEN IN BY A RICH OIL MERCHANT... BUT HE MADE ME SLAVE FROM DAWN TO MIDNIGHT...
IT WAS SO HARD...AND I WAS SO HUNGRY ALL THE TIME...
I CRIED EVERY DAY.
THEN, ONE DAY...
HERE. EAT THIS.
LORD MIROKU CAME TO THE VILLAGE TO DO AN EXORCISM...

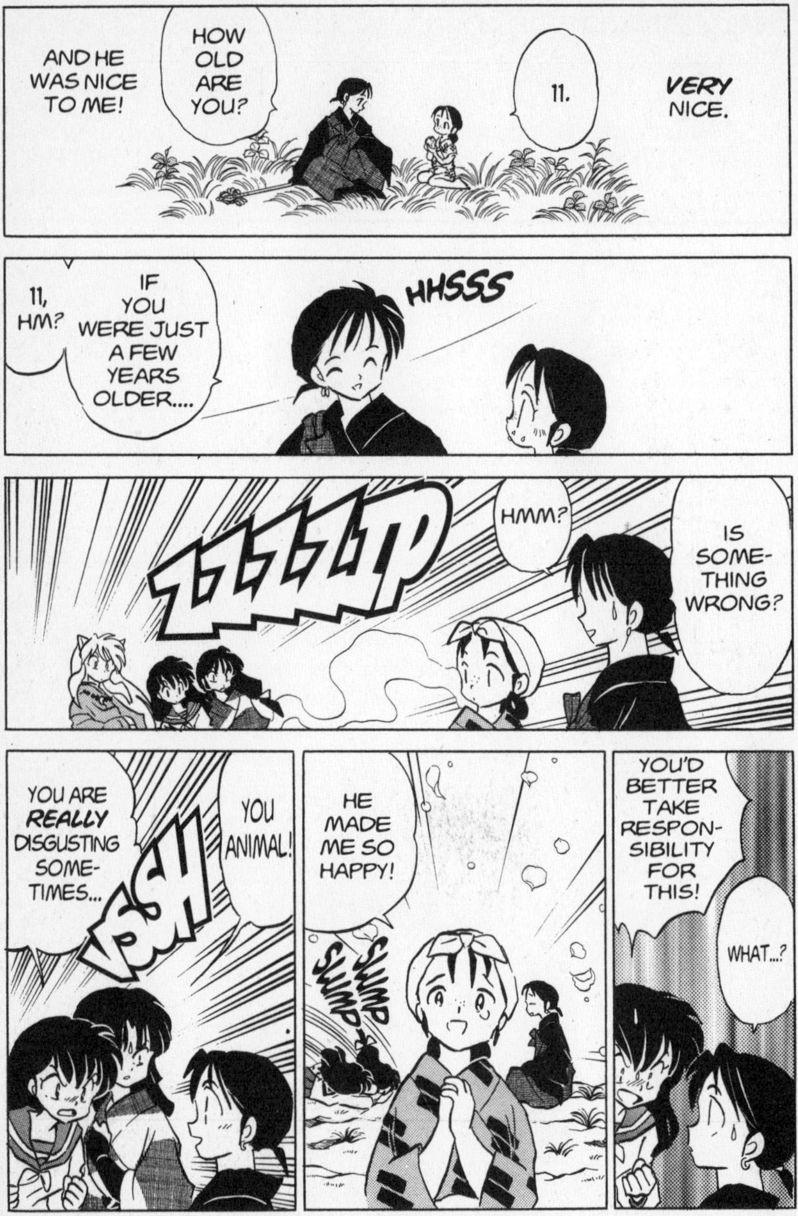
AND HE WAS NICE TO ME!
HOW OLD ARE YOU?
11.
VERY NICE.
11, HM?
IF YOU WERE JUST A FEW YEARS OLDER....
HHSSS
ZZZZIP
HMM?
IS SOME-THING WRONG?
YOU ARE REALLY DISGUSTING SOME-TIMES...
VSSH
YOU ANIMAL!
HE MADE ME SO HAPPY!
SWUMP SWUMP
YOU'D BETTER TAKE RESPON-SIBILITY FOR THIS!
WHAT...?

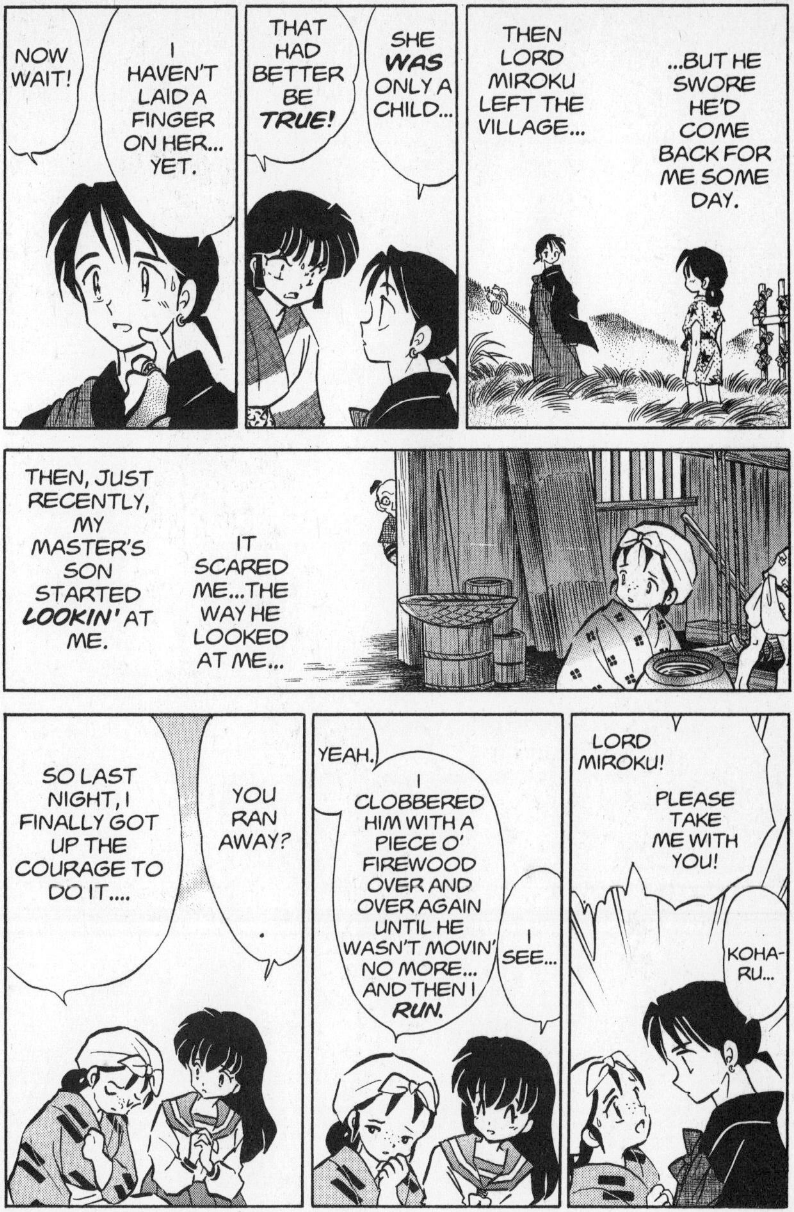
NOW WAIT!
I HAVEN'T LAID A FINGER ON HER... YET.
THAT HAD BETTER BE TRUE!
SHE WAS ONLY A CHILD...
THEN LORD MIROKU LEFT THE VILLAGE...
...BUT HE SWORE HE'D COME BACK FOR ME SOME DAY.
THEN, JUST RECENTLY, MY MASTER'S SON STARTED LOOKIN' AT ME.
IT SCARED ME...THE WAY HE LOOKED AT ME...
SO LAST NIGHT, I FINALLY GOT UP THE COURAGE TO DO IT....
YOU RAN AWAY?
YEAH.
I CLOBBERED HIM WITH A PIECE O' FIREWOOD OVER AND OVER AGAIN UNTIL HE WASN'T MOVIN' NO MORE... AND THEN I RUN.
I SEE...
LORD MIROKU!
PLEASE TAKE ME WITH YOU!
KOHA-RU...

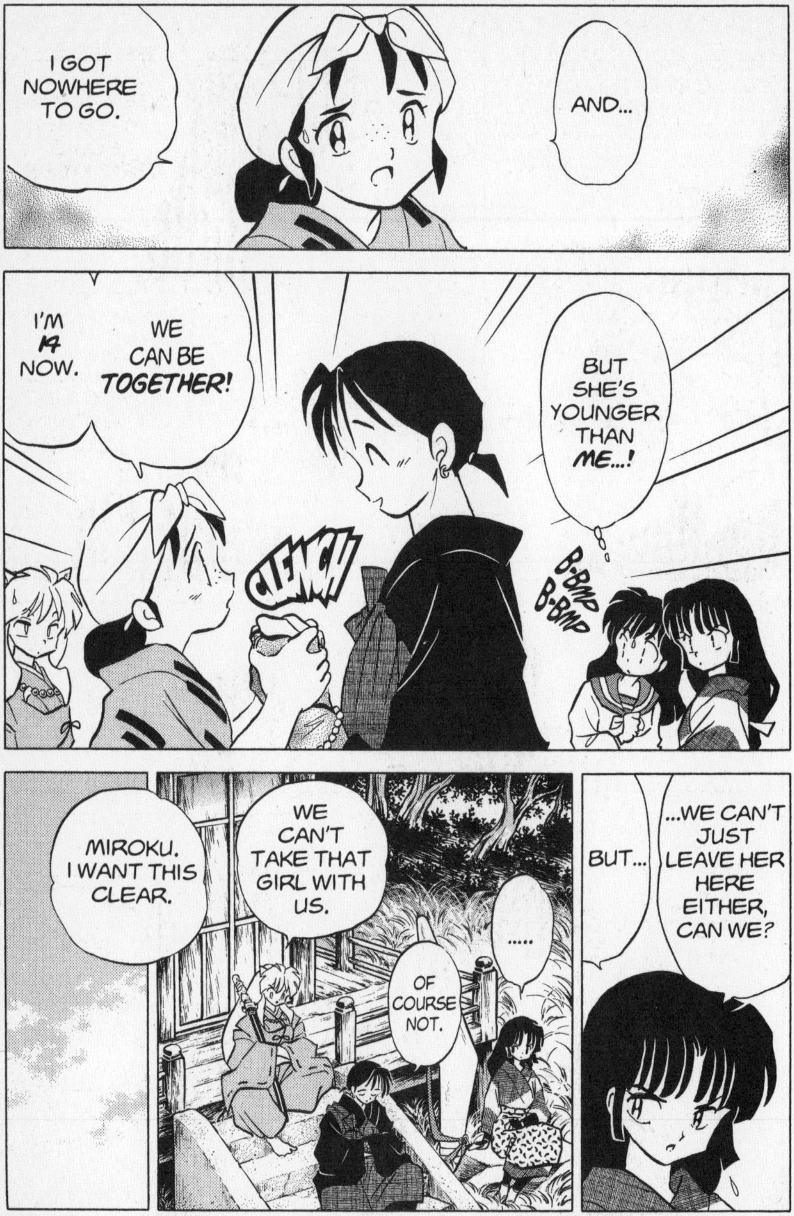
I GOT NOWHERE TO GO.
AND...
I'M 14 NOW.
WE CAN BE TOGETHER!
BUT SHE'S YOUNGER THAN ME...!
CLENCH
B-BMP B-BMP
MIROKU. I WANT THIS CLEAR.
WE CAN'T TAKE THAT GIRL WITH US.
.....
OF COURSE NOT.
BUT...
...WE CAN'T JUST LEAVE HER HERE EITHER, CAN WE?

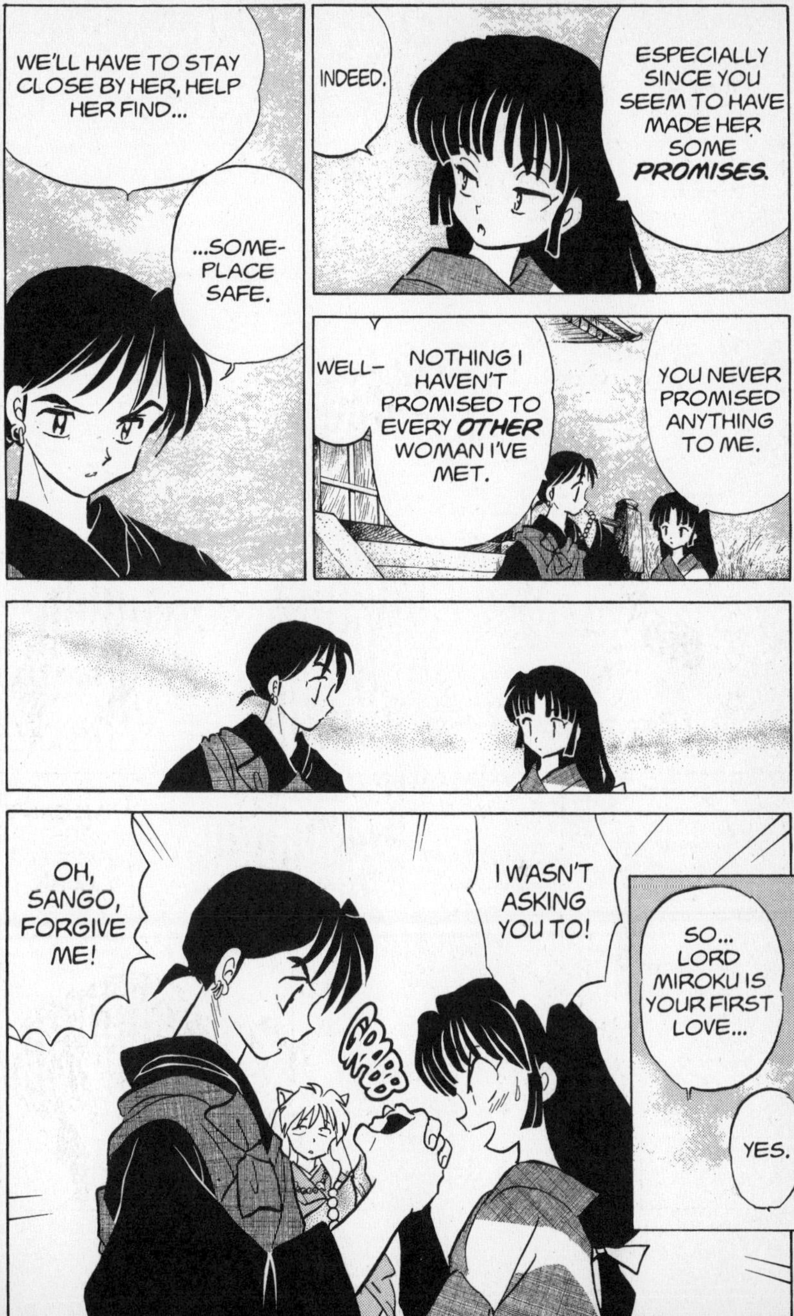
WE'LL HAVE TO STAY CLOSE BY HER, HELP HER FIND...
...SOME-PLACE SAFE.
INDEED.
ESPECIALLY SINCE YOU SEEM TO HAVE MADE HER SOME PROMISES.
WELL-
NOTHING I HAVEN'T PROMISED TO EVERY OTHER WOMAN I'VE MET.
YOU NEVER PROMISED ANYTHING TO ME.
OH, SANGO, FORGIVE ME!
I WASN'T ASKING YOU TO!
SO... LORD MIROKU IS YOUR FIRST LOVE...
YES.

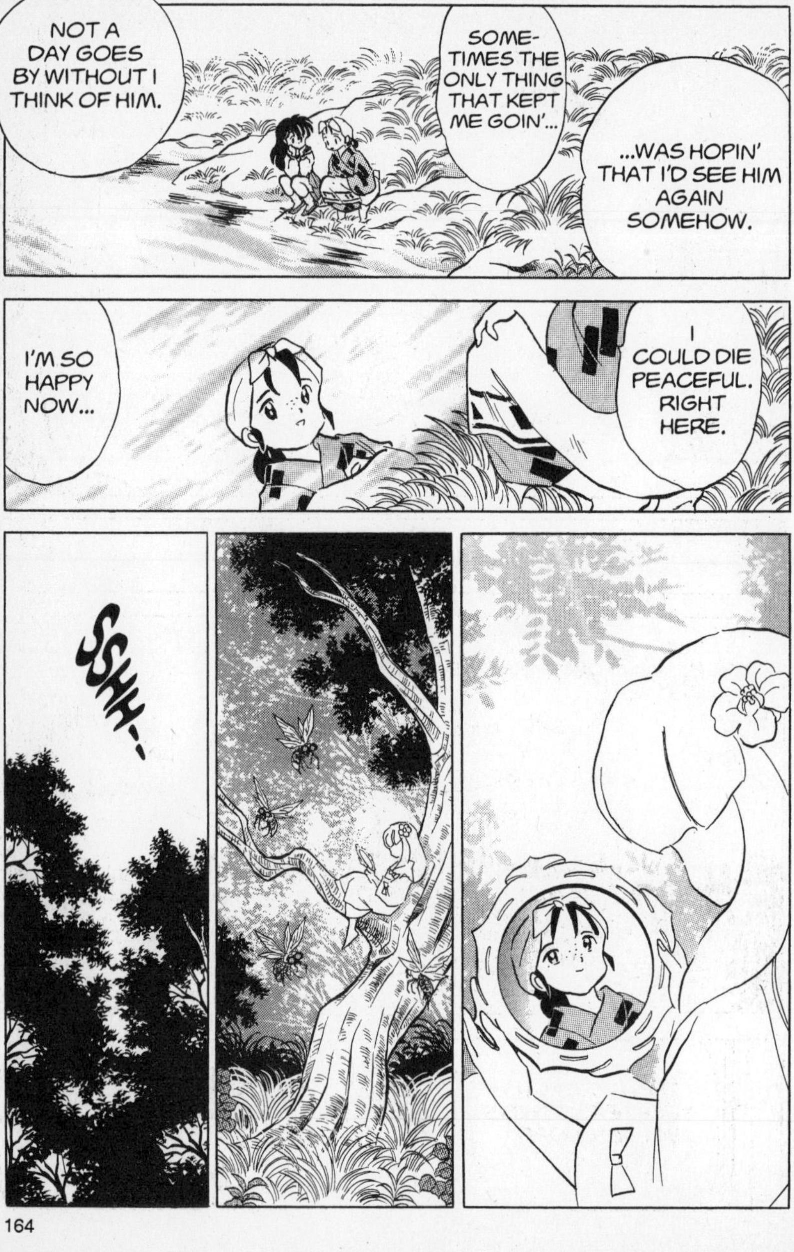
NOT A DAY GOES BY WITHOUT I THINK OF HIM.
SOME-TIMES THE ONLY THING THAT KEPT ME GOIN'...
...WAS HOPIN' THAT I'D SEE HIM AGAIN SOMEHOW.
I'M SO HAPPY NOW...
I COULD DIE PEACEFUL. RIGHT HERE.
SSHH--

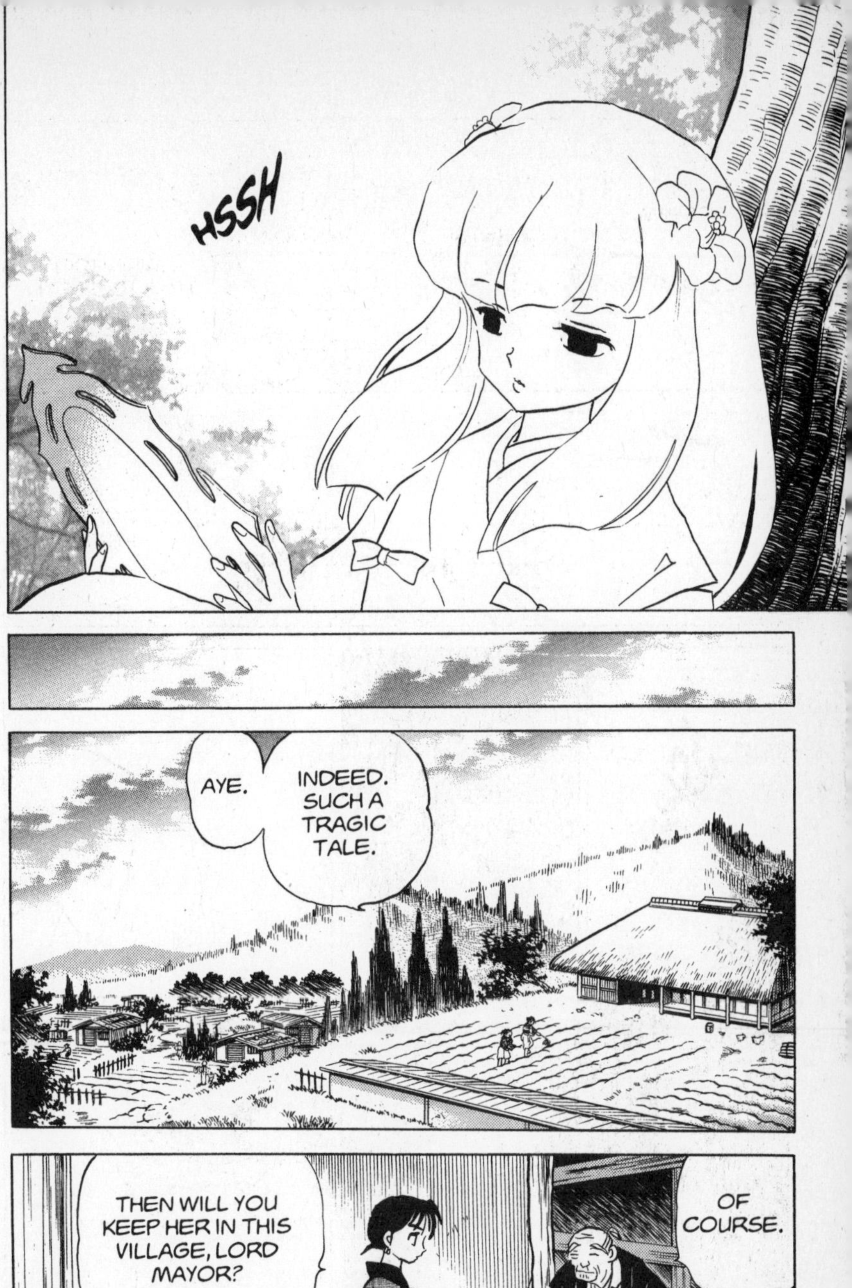
HSSH
AYE.
INDEED. SUCH A TRAGIC TALE.
THEN WILL YOU KEEP HER IN THIS VILLAGE, LORD MAYOR?
OF COURSE.

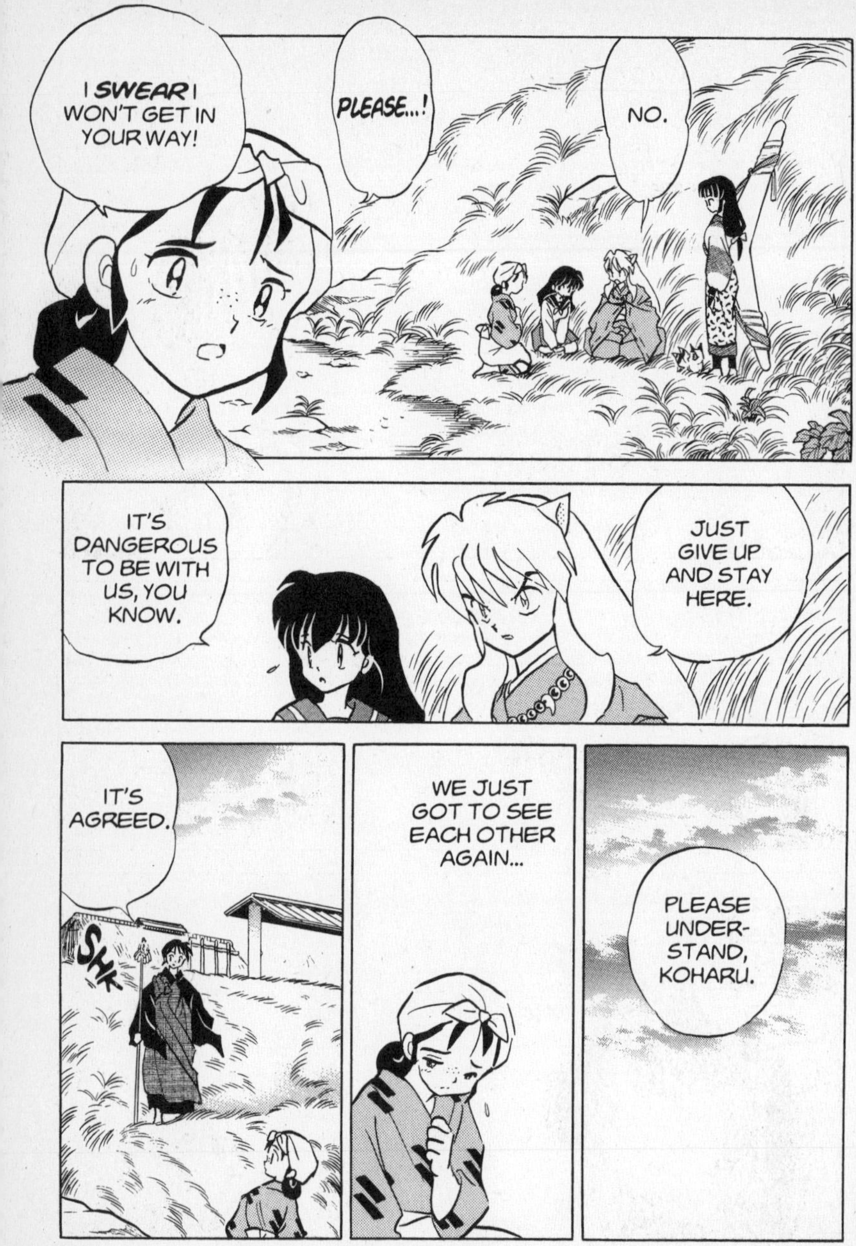

I SWEAR I WON'T GET IN YOUR WAY!
PLEASE...!
NO.
IT'S DANGEROUS TO BE WITH US, YOU KNOW.
JUST GIVE UP AND STAY HERE.
IT'S AGREED.
SHK
WE JUST GOT TO SEE EACH OTHER AGAIN...
PLEASE UNDER-STAND, KOHARU.

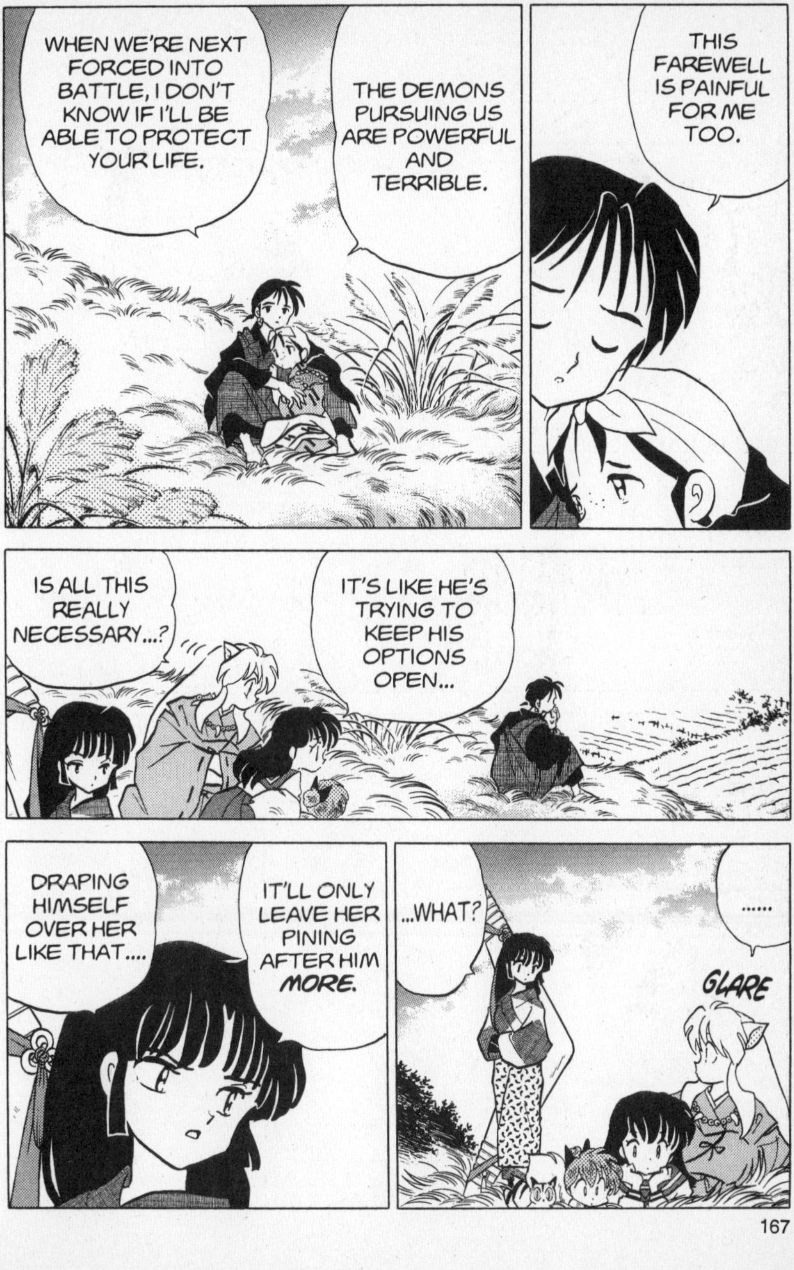
WHEN WE'RE NEXT FORCED INTO BATTLE, I DON'T KNOW IF I'LL BE ABLE TO PROTECT YOUR LIFE.
THE DEMONS PURSUING US ARE POWERFUL AND TERRIBLE.
THIS FAREWELL IS PAINFUL FOR ME TOO.
IS ALL THIS REALLY NECESSARY...?
IT'S LIKE HE'S TRYING TO KEEP HIS OPTIONS OPEN...
DRAPING HIMSELF OVER HER LIKE THAT....
IT'LL ONLY LEAVE HER PINING AFTER HIM MORE.
...WHAT?
......
GLARE

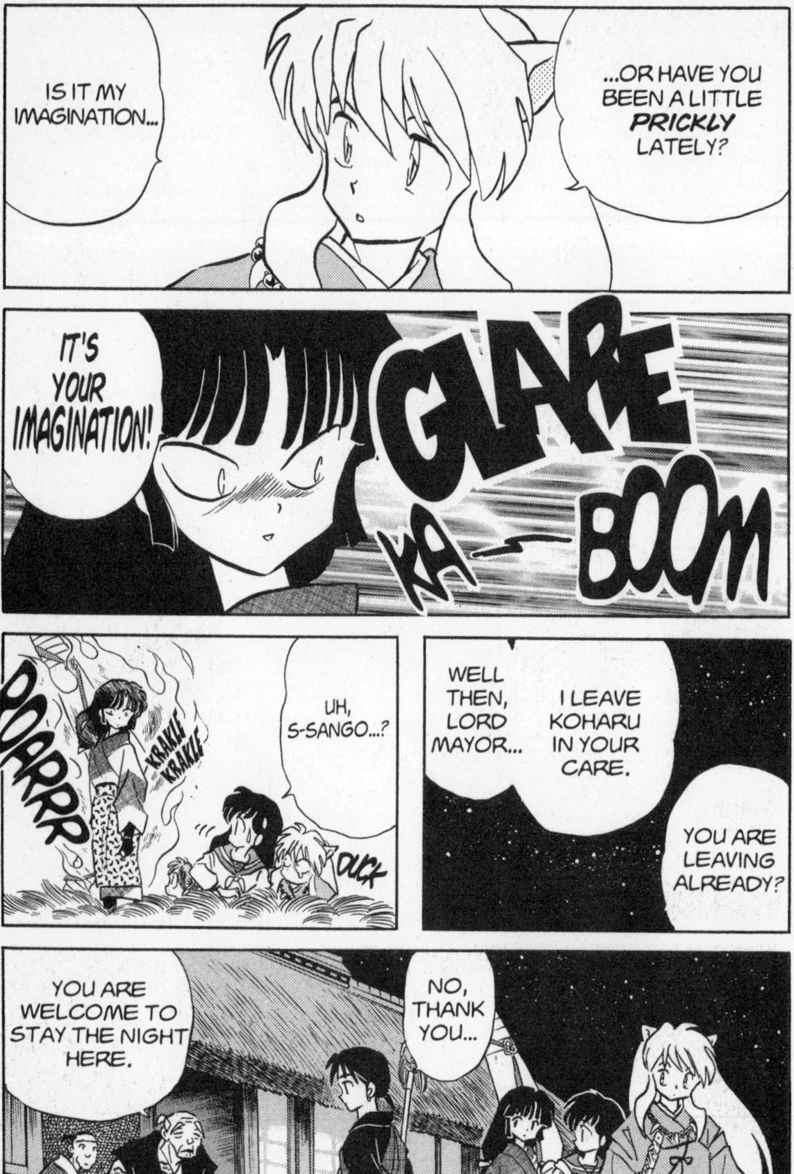
IS IT MY IMAGINATION...
...OR HAVE YOU BEEN A LITTLE PRICKLY LATELY?
IT'S YOUR IMAGINATION!
GLARE
KA-BOOM
ROARRR
KRAKLE KRAKLE
UH, S-SANGO...?
DUCK
WELL THEN, LORD MAYOR...
I LEAVE KOHARU IN YOUR CARE.
YOU ARE LEAVING ALREADY?
YOU ARE WELCOME TO STAY THE NIGHT HERE.
NO, THANK YOU...

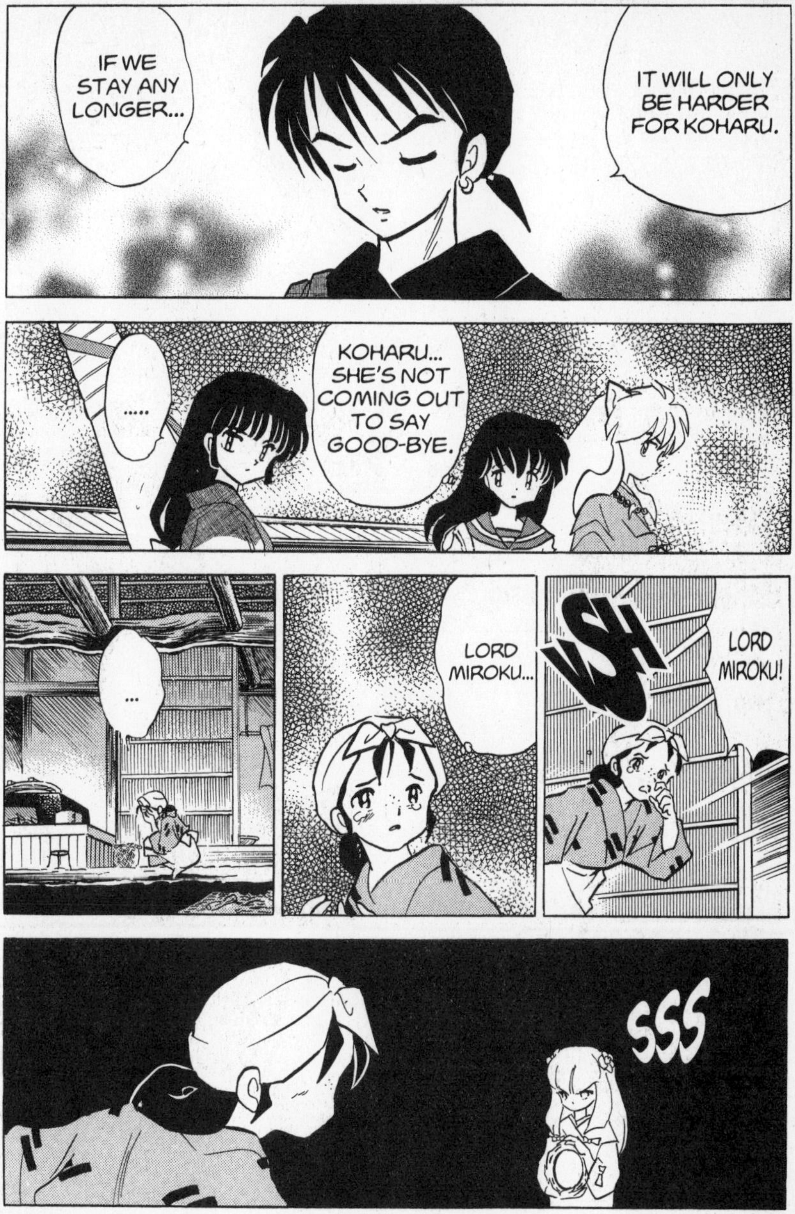
IF WE STAY ANY LONGER...
IT WILL ONLY BE HARDER FOR KOHARU.
.....
KOHARU... SHE'S NOT COMING OUT TO SAY GOOD-BYE.
...
LORD MIROKU...
VSH
LORD MIROKU!
SSS

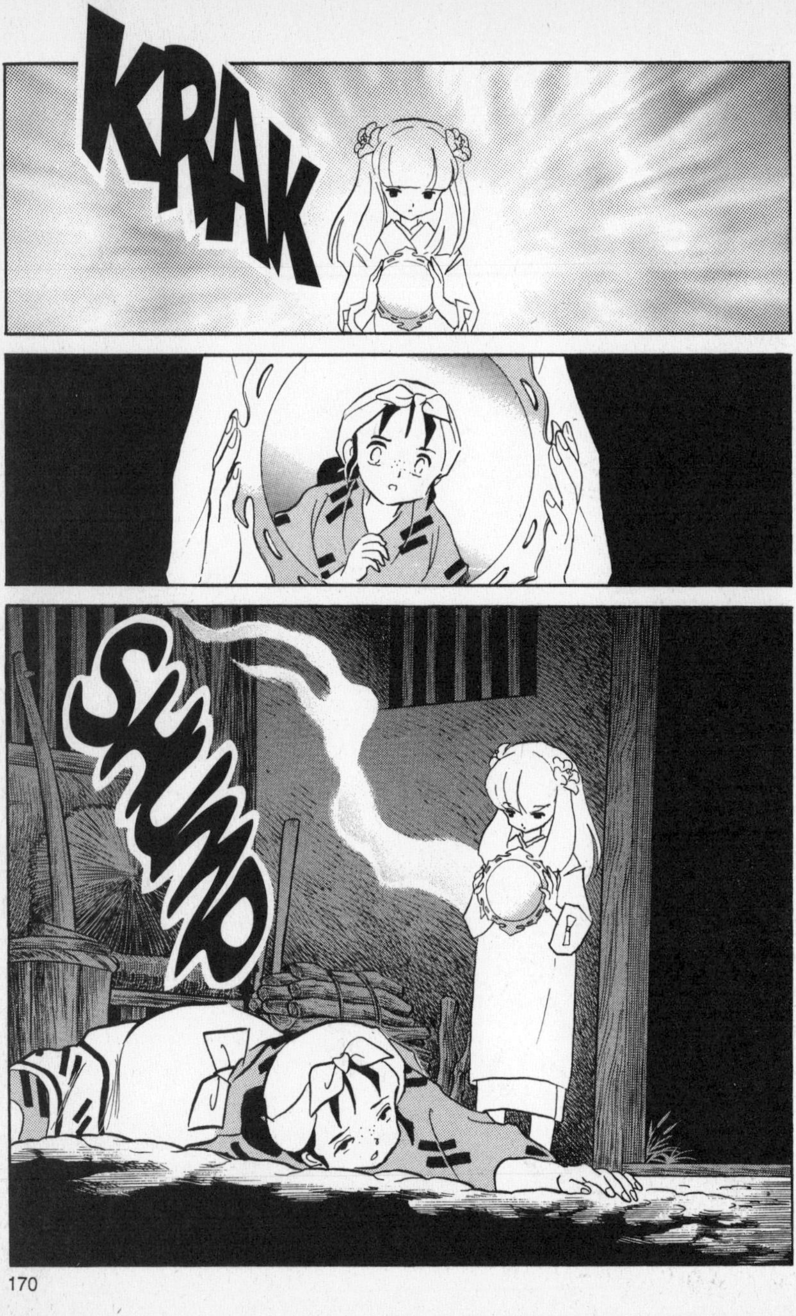
KRAK
SHUMP

SCROLL TEN
KANNA

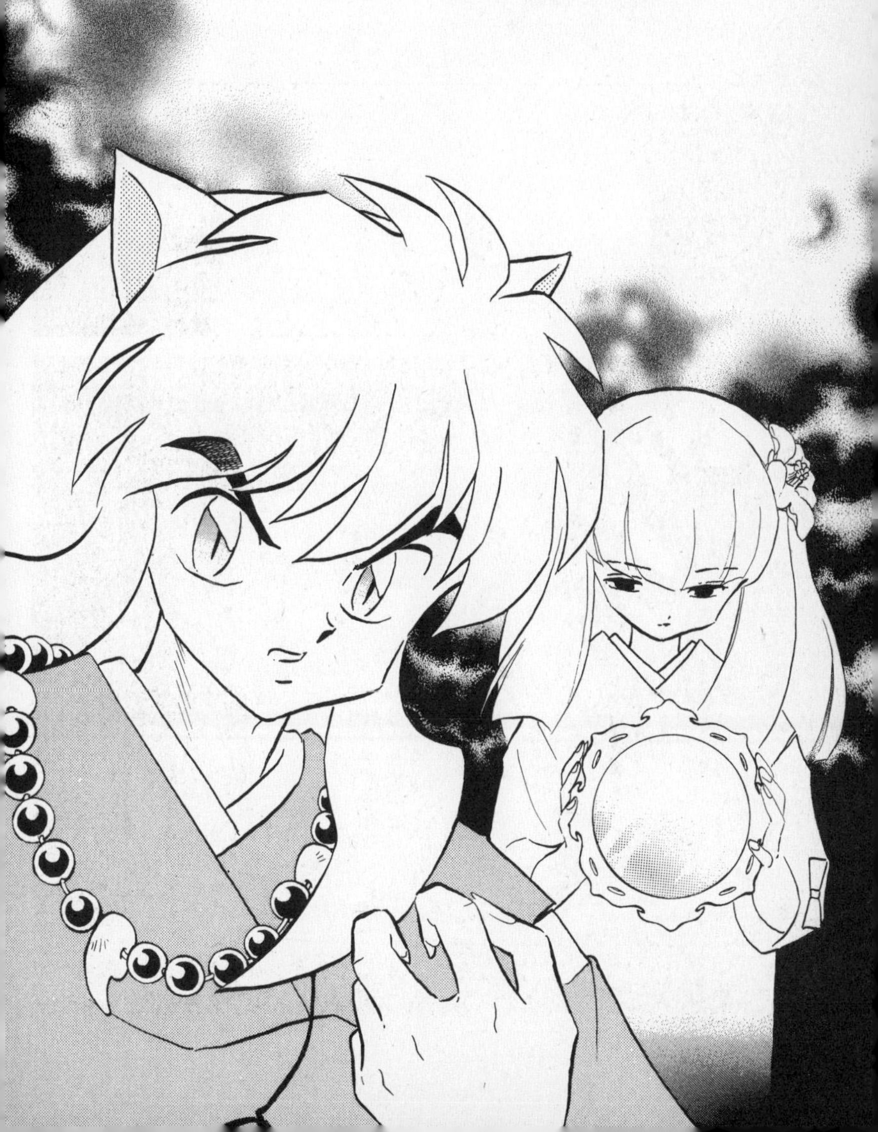

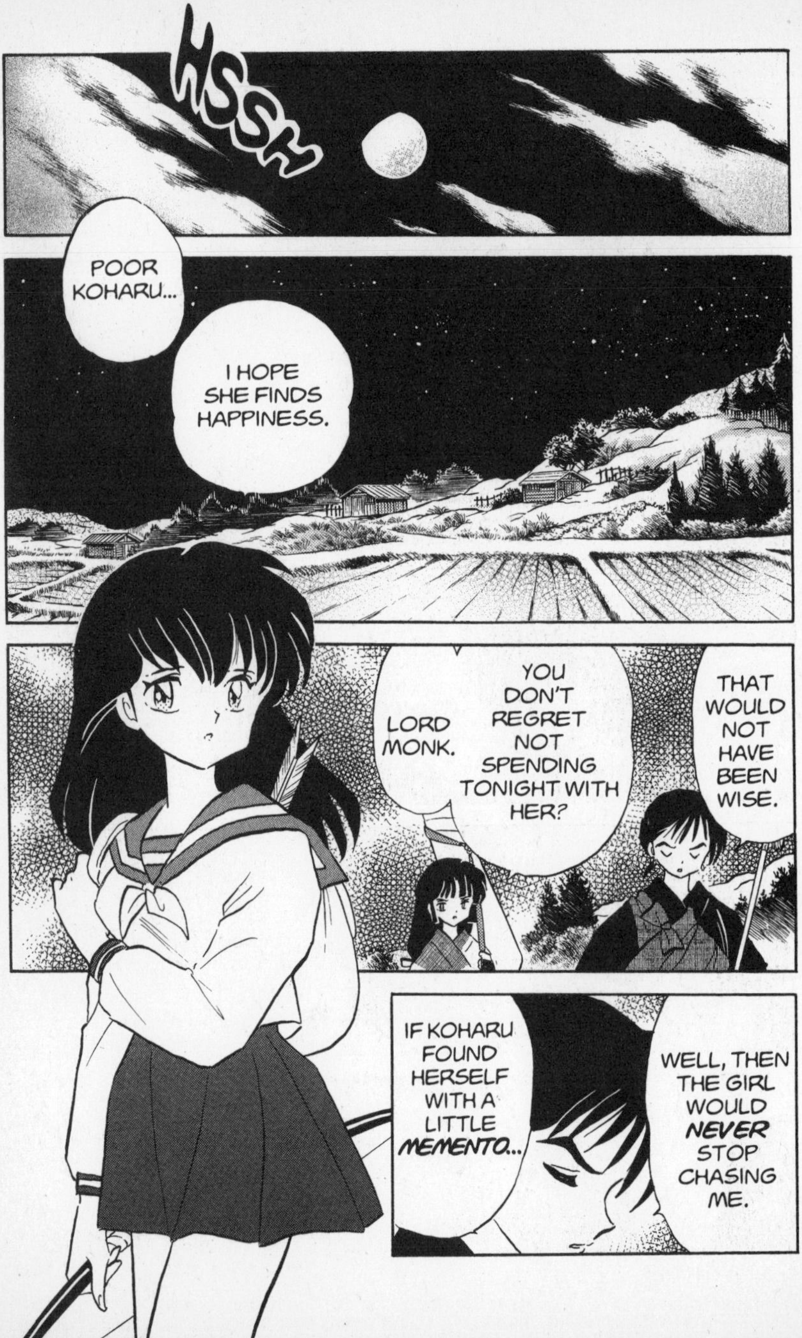
HSSH
POOR KOHARU...
I HOPE SHE FINDS HAPPINESS.
LORD MONK.
YOU DON'T REGRET NOT SPENDING TONIGHT WITH HER?
THAT WOULD NOT HAVE BEEN WISE.
IF KOHARU FOUND HERSELF WITH A LITTLE *MEMENTO*...
WELL, THEN THE GIRL WOULD ***NEVER*** STOP CHASING ME.

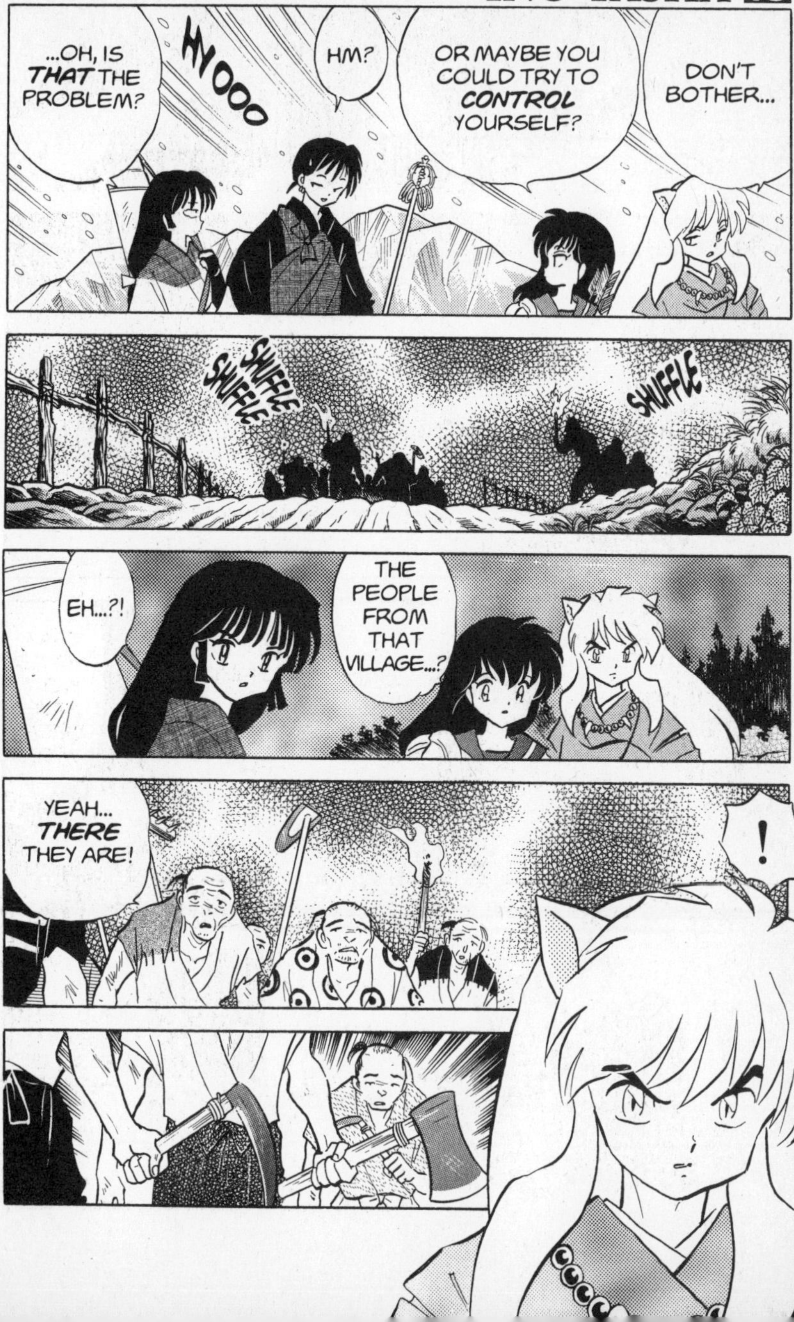
...OH, IS *THAT* THE PROBLEM?
HYOOO
HM?
OR MAYBE YOU COULD TRY TO *CONTROL* YOURSELF?
DON'T BOTHER...
SHUFFLE SHUFFLE
SHUFFLE
EH...?!
THE PEOPLE FROM THAT VILLAGE...?
YEAH... *THERE* THEY ARE!
!

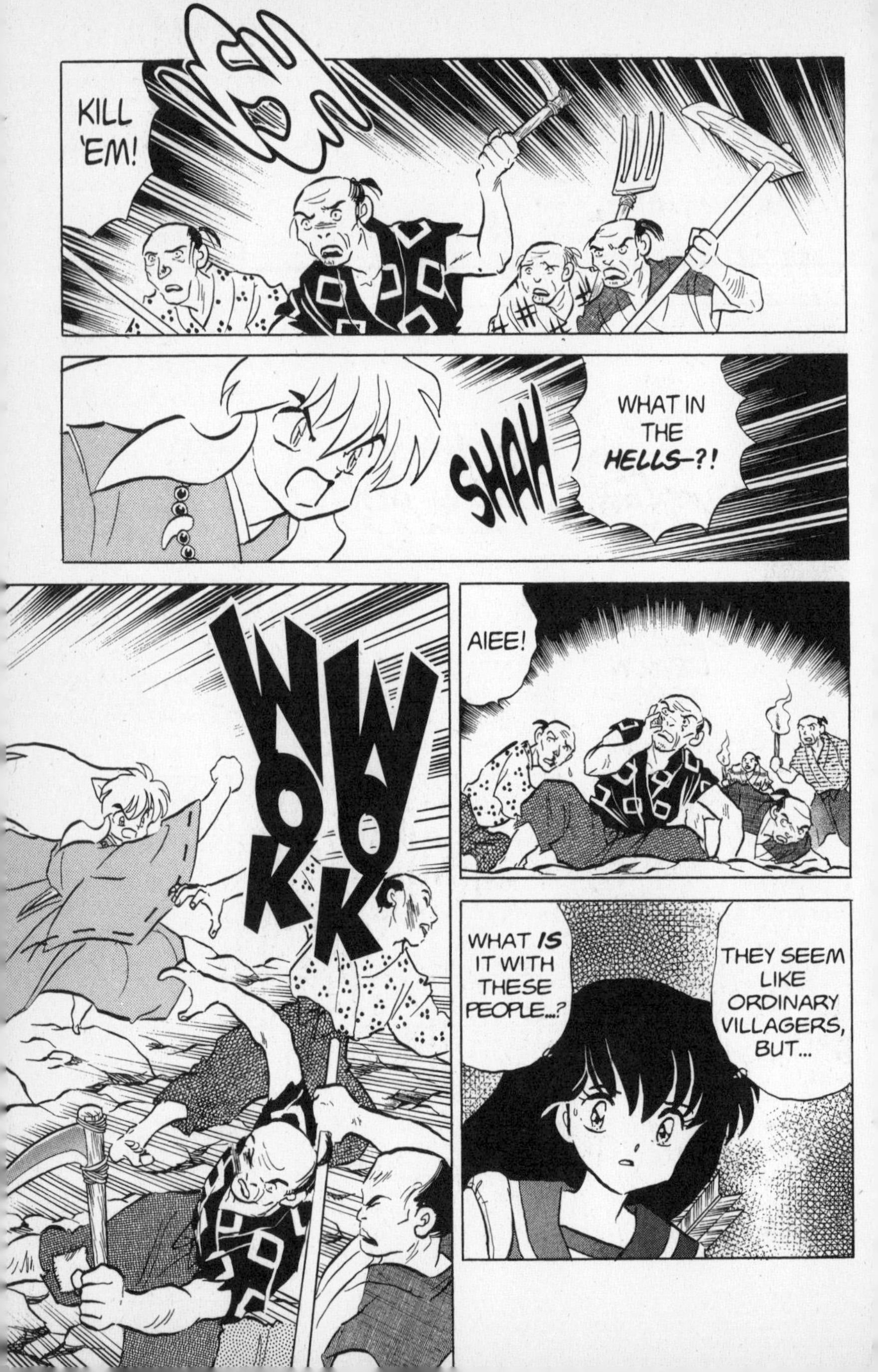
KILL 'EM!
SHAH
WHAT IN THE *HELLS*-?!
WOK
WOK
AIEE!
WHAT *IS* IT WITH THESE PEOPLE...?
THEY SEEM LIKE ORDINARY VILLAGERS, BUT...

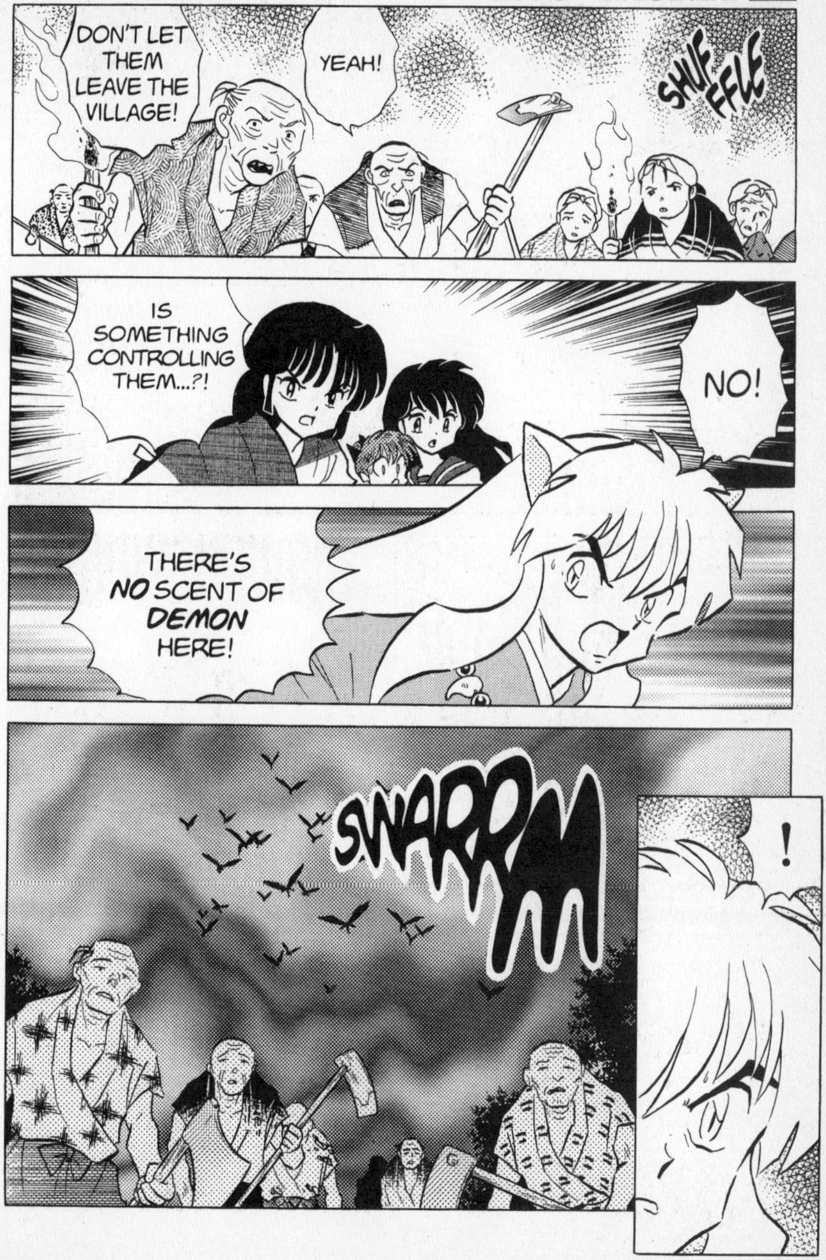
DON'T LET THEM LEAVE THE VILLAGE!
YEAH!
SHUFFFLE
IS SOMETHING CONTROLLING THEM...?!
NO!
THERE'S **NO** SCENT OF **DEMON** HERE!
SWARRM
!

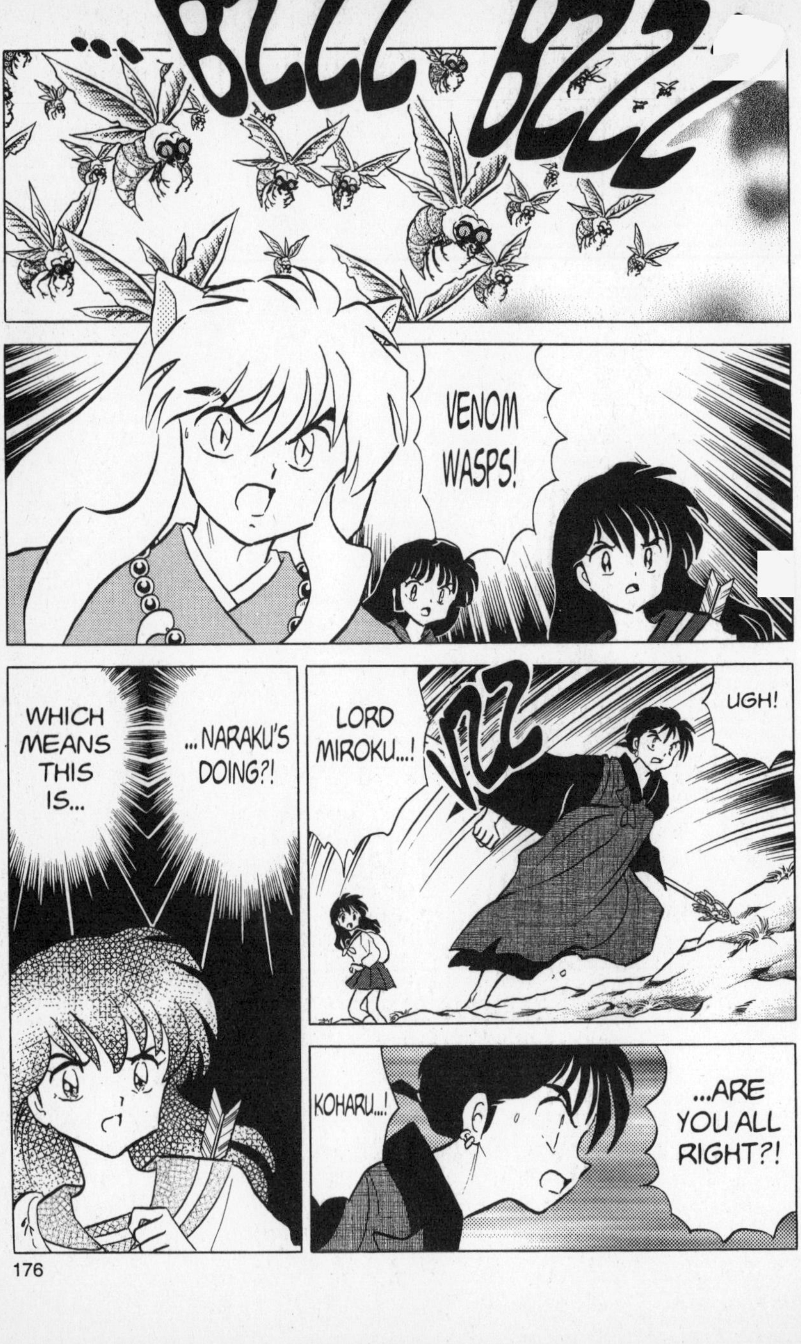
...BZZZ BZZZ
VENOM WASPS!
WHICH MEANS THIS IS...
...NARAKU'S DOING?!
LORD MIROKU...!
VZZ
UGH!
KOHARU...!
...ARE YOU ALL RIGHT?!

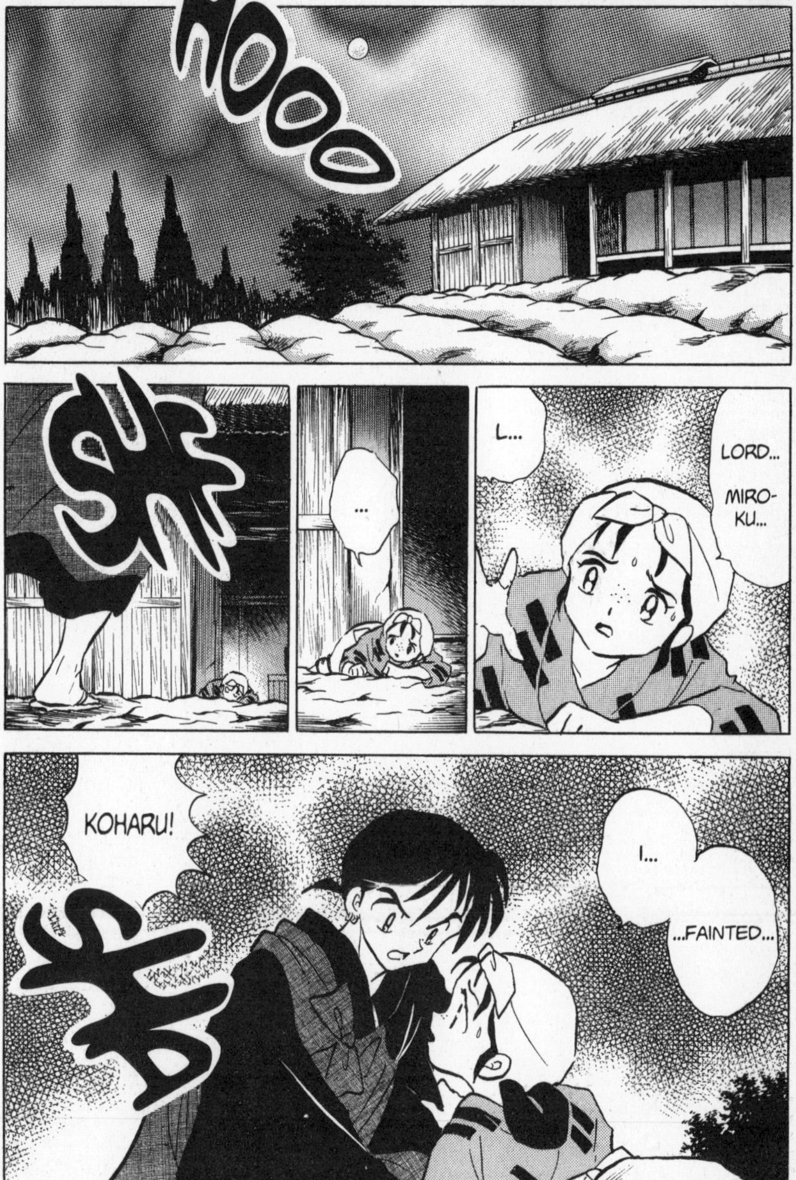
HOOO
...
L...
LORD...
MIRO-
KU...
KOHARU!
I...
...FAINTED...

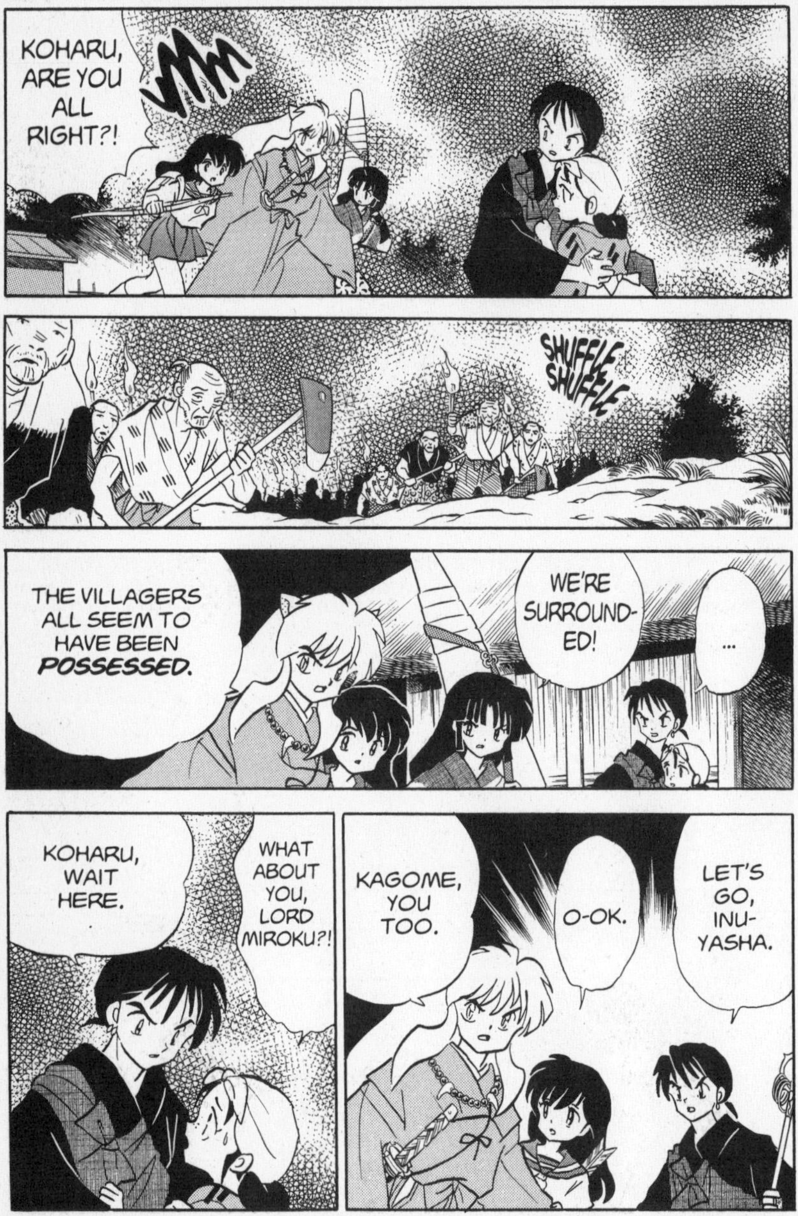
KOHARU, ARE YOU ALL RIGHT?!
SHUFFLE SHUFFLE
THE VILLAGERS ALL SEEM TO HAVE BEEN POSSESSED.
WE'RE SURROUNDED!
...
KOHARU, WAIT HERE.
WHAT ABOUT YOU, LORD MIROKU?!
KAGOME, YOU TOO.
O-OK.
LET'S GO, INU-YASHA.

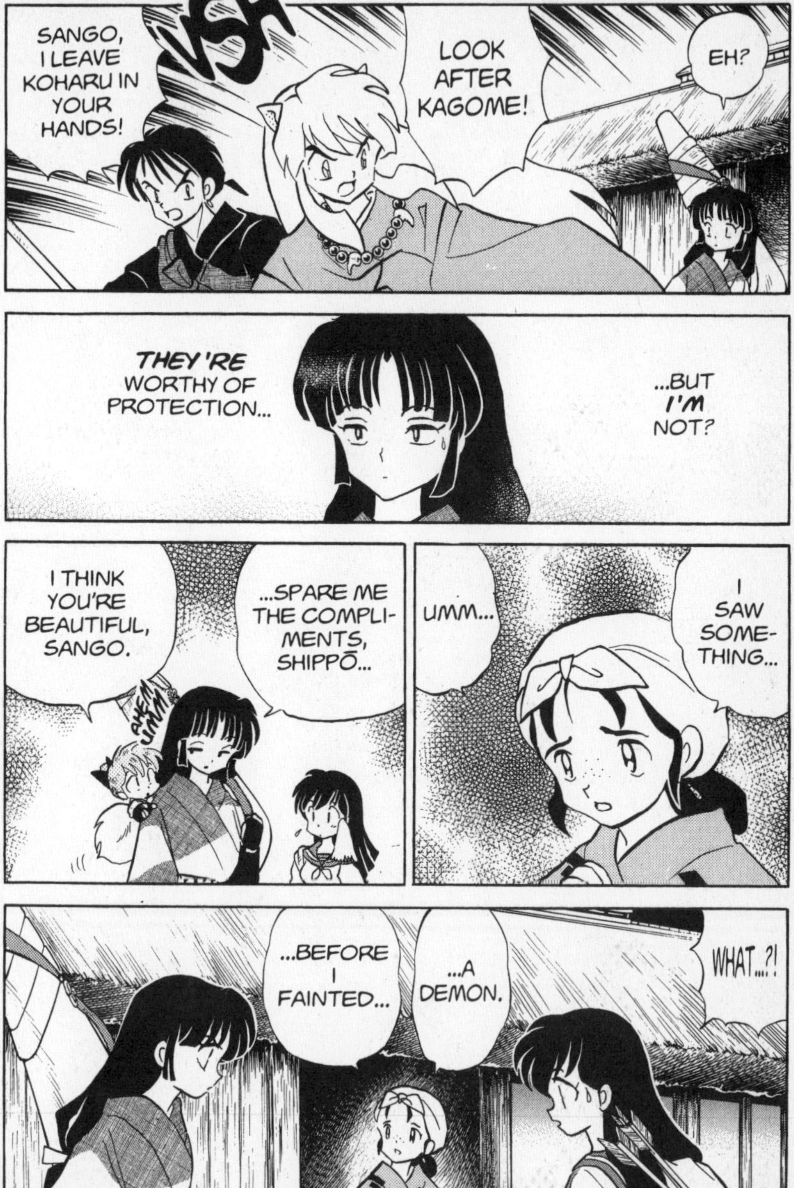
SANGO, I LEAVE KOHARU IN YOUR HANDS!
LOOK AFTER KAGOME!
EH?
THEY'RE WORTHY OF PROTECTION...
...BUT *I'M* NOT?
I THINK YOU'RE BEAUTIFUL, SANGO.
AHEM UMM
...SPARE ME THE COMPLI-MENTS, SHIPPŌ...
UMM...
I SAW SOME-THING...
...BEFORE I FAINTED...
...A DEMON.
WHAT...?!

THE MAYOR AND EVERYONE...

HWOOO

...THEY WERE KNOCKED OUT TOO.

IT MIGHT STILL BE IN THERE...

KRIII!

AND THAT'S WHAT'S MANIPULATING THE VILLAGERS...?

BUT HOW...?

INU-YASHA SAID THERE WAS NO SCENT OF DEMONS...

!

GLEEM

VSH VSH

THERE! THAT'S THE ONE!

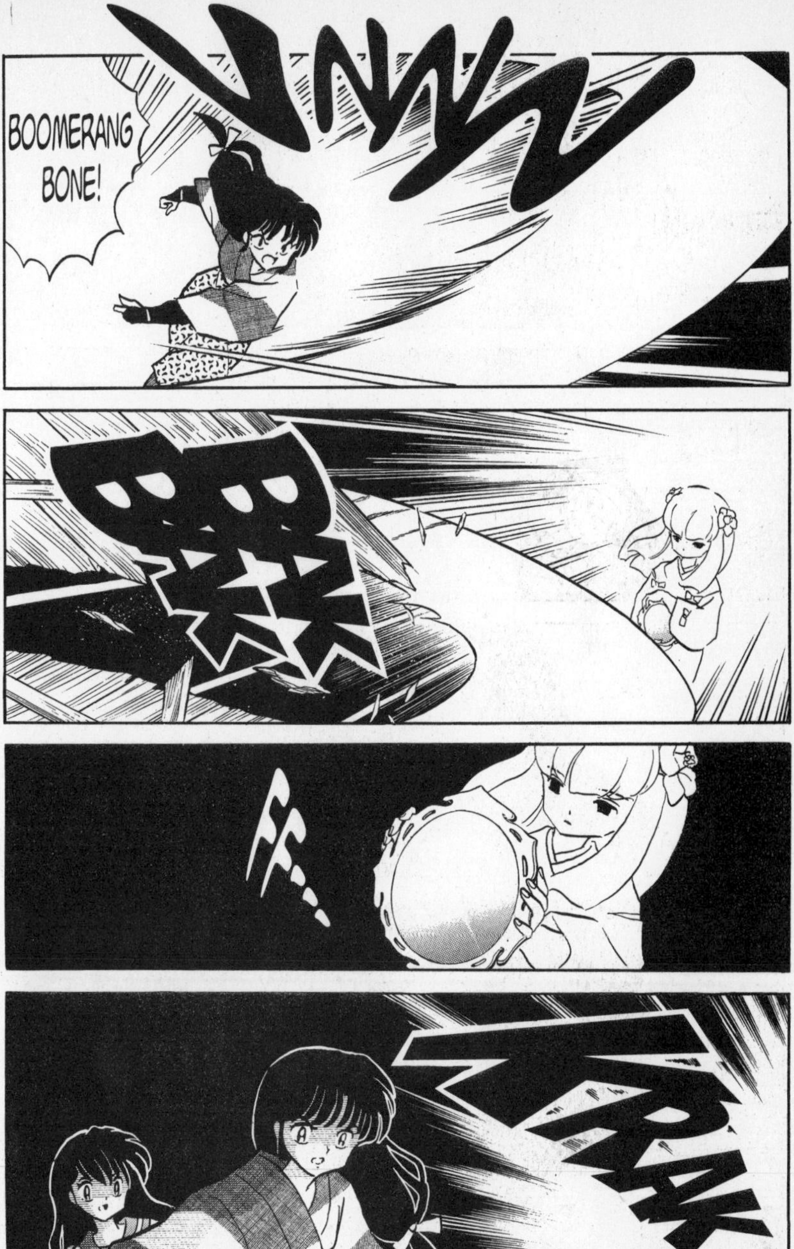
VWWW
BOOMERANG BONE!
BK
FF...
KRAK

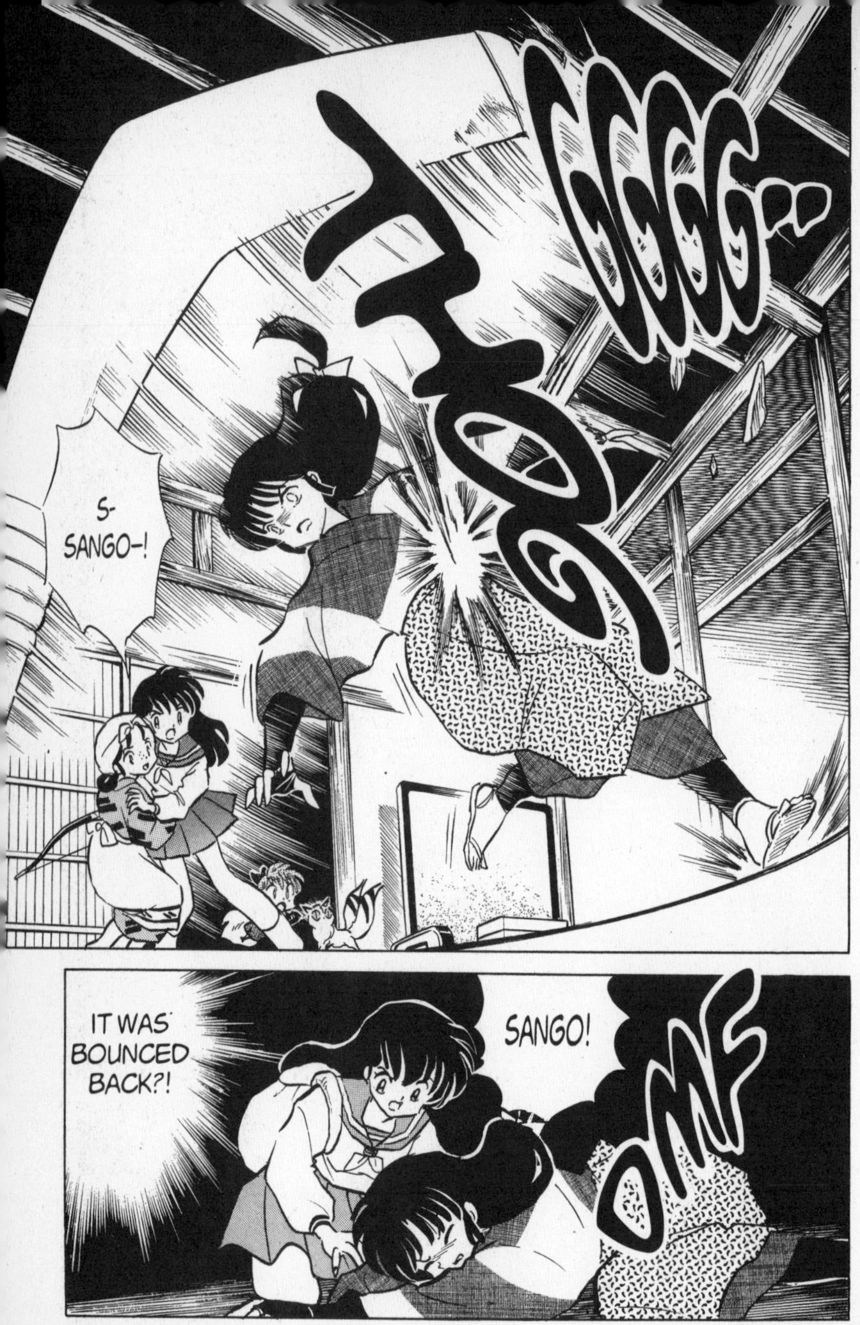
S-SANGO-!
IT WAS BOUNCED BACK?!
SANGO!

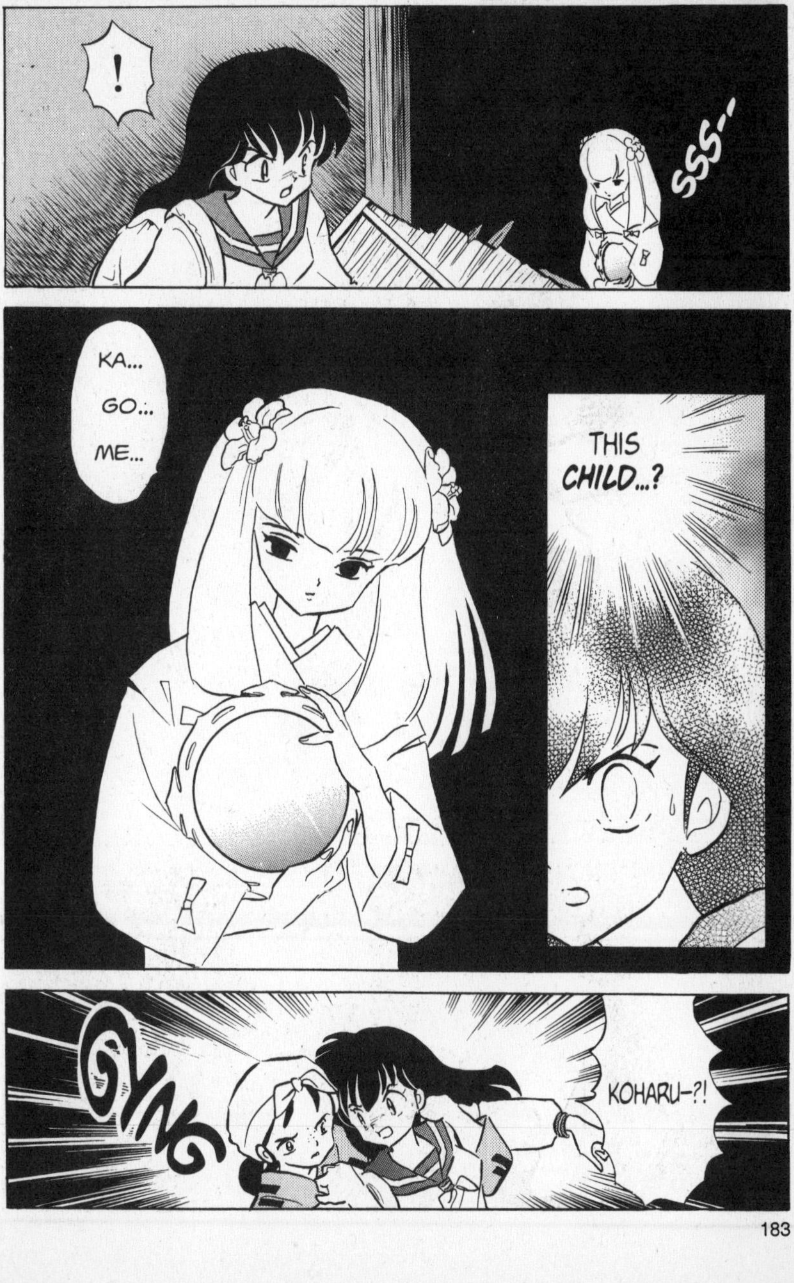
!
SSS-..
KA...
GO...
ME...
THIS CHILD...?
GYNG
KOHARU-?!

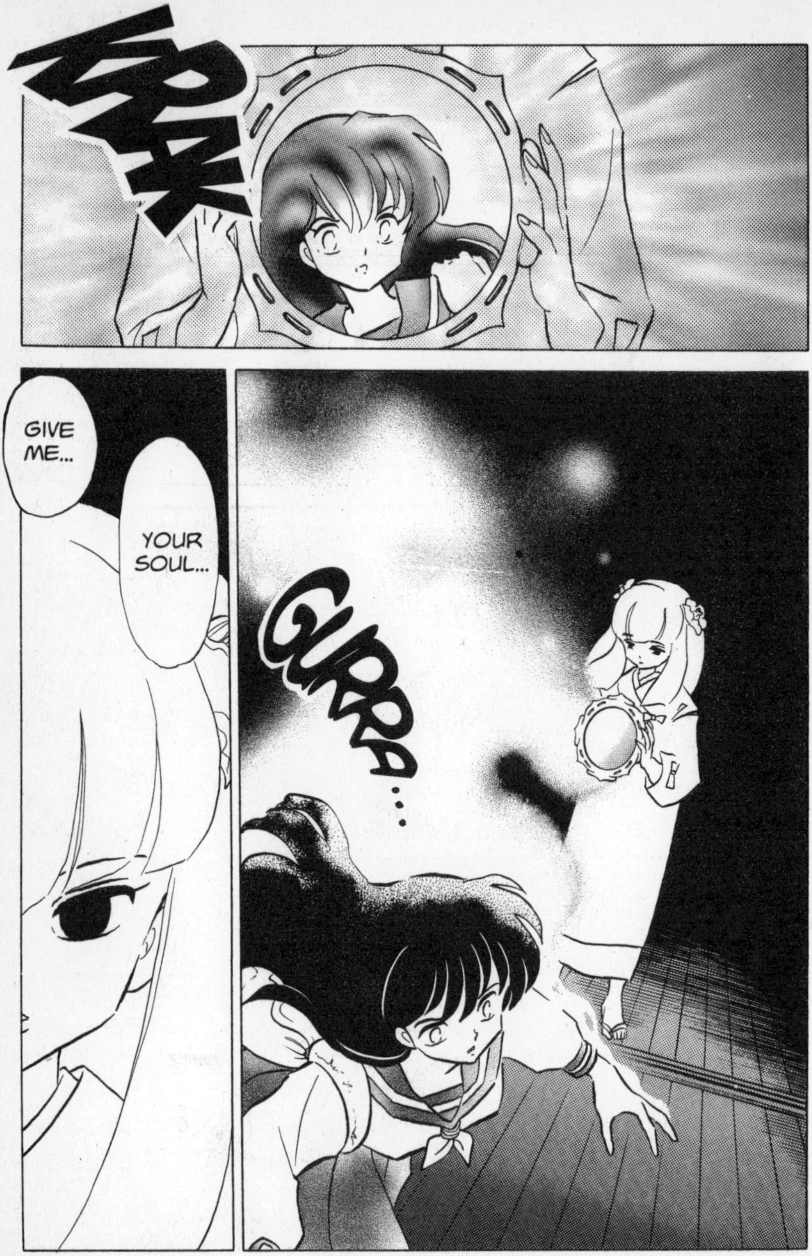
KRAK
GIVE ME...
YOUR SOUL...
GURRA...

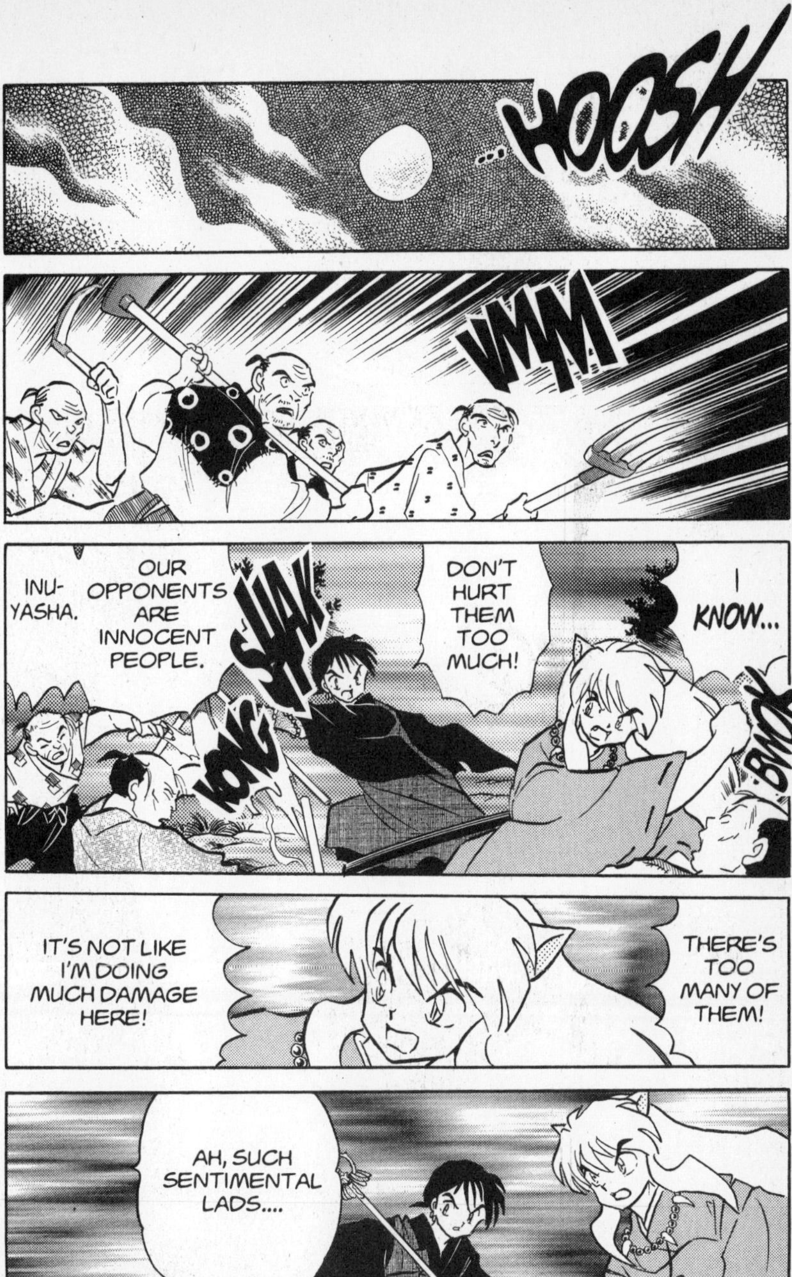
...HOOSH
VMM
INU-YASHA.
OUR OPPONENTS ARE INNOCENT PEOPLE.
KONG
SHAK
DON'T HURT THEM TOO MUCH!
I KNOW...
BWOK
IT'S NOT LIKE I'M DOING MUCH DAMAGE HERE!
THERE'S TOO MANY OF THEM!
AH, SUCH SENTIMENTAL LADS....

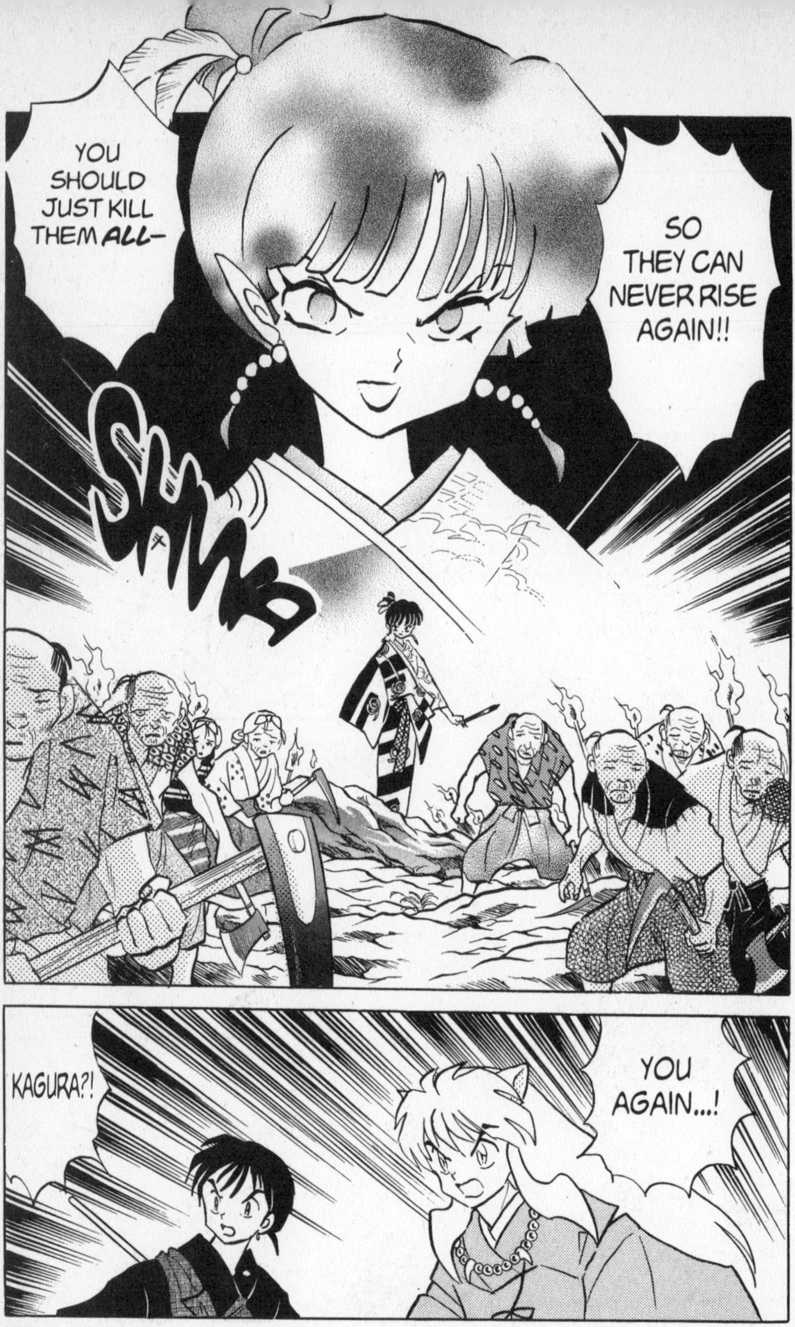
YOU SHOULD JUST KILL THEM ALL—
SO THEY CAN NEVER RISE AGAIN!!
KAGURA?!
YOU AGAIN...!

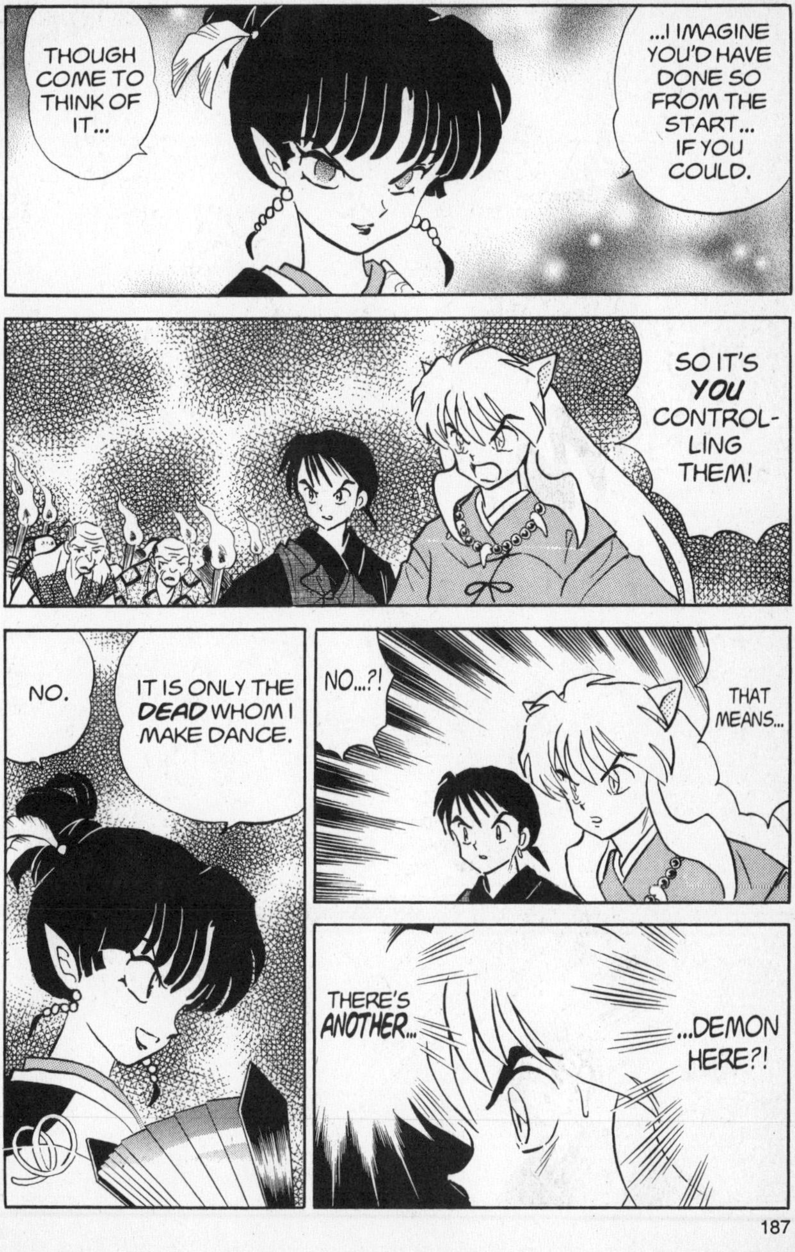
THOUGH COME TO THINK OF IT...
...I IMAGINE YOU'D HAVE DONE SO FROM THE START... IF YOU COULD.
SO IT'S YOU CONTROLLING THEM!
NO.
IT IS ONLY THE DEAD WHOM I MAKE DANCE.
NO...?!
THAT MEANS...
THERE'S ANOTHER...
...DEMON HERE?!

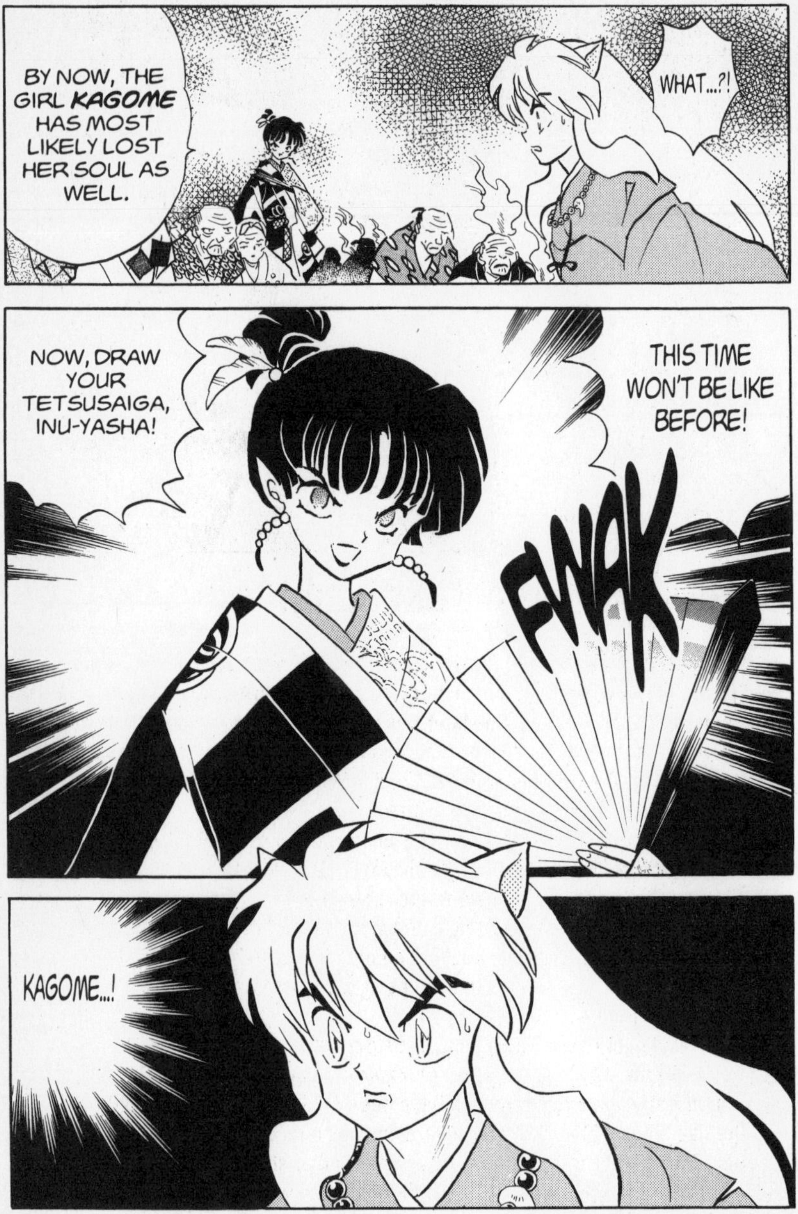
BY NOW, THE GIRL KAGOME HAS MOST LIKELY LOST HER SOUL AS WELL.
WHAT...?!
NOW, DRAW YOUR TETSUSAIGA, INU-YASHA!
THIS TIME WON'T BE LIKE BEFORE!
FWAK
KAGOME...!

TO BE CONTINUED...

About Rumiko Takahashi

Born in 1957 in Niigata, Japan, Rumiko Takahashi attended women's college in Tokyo, where she began studying comics with Kazuo Koike, author of *Crying Freeman*. She later became an assistant to horror-manga artist Kazuo Umezu (*Orochi*). In 1978, she won a prize in Shogakukan's annual "New Comic Artist Contest," and in that same year her boy-meets-alien comedy series *Urusei Yatsura* began appearing in the weekly manga magazine *Shônen Sunday*. This phenomenally successful series ran for nine years and sold over 22 million copies. Takahashi's later *Ranma 1/2* series enjoyed even greater popularity.

Takahashi is considered by many to be one of the world's most popular manga artists. With the publication of Volume 34 of her *Ranma 1/2* series in Japan, Takahashi's total sales passed *one hundred million* copies of her compiled works.

Takahashi's serial titles include *Urusei Yatsura, Ranma 1/2, One-Pound Gospel, Maison Ikkoku* and *InuYasha*. Additionally, Takahashi has drawn many short stories which have been published in America under the title "Rumic Theater," and several installments of a saga known as her "Mermaid" series. Most of Takahashi's major stories have also been animated, and are widely available in translation worldwide. *InuYasha* is her most recent serial story, first published in *Shônen Sunday* in 1996.

EDITOR'S RECOMMENDATIONS

Did you like INUYASHA? Here's what we recommend you try next:

RANMA 1/2 is the manga Rumiko Takahashi was working on previous to *INUYASHA*. It's more comedic than *INUYASHA*—sort of a cross between a screwball comedy and a martial-arts action movie—but it's chock full of unique characters and complicated romantic entanglements.

© 1988 Rumiko Takahashi/Shogakukan

MAISON IKKOKU is Takahashi's most romantic series. It's set in modern-day Japan, and traces the lives of the residents of a boarding house. It's intense, it's angsty, and it's one of the most absorbing manga romances ever written.

© 1984 Rumiko Takahashi/Shogakukan

CERES: CELESTIAL LEGEND is a sort of supernatural mystery by *FUSHIGI YÛGI*'s creator, Yû Watase. It's about a modern-day 16-year-old girl whose body houses a legendary power, and her family is determined to kill her in order to suppress it. The story draws heavily on Japanese legends.

© 1997 Yuu Watase/Shogakukan

COMPLETE OUR SURVEY AND LET US KNOW WHAT YOU THINK!

☐ Please check here if you DO NOT wish to receive information or future offers from VIZ

Name: _____

Address: _____

City: _____ State: _____ Zip: _____

E-mail: _____

☐ Male ☐ Female Date of Birth (mm/dd/yyyy): ___ / ___ / ___ (Under 13? Parental consent required)

What race/ethnicity do you consider yourself? (please check one)

☐ Asian/Pacific Islander ☐ Black/African American ☐ Hispanic/Latino

☐ Native American/Alaskan Native ☐ White/Caucasian ☐ Other: _____

What VIZ product did you purchase? (check all that apply and indicate title purchased)

☐ DVD/VHS _____

☐ Graphic Novel _____

☐ Magazines _____

☐ Merchandise _____

Reason for purchase: (check all that apply)

☐ Special offer ☐ Favorite title ☐ Gift

☐ Recommendation ☐ Other _____

Where did you make your purchase? (please check one)

☐ Comic store ☐ Bookstore ☐ Mass/Grocery Store

☐ Newsstand ☐ Video/Video Game Store ☐ Other: _____

☐ Online (site: _____)

What other VIZ properties have you purchased/own? _____

_____

How many anime and/or manga titles have you purchased in the last year? How many were VIZ titles? (please check one from each column)

ANIME	MANGA	VIZ
☐ None	☐ None	☐ None
☐ 1-4	☐ 1-4	☐ 1-4
☐ 5-10	☐ 5-10	☐ 5-10
☐ 11+	☐ 11+	☐ 11+

I find the pricing of VIZ products to be: (please check one)

☐ Cheap ☐ Reasonable ☐ Expensive

What genre of manga and anime would you like to see from VIZ? (please check two)

☐ Adventure ☐ Comic Strip ☐ Detective ☐ Fighting

☐ Horror ☐ Romance ☐ Sci-Fi/Fantasy ☐ Sports

What do you think of VIZ's new look?

☐ Love It ☐ It's OK ☐ Hate It ☐ Didn't Notice ☐ No Opinion

THANK YOU! Please send the completed form to:

NJW Research
42 Catharine St.
Poughkeepsie, NY 12601

All information provided will be used for internal purposes only. We promise not to sell or otherwise divulge your information.